Behavior Theory and Philosophy

Behavior Theory and Philosophy

Edited by

Kennon A. Lattal

and

Philip N. Chase
West Virginia University Morgantown, West Virginia

Kluwer Academic / Plenum Publishers
New York, Boston, Dordrecht, London, Moscow

Library of Congress Cataloging-in-Publication Data

Behavior theory and philosophy / edited by Kennon A. Lattal and Philip N. Chase.
    p. cm.
    Includes bibliographical references and index.
    ISBN 0-306-47780-7
1. Psychology–Philosophy–Congresses.   I. Lattal, Kennon A.   II. Chase, Philip N.

BF38.B42 2003   2003050648

ISBN HB: 0-306-47780-7

© 2003 Kluwer Academic/Plenum Publishers, New York
233 Spring Street, New York, New York 10013

http://www.wkap.nl/

10 9 8 7 6 5 4 3 2 1

A C.I.P. record for this book is available from the Library of Congress

Permissions for books published in Europe: permissions@wkap.nl
Permissions for books published in the United States of America: permissions@wkap.com

Printed in the United States of America.

This volume is dedicated to Hayne W. Reese, with affection and with admiration for all that he has done for the discipline of psychology

Hayne W. Reese was appointed Centennial Professor of Psychology at West Virginia University in 1970 and held that position until his retirement in May, 2000. His distinguished chair was one of four established by the West Virginia legislature to celebrate the 100th anniversary of the University. Professor Reese received his B.A. and M.A. degrees in psychology from the University of Texas at Austin and his Ph.D. degree in psychology from the University of Iowa in 1958. Prior to coming to West Virginia, he served on the faculties of the State University of New york at Buffalo and the University of Kansas. His extensive editorial service includes a term as editor of the *Journal of Experimental Child Psychology* from 1983 to 1997, editor of *Advances in Child Development and Behavior* from 1969 to 2002, and positions on the editorial boards of 10 professional journals. Professor Reese is the author of more than 165 books, chapters, and scientific articles and more than 215 professional presentations in the areas of learning, developmental psychology, philosophical and theoretical psychology, and the history of psychology. He has, in addition, provided exceptional intellectual and academic leadership to both the Department of Psychology and the University throughout his many years of service to West Virginia University.

Contributors

Donald M. Baer • (deceased) formerly of the Department of Human Development, University of Kansas, Lawrence, Kansas 66045-2133

A. Charles Catania • Department of Psychology, University of Maryland Baltimore County, Baltimore, Maryland 21250

Philip N. Chase • Department of Psychology, West Virginia University, Morgantown, West Virginia 26506-6040

Mecca Chiesa • Applied Social Science, University of Paisley, Paisley, Scotland, United Kingdom

John W. Donahoe • Department of Psychology, University of Massachusetts, Amherst, Massachusetts 01003-7710

Chad M. Galuska • Department of Psychology, West Virginia University, Morgantown, West Virginia 26506-6040

Sigrid S. Glenn • Department of Behavior Analysis, University of North Texas, Denton, Texas 76205

Philip N. Hineline • Department of Psychology, Temple University, Philadelphia, Pennsylvania 19122

Jon E. Krapfl • Williamsburg, Virginia 23185

Joseph S. Laipple • Aubrey Daniels International, Atlanta, Georgia 30084

Kennon A. Lattal • Department of Psychology, West Virginia University, Morgantown, West Virginia 26506-6040

Jack Marr • School of Psychology, Georgia Tech, Atlanta, GA 30332-0170

J. Moore • Department of Psychology, University of Wisconsin-Milwaukee, Milwaukee, WI 53201

Edward K. Morris • Department of Human Development, University of Kansas, Lawrence, Kansas 66045-2133

Nancy A. Neef • College of Education, The Ohio State University, Columbus, Ohio 43210

Allen Neuringer • Department of Psychology, Reed College, Portland, Oregon 97202

David C. Palmer • Department of Psychology, Smith College, Northampton, Massachusetts 01063

Stephanie M. Peterson • College of Education, The Ohio State University, Columbus, Ohio 43210

Howard Rachlin • Department of Psychology, State University of New York at Stony Brook, Stony Brook, New York 11974-2500

Emilio Ribes-Iñesta • Centro de Estudios e Investigaciones en Comportamento, Universidad de Guadalajara, Zapopan, Mexico 45030

Jesús Rosales-Ruiz • Department of Behavior Analysis, University of North Texas, Denton, Texas 76203

David W. Schaal • Department of Psychology, West Virginia University, Morgantown, West Virginia 26506-6040

J. E. R. Staddon • Department of Psychological and Brain Sciences, Duke University, Durham North Carolina 27708-0086

Conference Participants

April 7, 2000

(Left to right) Front row: Kennon A. Lattal, Steven C. Hayes, Sigrid S. Glenn, Willis Overton, Hayne W. Reese, Emilio Ribes-Iñesta, Mecca Chiesa, Philip N. Chase.
Middle row: Allen Neuringer, Donald M. Baer, Nancy A. Neef, Jon E. Krapfl, David C. Palmer, Philip N. Hineline, A. Charles Catania
Back row: John W. Donahoe, J. E. R. Staddon, Howard Rachlin, J. Moore, Jack Marr, Edward K. Morris.
(Authors not in photograph: Chad M. Galuska, Joseph S. Laipple, Stephanie M. Peterson, Jesús Rosales-Ruíz, David W. Schaal).

Preface

This volume is based on a conference held at West Virginia University in April, 2000 in recognition of the career-long contributions to psychology of Hayne W. Reese, Centennial Professor of Psychology, who retired from the University at the end of the 1999–2000 academic year. Although Professor Reese may be even better known for his contributions to developmental psychology, his influential scholarly work on philosophical and conceptual issues that impact all of psychology provided the impetus for the conference. *Behavior theory and philosophy* was the name given by Professor Reese and one of the authors in this volume, Jon Krapfl, to a course that they developed at West Virginia University in the late 1970s. It seemed appropriate to adopt its title for both the conference and this volume as the shared theme involves the ideas that have shaped modern behavior analysis.

A number of people contributed to the success of the May, 2000 conference honoring Hayne Reese and we thank them all for their efforts: Dean Duane Nellis of the Eberly College of Arts and Sciences at WVU offered enthusiastic support for the project both financially and through his assignment of staff to help with the conference. Mark Dalessandro, Relations Director for the Eberly College of Arts and Sciences, served as the "point man" for the conference and made all of the local arrangements both within the university and the community. The Chair of the Department of Psychology, Michael Perone, worked closely with us to ensure that every detail of the conference was perfectly planned and never said no to a request for either additional support or work on his part. Our colleagues in the Department of Psychology, and especially those in the Developmental Psychology Program, the program that Dr. Reese led for 28 years, offered invaluable advice and assistance. Tyler Feola managed the registration for the conference, and students Carolina Aguilera, Lori Lieving, Megan Meginley, and Stephen Scherer from the Behavior Analysis Program contributed their time and energy to transporting, hosting, and in general helping out with the nitty gritty operations of the conference.

We also thank Fred King, Assistant Dean of the Eberly College of Arts and Sciences, for providing a grant that helped cover the costs of preparing the volume for publication and Stephanie da Silva for her editorial assistance with the volume. Sharon Panulla, Senior Editor for the Behavioral Sciences with Kluwer Academic/Plenum in New York was both patient and helpful as we worked through the various stages of preparing the volume. Without the efforts of all these people, the conference and this book, which represents the intellectual components of the conference, would not have been possible.

Kennon A. Lattal
Philip N. Chase

Contents

PART II.   INTERPRETATIONS

PART III.   EXTENSIONS TO RESEARCH AND APPLICATION

1

Themes in Behavior Theory
and Philosophy

Kennon A. Lattal and Philip N. Chase

Psychology made its famous break from philosophy in 1879 and since then has faired well as an independent discipline. There remains, however, considerable evidence of its philosophical roots in many of the issues and problems that even its most hard-nosed scientists tackle. B. F. Skinner is a case in point. Even though his work exemplifies the effective application of scientific methods to the subject matter of psychology, much of his extrapolation and interpretation led inevitably to philosophical questions about both science and human behavior, whether observed in a clinic, a laboratory, or everyday settings. Some questions relate to the nature of scientific practices, others to the nature of psychological constructs and interpretations, and still others to the relations between psychology and other disciplines, both in the sciences and in the humanities. All of these topics are incorporated under the general heading of this book's title, *Behavior Theory and Philosophy*. The chapters that follow consider aspects of one or more of the preceding questions, addressed by scientists and practitioners trained and functioning within the scientific traditions associated with behavior analysis.

Kennon A. Lattal and Philip N. Chase • Department of Psychology, West Virginia University, Morgantown, WV 26506-6040.

Behavior Theory and Philosophy

Behavior analysis began as a branch of experimental psychology that studies how environmental variables influence behavior. It is internally consistent, has produced successful experiments, and generally has flourished for decades. Its success as an experimental science has been complemented by successful applications. It is the issues in philosophy and theory, however, that integrate significant problems in behavior analysis. Some of these issues are derived from general philosophy and from the philosophy of science. Others are derived from problems of longstanding interest to general psychology, and their discussion in behavior analysis involves providing interpretations of how behavioral processes, including some processes that have not yet have been subjected to experimental analysis, can be applied to these problems. Still others are related to whether and how the successes of applied behavior analysis can be integrated with the philosophical underpinnings of behavior analysis. In light of these issues, three major themes comprise this volume, and these themes constitute its three sections: Topics derived from general philosophy and from the philosophy of science that impact behavior analysis, the interpretation of psychological/behavioral processes of general interest among psychologists, and the manifestation of themes from behavior theory and philosophy in applied settings. As with any edited volume, a recurring issue is that, although the individual chapters may contribute to the understanding of the topic under discussion, it is easy to underplay, or even overlook, common themes that weave the chapters together to create a more molar overview of behavior theory and philosophy. Below we discuss a few of these common themes in order to interest the reader in exploring behavior theory and philosophy as a whole.

Some Common Themes Among the Chapters

Environment as context

Whether behavior analysis is more closely aligned with a mechanistic or contextualistic world view remains a matter of debate (Hayes, Hayes, & Reese, 1988; Marr, 1993; Morris, 1993; Pepper, 1942). Regardless of which of these world views better subsumes behavior analysis or whether behavior analysis is a world view of its own, the importance of context integrates several of the chapters. From a behavior-analytic perspective, context is fundamentally important in that, broadly speaking, the environment provides the context in which behavior occurs. Every chapter in this book is grounded in this fundamental relation between the environment and behavior. In order to account for complex behavior, particularly in applied settings, the environment that is described is often a conditional or contextual environment. Chase's chapter provides examples of this conditionality in his attempts to account for teaching novel behavior. Chiesa and Galuska discuss the need for considering context for fair and equitable decisions to be made on legal issues related to ethics and morality. Such basic scientific issues as the nature of observation (Marr), explanation (Moore), and meaning (Ribes), all are considered in this volume within the context of a behavior-analytic verbal community. More generally, the chapters all illustrate how behavior analysis can provide a useful context in which many traditional philosophical and psychological problems can be interpreted and discussed.

Selectionism

Darwin's fundamental principle of organic evolution has proven a useful metaphor for both ontogenic (Skinner, 1987), cultural (e.g., Campbell, 1965; Skinner, 1986), and technological (Petroski, 1994) change as well. Donahoe's chapter describes how selectionism provides a useful framework for understanding basic learning and memory processes, and others discuss selectionist principles at work in both the general culture and in specific everyday settings. Glenn and Catania discuss the role of selection in the interlocking concerns of culture and verbal behavior, respectively. Krapfl expands on the theme of selectionism as it relates to corporate cultures and Neuringer's research on variation adds experimental details with respect to understanding the process of variation, on which selection depends. But not all the authors agree that selectionism is important for behavior analysis. Staddon offers a critique of the metaphorical use of selectionism and his views form an important contrast to the other chapters for the reader to consider.

Pragmatism

Pragmatism in both philosophy and behavior analysis is discussed specifically by Lattal and Laipple, but many other chapters continue this theme with respect to other topics and problems within behavior analysis. Following along pragmatic lines, Schaal suggests how an understanding of physiological processes can contribute to the pragmatic behavior-analytic goals of prediction and control of behavior. Both Marr and Staddon propose pragmatic truth criteria and contrast these criteria with postmodernist views of observation and understanding. They conclude that the truth of an idea is not just its persistence, but whether the idea passes critical tests of its worth. Staddon, however, also takes simple pragmatism to task, claiming that the issues of truth, value, and free will, which are the concern of the humanities, cannot be answered by a pragmatic science. He, therefore, supports an intellectual dualism, which has a long history within western culture, between the questions addressed by a science like behavior analysis and those addressed by religion, philosophy, and other humanities. Applied topics, though, are almost by definition pragmatically driven ones; indeed, the chapters by Chase and Krapfl illustrate some important pragmatic tests that have faced and still face the application of behavior-analytic theory. Functional, pragmatic interpretations of complex human behavior such as cognition (Palmer), intention (Hineline), and privacy (Rachlin) reflect a pragmatic point of view.

Structure and Function

A part of behavior-analytic pragmatism involves a focus on behavioral function over structure, a theme in psychology that is traced at least to the turn of the 20th century. The relation between structure and function, however, is neither simple nor linear, as both Catania (1973) and Baer (1981) have discussed previously. In the present volume, Catania describes a functional analysis of verbal behavior and Ribes uses a related analysis, based on the philosophical writings of Ryle, to examine and critique the construction of concepts in behavior analysis. In addition, conventional interpretations of both ethics and religion are questioned by Chiesa and Galuska in part because issues of structure and form seem prepotent over the functions of such behavior. Baer and Rosales-Ruiz suggest how developmental stages might be "destructured" and considered more functionally. Schaal's chapter on reductionism, in particular, addresses how biological structure might complement a functional analysis of behavior to realize Skinner's (1938) early suggestion that the juxtaposing of physiology and behavior analysis may lead to a more complete understanding of the subject matter of both disciplines.

Behavioral interpretation

Some of the questions raised in this volume concern long-standing questions about the nature of behavior that require interpretation of behavioral phenomena. Such interpretations are described and discussed in the second section of this book. Palmer makes a strong case for the proper use of interpretation within a science to explain phenomena that have not been subject to an experimental analysis. The concept of *intention* (Hineline) is such a phenomenon. It raises both conceptual and practical questions. In brief, how does behavior analysis account for what in everyday terms appears as intent in the actions of people? The nature of ethics and legal responsibility in a deterministic world view is another such philosophical question with many societal implications. As one of the "sticky wickets" for environmental determinism, it is not surprising that the chapters on intentions, religion, and values, Hineline, Galuska, and Chiesa respectively, address the idea that just because the causes of behavior are found external to the behaver does not mean that society has to forgo its role in providing consequences for behavior. These chapters are consistent in insisting that a behavior-analytic stance does not excuse individuals from legal and moral responsibility. More importantly behavior analysis leads to a view of society and community that fosters fair and conditional forms of reinforcement and punishment from the community for behavior it has found to be exemplary and repulsive. Communities and societies are formed on the basis of the behavior they select, and its systems of reinforcement and punishment define this selection.

Applications within behavior theory and philosophy

Although the relation between basic research in behavior analysis and the applications of principles derived from the basic science has been explored in some detail elsewhere (e.g., Epling & Pierce, 1983; Johnston, 2000; Hayes, 1978; Pennypacker, 1986), important issues about these relations are addressed in the third section of this volume. In the context of a philosophy of technology, Neef and Peterson describe a range of possible relations between basic and applied behavior analysis that suggests many permutations of influence. These permutations replace the more conventional view that there is a linear progression of basic research to applied research to clinical practice and demonstrate how these influences have worked in one area of applied behavior analysis, developmental disabilities. Krapfl also proposes a break with more conventional applications of behavior analysis in organizational settings. Whereas in most applications of behavior analysis the attempt is to carry over the *methods* used in more controlled scientific settings to the applied site, Krapfl describes his experiences in carrying over the *philosophy* of the approach, and in so doing expanding the analysis from that of individuals to conceptually treating organizations or systems as behavior analysts typically treat individuals. Chase suggests how behavior-analytic concepts might be applied to problems of education. He starts with questions posed from those outside the field, and rather than dismissing them, argues that they are important pragmatic questions. This chapter then proceeds to illustrate some of the modern concepts of behavior analysis that have been developed to answer these questions.

Criticisms and defenses of behavioral psychology

Behavior analysis has never wanted for critics, both constructive and distractive, and one example has been within the general critique of modern scientific practices by postmodernists. The reaction of the authors in this book to postmodernism is consistent with Zuriff (1998); although behavior analysis shares commonalities with some forms of social constructionism, those forms of postmodernism that seemingly undermine a scientific approach to knowing (cf. Gross & Levitt, 1997) are the antithesis of behavior analysis. These issues are addressed specifically in the chapters by Marr and Staddon. Other criticisms of behavior analysis are also addressed. Often the initial criticism is provided by someone outside the field, for example, Chomsky's (1959) infamous review of Skinner (1957), but then the criticism is integrated into the field in the form of important questions that form the pragmatic criteria that need to be met by the field. In light of recent developments in behavioral education, for example, Chase responds to some of the earlier criticisms of behavior analysis made by Chomsky.

Self-criticism seems especially valuable because the weaknesses of the discipline are explored by those most familiar with it. Such criticisms provide some of best pragmatic tests for a field because they are informed, precise, and are more easily specified as pragmatic goals. Staddon addresses such issues with his critique of selectionism as a root metaphor of behavior analysis. Similarly, Ribes asks pertinent questions about the use and misuse of concepts in behavior analysis. Both Neuringer and Staddon point out Skinner's inconsistency in treating variability as a dimension of behavior. Skinner (1938) assumed that variability is affected by nonenvironmental factors. As a dimension of behavior, however, variability should be influenced by the environment and, in fact, Neuringer's review demonstrates this relation. Readers may or may not agree with all the conclusions about these issues, but they certainly form important challenges for the field.

In addition to these criticisms, there are also some contrasting views on a few fundamental issues reflected in the chapters of this book. One of these issues formed the gist of much debate at the Reese conference: the issue of molecular versus molar levels of analysis. Although most behaviorists take the evolutionary view that complex events are explained by the sum, product, or interaction of simpler events (see Donahoe's and Palmer's chapters), the nature of control by simpler events remains arguable. The molecular view specifies that control can be identified only at the most fine-grained level of behavior and contiguous environmental events. This kind of control is then repeated within complex events and the difficulty of examining complex events is making the relevant environmental events observable and measurable. This is the kind of view that leads to the reductionist views expressed by Donahoe and Schaal. Others take a molar view, the view that behavioral units can be integrated across time and space to form units that are themselves influenced by contiguous environmental events. Many of the chapters that deal with interpretation of psychological phenomena, like Hineline's chapter on intention, take this view. Both views are consistent with the simple to complex perspective of evolutionary epistemology. Both are consistent with the explanatory primacy of contiguity and contingency. They differ in terms of what the environment controls: the small units of behavior of the molecular view or the larger units of the molar view. This debate is by no means solved here, but the positions are described.

Connecting with other areas of psychology

Behavior analysis has sometimes been singled out as being outside the intellectual mainstream. For example, Krantz (1971) was among the first to point out the separation between what then was called operant and nonoperant psychology. Without assigning blame for the separation, he noted the infrequency of citations in the primary literature between the two worlds. Such a finding is not surprising in either the basic or applied areas of behavior analysis because of the specificity of the problems under investigation. When behavior analysis is represented in the nonoperant literature, however, the usual "steady misrepresentation" of the world view and the findings derived from them (Todd & Morris, 1983) illustrates the separation between behavior analysis and other areas of psychology. Nonetheless, from the Editors' vantage, a most important general theme in this book is the continuity of the ideas of behavioral psychology with many broader trends in the intellectual environment. As Sidman (1960) noted with respect to species differences in learning, differences between species, and in the present case, intellectual positions, are easy to find. The better criterion in terms of constructing a theory of learning or an epistemological position is that of its similarities or connections to extant positions, particularly similarities that expand and develop those extant themes.

Several of the chapters represent an attempt to reconcile such ideas from traditional psychology into behavior analysis. Whether this has been achieved without the perceived misrepresentation that characterizes some nonbehavioral interpretations of behavioral approaches is for the reader to judge. Many of the chapters in the second section represent a general attempt at reconciling concepts important to general psychology with a behavior-analytic world view. Morris's chapter directly emphasizes the importance of seeking common ground with mainstream psychology. Morris describes the similarities between behavior analysis and other areas of psychology through the concept of direct action. Direct action is the description of unmediated functional relations, except where those are "mediated" by other functional relations. Of special interest are the similarities and differences between behavior-analytic descriptions of direct action and those of other psychological workers including Gibson's theory of perception, Watkins' direct memory theorizing, certain aspects of social constructionism, and developmental systems analysis. In order to present the relations among these various parts of psychology, Morris reviews the basic tenets of each. Galuska addresses the issue of rapprochement with respect to the connections between science and religion, emphasizing a search for similarities rather than differences. These themes in behavior analysis build important bridges with other areas of intellectual life.

Another connection between behavior analysis and other points of view is found in the discussions in the first section of the volume where important general concepts in science and philosophy are discussed in the context of behavior analysis. For example, selectionism ties not only several of the present chapters together, as discussed above, but also relates behavior analysis to other disciplines concerned with how phenomena of different types evolve and change over time. Another example is that of contextualism, which as described earlier has an important place not only in behavior analysis, but also in the postmodernist movement that many behavior analysts and other scientists find antithetical to their world view. The philosophical traditions of behavior analysis tie it explicitly to other sciences.

Conclusions

This volume was designed as a textbook for students and professionals interested in a further understanding of behavior theory and philosophy. The chapters provide a mixture of some topics old, some new, and others borrowed. Although we can provide nothing "blue" to complete the folk rhyme repeated at generations of weddings, we hope that the marriage of these topics will enrich those who read about them and further the understanding of behavior theory and philosophy. We invite the reader to consider not only the chapters individually for their pithy development of specific problems in behavior theory and philosophy, but also consider them together as a whole. Like many of the best conferences, whether it is the annual meeting of the Association for Behavior Analysis or smaller more focused conferences, like the Reese conference that served the basis for this book, this book provides an exciting cross section of behavior-analytic work. Morris' synthesis of natural science and natural history applies to the integrative theme that we have attempted: "Together, . . . , they may contribute to a complete, thoroughgoing, unified, and naturalized psychology" (p. 290). It is this unified whole that defines behavior theory and philosophy.

References

Baer, D. M. (1981). The imposition of structure on behavior and demolition of behavioral structures. In John H. Flowers (Ed.) *Nebraska Symposium on Motivation* (pp. 217–254). Lincoln, NE: University of Nebraska Press.

Campbell, D. T. (1965). Variation and selection in sociocultural evolution. *Psychological Review, 67,* 380–400.

Catania, A. C. (1973). The psychologies of structure, function, and development. *American Psychologist, 28,* 434–443.

Chomsky, N. (1959). Verbal Behavior. By B. F. Skinner. *Language, 35,* 26–58.

Epling, W. F., & Pierce, W. D. (1983). Applied behavior analysis: New directions from the laboratory. *The Behavior Analyst, 6,* 27–37.

Gross, P. R., & Levitt, N. (1997). *Higher superstition: The academic left and its quarrels with science.* Baltimore: Johns Hopkins University Press.

Hayes, S. C. (1978). Theory and technology in behavior analysis. *The Behavior Analyst, 1978, 1,* 25–33.

Hayes, S. C., Hayes, L. J., & Reese, H. W. (1988). Finding the philosophical core: A review of Stephen C. Pepper's *World Hypotheses: A study in evidence. Journal of the Experimental Analysis of Behavior, 50,* 97–111.

Johnston, J. M. (2000). Behavior analysis and the R & D paradigm. *The Behavior Analyst, 23,* 141–148.

Krantz, D. L. (1971). The separate worlds of operant and nonoperant psychology. *Journal of Applied Behavior Analysis, 4,* 61–70.

Marr, M. J. (1993). Contextualistic mechanism or mechanistic contextualism?: The straw machine as tar baby. *The Behavior Analyst, 16,* 59–65.

Morris, E. K. (1993). Behavior analysis and mechanism: One is not the other. *The Behavior Analyst, 16,* 25–43.

Pennypacker, H. S. (1986). The challenge of technology transfer: Buying in without selling out. *The Behavior Analyst, 9,* 147–156.

Pepper, S. C. (1942). *World hypotheses: A study in evidence.* Berkeley, CA: University of California Press.

Petroski, H. (1994). *The evolution of useful things.* New York: Vintage Books.

Sidman, M. (1960). *Tactics of scientific research.* New York: Basic Books.

Skinner, B. F. (1938). *The behavior of organisms: An experimental analysis.* New York: Prentice Hall.

Skinner, B. F. (1957). *Verbal behavior.* Englewood Cliffs, NJ: Prentice-Hall.

Skinner, B. F. (1987). *Upon further reflection.* Englewood Cliffs, NJ: Prentice-Hall.

Todd, J. T., & Morris, E. K. (1983). Misconception and miseducation: Presentations of radical behaviorism in psychology textbooks. *The Behavior Analyst, 6,* 153–160.

Zuriff, G. (1998). Against metaphysical social constructionism in psychology. *Behavior and Philosophy, 26,* 5–28.

I

Philosophical Foundations

2

Explanation and Description in Traditional Neobehaviorism, Cognitive Psychology, and Behavior Analysis

J. Moore

Reese (1999) has noted that the nature of explanation and its relation to description have been hotly debated for many years. The present chapter critically examines the status of explanation and description in contemporary behavioral science, particularly traditional neobehaviorism, cognitive psychology, and behavior analysis.

Historical Background

The chapter begins with a review of certain themes in the historical background of explanation. The purpose of this historical review is to briefly draw attention to certain themes in the literature of causal explanation that are relevant to the latter stages of the paper, rather than to exhaustively survey the topic. Not surprisingly, I start with Aristotle.

Aristotle

Aristotle (ca. 385–322 BCE) is often given a treasured place in discussions about the origin of scientific knowledge and methodology, and

J. Moore, • Department of Psychology, University of Wisconsin-Milwaukee, Milwaukee, WI 53201.

rightfully so. According to Aristotle, one has knowledge of the fact, which is essentially observational or perceptual knowledge, and knowledge of the reasoned fact, which is demonstrated knowledge. Demonstrated knowledge is not experimental demonstration, but rather a rational demonstration or logical proof. The demonstration takes the form of a syllogism in which the major premise is a law of nature, the minor premise is the observed fact of nature, and the conclusion is the reasoned fact:

> All men are mortal
> Socrates is a man
> _____
> Socrates is mortal

The syllogism is taken to explain why Socrates is mortal. Knowledge of the highest order, or scientific knowledge, is knowledge of the reasoned fact, demonstrated according to such syllogisms (Wallace, 1972, p. 12).

In addition, scientific knowledge has another feature. Aristotle indicated that this feature concerns the identification of the causes of the phenomenon to be explained:

> We suppose ourselves to possess unqualified scientific knowledge of a thing, as opposed to knowing it in the accidental way in which the sophist knows, when we think that we know the cause on which the fact depends, as the cause of that fact and no other, and, further, that the fact could not be other than it is. (Ross, 1938, p. 25)

Thus, the implication is that a thing can be scientifically understood only when its causes are known. Aristotle suggested, however, the use of the word *cause* in four different senses. In informal language, these four causes are

1. The material cause, or that substance from which a thing is made;
2. The formal cause, or the antecedent conditions that attend to the form of the thing.
3. The efficient cause, or the action by which a thing is made; and
4. The final cause, or the consequence for the sake of which a thing is made.

Typically, the explanatory statement identifies as many of these causal explanatory factors as is appropriate to the matter at hand.

The common illustration is a statue. The material cause would be the substance of which the statue is made: clay, bronze, or marble. The formal cause would be a smaller copy or model of the statue that the sculptor made to guide the production of the full-size statue. The efficient cause would the hammering, chiseling, molding by the sculptor. The final cause would be the ultimate use or function of the statue, such as to honor a distinguished figure in a public park or building.

Note that the illustration above of a statue concerns the cause of an artifact, rather than the cause of an event. Aristotle's system went beyond the present simple illustration of making some artifact, of course. The event of going for a walk might be explained by appealing to several causes, and noting the relation among them. Persons might go for a walk because they have legs (a material cause), because they always walk at this time of day (a formal cause), because they socialize with others when they walk (an efficient cause), and because walking will improve their health (a final cause). Whether final causes are essentially teleological, and whether they are appropriate for science, if at all, is a matter of continuing debate. In any case, the most comprehensive answer to any *Why?* question would be in terms of the four types of explanatory factors, if knowledge of these factors is appropriate from the point of view being analyzed and can be attained (Wallace, 1972, pp. 13 ff.).

Bacon

Sir Francis Bacon (1561–1626) was a strict empiricist, advocating the direct and objective study of nature. Bacon believed that accounts of how nature should be studied that were based on Scripture, faith, or theological authority would only interfere with learning how nature actually functions. Smith (1995) points out that for Bacon, the appropriate method of science is induction, in which knowledge arises "by gradual and unbroken ascent" (Bacon, 1620/1960, p. 43) from particular observations to cautiously tested generalizations. No other approach to procuring knowledge would suffice, for "the intellect is not qualified to judge except by means of induction" (Bacon, p. 23). This is not to say that Bacon advocated that scientists should avoid classifying observations. Rather, he advocated proceeding inductively from observation to generalization, but very cautiously.

Before induction could begin, however, Bacon (1620/1960, p. 105) believed the mind must be purged and swept, and the floor of the mind must be leveled. These actions remove preconditions derived from everyday life that obstruct understanding and that lead investigators into "numberless empty controversies and idle fancies" (Bacon, p. 49) that interfere with learning about nature. Bacon identified four types of such preconditions, which he metaphorically labeled *Idols*. His choice of the term *Idol* was presumably based on their ability to inspire so much mischievous devotion (Bacon, pp. 48 ff.). The first was *Idols of the Tribe*, so named because he believed they were intrinsic to human nature. An example is the tendency to be overly influenced by sensational but unrepresentative occurrences.

The second was *Idols of the Cave,* so named to relate them to the Platonic myth of people living in a cave and mistaking shadows on the wall for reality. An example is the tendency of individuals to interpret the whole in light of the particular part with which they are especially acquainted. The third was *Idols of the Marketplace,* so named because the ill and unfit words and concepts that are used in daily life may not suit the task of understanding nature. An example is individuals who accept the words used in everyday language as naming real things, when in fact they only name fictions. The fourth is *Idols of the Theater,* so named because most formal philosophical systems offer dogmas that do not picture nature as it really is; rather, they offer only a representation of nature, much like a stage play in a theater offers only a representation of an event. An example would be accepting a particular philosophical system as comprehensive and valuable, when in actuality it is based on scholastic authority and too few observations to be useful. In any case, once the arbitrary abstractions of common parlance and of philosophical systems have been rejected, the process of Baconian induction could commence. This method, in Bacon's words, "depends on keeping the eye steadily fixed upon the facts of nature and so receiving their images as simply as they are" (Bacon, p. 29).

Smith (1995) notes that Bacon also advocated the practical aspects of scientific activity. "Nature to be commanded must be obeyed; and that which in contemplation is as the cause is in operation as the rule," said Bacon (1620/1960, p. 39). Science becomes an activity in which the inquisition of causes, "searching into the bowels of nature," merges with the production of effects, "shaping nature as on an anvil" (Bacon, 1623/1937, p. 413). If humans are to learn efficiently from nature, says Bacon, it will be from nature "forced out of her natural state, and squeezed and moulded" because "the nature of things betrays itself more readily under the vexations of art [i.e., experiments] than in its natural freedom" (Bacon, 1620/1960, p. 25). In Bacon's philosophy, therefore, the human capacity to inquire into causes, and knowing those causes, to produce effects, is the beginning and end of science. It is the beginning when nature is squeezed and moulded by experiments to reveal its order, and it is the end when its laws permit the shaping of nature as on an anvil for the betterment of the human condition.

Hume

The British empiricist philosopher David Hume (1711–1776) contributed much to the background of scientific explanation, particularly concerning the topic of causation and scientific knowledge. He did not deny the existence of causal relations and thereby undermine science, which presumably searches for those relations. Rather, Hume questioned whether people actually know a thing when they say they know the cause of an event. More specifically, he sought to specify what is meant by a causal relation and how beliefs in such relations develop: "The idea, then, of causation must be deriv'd from some *relation* among objects; and that relation we must now endeavour to discover" (Hume, 1888/1964, p. 75).

Hume (1888/1964) identified eight bases by which people come to use the language of cause and effect. The first four are well known and the ones generally cited. The last four are included here for completeness:

1. The cause and effect must be contiguous in space and time.
2. The cause must be prior to the effect.
3. There must be a constant union betwixt the cause and effect. 'Tis chiefly this quality that constitutes the relation.
4. The same cause always produces the same effect, and the same effect never arises but from the same cause...
5. There is another principle, which hangs upon this, *viz.* that where several different objects produce the same effect, it must be by means of some quality, which we discover to be common amongst them. For as like effects imply like causes, we must always ascribe the causation to the circumstance, wherein we discover the resemblance.
6. The following principle is founded on the same reason. The difference in the effects of two resembling objects must proceed from that particular, in which they differ. For as like causes always produce like effects, when in any instance we find our expectation to be disappointed, we must conclude that this irregularity proceeds from some difference in the causes.
7. When any object encreases or diminishes with the encrease or diminution of its cause, 'tis to be regarded as a compounded effect, deriv'd from the unition of several different effects, which arise from the several different parts of the cause....
8. The eighth and last rule I shall take notice of is, that an object, which exists for any time in its full perfection without any effect, is not the sole cause of the effect, but requires to be assisted by some other principle, which may forward its influence and operation. For as like effects necessarily follow from like causes, and in a contiguous time and place, their separation for a moment shews, that these causes are not compleat ones. (pp. 173–175)

Strictly speaking, then, people do not experience cause and effect. Rather, their knowledge of cause and effect is derived from experiences of the sort identified above.

In addition, Hume (1777/1902) identified two kinds of knowledge: empirical and demonstrative. Empirical knowledge is based on our experience in the world at large. It alone can furnish knowledge that can effectively guide our conduct. In contrast, demonstrative knowledge is the abstract product of the imagination. An example of demonstrative knowledge would be knowledge of relations in mathematics that are based on logical deduction from one idea to another. Demonstrative knowledge implied nothing about actual events in the world at large or objects outside the mind. According to Hume, knowledge must be either empirical or demonstrative to be considered genuine. As Hume stated in a famous passage,

> When we run over libraries, persuaded of these principles, what havoc must we make? If we take in our hand any volume; of divinity or school metaphysics, for instance; let us ask, Does it contain any abstract reasoning concerning quantity or number? No. Does it contain any experimental reasoning concerning matter of fact and existence? No. Commit it then to the flames; for it can contain nothing but sophistry and illusion. (p. 165)

Comte

The Frenchman August Comte (1798–1857) is generally associated with the development of the viewpoint known as positivism. According to Comte's positivism, societies pass through stages that are defined by the ways its members explain natural events. The first stage is the theological. Explanations during this stage are based on supernatural religious principles and mysticism. The second stage is the metaphysical. Explanations during this stage are based on unseen essences, principles, or forces. The third stage is the scientific. Explanations during the third stage are based on the scientific description of events as they are observed. The third stage is the stage of positivism, in which only events that can be positively and directly experienced (i.e., publicly observed) are worthy of scientific attention. Readers may note that Comte's ideas about first and second stages are compatible with Bacon's Idols and add that his ideas about a third stage are compatible with more modern positivistic treatments, such as that of Popper's (1963) emphasis on the falsifiability of deductions via publicly observable tests. In any case, Comte held that just as societies pass through this sequence of three stages, so also does human intellectual development. People tend to be theologians as children, metaphysicians as youths, and scientists only as adults, if at all.

Comte's positivism holds that the only things one can be sure of are those that are publicly observable. Insofar as science is concerned with the publicly observable, its explanations can be trusted and used as the basis for improving society. Indeed, science should become the religion for humanity, and science should be based on what is publicly observable, to prevent unwarranted diversions into theological or metaphysical dimensions (Hergenhahn, 1997).

Mill

John Stuart Mill (1806–1873) was an associationist in the British empiricist tradition of Locke, Berkeley, and Hume. With regard to scientific methodology, Mill proposed five canons, or Methods of Inductive Inference, by means of which one could investigate possible causes and lay the foundation for scientific explanations. These methods are those of Agreement, Difference, Joint Method of Agreement and Difference, Residues, and Concomitant Variation (Wallace, 1974). By following these Methods one could identify the causes of an event and thereby explain it.

According to the Method of Agreement, one looks to see if some suspected causal factor is present when the effect in question occurs. According to the Method of Difference, one looks to see if some suspected causal factor is absent when the effect fails to occur. According to the Joint Method, one conducts both operations simultaneously. According to the Method of Residues, one eliminates factors when the effect occurs, and the last factor that remains when the effect in question occurs is the cause. According to the Method of Concomitant Variation, one manipulates the degree to which a presumed causal factor is present, and if the degree of the effect also varies, then one can conclude the factor is indeed causal. If anyone believes these techniques are of historical interest only, consider various manipulations used in psychological research, both traditional and behavior analytic: (a) discrimination and reversal as control procedures in conditioning and stimulus control research, (b) A-B-A designs; and (c) parametric variations of independent variables.

Mach

Ernst Mach (1838–1916) was an eminent Austrian physicist and mathematician who sought to use the philosophical-historical method to resolve scientific problems and purify scientific concepts. Mach proposed a brand of positivism whereby science was viewed as the phenomenological experience of scientists. He further adopted a number of views in his life that followed directly from his position, but that strike us today as exceedingly curious. For example, he strenuously opposed the proliferation of unseen explanatory entities, such as atoms and genes, which were entirely too speculative for his tastes. Despite his reticence, he nevertheless accepted Lamarck's ideas about the inheritance of acquired characteristics as an approach to genetics and Wundt's introspectionism as an approach to psychology.

As Smith (1995, p. 42) and Marr (1985, p. 131) point out, the aim of Mach's method was to "clear up ideas, expose the real significance of the matter, and get rid of metaphysical obscurities" (Mach, 1883/1942, p. xiii). Mach's positivistic treatment of the concept of *cause* stands as a case in point. Mach argued that most thinkers conceive of cause in terms of some power or force that pushes or pulls entities toward some characteristic effect. Mach believed that this notion of cause, however, is metaphorical, superfluous, and must be rejected in scientific formulations. Instead, Mach advocated a purely descriptive notion of cause and effect in terms of the observed, correlated changes in two classes of phenomena. These observed, correlated changes could be represented economically as the functional relation between two variables in a mathematical equation (e.g., Mach, 1883/1942).

According to Mach, then, an explanation of an event was useful only if it carefully described how the event took place. An explanation of an event purportedly addressing the question of why the event took place ran the risk of sinking into a morass of metaphysical speculation about occult causal powers and forces. An effective explanation/description would use economical concepts derived from actual observation and human experience, rather than invoke hypotheses about unseen causal powers and forces. As had Bacon and other empiricists/positivists before him, Mach urged the direct study of nature, rather than the study of verbalizations about nature: "We err when we expect more enlightenment from an hypothesis than from the facts themselves" (Mach, 1883/1942, p. 600).

Russell

Bertrand Russell (1872–1970) was a philosopher of enormous interests, prodigious ability, and uncommon influence who wrote on topics ranging from the foundations of mathematics to nuclear disarmament. When discussing the philosophical basis of causation in science, Russell (1932) noted that paradoxically, "All philosophers, of every school, imagine that causation is one of the fundamental axioms or postulates of science, yet, oddly enough, in advanced sciences such as gravitational astronomy, the word *cause* never occurs" (p. 180). What was his alternative? In the empiricist tradition of his time, Russell embraced the position noted earlier by Mach:

> We then considered the nature of scientific laws, and found that, instead of stating that one event A is always followed by another event B, they stated functional relations between certain events at certain times, which we called determinants, and other events at earlier or later times or at the same time. (pp. 207–208)

Of course, mere observation was not always going to be adequate. It had to be supplemented by the application of rigorous logic. Hence, Russell noted,

"Whenever possible, logical constructions are to be substituted for inferred entities" (p. 155). Description supplemented by logical/mathematical formulations of functional relations became the benchmark for scientific explanation.

Modern Treatments

Many modern treatments of causation and explanation include some reference to necessary and sufficient conditions. As in many of the preceding strategies, the to-be-explained phenomenon is an event. One is said to have explained an event when one has identified its cause, in terms of the necessary and sufficient conditions. P is said to be a necessary condition for event Q if Q never occurs in the absence of P (Copi, 1982). P is said to be a sufficient condition for event Q if Q always occurs whenever P occurs. As Copi has described it, there may be several necessary conditions for the occurrence of an event, and they must all be included in the sufficient condition. The predecessors to an explanatory approach concerned with identifying necessary and sufficient conditions would presumably include Aristotle, Mill, and Russell for their emphasis on logic (e.g., Mill's Method of Agreement is concerned with eliminating some factor as a necessary condition, and his Method of Difference is concerned with eliminating some factor as a sufficient condition), Bacon for his pragmatic concerns, and Hume for his phenomenology (see also summaries in Pitt, 1988; Salmon, 1984, 1989; Sosa & Tooley, 1993). For example, with regard to Hume, the succession of contiguous events, the temporal priority of cause, and the constant union (i.e., constant conjunction) of cause and effect imply causation in the sense of either the final necessary condition or the sufficient condition.

To recapitulate, then, the phenomenon that is to be explained is an event. An event implies some sort of a change has taken place from t1 to t2. In a common example, suppose there has been an explosion of gasoline vapor. There was no explosion at t1, but there was at t2. One asks why the vapor exploded at t2, and identifies such factors as the striking of a match on a rough surface, the presence of oxygen, the presence of the vapor itself, and so on. It was necessary that the match be dry, but the presence of a dry match in and of itself, without the other factors, is not sufficient to explain the event of why the vapor exploded at t2.

In everyday usage, cause sometimes means a necessary condition and sometimes a sufficient condition (Copi, 1982). It is most often used in the sense of a necessary condition when one wants to eliminate some undesirable event. In such a case, one identifies a necessary condition and thereby eliminates it, eliminating the event. Thus, if one wants to eliminate an explosion of vapor, one eliminates the oxygen.

Cause is most often used in the sense of a sufficient condition when one wants to produce some desirable event (Copi, 1982). In such a case, one provides all the appropriate conditions. In the cylinder of an internal combustion engine, for example, one causes vapor to explode by bringing together a mixture of vapor and air from the carburetor, a spark from a plug, and so on.

In everyday usage, cause can sometimes also have a third meaning, traceable presumably to Hume: the (final necessary) condition that makes the difference between the occurrence or nonoccurrence of the event, in the context of the other necessary conditions that usually prevail. Thus, to continue with the analogy of the explosion of gasoline vapor, if one's lawn mower does not start and there is no problem with the carburetor, then one looks to the spark plug. Suppose it is fouled with carbon deposits from using an incorrect grade of gasoline. In such a case, one might say that changing the fouled spark plug causes the lawn mower to work.

Causes also have a temporal dimension that modern treatments typically take into account by the adjectives *remote* and *proximal*. The adjectives concern how far back into the causal chain of necessary or sufficient conditions one wants to go. If one goes back quite far, one is inquiring into remote causes, and the more one is concerned with immediate factors, the more one is concerned with proximal causes. A remote cause of a fouled spark plug resulting in the lawn mower not starting might be the incorrect grade of gasoline. A proximal cause might be the fouled spark plug itself.

Finally, questions are sometimes raised about the plurality of causes, and its relation to explanatory treatments in terms of necessary and sufficient conditions. At face value, the doctrine of necessary and sufficient conditions suggests a unique cause for an event. But what if there are alternative causes for an event? Presumably, gasoline vapor could be caused to explode (given other necessary conditions) by either the flame of a match or the spark from a plug. As Copi (1982) noted, if there can be a plurality of causes, then inferences about necessary and sufficient cause-effect relations are not possible. This question of the plurality of causes is ordinarily answered by focusing on a specific, particular event, with specific, particular participating factors. The vapor exploded. That was a particular event. In the explosion in question, was a match or spark present? The answer identifies a specific, particular causal factor in a specific, particular event. It may well be that in another event, another factor might assume a specific, particular causal role, but that would lead either to another analysis that identified necessary and specific conditions for that event or a factor common to all of these factors, for example, temperature.

Summary

As suggested in the review above, the relation between description and explanation has an interesting and lengthy past in scientific epistemology. Often one reads that description deals with matters of *How* and explanation deals with matters of *Why*, but the relation seems decidedly complex. Most scholars regard sense perceptions as the source of the data for explanations. Indeed, some empiricists and positivists like Comte and Mach would say that to properly explain an event one gives as precise a description as possible of how the event took place; to go beyond is to invite metaphysical speculation and epistemological disaster. A large number of scholars, however, have not regarded sense perceptions as adequate by themselves. For example, the treatments of Aristotle and Mill, which are separated by 2000 years, as well as more modern treatments (e.g., in the logical positivist tradition), argue that empiricism and positivism are much recommended, but empiricism and positivism ultimately need the rigor of logic to impart order into the observations and to ensure that unobserved causal powers and forces from other dimensions do not intrude into the explanation. Interestingly, despite the noble objective to bring order to empiricism through logic, scholars through the years have remained divided as to whether there really are causal phenomena (e.g., essences, powers, forces, entities, or agents) in other dimensions that are not publicly observable. Given this division of the scientific house, scholars have further debated such questions as (a) whether science can deal *directly* with the causal phenomena from those other dimensions, (b) whether science must deal *indirectly* with the phenomena as logical constructions, and (c) whether an explanation that appeals to the phenomena from other dimensions can still be regarded as adequate if it is logically rigorous. These questions apply to description and explanation in behavioral psychology, topics to which I now turn.

Two Explanatory Strategies in Traditional Neobehaviorism

In more modern approaches to explanation, two strategies have become prominent (e.g., Kaplan, 1964; Turner, 1967). One is here called *instantiation*, according to which an event is regarded as explained when its quantitative features are symbolically represented using some specific value of a variable in a general proposition, equation, or law. This strategy is descended from the basic observational, descriptive nature of science evident in Bacon's inductivism, Comte's positivism, Mill's methods of inductive inference, and Mach's descriptive positivism, described above.

Consider, for example, the neobehavioristic learning theory of C. L. Hull. Hull was interested in devising a theoretical system of behavior in which interlocking theoretical equations fit observations. In this regard, his famous Postulate 4 on reinforcement may be paraphrased as follows: "Whenever effector and receptor activity occur in close temporal contiguity, and this activity is closely associated with need reduction, there will result an increment in the tendency for that afferent impulse on later occasions to evoke that response" (Hull, 1943, pp. 177–178). The specific mathematical form of the equation that described the increasing tendency of the stimulus to evoke the response (a simple *positive growth function* that was negatively accelerated) was $_SH_R = 1 - 10^{-.0305N}$. In this equation, $_SH_R$ was the term for habit strength, and N was the number of prior trials on which reinforcement had been delivered (i.e., drive had been reduced). Instantiation contributed to Hull's explanations of behavior when he used specific instances of the variables from the equations in the system to describe the characteristics of an event, such as the speed with which a rat runs down a straight alley, given a series of trials in which the rat had received reinforcement (e.g., Hull, 1952).

The second explanatory strategy is to deduce an event from a *covering law* (e.g., Hempel & Oppenheim, 1948). According to this form of explanation, a behavioral event is regarded as explained when its description follows as a valid deduction in a logical argument in which one of the premises is a covering law and another premise is a statement of observed antecedent conditions. This strategy is descended from Aristotle's knowledge of the reasoned fact, Hume's demonstrative knowledge, and modern treatments of logic following in the tradition of Mach's and Russell's versions of positivism, described above. It is particularly related to logical positivism's blending of empiricism with formal symbolic logic and hypothetico-deductive techniques. A covering-law explanation might be said to be a higher level of explanation than instantiation in that a covering law typically includes premises that are derived from a wide range of observations, or perhaps even second order statements that are logically derived from the kind of first order statements found in explanations by instantiation (cf. Turner, 1967; Kaplan, 1964). The generality and logical derivation of the covering law and other premises contributes to a higher order theoretical network with additional implications. These kinds of networks and implications extend beyond the abstract descriptions of instantiation.

The covering-law model also contributed to Hull's neobehavioristic explanations in that his overall goal was to devise a hypothetico-deductive system in which behavioral events could be subsumed under an interlocking network of covering laws, much as Euclidean geometry consisted of deductions based on an interlocking network of postulates, axioms, theorems, and corollaries. For example, in one of his seminal papers, Hull (1937) wrote that:

1. A satisfactory scientific theory should begin with a set of explicitly stated postulates accompanied by specific or operational definitions of the critical terms employed.
2. From these postulates there should be deduced by the most rigorous logic possible under the circumstances, a series of interlocking theorems covering the major concrete phenomena of the field in question.
3. The statements in the theorems should agree in detail with the observationally known facts of the discipline under consideration.... (p. 5)

Given this stance, one can readily see why Kendler and Spence (1971) identified the focal importance of deductive processes in neobehavioristic explanations:

The neobehavioristic decision concerning the nature of explanation is, in principle, both clear and simple. Explanation is equated with theoretical deduction: an event is explained by deducing it from one or more general propositions. The deductive process is analogous to mathematical proof although its precision can vary from mathematical verification to the logical use of ordinary language. The constructs used in the theoretical propositions must in some manner be representative of the concepts involved in the events to be explained. In other words the theoretical constructs must be coordinated with the empirical events. (p. 21)

One particularly noteworthy feature of covering-law explanations is the symmetry among description, explanation, and prediction. For example, if the conclusion of the argument is expressed in the past tense, the conclusion is in fact a description of what has already been observed, and the event is said to explained. If the conclusion of the argument is expressed in the future tense, the conclusion is in fact a description of something that has not yet happened, but will happen if the designated antecedent conditions prevail, and the event is said to have been predicted. Moreover, the positions of (a) the statement of antecedent conditions and (b) the conclusion can technically be reversed in the argument, with no loss of validity. The covering-law model sidesteps these matters by emphasizing simply the logical structure of the argument. As shown below, however, this symmetry raises a technical question about the relation between explanation and description.

Explanations in Cognitive Psychology

As most readers are no doubt aware, cognitive and behavioral psychology are at considerable odds about the subject matter and methods of behavioral science. For example, Schnaitter (1986) suggests that cognitivists make two rather fundamental assumptions about behavior. The first is that prevailing environmental circumstances radically underdetermine behavior. The second is that appeals to empirical-associative principles cannot account for psychologically interesting behavior, such as engaging in a temporally extended sequence of actions like uttering a sentence. Thus, cognitivists argue vigorously that any viewpoint that embraces these two features, as they believe any form of behaviorism does, is limited at best, if not hopelessly inadequate. Let us now examine these two issues in more detail.

The first issue is that behavior is relatively independent of environmental stimuli. Consequently, cognitivists argue that any substantial appeal to environmental stimuli in an explanation cannot possibly be correct. Rather, one needs to take into account some postulated internal phenomenon, such as an internal state or mechanism, to properly explain any order in behavior. Fodor (1981) makes this point by describing the action of a machine that dispenses cans of soda. If Individual A puts in coins that constitute the purchase price, the machine dispenses a can of soda. Suppose, however, that Individual B has put in some number of coins first, but less than the purchase price, and then A starts to put in coins. The machine will dispense a can of soda before A has put in coins constituting the ordinary purchase price. Fodor argues that the appropriate way to characterize the operation of the soda machine is in terms of its internal state: How far along to the ordinary purchase price is it? By knowing this state, one can understand what input will produce the output.

In the same way, many cognitivists argue, one must know the functional state of the individual, the principles by which new states develop from old, and the principles by which the state generates its output, in order to understand why behavior occurs. Just knowing the input is never enough to explain the output (see alternatives to this view in this volume: Catania, Chase, Donahoe, Neef, Neuringer, Palmer, and Rachlin).

The second issue raised by cognitivists is that associative principles cannot account for temporally extended sequences of behavior. Cognitivists then argue that any position appealing to associative principles, as they assert behaviorism manifestly does, cannot possibly be correct. For example, Hull's Postulate 4 on reinforcement, previously cited, specifies an underlying associative connection (habit strength) forged by drive reduction. Similarly, consider an explanation of a series of movements that says one movement serves as the associated stimulus for another movement, like beads on a chain, until the sequence is completed. Moore (2000a) reviews how J. B. Watson often spoke of this sort of chaining mechanism in an effort to be objective (see also Schnaitter, 1986). Lashley (1951) has pointed out, however, that the temporal interval between individual responses in typing or playing a piano is far too short for the stimulating neural after-trace from one response to affect the next. Moreover, sentences seem not to be produced according to a simple, linear sequence whereby the first word serves as a stimulus for the second, the second for the third, and so on, until the sentence is completed (see Moore, 2000a). In these sorts of cases, the temporally extended sequence of behavior is obviously attributable to another, nonassociative principle. Consequently, given that an assumption of associationism is defective, so also must be behaviorism and any of its explanations that seek to incorporate that assumption.

Cognitive Explanations

To better understand the basis of the cognitive concerns, let us consider the argument advanced by Wessells (1982). Wessells suggested there are three stages in the research strategy of cognitive psychology. In the first stage, cognitivists define the area of inquiry, develop the methodology, and collect the basic observations. In the second stage, cognitivists propose on an essentially descriptive level, potential processing mechanisms responsible for generating the observed behavior. In the third stage, cognitivists construct a formal explanatory account that specifies an underlying internal phenomenon capable of generating the external phenomenon of interest, with particular attention to an abstract rendering of the functional principles attending the internal phenomenon.

Thus, many cognitivists have adopted a different approach to scientific activity than have behaviorists. Indeed, in a related analysis Wessells (1981) earlier stated that

> One of the chief points made above is that the two approaches [cognitive and behavioral] diverge sharply in their metatheoretical claims and their conceptions about explanation. The chief aims of radical behaviorism are to predict and control behavior. . . . In contrast, the principal aim of cognitive psychology is to explain behavior by specifying on a conceptual level the universal, internal structures and processes through which the environment exerts its effects. . . . In order to achieve extensive cooperation between behaviorists and cognitivists, these differences in conceptions of explanation will have to be reconciled. (pp. 167–168)

What explanatory strategies do cognitivists favor as alternatives?

As implied in the Wessells (1981) passage above, cognitivists favor mechanistic explanatory statements that identify on an abstract level a set of internal acts, states, mechanisms, processes, structures, capacities, and properties purportedly responsible for the observed behavioral events. Thus, the question of *Why does behavior x occur?* is taken to mean *In virtue of what properties in the internal structures, processes, and states of the subject under observation can behavior x occur?* Simon (1992) states the matter clearly:

> For systems that change through time, explanation takes the form of laws acting on the current state of the system to produce a new state—endlessly. Such explanations can be formalized with differential or difference equations.
>
> A properly programmed computer can be used to explain the behavior of the dynamic system that it simulates. Theories can be stated as computer programs. (p. 160)

A particularly important issue in cognitive psychology is postulating a set of mediating organismic states and principles that afford *competence.* Chomsky (1980) defined competence as:

> the cognitive state that encompasses all those aspects of form and meaning and their relation, including underlying structures that enter into that relation, which are properly assigned to the specific subsystem of the human mind that relates representations of form and meaning. (p. 59)

For example, with regard to language, competence is ordinarily taken to refer to the ability of a speaker to derive meaning from sounds or the linguistic tokens called words, according to the rules of the language. Chomsky (1965) was extraordinarily influential in the development of this approach, and although he has since revised his position substantially (Schoneberger, 2000), the concepts of rules and cognitive states they generate remains central in the field of psycholinguistics and by implication cognitive psychology generally. Rules, then, are the principles by which language may be generated and understood. For example, if one wanted to produce a series of even numbers, one might describe the algorithm according to which they are generated as $y = x + 2$, where the first x is an even number. The set would be complete and infinite. The algorithm does not produce any specific even number. Rather, it just describes how the set of such numbers is produced. In this same sense, language is a system of rules for generating a presumably infinite set of grammatically and syntactically correct and meaningful sentences. To explain language one would specify the internalized rules the speaker knows that underlie the generating of that language (Schoneberger, 2000).

The internalized concern with competence is distinguished from an externalized concern with performance, which would focus on analyzing the relation between observed concrete behavior of speaking as an event and any environmental circumstances that accompany that behavior. Observed performance is merely the evidence of that competence, but is not of any special concern beyond being evidence (Cummins, 1983; Schnaitter, 1984).

Ostensible Differences Between Cognitive, Instantiation, and Covering-Law Explanations

I have shown that traditional neobehavioristic explanations in psychology tend to embrace instantiation or the covering-law model, and that cognitivists dispute the adequacy of such explanations. Cognitivists also find the explanatory strategies of instantiation and covering laws to be unsatisfactory. In general, cognitivists believe instantiation is unsatisfactory because it is principally descriptive, as opposed to genuinely explanatory. On a cognitive view, genuine explanations must identify causal mental phenomena, for example, as a functional state, mechanism, or structure. If a statement does not do so, it cannot be regarded as explanatory. Hence, many cognitivists, along with others, reject instantiation because little if anything is said about an underlying mental state, mechanism, or structure that could have generated the data being described. When cognitivists do develop a formal mathematical model, the model serves primarily as a means to support the proposition of an underlying mental mechanism, rather than as an end in itself.

Cognitivists also find covering-law explanations unsatisfactory. As noted in the earlier section, covering-law explanations are generally concerned with events. An event is defined by some collection of stimulus circumstances in the environment that constitutes an input and behavior that constitutes an output. Moreover, cognitivists argue that from a behaviorist view, elements in an event are associated with each other. Cognitivists have essentially three sorts of objections to this sort of approach. The first two have been described already: one cannot explain behavior as output purely on the basis of stimulus inputs, and talk of associations providing the link between the elements of these events is defective (e.g., Lashley, 1951). Third, the symmetry among description, explanation, and prediction in covering-law explanations manifestly shows that covering-law explanations are essentially descriptions that are ultimately devoid of any explanatory power. They are just different ways of framing descriptions, without identifying an underlying causal state or mechanism.

In sum, many cognitivists contend that to regard explanation as fundamentally a matter of describing publicly observable events and presumed associations among the publicly observable elements making up the event is simple minded and totally inadequate. These inadequacies hold even if (a) the description instantiates a general mathematical formula or (b) the description may be subsumed as a deduction from a covering law given a set of antecedent conditions. Rather, explanation should more properly be regarded as a matter of proposing the underlying structures and states

of the organism and the principles by which they operate, such that publicly observable events like behavior are assumed to follow naturally from
them.[1]

Explanatory Strategies in Behavior Analysis

The distinctions and practices of behavior-analytic epistemology generally and behavior-analytic explanatory strategies particularly often do
not map neatly onto traditional distinctions and practices. In brief, for behavior analysis the term *explanation* is regarded as a verbal phenomenon
(Catania, 1993). To analyze the meaning of explanation, one analyzes the
discriminative stimuli that occasion the use of the term and the reinforcers
that maintain it.

In the most general conventional sense of the term, then, an instance
of verbal behavior is said to be an explanation when the verbal behavior in question is occasioned by the functional influence of environmental
factors on behavior at the level of phylogeny, ontogeny, or culture. Typically, that influence takes the form of a functional relation. For instance, in
talking of behavior that developed during an organism's lifetime, Skinner
(1964) stated, "When I said explanation, I simply meant the causal account.
An explanation is the demonstration of a functional relationship between
behavior and manipulable or controllable variables" (p. 102). Thus, causal
explanation plays a central role in Skinner's system, given the fundamental
concern with practical outcomes, and causation is expressed as a functional
relation, in the fashion of Mach and Russell.

A further understanding of behavior-analytic explanatory strategies
may be gained by examining Skinner's writings on scientific epistemology,

---

[1] As an important aside, we can note that traditional neobehaviorists might defend themselves against these sorts of charges by saying that their explanations include theoretical
terms, which mediate the relation between input and output. These terms can conceivably
be taken to identify such factors as internal states, so neobehaviorists might argue they are
actually not guilty of the charges levied against them. Cognitivists disparage these sorts of
defenses by arguing that behaviorist theoretical terms are just puny facsimiles of stimuli
and responses, so the theoretical terms are not really mental states at all. The cognitivist
criticism, however, is inadequate because neobehaviorist theoretical terms are generally
hypothetical constructs, whose referents are open ended. Stimuli and responses may be the
license for invoking the construct, but they do not constitute the referents of the construct,
which can be anything, even mental states. Thus, in the end, the explanatory strategies of
traditional neobehaviorism as it eventually evolved and cognitive psychology, which are
conventionally regarded as diametrically opposed, may differ primarily in degree of emphasis, and not differ in kind after all (for complete development of this point, see Moore,
1996).

for example, concerning the use of the term theory. In this regard, Skinner (1953) wrote that science

> is a search for order, for uniformities, for lawful relations among the events in nature. It begins, as we all begin, by observing single episodes, but it quickly passes on to the general rule, to scientific law. . . . In a later stage science advances from the collection of rules or laws to larger systematic arrangements. Not only does it make statements about the world, it makes statements about statements. (pp. 13–14)

This claim about more advanced stage scientific statements is presumably consistent with Russell's (1932) comment that cause and effect statements may turn out to be absent from science. Cause and effect statements may well be conspicuous at the lower stages, but the terms cause and effect may disappear from higher order statements taken as theories and explanations because the higher order statements are less precise and more general.

Skinner (1947/1972) also noted that three important steps occur in the development of higher order scientific statements like theories and explanations. The first step is to identify the basic data. This step is surprisingly difficult, and many sciences have started off on the wrong foot precisely because they have incorrectly identified their basic data. The second step is to express uniform relations among the data. The expression of these relations typically takes the form of the laws of the science. The third step is to develop abstract concepts. Relying on Mach, Skinner identified *acceleration* and *force* as examples. These concepts are something more than the second step laws from which they are derived. Importantly, these concepts "are peculiarly the product of theory-making in the best sense, and they cannot be arrived at through any other process" (Skinner, 1947/1972, p. 307). They help the scientific statement go beyond the expression of uniform relations by providing "a formal representation of the data reduced to a minimal number of terms" (Skinner, 1950, p. 216). They can even be conjoined with laws for ever more complex statements. Whether one wants to call the resulting higher order statements theories or explanations is to some extent a matter of personal preference.

In any event, Skinner's early writing and its unselfconscious embrace of Baconian induction and Machian positivism created some confusion about the roles of description and explanation in behavior analysis (see Moore, 2000b). For example, Chapter 2 of *The Behavior of Organisms* (Skinner, 1938) opens as follows: "So far as scientific method is concerned, the system set up in the preceding chapter may be characterized as follows. It is positivistic. It confines itself to description rather than explanation" (p. 44). The relation between description and explanation was clarified, however, in Skinner's later writings. For example, Skinner (1957) distinguishes between descriptive and explanatory practices in *Verbal Behavior*:

> The direction to be taken in an alternative approach is dictated by the task itself. Our first responsibility is simple description: What is the topography of this subdivision of human behavior? Once that question has been answered in at least a preliminary fashion we may advance to the stage called explanation: What conditions are relevant to the occurrence of the behavior–what are the variables of which it is a function? (p. 10)

Thus, for behavior analysis, description and explanation are not isomorphic, but rather on a continuum of scientific activity (see also Skinner, 1953, and Moore, 1998).

In behavior analysis, therefore, when one is explaining, one is doing something more than when one is describing. A description might very well be offered on the basis of just a single observation, whereas an explanation is ordinarily never so offered. An explanation of behavior goes beyond description by specifying the functional relations between the to-be-explained response and its controlling variables. Explanation therefore involves more complex and presumably abstract stimulus control than description (Skinner, 1957). A description might well identify prevailing antecedent conditions and consequent conditions, but not a functional relation per se. The identification and further specification of causes and effects in terms of functional relations constitutes explanation in the ordinary usage of the term. Higher order explanations and theories may well take the form of statements about organizations of functional relations. Nevertheless, that specification involves a consistent level of observation and analysis. Behavior in particular is explained at the level of behavior, that is, at the level of the operations and prevailing stimulus conditions that impinge upon the organism and that may be considered as responsible for the behavior. One explains behavior by locating it "in a frame of reference provided by the [object] itself or by various external objects or fields of force" (Skinner, 1938, p. 6).

Why are explanations offered? This is a question about what reinforces the verbal behavior of explaining. Again, in conventional usage explanations are offered because they contribute, perhaps only indirectly, to understanding, prediction, and control. In short, an explanation provides the basis for effective interaction with nature. In an extension of the influence of Bacon and Mach, Skinner (1979) spoke about these and other more subtle factors that might maintain the behavior of explaining:

> Was not confirmation the be-all and end-all of science? It was a question concerning my own behavior, and I thought I had an answer: " . . . . What is the motivational substitute for thing-confirmation? Pretty important in teaching

> method to graduate students. Resulting *order* instead of *confirmation*?" My rein-
> forcers were the discovery of uniformities, the ordering of confusing data, the
> resolution of puzzlement. (p. 282)

In any event, the point is that always at issue in any analysis of explanation are the contingencies governing the verbal behavior regarded as
explanatory (Moore, 1990a).

Causal Explanation, Prediction, and Description

As the traditional covering-law model of explanation has been presented above, one of its principal features is that it mediates prediction.
Where does behavior analysis stand with respect to the important feature
of prediction? For behavior analysis, prediction is important as a practical matter. Skinner (1953) explicitly acknowledged the importance of the
matter as follows:

> [Science] begins, as we all begin, by observing single episodes, but it quickly
> passes on to the general rule, to scientific law.... As Ernst Mach showed in
> tracing the history of the science of mechanics, the earliest laws of science were
> probably the rules used by craftsmen and artisans in training apprentices....
> The scientific "system," like the law, is designed to enable us to handle a subject
> matter more efficiently. What we call the scientific conception of a thing is not
> passive knowledge. Science is not concerned with contemplation. When we
> have discovered the laws which govern a part of the world about us, we are
> then ready to deal effectively with that part of the world. By predicting the
> occurrence of an event we are able to prepare for it. By arranging conditions
> in ways specified by the laws of a system, we not only predict, we control: we
> "cause" an event to occur or to assume certain characteristics. (pp. 13–14)

Hence, behavior analysis is not simply interested in post hoc description.
Behavior analysis is concerned with prediction by virtue of its practical
implications. Interested readers may also want to review related arguments
in Moore (1998), which further discuss the pragmatic character of scientific
verbal behavior.

Staddon (1973, 2001) has argued that the proper concern for behavioral
psychology is the study of *behavioral mechanisms*. A behavioral mechanism
refers to a real-time principle of operation that describes the actual behavior of a living organism (Staddon, 2001). Thus, a behavioral mechanism
is a comprehensive statement of the relations among inputs, outputs, and
internal states of the organism at hand, where each state is defined by a set
of equivalent histories (e.g., Staddon, 1973, 2001). The causes are the inputs
together with the internal states. The states and resulting mechanisms are
not necessarily physiological, although they may ultimately make some
connection with brain physiology. Similarly, they are not cognitive, in that

they do not appeal to elements of mental life, like representations and expectancies (Staddon, 2001). Explanation consists of theoretical specification of the underlying behavioral mechanisms, using the inputs and internal states as the calculus. At issue for present purposes is the relation between Staddon's approach and behavior analysis, insofar as Staddon (e.g., 2001) has explicitly distanced himself from Skinner (see Staddon, this volume).

In actuality, behavior analysis has no dispute with internal states, provided the states are not assumed to be in another dimension, such as mental or conceptual (see Palmer, this volume). Behavior analysis simply calls attention to the necessity of dealing with the source of any internal states that are taken to exist, and the practical contribution of such states to prediction and control. For example, the internal state itself is presumably the result of the way that (a) prior contact with stimulating circumstances or (b) time/maturation has affected the organism in question. The organism's physiology has changed, but in principle the changes in that physiology are attributable to a set of conditions and those changes can be known. Thus, knowledge of internal states can enter into prediction and control, just as can other factors. Schnaitter (1986) has further described why the behavior-analytic approach is reasonable. For example, Schnaitter points out that the internal state of Fodor's (1981) soda machine given input from an insufficient number of coins is, after all, nothing less than a functionally equivalent way of specifying the environmental history of the machine. In addition, distributed throughout the behavior-analytic literature are such statements as "It is a given organism at a given moment that behaves, and it behaves because of its 'biological equipment' at that moment" (Skinner as cited in Catania & Harnad, 1988, p. 301); "The organism behaves as it does because of its current state" (Skinner as cited in Catania & Harnad, 1988, p. 305); "I agree that at any given moment a person's behavior is due to the state of his body at that moment" (Skinner as cited in Catania & Harnad, 1988, p. 327); and

> This is not to question the importance of physiology in a science of behavior. In a more advanced account of a behaving organism "historical" variables will be replace by "causal." When we can observe the momentary state of an organism, we shall be able to use it instead of the history responsible for it in predicting behavior. When we can generate or change a state directly, we shall be able to use it to control behavior. Neither the science nor the technology of behavior will then vanish, however. Physiological manipulations will simply be added to the armamentarium of the behavioral scientist (Skinner, 1969, p. 283).

Indeed, it would seem that behavior analysis has done a reasonably acceptable job of acknowledging the functional relevance of internal states all along (cf. Donahoe, this volume; Palmer, this volume; Schaal, this volume).

Behavior Analysis and Cognitive Explanations

How then does behavior analysis view cognitive explanations? Is a cognitive explanation in terms of mental acts, states, mechanisms, processes, or entities superior to instantiation or a covering-law explanation? In what sense is it appropriate to ask in virtue of what properties in the subject under observation does behavior X occur? Do behavior analysts actually disregard internal states?

From a behavior-analytic view, as I have noted above, a concern with internal states is a concern with physiology, not with hypothetical states or information processing mechanisms in a mental dimension (see also Moore, 1984, 1990b). Knowledge of physiological states is important because such knowledge may complement knowledge of an organism's history and nature of interaction with the environment in efforts to predict and control. In an ontological sense, there is no mental dimension. Consequently, talk of mental states or mechanisms cannot literally be occasioned by mental phenomena. Rather, such talk is occasioned by other factors, not all of which are relevant from a scientific perspective. At issue is whether cognitive psychology as it currently is practiced is genuinely a legitimate, theoretical neuroscience. For Skinner (1978), the answer is no: "cognitive constructs give physiologists a misleading account of what they will find inside" (p. 111).

The way to respond to the challenge of mentalism and cognitive psychology, however, is not to debate the alleged richness and freedom afforded by cognitive constructs and whether cognitive explanations pay their way by accounting for an intellectually satisfying percent of the variance in the data. That tactic concedes the nature of the battle to be fought as well as the ammunition that can be used in the battle. Rather, the way to respond is to pragmatically assess the source of control over the verbal behavior involved in developing and offering cognitive explanations. In this regard, Skinner identified the importance of spurious contingencies affecting the use of scientific terms, particularly the contingencies that involve a social/cultural dimension, when he talked about the origin of cognitive terms:

> The reasons for the popularity of cognitive psychology ... have nothing to do with scientific advances but rather with the release of the floodgates of mentalistic terms fed by the tributaries of philosophy, theology, history, letters, media, and worst of all, the English language (as cited in Catania & Harnad, 1988, p. 447).

In fact, much of Skinner's later writing was concerned with elucidating the prevalence of this form of stimulus control over the suspect verbal behavior called cognitive (e.g., Skinner, 1989, 1990). Thus, many of these terms are related to inappropriate metaphors, culturally established patterns of speech, and so on, none of which are consistent with the perspective of natural science (see also Hineline, 1984; Marr, 1983; Moore, 1990a, 1992; Schnaitter, 1984). As suggested earlier in the present paper, these mischievous forms of control over so-called explanatory verbal behavior need to be removed so that the facts at issue can be readily addressed. In this regard, Skinner shows the influence of Bacon's Idols and Comte's stages, described earlier in the present chapter.

The foregoing arguments show that behavior analysis embraces a pragmatic concern with what can be manipulated in space and time to better the human condition. One cannot manipulate the concepts of cognitive psychology, such as a hypothetical underlying state or processing mechanism. Indeed, by accepting causal factors from a mental dimension, one does not even investigate factors that can be manipulated in space and time. Chomsky's linguistic theories have garnered much attention in the world of academic psycholinguistics, but as he himself readily admits, they are not of much value when it comes to teaching language skills to developmentally disabled individuals. Whatever one manipulates to teach language, it is presumably something that exists in space and time. To be sure, one can take into account evolutionary history that has selected some receptive capacity to stimuli, some capacity to engage in motor activity, and so on, but these sorts of factors are not the same things as cognitive explanatory concepts derived from folk psychology. The cognitive objections to instantiations and covering-law explanations are simply beside the point. The influence of the pragmatic tradition associated with Bacon and Mach looms large here for behavior analysis. This tradition emphasizes that the activities called science are operant activities and find their ultimate support in environmental interaction of one sort or another, such as prediction, control, or just making sense out of the world.

Conclusions

In conclusion, explanation and description are not essentially identical activities for behavior analysis, although they may well be symmetrical for traditional mediational neobehaviorism that subscribes to instantiation and covering-law models of explanation. Cognitive psychology typically objects to all forms of behaviorism, whether neobehaviorism or behavior analysis, by asserting that behavioristic explanations achieved through instantiation and covering-law strategies are merely descriptions. Closer analysis of cognitive objections, however, indicates that they apply more to neobehaviorism than to behavior analysis. Moreover, cognitive explanations in terms of supposed underlying mental phenomena raise considerable dimensional problems of their own. Behavior analysis is ultimately concerned with the practical function of explanation. Explanations guide effective action, either directly by occasioning successful actions that control behavior or indirectly by occasioning successful actions when control is not feasible. Description may be the starting point for meaningful explanations, but not the ending point.

References

Bacon, F. (1937). De dignitate et augmentis scientarium. In R. F. Jones (Ed. and trans.), *Essays, Advancement of Learning, New Atlantis, and other pieces* (pp. 377–438). New York: Odyssey. (Original work published 1623.)

Bacon, F. (1960). *The new organon.* (F. H. Anderson, Ed.). Indianapolis, IN: Bobbs-Merrill. (Original work published 1620)

Catania, A. C. (1993). The unconventional philosophy of science of behavior analysis. *Journal of the Experimental Analysis of Behavior, 60,* 449–452.

Catania, A. C., & Harnad, S. (Eds.). (1988). *The selection of behavior: The operant behaviorism of B. F. Skinner: Comments and controversies.* Cambridge: Cambridge University Press.

Chomsky, N. (1965). *Aspects of a theory of syntax.* Cambridge, MA: MIT Press.

Chomsky, N. (1980). *Rules and representations.* New York: Columbia University Press.

Copi, I. (1982). *Introduction to logic* (6th ed.). New York: Macmillan.

Cummins, R. (1983). *The nature of psychological explanation.* MIT Press: Cambridge, MA.

Fodor, J. (1981). The mind-body problem. *Scientific American, 244,* 124–133.

Hempel, C. G., & Oppenheim, P. (1948). Studies in the logic of explanation. *Philosophy of Science, 15,* 135–175.

Hergenhahn, B. R. (1997). *An introduction to the history of psychology* (3rd ed.). Pacific Grove, CA: Brooks/Cole.

Hineline, P. N. (1984). Can a statement in cognitive terms be a behavior-analytic interpretation? *The Behavior Analyst, 7,* 97–100.

Hull, C. L. (1937). Mind, mechanism, and adaptive behavior. *Psychological Review, 44,* 1–32.

Hull, C. L. (1943). *Principles of behavior.* New York: Appleton-Century-Crofts.

Hull, C. L. (1952). *A behavior system.* New York: Appleton-Century-Crofts.

Hume, D. (1964). *A treatise of human nature.* (L. A. Selby-Brigge, Ed., reprinted). Oxford: Clarendon Press. (Earlier edition published 1888)

Hume, D. (1902). *Enquiries concerning the human understanding and concerning the principles of morals.* (L. A. Selby-Brigge, Ed., 2nd ed). Oxford: Clarendon Press. (Original work published 1777)

Kaplan, A. (1964). *The conduct of inquiry.* San Francisco, CA: Chandler.

Kendler, H. H., & Spence, J. T. (1971). Tenets of neobehaviorism. In H. H. Kendler & J. T. Spence (Eds.), *Essays in Neobehaviorism: A memorial volume to Kenneth W. Spence* (pp. 11–40). New York: Appleton-Century-Crofts.

Lashley, K. (1951). The problem of serial order in behavior. In L. A. Jeffress (Ed.), *Cerebral mechanisms in behavior* (pp. 112–146). New York: Wiley.

Mach, E. (1942). *The science of mechanics* (T. J. McCormack, Trans.; 5th ed.). LaSalle, IL: Open Court. (Original work published 1883)

Marr, M. J. (1983). Memory: Metaphors and models. *Psychological Record, 33*, 12–19.

Marr, M. J. (1985). 'Tis the gift to be simple: A retrospective appreciation of Mach's *The Science of Mechanics*. *Journal of the Experimental Analysis of Behavior, 44*, 129–138.

Moore, J. (1984). On behaviorism, knowledge, and causal explanation. *Psychological Record, 34*, 73–97.

Moore, J. (1990a). On mentalism, privacy, and behaviorism. *Journal of Mind and Behavior, 11*, 19–36.

Moore, J. (1990b). On the "causes" of behavior. *Psychological Record, 40*, 469–480.

Moore, J. (1992). On private events and theoretical terms. *Journal of Mind and Behavior, 13*, 329–346.

Moore, J. (1996). On the relation between behaviorism and cognitive psychology. *Journal of Mind and Behavior, 17*, 345–368.

Moore, J. (1998). On behaviorism, theories, and hypothetical constructs. *Journal of Mind and Behavior, 19*, 215–242.

Moore, J. (2000a). Behavior analysis and psycholinguistics. *European Journal of Behavior Analysis, 1*, 5–22.

Moore, J. (2000b). Varieties of scientific explanation. *The Behavior Analyst, 23*, 173–189.

Pitt, J. C. (Ed.). (1988). *Theories of explanation.* New York: Oxford University Press

Popper, K. R. (1963). *Conjectures and refutations.* London: Routledge & Kegan Paul.

Reese, H. W. (1999). Explanation is not description. *Behavioral Development Bulletin, 8(1)*, 3–7.

Ross, W. D. (Ed.). (1938). *Aristotle: Selections.* New York: Scribner.

Russell, B. (1932). *Mysticism and logic.* London: George Allen.

Salmon, W. (1984). *Scientific explanation and the causal structure of the world.* Princeton, NJ: Princeton University Press.

Salmon, W. (1989). *Four decades of scientific explanation.* Minneapolis, MN: University of Minnesota Press.

Schnaitter, R. M. (1984). Skinner on the "mental" and the "physical." *Behaviorism, 12*, 1–14.

Schnaitter, R. (1986). Behavior as a function of inner states and outer circumstances. In T. Thompson & M. D. Zeiler (Eds.), *Analysis and integration of behavioral units* (pp. 247–274). Hillsdale, NJ: Erlbaum.

Schoneberger, T. (2000). A departure from Cognitivism: Implications of Chomsky's second revolution in linguistics. *The Analysis of Verbal Behavior, 17*, 57–73.

Simon, H. A. (1992). What is an "explanation" of behavior? *Psychological Science, 3*, 150–161.

Skinner, B. F. (1938). *The behavior of organisms.* New York: Appleton-Century-Crofts.

Skinner, B. F. (1972). Experimental psychology. *Cumulative record* (pp. 295–313). New York: Appleton-Century-Crofts. (Reprinted from *Current trends in psychology*, pp. 16–49, by W. Dennis, Ed., 1947, Pittsburgh, PA: University of Pittsburgh Press)

Skinner, B. F. (1953). *Science and human behavior.* New York: Macmillan.

Skinner, B. F. (1957). *Verbal behavior.* New York: Appleton-Century-Crofts.

Skinner, B. F. (1964). Behaviorism at fifty. In T. W. Wann (Ed.), *Behaviorism and phenomenology* (pp. 79–108). Chicago: University of Chicago Press.

Skinner, B. F. (1969). *Contingencies of reinforcement.* New York: Appleton-Century-Crofts.

Skinner, B. F. (1978). *Reflections on behaviorism and society.* Englewood Cliffs, New Jersey: Prentice-Hall.

Skinner, B. F. (1979). *The shaping of a behaviorist.* New York: Knopf.

Skinner, B. F. (1989). The origins of cognitive thought. *American Psychologist, 44*, 13–18.

Skinner, B. F. (1990). Can psychology be a science of mind? *American Psychologist, 45*, 1206–1210.

Smith, L. D. (1995). Inquiry nearer the source: Bacon, Mach, and *The Behavior of Organisms*. In J. T. Todd & E. K. Morris (Eds.), *Modern perspectives on B. F. Skinner and contemporary behaviorism* (pp. 39–50). Westport, CT: Greenwood Press.

Sosa, E., & Tooley, M. (Eds.). (1993). *Causation*. New York: Oxford University Press.

Staddon, J. E. R. (1973). On the notion of cause, with application to behaviorism. *Behaviorism, 1*, 25–63.

Staddon, J. E. R. (2001). *The new behaviorism*. Philadelphia, PA: Taylor & Francis.

Turner, M. B. (1967). *Philosophy and the science of behavior*. New York: Appleton-Century-Crofts.

Wessells, M. (1981). A critique of Skinner's views on the explanatory inadequacy of cognitive theories. *Behaviorism, 9*, 153–170.

Wessells, M. (1982). A critique of Skinner's views on the obstructive character of cognitive theories. *Behaviorism, 10*, 65–84.

Wallace, W. A. (1972). *Causality and scientific explanation* (Vol. 1). Ann Arbor, MI: University of Michigan Press.

Wallace, W. A. (1974). *Causality and scientific explanation* (Vol. 2). Ann Arbor, MI: University of Michigan Press.

3

Pragmatism and Behavior Analysis

Kennon A. Lattal and Joseph S. Laipple

The American philosophical movement known as pragmatism has played a major role in psychology since the two developed together from the late 19th century through the early years of the 20th century. As B.F. Skinner shifted intellectually from his early positivist framework, pragmatism was strongly reflected in his mid-to-late 20th century behavior analysis. This chapter briefly reviews the history and major tenets of pragmatism before examining the continuing interplay between pragmatism and behavior-analytic research, application, and conceptual issues.

From Philosophy to Psychology

Pragmatism emerged in the late 19th century in the United States of America from a philosophical caldron that included liberal doses of British Empiricism, Kant, Hegel, and the German Romantic Idealists (cf. James, 1907/1963, p. 45), as well as positivists like de La Mettrie, Comte, and Mach. Each of its founders had one foot in philosophy and the other in areas such as science, education, psychology, and religion. Indeed, pragmatism invited a context, for it was a counterpoint to the abstract academic philosophy of the time. The context, however, was not necessarily one of social application, for pragmatism as a philosophy was not synonymous with an ordinary meaning of "practical." Pragmatism simmered

Kennon A. Lattal • Department of Psychology, West Virginia University, Morgantown, WV 26506-6040. Joseph S. Laipple • Aubrey Daniels International, Atlanta, GA 30084 in an American political environment of manifest destiny, an economic environment driven by the industrial revolution and the Big Business that revolution fostered, and a cultural-intellectual environment of invention and experimentation. By the early 20th century it had become virtually the defining philosophy of American life.

A series of discussions among a group known as the Metaphysical Club in Cambridge, Massachusetts in the 1870s laid the foundations of pragmatism. This group included William James, Charles W. Peirce, Chauncey Wright, F. E. Abbott, and Oliver Wendell Holmes. Although Peirce is credited with giving birth to the idea of pragmatism with his essay on "How to Make our Ideas Clear," published in *Popular Science Monthly* (Peirce, 1878), it was William James who became, in a manner of speaking, "Peirce's bulldog," articulating, defending, developing, and expanding the ideas of pragmatism through popular lectures and writings.

The developers of pragmatism included two giants of American psychology: William James and John Dewey. By the time James got around to philosophy, he had largely abandoned psychology, where he is widely acknowledged as the father of the American version of that discipline. He authored the first American psychology textbook, founded the first Department of Psychology, at Harvard, and trained the first Ph.D. in psychology, the indefatigable G. Stanley Hall. James wrote of a psychology emphasizing the study of the uses, or functions, of consciousness (James, 1890), a view signifying a philosophy of action over one of contemplation and conjecture.

John Dewey, trained as a philosopher rather than as a psychologist, was, along with Harvey Carr and James Angell, instrumental in establishing the functionalist school of psychology. Among his many activities, Dewey developed the University Elementary School at Chicago, a school described by Menand (2001)

> as a *philosophy* laboratory. Dewey wasn't conducting curricular experiments or collecting data on mental development. He was trying out a theory. It was a theory, as he said, of "the unity of knowledge".... By "unity of knowledge" Dewey... meant that knowledge is inseparably united with doing. (p. 322)

It was through this school that Dewey established "the validity of his hypothesis that thinking and acting are just two names for a single process—the process of making our way as best we can in a universe shot through with contingency" (Menand, p. 360).

During the period when pragmatism's star was at its zenith, John B. Watson formulated his transformation of psychology through behaviorism, and, only a little later, Skinner, as a beginning graduate student, first encountered the work of Watson. Watson had received his Ph.D.

from Chicago during the halcyon years of functionalism there. Although a defining feature of behaviorism became its pragmatism, the connection of Watson and behaviorism with Chicago and Dewey was coincidental. Watson was a thorough-going positivist with little sympathy for James's introspectionism, which he lumped together with Titchener's structuralism, describing both as being of "German origin" (Watson, 1924/1958, pp. 1–2). Of Dewey, Watson observed "I never knew what he was talking about then, and, unfortunately for me, I still don't know" (Watson, 1936/1961, p. 274). Moxley (2001) proposed that philosophical pragmatism came to radical behaviorism with Skinner's (1945) paper on operationism:

> Before 1945, Skinner made at least some positive associations with the views of Watson, Russell, and Carnap. From 1945, and afterwards, he strongly disassociated his views on verbal behavior from theirs. Before 1945 Skinner did not associate his views with those of Darwin or Peirce. After 1945, he strongly associated his views with those of Darwin and Peirce (in one published interview). (p. 201)

Schneider (1997) also noted commonalities between Dewey's views and those of the radical behaviorists. Skinner employed his increasingly pragmatic framework for a science of human behavior with remarkable vigor to an almost endless number of conceptual, social, and ethical problems faced by American psychology, and the larger society.

What is Pragmatism?

Varieties of Pragmatism

Although pragmatism, like behaviorism, often is presented as a uniform philosophy, also like behaviorism, it is not. Peirce, James, and Dewey each created variations on a theme. Lovejoy (1908a, b) distinguished 13 varieties of pragmatism, shades of nuance interspersed between the ideas of the triumvirate noted above. Some highlights of pragmatism from the standpoint of each of the three principals are presented below.

Pragmatism first was conceived by Peirce as a method for "how to make our ideas clear." Anticipating aspects of operationism, Peirce called for precise definitions of terms when describing concepts, which for him required conditional, or contextual, definition. "By translating ideas into behavior, pragmatism reduced meaning to something public and observable rather than private and personal" (E. C. Moore, 1961, pp. 57–58). More than this, however, meaning was to be found in actions, not merely talk about actions. Pragmatism was the method of achieving meaning, but not a definition of meaning per se: only concepts that are defined empirically, and not as abstractions, have pragmatic meaning. This can be compared to Skinner's (1974) observation that "the meaning of a response is not in its topography or form . . . it is to be found in its antecedent history" (p. 90).

Although pragmatism initially was offered by Peirce as a method for achieving clarity of meaning, it developed into a theory of truth, largely in the hands of James and Dewey. In contrast to the idealist position that truth existed independent of experience, these two pragmatists held that truth was not an abstraction, but rather was found *in* experience: "Truth is *made* just as health, wealth, and strength are made in the course of experience" (James 1907/1963, p. 143).

Where Peirce was concerned with experimental science, James was concerned with the human condition. James moved pragmatism from general cases, the *sine qua non* for Peirce, to particular, individual ones. For Peirce, a pragmatic truth statement about the characteristics of a chemical compound, for example, would be a general one on which all scientists would be likely to agree as to its utility. By contrast, James's application of the pragmatic truth criterion to such uniquely human events as religious experience or beliefs is specific to the individual. Because of this emphasis on the individual, James developed the position that truth is anything that gives satisfaction. It is important to note, however, that by satisfaction he meant not the emotion of satisfaction, but satisfaction as an outcome—in the terminology of pragmatism, a goal or purpose defined as successful action. In his view, then, an idea, or judgement, by a person was true if and only if (a) it led to a specific action and (b) the action led to a satisfactory (*useful, workable*) solution (see section below on *Truth as Successful or Useful Working*). The solution demonstrated the truth of the original idea. Truth, then, is determined after the fact, inductively rather than deductively. Something that happens earlier in time does not become true until it has worked. This is the same type of criterion used by Skinner to define reinforcement. A stimulus is not classified as a reinforcer until there are particular effects on behavior (cf. Skinner, 1938, p. 62).

In contrast to James, Dewey downplayed value-based and experiential references to useful working, focusing more on the individual in cultural and historical context. Dewey also disagreed with James's truth criterion on the grounds that it confused truth with value: A person could value something without it being true (Dewey, 1916, p. 320). As noted, Peirce conceived of pragmatism originally as a solution to problems of meaning for the "pure" scientist, working in a community of like-minded people. Dewey embraced the scientific applications suggested by Peirce. In contrast to him, however, Dewey also extended pragmatism to issues of human affairs, such as those encountered in education. Peirce did not consider such practical problems amenable to scientific inquiry (cf. C. Morris, 1970, pp. 64–65). James arguably went even further than Dewey, though, extending the idea of successful working to personal beliefs, where their truth depended on their effects on the individual espousing them.

Pragmatism also influenced the philosophy of science. In particular, Peirce's concern with scientific definitions based on differences in practice resonates to the later operationism of Bridgeman (1927) and to Mach's (e.g., 1893/1960) positivist ideas that influenced the young Skinner (cf. Chiesa, 1992). Bridgeman's work in turn influenced the logical positivists, although, there are marked differences between logical positivism and pragmatism. The former emphasizes linguistic concepts and the latter downplays linguistic analysis in favor of successful working. Furthermore, the logical positivists were concerned with verification of observations among observers, something not of concern to pragmatism. The pragmatic truth criterion of successful working does not require agreement between observers, only successful working for the individual, relative to the individual's purpose. In an iteration of the pragmatic view, Skinner (1945) noted that

> the ultimate criterion of goodness of a concept is not whether two people are brought into agreement but whether the scientist who uses the concept can operate successfully upon his material—all by himself if need be. What matters to Robinson Crusoe is not whether he is agreeing with himself but whether he is getting anywhere with his control over nature. (p. 552)

and later (Skinner, 1974) that "[behavior analysis] does not insist upon truth by agreement..." (p. 16).

Pragmatism and Practicality

We noted earlier in this chapter that, although *pragmatic* as a philosophical term and in its ordinary usage as practicality overlap with one another, they are not synonymous. If practical is used to describe a concern with ordinary activities then it describes only a subset of the concerns of pragmatism. For example, in a seminal article in the first issue of the *Journal of Applied Behavior Analysis* (*JABA*) delineating the dimensions of applied behavior analysis. Baer, Wolf, and Risley (1968) noted that "Behaviorism and pragmatism seem often to go hand in hand. Applied research is eminently pragmatic; it asks how to get an individual to do something effectively" (p. 93). The latter term then is discussed in relation to "applied value" (p. 93) and goals that are "socially important" (p. 93). Thus, even though it is not explicit in the quotation, there is, appropriately, considerable attention to the practical (as socially important) goals of effective intervention. Socially important goals certainly may be pragmatic as well as practical;

however, not all goals need be socially relevant to be pragmatic. From the standpoint of pragmatic philosophy, any solution, even ones that may not meet other criteria such as social acceptability (let alone relevance), can be pragmatic to the extent that it meets the goals of the goal setter.

Truth as Successful or Useful Working

The topic of this section is perhaps the most important common theme among the pragmatisms of Peirce, James, and Dewey. For Peirce, truth was achieving clarity of definition, or meaning, and the criterion was improved communication among scientists. For James (1907/1963) also,

> *True ideas are those that we can assimilate, validate, corroborate and verify. False ideas are those that we can not.* That is the practical difference it makes to us to have true ideas; that, therefore, is the meaning of truth, for it is all that truth is known as. (p. 133)

The test of successful (or useful—the two terms are used interchangeably in this chapter) working for James, then, was in terms of ideas having a *useful effect* on the individual: "[t]he pragmatic method . . . is to try to interpret each notion by tracing its respective practical consequences" (James 1907/1963, p. 42). For Dewey, broadly speaking, successful working involved having a *useful effect* on the community or, more generally, society.

Both *successful* (*useful*) and *working* require clarification. Working may be interpreted two ways. It may be used as a gerund to refer to an action in context (setting). The circumstances (the what, who, where, when, etc.) are in the "working" in this use. Success then is used to evaluate the action in context. Alternatively, it may be a noun modified by successful or useful, in which case it could refer to a type of outcome. Useful or successful implies that truth is not determined a priori, but rather in context and, importantly, *in comparison with the practical goals and purposes of the investigator*. Of success Schiller (1912) said:

> "Success," therefore, in validating a "truth," is a relative term, relative to the purposes with which the truth was claimed. The "same" prediction may be "true" for me and "false" for you, if our purposes are different. As for the truth in the abstract, and relative to no purpose, it is plainly unmeaning. (p. 193)

Thus, as developed in pragmatic *philosophy*, useful working refers to (is defined in terms of) the correspondence between a goal and an outcome. This definition obviates the criticism that the concept of useful working is circular: only outcomes that correspond to previous (typically verbal) statements are eligible to be instances of pragmatic truth. Furthermore, something can work usefully, but not be an instance of pragmatic truth. For example, an evolutionary adaptation, by definition, may be described as working usefully, but this is not useful working in the present pragmatic sense because the outcome (the adaptation) does not follow (meet or achieve) a goal or purpose (but see the section on *Selectionism* below for further considerations concerning this use).

Introducing the concept of goal-directed or purposive behavior to resolve the question of the circularity of the successful working truth criterion at first blush seems at odds with a behavior-analytic world view in two ways. The latter holds that an understanding of the determinants of action are to be found through selectionism as opposed to essentialism (Palmer & Donahoe, 1992; Zuriff, 1986). Reese (1997), however, has observed that "[p]urpose in humans is not problematic because it is antecedent to the behavior it affects" (p. 44). Even Skinner (1974) defined behavior analysis as "the very field of purpose and intention" (p. 55). Other radical behaviorists also have examined the concepts of purpose and teleology (see Hineline, this volume; Rachlin, 1992). At least two processes might be considered in accounting for purpose from a behavior-analytic perspective. First, in behavior analysis, purpose often is reconceptualized in terms of the control of actions by antecedents. More generally, verbal rules, generated either by the listener or by another speaker, are often conceptualized as discriminative stimuli that set the occasion for a subsequent response. Thus, purpose may be another way of stating control by antecedent events, with the antecedent events determined by the organism's history. A second, related, process is that of say-do correspondence whereby subsequent behavior is determined by initial choices. For example, in laboratory studies of say-do correspondence, a response is reinforced if it corresponds to a previous action that sets the occasion for that subsequent response to be reinforced. Lattal and Doepke (2001) have suggested that correspondence of this sort (the use of the term correspondence here should not be confused with a correspondence theory of truth) may function as a higher-order, two-element operant in which the elements together are determined by their consequences. Stating goals and their subsequent attainment might be maintained by the consequences of attainment. In these ways, both antecedent and consequent control can give meaning to purposes and goals in discussions of useful working.

Useful working as the goals-to-outcome correspondence also may seem more compatible with a deductive as opposed to an inductive approach to science, in that the action leading to the useful working may be considered as derived from the goal or purpose. In psychology, the hypothetico-deductive method of the Hullian tradition often is contrasted to Skinner's inductive, positivist approach to science, but it is Skinner who is described as the pragmatist and Hull who is not (cf. Zuriff, 1986, p. 259). Cohen and Nagel (1934, pp. 275–279; for a related discussion, see also Staddon, 1993) suggested that the two approaches are complementary rather than contradictory. They noted that inductive statements are often based on prior (often implicit) formulations of principles that, for the present purposes could be construed as goals or purposes. Furthermore, simply because goals are either unstated or are very general ones does not mean that they could not be articulated. At the most basic level, the (pragmatic) goal of science of modern science is often stated as "discovery" or "exploration." More specific goals related to generality and extension can be implicitly drawn from earlier observations. Put into more radical behavioral language, prior observations serve as discriminative stimuli controlling subsequent scientific practice.

Explanation and Theory

There is consensus among neither scientists nor philosophers as to what constitutes an explanation of a phenomenon. Pragmatism has nothing to say about the contents of an explanation because pragmatism "is primarily a *method* of settling metaphysical disputes that otherwise might be interminable" (James, 1907/1963, p. 43, italics added). Pragmatism contributes to the understanding of explanation in that successful working shows that an explanation is true. Because competing explanations may each lead to successful working, there may be multiple "truths." This latter idea is found in Pepper's (e.g., 1942) writings wherein he suggests that different world views with different truths may coexist, but it is important to remember that these truths exist *within* world views, but not necessarily *across* them.

Explanations appealing to concepts that are fixed, that is, established out of context, are not consistent with pragmatism. Such noncontextual explanations involve a correspondence view of the truth of a statement in that the present circumstances are thought to correspond to a model or other representation of which the present instance is but an example. For James (1907/1963), pragmatism was an *"attitude of looking away from first things, principles, 'categories,' supposed necessities; and of looking towards last things, fruits, consequences, facts"* (p. 47).

Developing a scientific theory requires identifying the basic data, describing systematic relations among the data, and, finally, articulating abstract concepts (e.g., Moore, 1998; this volume). Pragmatism is consistent with the first two steps, and it may be consistent with the third. To the extent that abstract concepts lead to prediction and control of behavior, they may be pragmatic. Such abstractions are verbal statements about nature, not rules that nature must obey (cf. Moore, 1998, p. 234). As verbal statements they can have a direct effect on the behavior of the scientist and serve to predict and control the behavior of that scientist. Thus, from a pragmatic stance, the truth or value of abstractions is measured tested against the criterion of successful working.

James (1907/1963) considered theories as *"instruments, not answers to enigmas..."* (p. 46), thus they were not ends but means to ends. Moore (1998) suggested that pragmatic theories are testable, valid, useful, and have heuristic value. The heuristic function of a theory, that is, its propensity to stimulate further experimentation or other investigation, is pragmatic to the extent that it leads to the useful action of further investigation; however, pragmatism and heuristic value are not isomorphic because research may be stimulated by theories that are based on other than pragmatically (or functionally) defined concepts (cf. Skinner, 1950, 1956).

Pragmatism and Behaviorism

By the 1930s, behaviorism was in full swing, but pragmatism had lost some favor in intellectual, especially scientific, circles to the logical positivism of the Vienna Circle of philosophers and scientists. The various forms of behaviorism developed with differing views on the dependence on "theory." The so-called methodological behavioral views became more theory-laden and mentalistic and ultimately contributed to the emergence of cognitive psychology. By contrast, radical behaviorism continued to eschew mentalism and favor a pragmatic view of science with the Watsonian goals of prediction and control of behavior. To the extent that all of the behaviorisms are empirical and concerned with these goals they are consistent with a pragmatic view.

The behaviorisms differ, however, with respect to their positions on the nature of knowledge and scientific explanation. Smith (1986) concluded that the three major learning theories of the 1930s, those of Tolman, Hull, and Skinner, all are better characterized as pragmatic than as logical positivistic. Zuriff (1986) reached a similar conclusion with respect to Tolman and Skinner, and added Guthrie to the list. Zuriff also identified several pragmatic themes in Hull's neobehaviorism, but he suggested that Hull did not subscribe to the view that "scientific knowledge is an instrument... whose function is to enable us to adjust to our world and whose truth depends on its usefulness in satisfying our needs" (p. 259).

Skinner's Pragmatism

Skinner's (1956) autobiographical case study describing his approach to psychology is a powerful endorsement of pragmatism. He described the development of his research methods, beginning with a rat restrained on an activity tambour and ending with the ubiquitous operant conditioning chamber (see also Iversen, 1992). The description is of research methods designed to obtain useful results, that is, results that lead to the prediction and control of behavior. The greater significance of the review is that it is an epistemological statement: Knowing about something is achieved by making it work.

In discussing functional relations, which replace causal relations in his system, Skinner (1956) observed that

> Science is not concerned with contemplation. When we have discovered the laws which govern a part of the world about us, and . . . organized those laws into a system, we are then ready to deal effectively with that part of the world. By predicting an event we are able to prepare for it. By arranging conditions in ways specified by the laws of a system, we not only predict, we control: we "cause" an event to occur or to assume certain characteristics. (p. 14)

Thus, science is not concerned with abstract knowledge but rather with action and "doing": arranging conditions, observing effects, and organizing laws into a system. The utility of science is in predicting and controlling behavior, goals that echo, in different words, the ideas of those early pragmatists already described.

Theories and philosophies were not the basis of Skinner's science. Skinner found theories useful only if they referred to the same universe of discourse (the same dimensional system) as the data:

> A more general analysis is also possible which answers the question of *why* a given schedule generates a given performance. It is in one sense a theoretical analysis; but it is not theoretical in the sense of speculating about corresponding events in some other universe of discourse. It simply reduces a large number of schedules to a formulation in terms of certain common features. It does this by a closer analysis of the actual contingencies of reinforcement prevailing under any given schedule. (Ferster & Skinner, 1957, p. 2)

Skinner was neither anti- nor a-theoretical, as some have suggested, but, rather, he argued for a particular type of theory:

> Beyond the collection of uniform relationships lies the need for a formal representation of the data reduced to a minimum number of terms. A theoretical construction may yield greater generality than any assemblage of facts. But, such a construction will not refer to another dimensional system and will not, therefore, fall within our present definition [of a theory]. (1950, pp. 215–216)

Skinner summed up his skepticism about science that relies on deductive theories and logic as follows: "When we have achieved a practical control over the organism, theories of behavior lose their point. In representing and managing relevant variables, a conceptual model is useless, we come to grips with behavior itself" (1956, p. 531) and "Research designed with respect to theory likely to be wasteful. That a theory generates research does not prove its value unless the research is valuable" (1950, p. 194). This last sentence also describes the limits of a pragmatic view of the heuristic value of a theory described previously on page 49.

Skinner's position with respect to theory and in more general terms is thoroughly and undeniably pragmatic; however, the direct influence of pragmatism as a *guiding* philosophy on the development of behavior analysis is more an open question. Rachlin (1995) portrayed Skinner as a "true descendant" (p. 3) of James, Dewey, and Peirce, which he certainly was in terms of how his position evolved. Thompson (1984), however, proposed that it was the French physiologist and methodologist Bernard who had the greater antecedent effect on the development of behavior analysis than did either James or Pavlov. As a graduate student Skinner worked in the experimental physiology laboratory of Crozier, from which the strong influence of Bernard's *methods* of experimental physiology on Skinner is obvious. Degrees of influence are open to interpretation, but it is clear that both pragmatism and the subtleties of experimental science meld in Skinner's work. Skinner's pragmatism seems to have been contingency-, rather than rule-, governed (see Catania, this volume); that is, pragmatism did not serve as a guide in developing the science of behavior, but rather as a consequence (cf. Moxley, 2001), and it describes Skinner's interactions with his subject matter.

Pragmatism in Contemporary Behavior Analysis

Following Skinner's lead, modern behavior analysts describe themselves as pragmatic. Baum (1994) noted that

> To the question "What is science?" [radical behaviorism] gives the answer of James and Mach: Science is the pursuit of economical and comprehensible descriptions of natural experience... The pragmatist (radical behaviorist)... asks only which way of describing man's behavior is most useful..." (p. 25)

Indeed, pragmatism is one of the common themes that contributes to a cohesive intellectual system despite differences between basic, applied, and conceptually-oriented behavior analysts in their content, methods, immediate goals, and populations studied. The older sibling of the group, the experimental analysis of behavior, largely has followed Skinner's lead in terms of both method and theory. Applied behavior analysis is philosophically pragmatic, but also practical to the extent that its goal is contributing to the solution of social problems. For example, the *raison d'être* of *JABA*, as stated on its cover page, is "primarily for the original publication of reports of experimental research involving application of the analysis of behavior to problems of social importance." In the conceptual area, Moxley (2001) has traced the close relation between the conceptual/interpretive analysis of verbal behavior and pragmatism.

To illustrate some different aspects of pragmatism and its relation to behavior analysis, we now turn to two controversial issues in modern behavior analysis, one that has developed in the experimental analysis of behavior and the other in applied behavior analysis. The first is the discussion among basic researchers about levels of analysis and related mechanisms of behavioral control, sometimes described as the molar-molecular controversy. The second is the use of aversive control procedures, particularly punishment, to ameliorate behavior problems in applied settings. Both show how the pragmatic position allows multiple solutions to a problem and how different pragmatic truths may conflict with one another.

Levels of Behavioral Analysis

A critical issue in any science is what to measure, because what is measured defines the subject matter. Thus, one of the first issues to be addressed in constructing a science of behavior was identifying a common unit of analysis. Skinner's (1935) elegant solution to the unit of analysis problem was to define the unit functionally, in terms of its effects rather than in a formal structural way. This analysis of the operant allowed for units of unlimited sizes and types. When prediction and control of behavior are the goals, in any particular investigation or application of one type of unit, or, more generally, one level of analysis may prove more orderly or useful than another. Although the analysis allows a selection of the best unit for a particular purpose (that which results in optimal control of the behavior vis à vis that purpose), other criteria (e.g., practical considerations related to cost) may outweigh gains in precision accruing from more refined units. Taking into account the various factors will yield a unit sufficient to accomplish the goal of the work. Such unit selection illustrates the *good enough* criterion described by evolutionary biologists like Dawkins (1986) whereby the design of a given biological structure may not be as elegant or theoretically perfect as it could be, but it is sufficient to get the job done.

Levels of behavioral analysis have been debated for some time among those concerned with the experimental analysis of behavior. The portion of the debate relevant to the present purpose concerns the relative merits of an account of reinforcement based on the primacy of response-reinforcer temporal contiguity (a molecular variable) versus one based on the integrated effect of multiple reinforcers on responding over noninstantaneous time frames (a molar variable).

Each level has its supporters and detractors (e.g., Anger, 1956; Baum, 1973, 1994, 1995, 2001, 2002; Dinsmoor, 2001; Herrnstein & Hineline, 1966; Hineline, 1977, 2001; Iversen, 1991; Lattal & Gleeson, 1990) at both empirical and theoretical levels. Some of the arguments for either position are in the pragmatic terms of which account offers the best account of the data, that is, offers the better prediction and control of behavior. Other arguments, however, are based more in epistemology, having to do with which analysis fits better with a behavior-analytic world view. Some theorists favor a molar point of view in part because it breaks so clearly with explanatory reductionism (e.g., Baum, 1973; see Schaal, this volume) that involves a linear causality model wherein mediating psychological or quasineurological entities, like memory, are constructed to fill the temporal gaps between response and consequence.

In the final analysis the resolution of the question of levels of analysis controversy is pragmatic: "we do not choose rate of response as a basic datum merely from an analysis of the fundamental task of a science of behavior. The ultimate appeal is to its success in an experimental science" (Skinner, 1950, p. 199). The selection of an appropriate level of analysis is dictated by the effect that such selection allows in terms of prediction and control of behavior. The matching law (Herrnstein, 1970) usefully describes many aspects of behavior; however, some aspects, such as concurrent-schedule responding during and after a changeover between the alternatives, may be more accurately described at a molecular level (e.g., Silberberg & Fantino, 1970; see Iversen, 1991 for other examples). The level of analysis need not be construed as an either/or choice, but is better discussed as a problem in useful working. Selecting one level over the other depends on which level allows the researcher's or practitioner's goals to be accomplished.

The Use of Aversive Control in Applied Behavior Analysis

Applied behavior analysts have struggled for some time over whether (or in some cases to what extent) to use procedures based in the *aversive control of behavior*, notably punishment, in the management of behavior problems of humans—adults or children. The controversy illustrates how different pragmatic goals often coexist while conflicting with one another.

Aversive control was defined by Horner et al. (1990) as involving "the delivery of pain, withholding basic human needs, or social humiliation" (p. 126). There is not a consensus as to whether aversive procedures of behavior management include "presumptions of physical or emotional distress" (Horner et al., p. 126).

Advocates of minimizing the use of aversive control procedures contend "... that the delivery of punishers for challenging behaviors is not desirable" (Horner et al., 1990, p. 128) and that "... the time has come for limiting the use of stimuli and procedures that are painful, damaging, and dehumanizing" (Horner et al., p. 130). Other points made by these advocates emphasize that nonaversive procedures have developed (or should be developed) to the extent that aversive techniques are not necessary, that aversive control has side effects that make the cure worse than the presenting behavior, and that such procedures are inhumane and therefore unethical. Arguments supporting, or at least less consistently opposing, the use of aversive control include the assertion that aversive control is effective (although this definition of effective might be somewhat different by comparison to its definition by those who oppose its use), that extremely deviant behavior (such as self-injurious behavior) calls for extreme methods of behavior management; that, properly employed, potentially harmful side effects of aversive control can be managed; that aversive control has to be viewed in context; and that aversive control *is* humane and in keeping with current ethical practices of both psychology and behavior analysis. The disagreements between the two sides are based in part on two different pragmatic goals: The short-term goal of rapid cessation of the problem behavior (which presumably cannot be achieved efficaciously with strictly positive procedures) and the longer-term goal of having positive effects on the individual and on society.

Azrin's pioneering work on punishment (e.g., Azrin, 1956; Azrin & Holz, 1966) demonstrated the functional properties of response-dependent stimuli (notably, in his research, electric shock) presented following responses in suppressing responding (which is the functional definition of punishment) in the laboratory setting with experimental animals. The utility of punishment, where utility is defined as rapidly reducing undesirable behavior, also has been shown in some applied settings. Iwata (e.g., 1988) pioneered the use of a self-contained portable device (self-injurious behavior inhibiting system, or SIBIS) that immediately punished, with electric sock, self-injurious responses of children with severe mental retardation. Summarizing a number of applied studies, van Houten (1983) observed that, "When used in conjunction with reinforcement it [punishment] is probably the most effective way to reduce and eliminate aggressive, oppositional, highly disruptive, and tantrum behavior" (p. 39).

The pragmatic arguments against using aversive control are based in part on the assertion that, even if there is short-term suppression of inappropriate responses, in the long run, it is detrimental (i.e., does not "work usefully"). One part of this failure to work usefully is reflected in the question raised in the Book of St. Matthew in the Bible (Chapter 16, verse 26) of "... what is a man profited, if he shall gain the whole world, and lose his own soul?" That is, even if aversive control is beneficial (effective) in the short term (a point that many opposed to aversive control will not concede either), can these benefits outweigh the long-term detrimental effects? To Horner et al. (1990) and others, the answer is no. If, for example, the goal of applied behavior analysis is to do "great good" for society, using aversive control is inconsistent with this pragmatic goal in the long run. Both Skinner (1953) and Sidman (1989) have suggested that aversive control is costly to the individual *and* to society. Thus, any short-term gains of reducing problem behavior with aversive control in the short term pales in comparison to its longer-term detrimental effects on dignity of and respect for the individual (e.g., Horner et al., 1990). An argument for longer-term pragmatic goals, however, also has been proposed by those unopposed to using aversive control. If the useful working is societal benefit, and aversive procedures ameliorate behavior, then aversive control is effective not only in the short term, but it also achieves a long-term goal of improved functioning and personal adjustment, with society ultimately benefitting from the individual's personal benefits.

Although the controversy may be resolvable in other ways, it is difficult to select between these two positions regarding aversive control procedures on pragmatic grounds because the rules of pragmatism are relative and contextual. Both positions have pragmatic merit in the context of their asserted goals.

Pragmatism in Relation to Other Points of View Important in Behavior Analysis

Selectionism

Selectionism, that is, the process whereby physical characteristics and behavior are made more or less likely by their interactions with environments is a central theme in the writings of both Darwin and Skinner. James is credited with, if not introducing Darwinism to American psychology, at least enabling its acceptance. His classic textbook, *Principles of Psychology* (James, 1890), is firmly grounded in biological science (the first part describes in detail the senses and the brain). The acceptance of biological evolution was one of the precursors to the development of pragmatic philosophy (cf. C. Morris, 1970). Although specific references to Darwin are minimal, James (1892) believed that human consciousness was selected by an evolutionary process because of its survival value. On an ontogenic level, he held that "**mental life is primarily teleological;** ... our various

ways of feeling and thinking have grown to be what they are because of
their utility in shaping our *reactions* on the outer world" (p. 4). For James
and Dewey, ideas exist because humans *must* act to achieve ends. Thus,
ideas have been selected ("grown to be what they are") as a result of their
effects ("their utility in shaping . . . *reactions* . . ."). James's position was that
both consciousness for the human species and ideas for the individual were
selected because of their survival value. The problem is that survival value
is not defined independently of the *prima facie* evidence of survival—the
presence of the product of the process.

Extrapolating this idea, biological structures and behavior often are
described as adaptive, and adaptive might be taken to mean "work usefully." Such a definition of adaptive, however, is circular. Furthermore, if
useful working is interpreted in terms of a relation between a stated goal
and an outcome, then the products of selectionism are not, on the surface
at least, pragmatic—even though in other terms they "work usefully"—
because selectionism is not teleological: It operates without purpose in the
usual sense of an efficient cause and thus without goals.

Indeed, pragmatism and selectionism typically are viewed as compatible with one another. Moxley (2001) referred to Skinner's "pragmatic
selectionism" and Baum (1994) described behavior analysis as both pragmatic and selectionistic. Both James and Dewey interpreted Darwinian
theory in relation to a final cause in that the purpose of evolution was
survival (Menand, 2001, p. 364). It is with this type of final cause that selectionism melds easily with pragmatism. By reconsidering purposes and
goals in behavioral terms as discussed under the topic of *Truth as Successful or Useful Working* above, a fit between selectionism and pragmatism
may be constructed. Rachlin's (1992) teleological behaviorism also may
offer a potential conceptual rapprochement between pragmatism and selectionism because he suggested the interjection of Aristotelian final causes,
like survival, in a behavioristic world view otherwise constructed around
the notion of efficient causes. Furthermore, it is important not to confuse
the process of selection, which operates without purpose or goals, with the
epistemology that is used to discover and describe that process.

Realism

Realism is an ontological position addressing the question of "what
exists?" Materialistic realism holds that only matter exists, and idealistic
realism holds that only ideas or ideal forms exist. Naive realism is materialistic realism with an epistemological component asserting that we know
about matter through observation. Baum (1994) suggested that some mix
of the above types of realism ("there is some real behavior that goes on in

the real world, and ... our senses ... provide us only with sense data about that real behavior, which we never know directly" (p. 26) was associated with the methodological behaviorism of Watson, Hull, and Tolman, among others. Baum then contrasted this view of realism to pragmatism, asserting that radical behaviorism is more consistent with pragmatism.

Juxtaposing realism and pragmatism in this way, however, may be questioned. First the founder of pragmatism, Peirce, for example, considered himself to be a realist, one who believed in "truth as an ideal and absolute limit of scientific investigation" (Scheffler, 1974, p. 112). James proposed the notion of mutability of truth, by which he suggested that our evaluation of truth changes as a function of new evidence, or context. Scheffler, however, has noted that the mutability of truth idea has more to do with verification or confirmation than it does with the truth of a set of observations, thereby preserving, for him, the notion of truth as an ideal, that is, as an independent reality outside personal experience. Marr (1998; this volume) discussed a number of semantic and logical issues in describing the relation between realism and pragmatism suggesting that, at the very least, the two are not, of necessity, incompatible with one another. He observed that the views of both Skinner and Mach featured aspects of realist philosophy (though there are fundamental differences between them). In addition, Smith (1986) and Zuriff (1986) both observed that many of the methodological behaviorists, described by Baum (1994) as realists, also were pragmatists.

Contextualism

Pepper (1942) identified four world hypotheses, or world views, in terms of the root metaphor employed in each: Mechanism involves a machine metaphor, in formism the metaphor is similarity; and in organicism the metaphor is the process of organic development. The fourth world view, contextualism, takes as its metaphor the ongoing act in context. Reese (1986, p. 169) equated contextualism with pragmatism. There have been lengthy discussions about whether behavior analysis is described most usefully as mechanistic or contextualistic (e.g., Marr, 1993; Morris, 1993; Reese, 1993). Hayes, Hayes, and Reese (1988) note features of both contextualism and mechanism in behavior analysis, but in the end they conclude that it is more contextualistic than not. The conclusion of Hayes et al. is based in part on the presence of a pragmatic truth criterion in behavior analysis. They note that in mechanistic world hypotheses the "knower relates to the world [the known] by producing an internal copy of it, through mechanical transformation" (p. 99). Truth is determined by the correspondence between the copy and the world "as evaluated by corroboration among independent knowers" (Hayes et al., p. 99), a point of view reminiscent of logical positivism, a philosophical position to which behavior analysis does not subscribe (e.g., Skinner, 1945). By contrast, successful working is the truth criterion of both contextualism and behavior analysis.

Conclusion: The Value of Pragmatism in Behavior Analysis

After more than a hundred years as an intellectual position in both philosophy and psychology, in concert with other conceptual and empirical developments, pragmatism continues to perform yeoman's duty in contributing to the functional study of behavior. It has helped underwrite the goals of prediction and control as being worthwhile ones for a science of behavior. It has helped clarify definitions of concepts and constructs in behavior analysis. It has freed behavior analysis from a simple linear cause-effect model of science by emphasizing function over structure. It is like Skinner's concept of the operant: It provides a method allowing sufficient precision to address important questions through experimental science while simultaneously allowing broad scope through its application to a seemingly limitless variety of issues and problems both and outside the laboratory. In short, it continues to work usefully.

Acknowledgments

We thank Cindy Anderson, Adam Doughty, Darnell Lattal, Jack Marr, and Ed Morris for helpful comments on various issues discussed herein. We are especially grateful to Hayne Reese, our colleague and perpetual mentor, for a thorough critique of an earlier version of this chapter.

References

Anger, D. (1956). The dependence of interresponse times upon the relative reinforcement of different interresponse times. *Journal of Experimental Psychology, 52,* 145–161.

Azrin, N. H. (1956). Effects of two intermittent schedules of immediate and nonimmediate punishment. *Journal of Psychology, 42,* 3–21.

Azrin, N. H., & Holz, W. C. (1966). Punishment. In W. K. Honig (Ed.), *Operant behavior: Areas of research and application* (pp. 380–447). New York: Appleton-Century-Crofts.

Baer, D. M., Wolf, M. M., & Risley, T. R. (1968). Some current dimensions of applied behavior analysis. *Journal of Applied Behavior Analysis, 1,* 91–97.

Baum, W. M. (1973). The correlation-based law of effect. *Journal of the Experimental Analysis of Behavior, 20.*

Baum, W. M. (1994). *Understanding behaviorism: Science, behavior, and culture*. New York: Harper-Collins.

Baum, W. M. (1995). Introduction to molar behavior analysis. *Mexican Journal of Behavior Analysis, 21*, 7–25.

Baum, W. M. (2001). Molar versus molecular as a paradigm clash. *Journal of the Experimental Analysis of Behavior, 75*, 338–341.

Baum, W. M. (2002). From molecular to molar: A paradigm shift in behavior analysis. *Journal of the Experimental Analysis of Behavior, 78*, 95–116.

Bridgeman, P. W. (1927). *The logic of modern physics*. New York: Macmillan.

Chiesa, M. (1992). *Radical behaviorism: The philosophy and the science*. Boston: Author's Cooperative.

Cohen, M. R., & Nagel, E. (1934). *An introduction to logic and scientific method*. New York: Harcourt, Brace, & World.

Dawkins, R. (1986). *The blind watchmaker*. New York: Norton.

Dewey, J. (1916). *Essays in experimental logic*. Chicago: University of Chicago Press.

Dinsmoor, J. A. (2001). Stimuli inevitably generated by behavior that avoids electric shock are inherently reinforcing. *Journal of the Experimental Analysis of Behavior, 75*, 311–333.

Ferster, C. B., & Skinner, B. F. (1957). *Schedules of reinforcement*. New York: Appleton Century Crofts.

Hayes, S. C., Hayes, L. J., & Reese, H. W. (1988). Finding the philosophical core: A review of Stephen C. Pepper's *World Hypotheses: A Study in Evidence. Journal of the Experimental Analysis of Behavior, 50*, 97–111.

Herrnstein, R. J. (1970). On the law of effect. *Journal of the Experimental Analysis of Behavior, 13*, 243–266.

Herrnstein, R. J., & Hineline, P. N. (1966). Negative reinforcement as shock frequency reduction. *Journal of the Experimental Analysis of Behavior, 9*, 421–430.

Hineline, P. N. (1977). Negative reinforcement and avoidance. In W. K. Honig & J. E. R. Staddon (Eds.), *Handbook of operant behavior* (pp. 364–414). Englewood Cliffs, NJ: Prentice Hall.

Hineline, P. N. (2001). Beyond the molar-molecular distinction: We need multiscaled analyses. *Journal of the Experimental Analysis of Behavior, 75*, 342–347.

Horner, R. H., Dunlap, G., Koegel, R. L., Carr, E. G., Sailor, W., Anderson, J., Albin, R. W., & O'Neill, R. E. (1990). *Journal of the Association for Persons with Severe Handicaps, 15*, 125–132.

Iversen, I. H. (1991). Methods of analyzing behavior patterns. In Iversen, I. H. & Lattal, K. A. (Eds.), *Techniques in the behavioral and neural sciences vol. 6: Experimental analysis of behavior* (Part 2, pp. 193–241). Amsterdam: Elsevier.

Iversen, I. H. (1992). Skinner's early research: From reflexology to operant conditioning. *American Psychologist, 47*, 1318–1327.

Iwata, B. (1988). The development and adoption of controversial default technologies. *The Behavior Analyst, 11*, 149–157.

James, W. (1890). *Principles of Psychology*. New York: Holt.

James, W. (1892). *Psychology*. New York: Holt.

James, W. (1963) *Pragmatism*. Cleveland, OH: Meridian. (Original work published 1907).

Lattal, K. A., & Doepke, K. A. (2001). Say-do correspondence as conditional discrimination: Insights from experiments with pigeons. *Journal of Applied Behavior Analysis, 34*, 127–144.

Lattal, K. A., & Gleeson, S. (1990). Response acquisition with delayed reinforcement. *Journal of Experimental Psychology: Animal Behavior Processes, 16*, 27–39.

Lovejoy, A. O. (1908a). The thirteen pragmatisms. I. *The Journal of Philosophy, 5*, 5–12.

Lovejoy, A. O. (1908b). The thirteen pragmatisms. II. *The Journal of Philosophy, 5*, 29–39.

Mach, E. (1960). *The science of mechanics: A critical and historical account of its development*. Peru, IL: Open Court. (Original work published 1893).

Marr, M. J. (1993). Contextualistic mechanism or mechanistic contextualism?: The straw machine as tar baby. *The Behavior Analyst, 16*, 59–65.

Marr, M. J. (1998, November). Realistic pragmatism or pragmatic realism: What in the world is there to talk about? Paper presented at the Fourth International Congress on Behaviorism and the Sciences of Behavior, Seville, Spain.

Menand, L. (2001). *The metaphysical club: A story of ideas in America*. New York: Farrar, Straus & Giroux.

Moore, E. C. (1961). *American pragmatism: Peirce, James, and Dewey*. New York: Columbia University Press.

Moore, J. (1998). On behaviorism, theories, and hypothetical constructs. *The Journal of Mind and Behavior, 19*, 215–242.

Morris, C. (1970). *The pragmatic movement in American philosophy*. New York: Braziller.

Morris, E. K. (1993). Behavior analysis and mechanism: One is not the other. *The Behavior Analyst, 16*, 25–43.

Moxley, R. A. (2001). Sources for Skinner's pragmatic selectionism in 1945. *The Behavior Analyst, 24*, 201–212.

Palmer, D. C., & Donahoe, J. W. (1992). Essentialism and selectionism in cognitive science and behavior analysis. *American Psychologist, 47*, 1344–1358.

Pepper, S. C. (1942). *World hypotheses: A study in evidence*. Berkeley, CA: University of California Press.

Peirce, C. S. (1878). How to make our ideas clear. *Popular Science Monthly, 12*, 286–302.

Rachlin, H. L. (1992). Teleological behaviorism. *American Psychologist, 47*, 1371–1382.

Rachlin, H. L. (1995). Burrhus Frederick Skinner 1904–1990. *Biographical Memoirs, 67*, 2–17.

Reese, H. W. (1986). Behavioral and dialectical psychologies. In L. P. Lipsitt & J. H. Cantor (Eds.), *Experimental child psychologist: Essays and experiments in honor of Charles C. Spiker* (pp. 157–195). Hillsdale, NJ: Erlbaum.

Reese, H. W. (1993). Comments about Morris's paper. *The Behavior Analyst, 16*, 67–74.

Reese, H. W. (1997). A belated response to Moxley. *The Behavior Analyst, 20*, 43–47.

Scheffler, I. (1974). *Four pragmatists: A critical introduction to Peirce, James, Mead, and Dewey*. New York: Humanities Press.

Schiller, F. C. S. (1912). *Studies in humanism*. London: Macmillan.

Schneider, S. M. (1997). Back to our philosophical roots: A journal review of *Transactions of the Charles S. Peirce Society*. *The Behavior Analyst, 20*, 17–23.

Silberberg, A., & Fantino, E. (1970). Choice, rate of reinforcement, and the changeover delay. *Journal of the Experimental Analysis of Behavior, 13*, 187–197.

Sidman, M. (1989). *Coercion and its fallout*. Boston, MA: Authors Cooperative.

Skinner, B. F. (1935). The generic nature of the concepts of stimulus and response. *Journal of General Psychology, 12*, 40–65.

Skinner, B. F. (1938). *The behavior of organisms: An experimental analysis*. New York: Prentice Hall.

Skinner, B. F. (1945). The operational analysis of psychological terms. *Psychological Review, 52*, 270–277, 291–294.

Skinner, B. F. (1950). Are theories of learning necessary? *Psychological Review, 57*, 193–216.

Skinner, B. F. (1953). *Science and human behavior*. New York: Macmillan.

Skinner, B. F. (1956). A case history in scientific method. *American Psychologist, 11*, 221–233.

Skinner, B. F. (1974). *About behaviorism*. New York: Knopf.

Smith, L. D. (1986). *Behaviorism and logical positivism: A reassessment of the alliance*. Stanford, CA: Stanford University Press.

Staddon, J. E. R. (1993).The conventional wisdom of behavior analysis. *Journal of the Experimental Analysis of Behavior,60*, 439–447.

Thompson, T. (1984). The examining magistrate for nature: A retrospective review of Claude Bernard's *An Introduction to the Study of Experimental Medicine. Journal of the Experimental Analysis of Behavior*, 41, 211–216.

van Houten, R. (1983). Punishment: From the animal laboratory to applied settings. In S. Axelrod, S., & J. Apsche (Eds.), *The effects of punishment on human behavior* (pp. 13–44). New York: Academic Press.

Watson, J. B. (1958). *Behaviorism.* Chicago: Phoenix. (Original version published 1924).

Watson, J. B. (1961). Autobiography. In C. Murchison (Ed.) *A history of psychology in autobiography Vol. 3., (pp. 271–281).* New York: Russell & Russell. (Original version 1936).

Zuriff, G. E. (1986). *Behaviorism: A conceptual reconstruction.* New York: Columbia University Press.

4

Empiricism

Jack Marr

Experience is the Angled Road—Emily Dickinson

The word *empiricist* comes from the Greek root meaning "experience" and appears to date from the middle seventeenth century. The emphasis on experience in the acquisition of any kind of knowledge, scientific or otherwise, became a basic pillar of *epistemology*, that philosophical domain addressing such questions as what *could* people know, how *could* they know it, what *do* they know, and how *do* they know it. "Empirical" was thus reified into *empiricism*, traditionally the doctrine asserting that most, if not all, of what counts as knowledge results from experience. Although there were certainly antecedents, the development of empiricism into systematic philosophical positions by Locke, Berkeley, and Hume in the seventeenth and eighteenth century paralleled, indeed was spurred by, the development of modern science.

In this brief essay I do not wish to treat the history of empiricism or the wide range of critical views (for just a few of these, see, e.g., Carruthers, 1992; Copleson, 1994; Curd & Cover, 1998; Dancy, 1985; Moser, Mulder & Trout, 1998; Rosenberg, 2000; Zuriff, 1985), but then, how should this topic be approached? Not only is the subject huge; but also if the major philosophical discussions of empiricism throughout its history are to be taken seriously, no conceivable aspect has gone unchallenged, and by very clever people. Given this deep and contentious history, what can be said about the place of empiricism in modern behaviorism and behavior

Jack Marr • School of Psychology, Georgia Tech, Atlanta, GA 30332-0170.

analysis? Why discuss this venerable and battle-weary topic at all? Empiricism, as indicated above, emphasizes the primary role of experience in the acquisition of knowledge. But just what is meant by "experience"? This question has been addressed in many ways, not a few antithetical to a behavioral perspective. Behavior analysts are concerned with the acquisition, maintenance, and modification of the behavior of organisms through their interaction with the environment, as well as the subsequent alteration of that environment through such interaction. "Men act upon the world to change it and are in turn changed by the consequences of their action." (Skinner, 1957, p. 1) I submit that this behavior-environment interaction encompasses much of what can be deemed "experience", and thus empiricism lies at the core of behavior analysis—basic and applied— as well as a background conceptual framework called behaviorism. So, then, beyond this simple rationale, why else might one wish to address this topic?

First, behaviorism, said to be the philosophy of the science of behavior analysis, is in a continuing struggle for its identity. In the past couple of decades and proceeding apace, many calling themselves radical behaviorists have debated endlessly just what holding such a view entails. The dimensions of these debates range widely but largely center on concerns of epistemology, and in particular those bearing on the topic of empiricism. Among the more contentious issues are: *realism vs. pragmatism, mechanism vs. contextualism, description vs. explanation, observables vs. unobservables, molarism vs. molecularism,* and *determinism vs. indeterminism* (e.g., Baum, 1989, 1994; Chiesa, 1994; Hayes, Hayes, & Reese, 1988; Morris, 1993; Staddon, 2001). Others address some of these issues in this volume, confirming that the quest goes on for some conceptual coherence to behaviorism. Based on the various views expressed in these debates, "behaviorism" is, at best, a family-resemblance term. Worse, the contrasting dimensions just mentioned and the rankling they engender often remind me of Aesop's fable of two men arguing over the shadow of an ass. The debates have too often hinged on conceptual confusions, category mistakes, and a common disorder one could call *genus simplex*—the tendency to amplify some distinctions to the neglect of others and to oversimplify that which is complex in order to make such distinctions.

All this verbal sparring over "conceptual issues" is often a lot of fun, but it rarely addresses, or affects how the science of behavior analysis is actually conducted, or any other science for that matter. Moreover, much of this contentious messiness seems far afield from Skinner's unachieved ambition for what he called a "scientific epistemology", his vision to apply a science of verbal behavior to improving the effectiveness of logical and scientific practice. In his own words:

> The verbal processes of logical and scientific thought deserve and require a more precise analysis than they have yet received. One of the ultimate accomplishments of a science of verbal behavior may be an empirical logic, or a descriptive and analytic scientific epistemology, the terms and practices of which will be adapted to human behavior as a subject matter. (Skinner, 1957, p. 431)

Regardless of one's view on whether such an enterprise would be valuable, or possible, or even make sense, most behaviorists share the notion that the conduct of science, that is, the behavior of those who are identified as scientists, is an appropriate subject for behavior analysts to consider, if only in an interpretive way. But, in reality, the science of behavior has given little attention to the behavior of scientists. Considering the complexity of the topic, this should not be surprising. Some treatment of this behavior, however, provides a second rationale for why one might address a dusty topic like empiricism.

A more immediate and compelling third reason follows from the second and returns to the first. There is a formidable and still very active movement in academe called "postmodernism" that threatens and abuses the scientific enterprise, including a science of behavior that might address that enterprise. One of postmodernism's facets is a radical social relativism that essentially repudiates any useful meaning of empiricism or, more generally, epistemology in a scientific context (e.g., Devitt, 1997; Gross & Levitt, 1994, Gross, Levitt, & Lewis, 1996; Kitcher, 1993; Laudan, 1990, 1996; Searle, 1995). This last reason to treat the topic of empiricism in many ways sets the agenda for what I have to say, so I will give it initial and special emphasis. Postmodernism's treatment of science raises disturbing questions about the practice of science, the meaning and value of its products, and what can be known, if anything, through experience with the world, that is, through the application of a systematic empiricism. With this goes any hope of Skinner's (or anyone else's) proposal for a "scientific epistemology", or, in general, an effective application of behavioral science to the analysis of science itself. As the reader will see, there is irony here in that programs emerging from the postmodernist movement purport to conduct a scientific (e.g., sociological) analysis of science. I will show that, in the main, their results are unsurprising, if not simply misleading. Moreover, as may be clear already, this "science" appears to be immune from the critiques it makes of other sciences. Perhaps even more ironic is that, for reasons I will outline, some behaviorists are attracted to features of the "sociology of science" movement. How does all this relate to empiricism?

At issue here is the extent to which practicing scientists might trust their experiences. Clearly, this extent should depend, at least in large measure, on the origins of that trust. This addresses the vital question of why scientific practices are so effective. I will provide an example of how this question might be approached. The conceptual issues involved here hark back to several of those listed earlier as bones of contention among behaviorists, as I will indicate. In a modest way, I want to sensitize the student of behavior analysis to some of the tensions and controversies centering on empiricism within behavior analysis and, in this process, indicate how behavior analysis relates and may contribute to more general scientific interests.

Worldmaking

Scientists do not as a rule see science as some lofty and sacred entity somehow independent from human action. That the acquisition, practice, dissemination, and application of science reflect social contingencies is a truism. For some, however, this fact has come to mean something a great deal more than most, if not all, practicing scientists would be willing to swallow. I am referring to the radical relativists (and a number of other possible appellations) espousing the "Sociology of Scientific Knowledge," including championing certain atavistic practices under the rationale of "other ways of knowing." This position sees scientific results and the methods used to achieve them as having all the arbitrariness and significance of Tibetan table manners or the rules of tiddly-winks. Worse yet, according to these views, whatever in its history science might claim to have accomplished *only* reflects the prevailing socio-politico-cultural-ethnic climate, the concerted subjugation of the downtrodden and unempowered, and the petty jealousies and power struggles among rival researches. Most scientists and the science they practice are untouched by these assertions, but apparently not some behaviorists and their followers (e.g., Andresen, 1991; Czubaroff, 1991; Moxley, 1999; Schnaitter, 1999). An emphasis on social and, in particular, verbal contingencies in the conduct of science strikes a resonant chord in the behaviorist's instrument. No behavioral scientist I know, however, would assert that the natural world and our scientific descriptions of it put *no* constraints on belief, or that the *only* entity is "text," and that any text can have *any* interpretation. I am reminded of an old story about Lincoln:

> "Sir, how many legs does this donkey have?"
> "Four, Mr. Lincoln."

"And how many tails does it have?"

"One, Mr. Lincoln."

"Now, sir, what if we were to call a tail a leg; how many legs would the donkey have?"

"Five, Mr. Lincoln.

"No, sir, for you cannot make a tail into a leg by calling it one."

The attempt of a few to cram any credible behavioral stance, Skinner included, into some postmodernist worldview is profoundly misguided, as all conceptual shoehorning must be. Behaviorists would be foolish, however, simply to dismiss this challenge, especially when it comes from within. To treat the threat seriously must involve consideration of a wide variety of interconnected and interactive topics, all, however, bearing on the behavioral dynamics of effective scientific practice. Empiricism, then, as emphasizing the role of what is deemed "experience," requires an analysis of those variables controlling this practice, in other words, the special history of the scientist, including the antecedents and consequences of scientific behavior. Antecedents include the rules of evidence, and what events count as evidence; consequences include the outcomes of applying those rules and of acting on the evidence obtained.

My allotted space precludes any detailed discussion of even the major issues, but what are some of those issues as I see them? I certainly should include all those putatively polar contentions mentioned before (contextualism versus mechanism, realism versus pragmatism, etc.). For radical social constructivists contextualism is the "foundational" view, and while some have also emphasized their pragmatic (as opposed to realistic) stance, I will argue that they are neither practical, nor realistic.

Their radical relativism has also gotten a boost, whether appropriate or not, from certain philosophers of science and their conceptual camp followers, among them Kuhn, Popper, Feyerabend, Lakatos, Bloor, and Rorty, as well as the so-called "sociologists of science," Woolgar, Aronowitz, Latour, and others (see, e.g., Pickering, 1992), including that gloomy Gallic folie à deux, Derrida (1982) and Foucoult (e.g., 1973). The questions and issues raised by this group include whether there is such a thing as scientific progress, whether the rules and other practices of scientists have any special reliability or validity, whether any assertion or belief about the world can have any justification, empirical or otherwise, and the generally holistic, incommensurable, and under-deterministic character of any so-called knowledge. One is immediately stuck, not only by the profound skepticism of these sorts of views, but their equally profound self-referential incoherence.

Why are some behaviorists attracted to these views? Basically, because they are taught that (a) science is a social practice itself subject to a behavioral analysis, (b) much of science is verbal behavior shaped by a verbal community, (c) any useful distinction between the "subjective" and the "objective" should be questioned, (d) any meaningful notion of "truth" is embodied only in pragmatics (more formally called "successful working" after Pepper, 1942), and (e) behavior analysts are "contextualists" as opposed to "mechanists." All of these assertions can put a smile on any postmodernist's face. The first four, however, as stated, conceal more than they reveal. All of them, when unpacked within the context of real scientific practice and its consequences are either irrelevant to a socially-constructed theory of knowledge, or antagonistic to it. The last assertion, about contextualism, is, shall I say, wholly uncompelling, but many apparently need to be reminded. In the following sections I comment briefly on the first four of these interlocking issues; as for the fifth, the reader is referred to Marr (1993a, 1993b).

Science as Social Practice

What perspectives are those calling themselves social relativists asserting? There are many hues here, but basically the principal thesis is that because science is a social practice, it has no special claim to knowledge. Another way of putting it is that the natural world and our scientific descriptions of it place *no* constraints on *any* belief.

That science is a social practice is incontestable. What else could it be? Even a Robinson Crusoe scientist would have learned scientific knowledge and practice elsewhere in a language shaped by a verbal community, all inherently social processes. As human social practices founded on verbal behavior, what are called the methods of science developed late in history (and continue to be developed), although many elements were already around in ancient times. Consider the construction of the pyramids in ancient Egypt (c. 2000 BCE), Euclid's *Elements of Geometry* (c. 300 BCE), Archimedes principle of displacement (c. 200 BCE), and the remarkably accurate calculation of the earth's circumference by Eratosthenes (c. 200 BCE). Nonetheless, the systematic development of science as an independent human endeavor was not achieved until perhaps the beginning of the 19th century (when the term "science" was first used). As indicated earlier, empiricism, in various conceptual forms, was the guiding force in this development.

The issue is not that science is a social practice, but the extent to which that fact supports the relativist's convictions. First of all there are, I believe, interesting questions about scientific practice that might draw and has drawn behavioral scientists to consider. For example, behavior analysts might certainly raise issues and questions about the origin of particular scientific practices, the conditions under which discoveries might be made and new practices introduced, the most effective practices for a given purpose, the social dynamics of scientific teams, the most effective means for teaching science and mathematics, how mathematicians go about solving problems and proving theorems, etc. These all seem like reasonable, albeit difficult, behaviorally relevant questions about how science is done. Regarding the development and practice of behavior analysis itself, the reader should consult, for example, Skinner's (1956) "A case history in scientific method" as well as his autobiography (1976, 1979, 1983). In general, autobiographies and biographies of eminent scientists provide a wealth of information on the enormous range of contingencies controlling effective (and ineffective) scientific practices.

One could go into the domain of socio-political inquiry and ask why, for example, one NSF grant might be funded as opposed to another of apparently equal scientific merit. In another area, historians still debate the issue of why the United States needed to drop the atom bomb on Japan, or even if the bomb should have been developed in the first place. In more recent times there is much debate about cell cloning and its possible consequences. In yet another domain, behavior analysts might read with delight Watson's (1968) *The Double Helix*, relating the achievement of a momentous scientific goal as a human drama. *The Double Helix* could serve as an object lesson in the role of social dynamics, as well as fortuitous events in the practice of science. In it there are diverse and conflicting personalities, rivalries, the "arrogance of office," bits of chicanery, mistakes, embarrassment, and, of course, triumph.

Here, however, is an essential point: The structure of DNA (no matter how it might be represented in the language of the chemist) and all that flowed from it did not depend on all these fascinating human dynamics. It is not a triple helix or an icosahedron comprised of sugarplums, or anything else than what it is. It is DNA in me, in you, in a silverfish, and in a frozen mammoth. In the same way, no matter where you might be on the earth—in West Virginia, in the Fiji Islands, in the backwaters of the Amazon, no matter in what culture or political system, people are not thrown off the earth as a result of its rotation. Whether the Democrats or Republicans were in office, or during the Han Dynasty, or the time of the Great Zimbabwe, one can be certain that polar bears did not roam around the broiling Sahara, nor anacondas slither across the arctic ice, nor walruses chat with carpenters over a meal of pleading oysters. Moreover, I would challenge anyone to show how any work by these "sociologists of scientific knowledge" can improve scientific methodology so as to lead to any scientific discovery, significant or not. Shall people look to Bloor, or Aronowitz, or Latour, or Woolgar to help with curing AIDs, mapping the human genome, finding whether life has existed on Mars, taming fusion reactions, proving Goldbach's conjecture, or even finding a convincing feedback function for a fixed-interval schedule?

Of course, what I am belaboring here is that the particular practices of scientists have been enormously successful wherever they have been applied, both in characterizing nature and in eliminating a host of possibilities, despite cries of "underdetermination" and "incommensurability." Neither the practices nor the knowledge won from them are considered by any scientist to be infallible or immutable. Indeed, these qualities, given the stringent contingencies for acceptable evidence, are what make science unique as a source of knowledge and understanding. The fallibility and mutability of science, however, certainly opens a crack in the door for an enterprising social constructivist to stick in his or her foot. Neither fallibility nor mutability, however, confers respectability to relativism or constructivism. To do so would, at the least, conflate "belief" with "evidence for belief," or, in scientific terms, tests of confirmation or falsifiability. These tests—empiricism harnessed and put to work—are part of scientific practice that has grown concurrently and reciprocally with scientific knowledge. As knowledge through practice grows, so practices themselves evolve to yield new knowledge, and so on, in a dynamic interplay of positive and negative feedback. Success in the growth of knowledge is conferred to method and vice versa. I am, of course, aware that relativists do not believe science is progressive or cumulative. I hold further comment on this view until later.

Some of the findings of the constructivists deeply reflect an ignorance of a particular science or engineering field in both method and content. I will not relate here, for example, Gross and Levitt's (1994) analysis of the works of Aronowitz and Latour, or the now notorious Sokal (1996) affair. Perhaps one of the strangest "revelations" to emerge from these kinds of efforts is that science, as conducted from day to day, is not really like what appears in the best, polished published form—an organized, systematic, coherent, scholarly, objective presentation! Anyone who has ever actually done science, alone or as a part of a team, would regard this so-called finding as stupefyingly insipid. If the reader is unconvinced, compare *The Double Helix* (Watson, 1968) with Watson and Crick's (1953) original publication in *Nature* or Skinner's (1956) "case history" with his technical papers. The distinctions between the processes of creation or discovery and the final products of these activities have never been in question.

Science as Verbal Behavior

That scientific behavior is principally verbal is, of course, another truism. Skinner (1957, 1969) seems to have been a pioneer in the analysis of scientific verbal behavior. He sets the stage for his discussion with the following:

> When a speaker accurately reports, identifies, or describes a given state of affairs, he increases the likelihood that a listener will act successfully with respect to it, and when the listener looks to the speaker for an extension of his own sensory capacities, or for contact with distant events, or for an accurate characterization of a puzzling situation, the speaker's behavior is most useful if the environmental control has not been disturbed by other variables. (Skinner, 1957, p. 418)

Later, he focuses on the scientific community itself: "The scientific community encourages the precise stimulus control under which an object or property of an object is identified or characterized in such a way that practical action will be most effective" (Skinner, 1957, p. 419). Skinner then treated various classes of verbal operants common to scientific discourse and practice, the manipulation of verbal material, the role of graphs, models, mathematics, and logical operations. Subsequently (Skinner, 1969, 1974), he discussed the roles of rule-governed and contingency-controlled behavior. Here is a particularly pertinent comment:

> Differences in thought processes have been attributed to the apparent differences between the laws of religions or governments and the laws of science. The first are said to be "made", the second merely discovered, but the difference is not in the laws, but in the contingencies the laws describe. The laws of religions and governments codify contingencies of reinforcement maintained by social environments. The laws of science describe contingencies which prevail in the environment *quite apart from any deliberate human action.* (Skinner, 1974, p. 124, italics added)

Now, there are several sources of criticism, or "deconstruction" that scientific "texts" and "representations" face from postmodernists. For example, the postmodernist forces inspired by Derrida and Foucault hold the skeptical perspective that all texts are, if not meaningless, then certainly untrustworthy, unstable, self-contradictory, and could in no way reflect a reality outside the texts themselves. Moreover, they are capable of *any* interpretation. (I have to point out here that these judgments do not seem to apply to the texts of the founders or contemporary practitioners of postmodernist criticism). Foucault saw language as both a source of political power and a blindfold to reality. All these assertions of the postmodernists directly apply to methods, theories, and data or results in science. The ideas applied here include "underdetermination" and "incommensurability."

Presumably, any data could be shown to be in accord with any theory. Moreover, theories cannot be compared for testing, etc., because each is a separate worldview without possibility of translation or cross interpretation.

It is difficult to know where to start here, but I will spend little time. *Moby Dick* is perhaps my favorite American novel and it certainly has many interpretations, but to assert that it can have any interpretation is simply nonsense. Any interpretation means no interpretation, because the term "interpretation" can have no use in such a scheme. Indeed, verbal behavior could never be shaped at all if those conditions prevailed. Nor would verbal behavior be shaped and maintained if it were basically meaningless, untrustworthy, unstable, self-contradictory, and had no relation to "given states of affairs."

The same can be said in response to Woolgar's (1988) assertion that: "... there is no sense in which the claim can be made that the phenomenon has an existence independent of its means of expression... there is no object beyond discourse, but that the organization of discourse is the object. Facts and objects in the world are inescapably textual constructions" (p. 73). Wow! What does Woolgar live on? Does he eat the words "eggs and bacon" for breakfast? Again, how would verbal behavior ever come about if he were right? What about the world of trees, birds, galaxies, dinosaurs, and, indeed words, that people have come to talk about? What about all those nonverbal creatures in the world without the benefit of a text to give life to crawling, walking, flying, mating, nest building, prey-catching, and all their other activities that have been going on for eons before there were texts? By claiming that there would not have been stars and rain and trilobites without an accompanying text, Woolgar certainly gives a unique spin on the opening of the Gospel According to Saint John: "In the beginning was the Word ... "

A more sophisticated perspective comes from Bloor (1983), whose book, *Wittgenstein: A Social Theory of Knowledge* has been influential in the social constructivism movement, and among some behavior analysts. In general, Wittgenstein is potential quick sand for those looking for the putative role of social convention in controlling human action. Phrases like "forms of life," "language games," and "family resemblances" are traps for the unwary, or for any with a particular axe to grind.

To simplify some lengthy arguments, Bloor (1983) interprets (and I think misinterprets) Wittgenstein's analysis of the place of rules and why they might be consistently followed, as reflective of social convention— whether the rules occur as in mathematical proofs or in the theories and practices of natural science. In the latter, for example, any finite collection of empirical results could be interpreted by an infinite number of different rules. Thus, let social convention decide, and the sociologists of scientific knowledge tell us why the decision was made. One obvious problem with this is: What rules would the sociologist (or, indeed, any other potential investigator, including a behavior analyst) use that did not suffer the vagaries of some other convention?

Wherefore Convention?

A more interesting issue is that of convention itself. What controls convention, especially in scientific or mathematical practice? This is, I believe, a deep issue that cannot be cast simply as reflective of a set of "arbitrary" social contingencies. To conform to a set of conventions, or, perhaps more formally, a collection of rules, has consequences the effects of which are to sustain conformity. The methods of science uniquely discipline experience with extraordinary consequences, including unprecedented control over manifold phenomena of nature. Such an outcome could hardly be the result of following a definable set of arbitrary social conventions. Moreover, doing productive science is not simply following a set of rules or even clearly specified conventions (again, e.g., see Skinner, 1956). Yes, scientists all learn scientific methods, research design, laboratory procedures, mathematics, and many other techniques for studying and describing nature. These are the means through which empiricism is harnessed. As with any high-level skill, however, including one initially under control of a set of rules, complex contingency-controlled behaviors come to play a major, if not predominant role in the expression of the skill. An effective scientist is more like an improvising jazz pianist than a cook dutifully following a recipe. The acquisition and exercise of scientific skill has special implications for how that skill can or should be studied. To do effective physics, biochemistry, or behavior analysis means, as Skinner has said, to describe contingencies that operate apart from human agency. Sociologists of a science are of no help here unless they also know physics, biochemistry, or behavior analysis. That is, they must acquire the verbal and nonverbal repertoires of their "subjects" to be sensitive to the same contingencies that control what their subjects do as physicists, biochemists, or behavior analysts in their attempts to capture the contingencies of nature.

To assert the role of convention in any practice should always beg the question of the source of that convention. I consider one of the most vexing questions in the philosophy of science and mathematics to highlight the sources of convention in scientific rules and practice: Why does mathematics work so well? (For more detail, see, e.g., Marr, 1986, 1995; Hersh, 1997.) I choose to treat this question not only because of its putative profundity and difficulty, but if this issue can be addressed with some degree of success, then less difficult problems regarding the practice of science should also yield to a similar analysis. Perhaps most important for the present purposes, consideration of this question indicates why, with proper harnessing of empiricism, people have reasons to trust their experience.

This issue was addressed in a classic essay by Wigner (1984) entitled "The unreasonable effectiveness of mathematics in the natural sciences". So, what is the problem here? Let me start with an anecdote from Wigner. A statistician was explaining to a nonmathematical friend the equation for the Gaussian, or normal distribution describing some characteristic of a population. The friend was skeptical and asked "How can you know that?" "And what is this symbol here?" "Oh," said the statistician, this is π." "What is that?" "The ratio of the circumference of a circle to its diameter." "Well, now you are pushing the joke too far—surely the population has nothing to do with the circumference of a circle." Not only is it the case that mathematical concepts turn up in unexpected places, but physicists, engineers, and others can develop mathematical models of startling effectiveness both in describing nature's contingencies and predicting previously unobserved phenomena. To Wigner and to many others who have practiced this art, it "borders on the mysterious and there... is no rational explanation for it" (p. 117). Einstein once said that the most incomprehensible thing about the world is that it is comprehensible. Wigner concludes his essay with the mystery remaining: "The miracle of the appropriateness of the language of mathematics for the formulation of the laws of physics is a wonderful gift which we neither understand nor deserve" (p. 124).

How, indeed, do scientists come to know so much about nature by properly talking about it? The answer seems mind-bogglingly simple: Because nature taught us how to talk. Emo Phillips, a comedian now mostly known to crossword puzzle solvers, once commented that he used to think that the most wonderful organ in the universe was the human brain—then he realized what was telling him that! How is it that natural selection yielded up fish with streamlined bodies, birds whose wings are structured in accordance with Bernoulli's Principle, and elephants with log-like legs? Whatever the origins of verbal behavior, the outcome is a class of behavior in accordance with and capable of describing the nature that shaped it. Behavior analysts characterize verbal behavior as behavior whose effectiveness is mediated through other people—the verbal community. This verbal community, however, shares the public world, the world independent of representations of it. And, of course, this in no way implies that the representations are independent of the world.

The mystery referred to by Wigner seems a long way from the grunts and groans of our early ancestors. Here is a modern example. Quantum mechanics, arguably the most successful scientific theory ever to be constructed has many fascinating questions of interpretation, but none of these have much, if anything, to do with the successes of the theory. These successes are demonstrated by numerous and astonishingly detailed accounts and predictions of a host of phenomena through the mathematics comprising the theory. The curious thing is that much, if not all of this mathematics seems very remote from human experience. Neils Bohr once said that anyone who claims to understand quantum physics does not understand it (Marr, 1995).

To get a picture of how this might be possible requires starting far back with the development of mathematics. Analogously with the development of a verbal repertoire in an individual through interaction with a verbal community, consider the development of a set of verbal practices in a community shaped through the consequences of those practices. What contingencies led to the development of behaviors like counting, measuring, etc.? Many of these activities in the context of cultural development had, and, of course, still have major economic consequences. Methods of determining lengths, areas, volumes, times, and so on, are considered foundational to cultural development. Presumably, people who were particularly clever at these tasks attained a certain respect, responsibility, and authority. Moreover, while these earlier mathematical activities were closely tied to such applications as those in construction, land measure, inventory, appraisal, military deployment, and money systems, the verbal behavior called mathematics, as with other verbal behavior, has verbal as well as nonverbal consequences. As Skinner (1969) stated, "...rules...are physical objects and they can be manipulated to produce other...rules" (p. 144). Mathematical behavior is, from a verbal operant perspective, not only a system of rules, including rules about rules, but a system of intraverbals, autoclitic, and relational frames, and a variety of tacts including metaphoric, generic, and, especially, abstract. Consider what developments were necessary to shape abstraction from, say, crude land measures to Euclid's *Geometry* and on to Ptolemaic, Copernican, Keplerian, Newtonian, and, most recently, Einsteinian "Systems of the World." As with all behavioral shaping, it is possible to trace the steps along the way. So, one can step backward from four-dimensional Riemannian geometry of general relativity to the scribblings of sand reckoners in Mesopotamia eons ago. This evolution of abstraction, which is the principal theme in the history of mathematics, does not imply that the course was smooth. For example, great resistance or, at least agitated perplexity, greeted the introduction and exploration of irrational, complex, and transfinite numbers; indeed, as late as the 17th century, mathematicians did not accept negative numbers as numbers (Klein, 1980).

Mathematics thus developed through effective consequences of its construction and exercise, occasioned by the solution of practical problems, and, as well, strongly maintained by its own verbal consequences. Unambiguous specifications of this latter form of reinforcement are elusive, but achieving control over verbal material can be at least as powerful as achieving control over any nonverbal domain, and mathematics has the advantages of doing both. As a result, mathematical creativity, like other forms of verbal behavior, has taken on a life of its own. Pure mathematicians are sometimes known for their disdain of application, but the remarkable fact is that some of their most abstract accomplishments end up becoming part of the common repertoire of the working scientist. Despite the goal of purity in abstraction, major portions of mathematics can be seen as outdistancing their applications, so that when more effective accounts of nature's contingencies were ultimately explored and constructed, appropriate mathematical repertoires are already available, now to be further strengthened by non-verbal consequences. Notable examples include complex variables for electromagnetic theory and hydrodynamics, non-Euclidian geometry and tensor analysis for general relativity, and Hilbert space and group theory for quantum mechanics. At each stage of advance, the pictures of nature given by everyday experience seem to retreat further into an impenetrable mathematical jungle. Nevertheless, this whole process can be described as a helix of discovery that finds its origins in nature and leads back to nature. Where is this helix going? I have no idea, but it is certain that scientific accounts, in the parlance of my behaviorist colleagues, are ever more successfully working.

Subjective-Objective Distinction

This contrast has relevance to what "experience" means. Radical behaviorists view the traditional subjective-objective distinction as an expression of dualism in the form of a "copy theory," separating an inner from an outer world, the outer world essentially inaccessible, only knowable through fallible senses. For the behaviorist, there is only one world and different behaviors in relation to it controlled by different contingencies and the rules derived from them. Skinner (1972), for example, asserted that the control of behavior by private events reflects the same processes descriptive of behavior with respect to public events. One can say that private events are observed in the same way as public ones. As for sensations comprising the basic datum of a science, Skinner, using the response "red" as an example, said:

> The response "red" is imparted and maintained by reinforcements which are contingent upon a certain property of stimuli. . . . The older psychological view, however, was that the speaker was reporting not a property of the stimulus, but a certain kind of private event, the sensation of red. . . . This seems like a gratuitous distinction. (p. 378)

Skinner's views on the observability of private events are counter to the generally accepted definition of an observable in terms of intersubjective agreement. Yet truth by agreement is not as "arid" (p. 363) as Skinner would have one believe—by his own analysis. First of all, control via private events is a function of interaction with the verbal community. Second, while I might take effective action by observing my private events, it will be less likely that anyone else could do so. The implication is that one is not in a position to develop a *science* based upon private events. As Skinner notes: "In a rigorous scientific vocabulary private effects are practically eliminated" (p. 377).

There is a sense, however, in which the terms *subjective* and *objective* have a proper use. Although the behaviorist proclaims but one world, a distinction is made between "public" and "private" events, at least on the basis of accessibility, if for no other reason. This has important implications. "I have a pain" is fundamentally distinguishable from "I have ten dollars." There are clear rules or criteria that can be applied to the latter, but there are none for the former. One could be wrong about how much money she has, but the judgment of correctness or error is not applicable to one's being in pain. This sounds like the domain of the postmodernist who eschews facts, rules, criteria, and interpretations; and, along with them, the possibility of any kind of positive knowledge. Why then, are they talking at all? There would seem to be nothing to say. It is a kind of idealism through the looking glass.

For Skinner, scientific practice is under the control of contingencies ultimately supplied by nature. The effectiveness of these practices is manifested in the degree of prediction and control over a phenomenon. Other practices concerned with the same phenomenon may be shown to be less successful. For example, I suspect that even the most ardent relativist suffering from a burst appendix is more likely to seek out a competent surgeon in an emergency room than request to be taken to a new-age faith healer.

Successful Working—The Pragmatic Stance

Most who are not postmodernists or social constructivists are impressed by what would seem to be an obvious fact—*science works*. What does this mean? Many things, actually, some of which I have already alluded to. For me, the success of science in its description of nature is the key issue in the behaviorist's debate over pragmatism versus realism. As has been indicated, the issue is not the assumed stance of infallibility; science is fallible. If, in fact, it were truly infallible, then there could be no accumulation of knowledge and method. Everything would already be known. The issue is not that the conduct of science stands beyond social contingencies to reside in some crystalline, pristine, and all-seeing God's eye. The issue is not that there are no conventions in science. Concepts like "length" or "time" and their units of measurement have a long history (Klein, 1974). But, through the application of such conventions, conclusions can be derived that would seem to be not simply a matter of convention, despite their residing in a complex nexus of rules, concepts, methods, etc. For example: "It is further from here to the moon than it is to my front door"; and, "I am younger than the earth."

The burden falls to the relativist to show that science is not progressive or accumulative, and in that effort he fails. No amount of metaphysical legerdemain with "undecidibility," "underdetermination," "holism," or "incommensurability" would succeed in convincing most modern philosophers of science (see, e.g., Laudan, 1977, 1990; Kitcher, 1993), and certainly not scientists themselves that what is known about electricity today is just as much as Benjamin Franklin knew in the 18th century. The 100th anniversary of J. J. Thompson's discovery of the electron was in 1997—Franklin would have been delighted!

Why is science so successful? Some of the reasons have to do with social contingencies, as Skinner asserted. Essential are the self-corrective aspects of scientific practice. Science has its share of fools and knaves, and the rest are more than capable of making honest mistakes. Nevertheless, if the problem is interesting enough, and the communication network is functioning, scientific claims are subject to intense scrutiny. One cannot claim to have discovered aliens from outer space in New Mexico, or superconductivity at room temperature, or a unified field theory, or life on Europa, without the scientific community demanding a lot of data, tests, replications, predictions, apparatus specifications, and the like. In other words, not without credible evidence. Would that politics, religion, education, and, especially, the "Sociology of Scientific Knowledge" be subject to those assessments.

There are more interesting reasons for the successes of science. Relativists seem to claim that social conventions, including language, are arbitrary. I assume by "arbitrary", they mean independently of any contingencies. Surely not. Harris (1979), for example, has asserted some very plausible reasons for a number of cultural practices, largely based on analysis of prevailing economic contingencies. More recently, Diamond (1999) and Landes (1999) have provided fascinating contingency analyses to account for differential cultural characteristics and accomplishments. Without surprise, people who live in cold climates not only dress warmly, but also have words and expressions relating to ice and snow, and other features of a wintry world. Likewise, such practices and expressions tend to be missing from a native of the Upper Congo.

The attribution of successful working not only depends on a set of criteria (and one might inquire whether they are chosen pragmatically, and by what criteria), but is parasitic on some form of realism. Even Laudan (e.g., 1977, 1990), a major and eloquent spokesman for pragmatism has commented as follows about the rules of scientific practice

> ... there must be something right about the rules ... since a randomly selected set of rules for judging beliefs would not exhibit the striking success shown by the theories of the natural sciences. Unless the rules of scientific method reflect something about the 'facts of the matter', scientific inquiry would be nothing like as successful as it is. (Laudan, 1990, p. 102; (See also Kitcher, 1993; Putnam, 1995.)

Thus the effective practices of the scientist deeply reflect not only what might be deemed the "experience" of the practitioner in the sense of a special history particularly focused on problem solving, but the sources of that history. The methods of science, including mathematics, with all their variety and complexity, are, in fact, ways people manipulate and are manipulated by verbal and non-verbal environments with the differential consequences they identify with the progress of science. This is a feedback system because nature initially shapes this behavior and dictates the constraints on what could constitute the pragmatist's "successful working" (see also Lattal & Laipple, this volume). This is the "boot strapping" operation described by Skinner as essential to a scientific epistemology. Verbal behavior is shaped by nature and that behavior is reflected back toward nature in scientific descriptions and explanations. In much the same way organisms are said to exploit their environment or ecological niche, but the organisms, including their behavior, are the product of the environment itself. This process lies at the heart of the question initially raised by empiricism—why should one trust experience? Healthy skepticism aside, evolution has selected physiology and behavior in dynamic conformity with the environment—the world as it is.

In sum, nature supplies the contingencies that shape language as well as other practices. What has been seen in mathematics and science in general, as Mach pointed out a century ago, is a gradual shaping of abstraction from contingencies to rules and rules about rules. These rules then help scientists explore more contingencies that further shape the development of rules. If there were no relations between nature's contingencies and the constraints on those rules, then the world would truly be incomprehensible.

References

Andresen, J. (1991). Skinner and Chomsky 30 years later. *The Behavior Analyst, 14,* 49–60.
Baum, W. M. (1989). Quantitative prediction and molar description of behavior. *The Behavior Analyst, 12,* 167–176.
Baum, W. M. (1994). *Understanding Behaviorism.* NY: Harper Collins.
Bloor, D. (1983). *Wittgenstein: A Social Theory of Knowledge.* New York: Columbia University Press.
Carruthers, P. (1992). *Human Knowledge and Human Nature.* NY: Oxford University Press.
Chiesa, M. (1994). *Radical Behaviorism: The philosophy and the science.* Boston: Authors Cooperative.
Copleston, F. (1994). *A History of Philosophy* (Vol. VIII). NY: Image Books.
Curd, M., & Cover, J.A. (Eds.) (1998). *Philosophy of Science.* NY: Norton.
Czubaroff, J. (1991). A post-modern behavior analysis? *The Behavior Analyst, 14,* 19–21.
Dancy, J. (1985). *Introduction to Contemporary Epistemology.* Oxford: Basil Blackwell.
Diamond, J. (1999). *Guns, Germs, and Steel.* NY: Norton.
Derrida, J. (1982). *Acts of Literature.* NY: Routledge.
Devitt, M. (1997). *Realism and Truth* (2nd Ed.). Princeton: Princeton University Press.
Foucault, M. (1973). *Madness and Civilization.* NY: Random House.
Gross, P. R., & Levitt, N. (1994). *Higher Superstition.* Baltimore: Johns Hopkins University Press.
Gross, P. R., Levitt, N., & Lewis, M. W. (Eds.) (1996). *The Flight from Science and Reason.* Baltimore: Johns Hopkins University Press.
Harris, M. (1979). *Cultural Materialism.* NY: Random House.
Hayes, S. C., Hayes, L. J., & Reese, H. W. (1988). Finding the philosophical core: A review of Stephen C. Pepper's *World Hypotheses: A Study in Evidence. Journal of the Experimental Analysis of Behavior, 50,* 97–111.
Hersh, R. (1997). *What is Mathematics, Really?* NY: Oxford University Press.
Klein, H. R. (1974). *The Science of Measurement.* NY: Dover
Kline, M. (1980). *Mathematics: The Loss of Certainty.* NY: Oxford University Press.
Kitcher, P. (1993). *The Advancement of Science.* NY: Oxford University Press.
Landes, D. S. (1999). *The Wealth and Poverty of Nations.* NY: Norton.
Laudan, L. (1977). *Progress and its Problems.* Berkeley, CA: University of California Press.
Laudan, L. (1990). *Science and Relativism.* Chicago: University of Chicago Press.
Laudan, L. (1996). *Beyond Positivism and Relativism.* Bolder, CO: Westview.
Marr, M. J. (1986). Mathematics and verbal behavior. In T. Thompson & M. Zeiler (Eds.), *Analysis and Integration of Behavioral Units,* (pp. 161–183). Hillsdale, NJ: Erlbaum.
Marr, M. J. (1993a). Contextualistic mechanism or mechanistic contextualism?: The straw machine as tar baby. *The Behavior Analyst, 16,* 59–65.
Marr, M. J. (1993b). A mote in the mind's eye. *The Behavior Analyst, 16,* 251–253.
Marr, M. J. (1995). Quantum physics and radical behaviorism: Some issues of scientific verbal behavior. In J. T. Todd & E. K. Morris (Eds.), *Modern perspectives on B. F. Skinner and contemporary behaviorism* (pp. 107–128). Westport, CT: Greenwood Press.

Morris, E. K. (1993). Mechanism and contextualism in behavior analysis: Just some observations. *The Behavior Analyst, 16*, 255–268.

Moser, P. K., Mulder, D. H., & Trout, J. D. (1988). *The theory of knowledge*, New York: Oxford University Press.

Moxley, R. A. (1999). The two Skinners, Modern and postmodern. *Behavior and Philosophy, 27*, 97–125.

Pepper, S. C. (1942). *World hypotheses: A study in evidence*. Berkeley, CA: University of California Press.

Putnam, H. (1995). *Pragmatism*. Cambridge, MA: Blackwell.

Pickering, A. (Ed.). (1992). *Science as Practice and Culture*. Chicago: University of Chicago Press.

Rosenberg, A. (2000). *Philosophy of Science*. NY: Routledge.

Searle, J. (1995). *The Construction of Social Reality*. New York: Free Press.

Schnaitter, R. (1999). Some criticisms of behaviorism. In B. A. Thyer (Ed.), *The philosophical legacy of behaviorism* (pp. 209–249). Dordrecht: Kluwer.

Skinner, B. F. (1956). A case history in scientific method. *American Psychologist, 11*, 221–233.

Skinner, B. F. (1957). *Verbal Behavior*. New York: Appleton-Century-Crofts.

Skinner, B. F. (1969). *Contingencies of Reinforcement: A Theoretical Analysis*. Englewood Cliffs, NJ: Prentice-Hall.

Skinner, B. F. (1974). *About Behaviorism*. New York: Knopf.

Skinner, B. F. (1976) *Particulars of My Life*. NY: Knopf.

Skinner, B. F. (1979). *The Shaping of a Behaviorist*. NY: Knopf.

Skinner, B. F. (1983). *A Matter of Consequences*. NY: Knopf.

Sokal, A. D. (1996). Transgressing the boundaries: Toward a transformative hermeneutics of quantum gravity. *Social Text, 46/47*, pp. 217–252.

Staddon, J. (2001). *The New Behaviorism*. Philadelphia: Taylor & Francis.

Watson, J. (1968). *The Double Helix*. New York: Signet.

Watson, J., & Crick, F. (1953). A structure for deoxyribose nucleic acid. *Nature, 171*, 737–738.

Wigner, E. P. (1984). The unreasonable effectiveness of mathematics. In D. M. Campbell & J. C. Higgins (Eds.), *Mathematics: People Problems Results* (Vol. 3, pp. 116–125). Belmont, CA: Wadsworth.

Woolgar, S. (1988). *Science: The Very Idea*. London: Routledge.

Zuriff, G. E. (1985). *Behaviorism: A Conceptual Reconstruction*. NY: Columbia University Press.

5

Explanatory Reductionism in Behavior Analysis

David W. Schaal

Radical behaviorism asserts the validity of a purely functional analytic approach to the science of behavior. Reliable, general functional relations between environmental and behavioral variables constitute behavior-analytic explanations, behavior principles. Temporal gaps exist between the terms in these relations, ranging on the order of seconds (e.g., in the case of delayed matching-to-sample performance) to hours, days, and years (e.g., in the case of the lasting effects of classical and operant conditioning). Those temporal gaps almost seem like badges of honor to radical behaviorists; they are compared to the spatial gaps over which celestial bodies exert their influence. Not only is it unnecessary for radical behaviorists to fill the gaps with brain events (or cognitive events), it is suspected that it might be misleading, or perhaps impossible, to do so. As graduate students several of us memorized word for word this quote from Wittgenstein:

> I saw this man years ago: now I see him again, I recognize him, I remember his name. And why does there have to be a cause of this remembering in my nervous system? Why must something or other, whatever it may be, be stored up there *in any form*? Why *must* a trace have been left behind? Why should there not be a psychological regularity to which no physiological regularity corresponds? If this overturns our concept of causality then it is time it was overturned. (cited in Malcolm, 1977, p. 166)

David W. Schaal • Department of Psychology, West Virginia University, Morgantown, WV 26506-6040.

Some radical behaviorists have been vaguely bothered that Skinner (1974) himself had made it clear that behavioral functional relations, as useful as they may be, are incomplete. Skinner stated,

> The physiologist of the future will tell us all that can be known about what is happening inside the behaving organism. His account will be an important advance over a behavioral analysis, because the latter is necessarily "historical"—that is to say, it is confined to functional relations showing temporal gaps. Something is done today which affects the behavior of an organism tomorrow. No matter how clearly that fact can be established, a step is missing, and we must wait for the physiologist to supply it. (pp. 236–237)

Today evidence from neuroscience research leads one to conclude, perhaps contrary to Wittgenstein and in agreement with Skinner, that many psychological regularities do, indeed, correspond to physiological regularities. The goal is to illuminate more completely what the two sets of regularities are, and to work out the details of their correspondence. In this chapter neuroreductive explanations of behavior will be reviewed briefly to determine what such explanations might look like. There are reasons to be skeptical of neurobiological reductionism, of course, and these will be addressed. Finally, a proposal for what both behavior analysts and neuroscientists would gain from working out the two sets of regularities will be offered.

Radical Behaviorism and Neurobiological Reductionism

Essays on reductionism (e.g., Branch & Schaal, 1990; Marr, 1990) have granted that behavior requires the participation of the brain, but have expressed wariness of more theoretical forms of reductionism, and neuroreductionism in particular. In a paper that argued that explanations of the behavioral effects of drugs could be couched profitably in behavioral terms (i.e., the notion of behavioral mechanisms of drug action; Thompson & Schuster, 1968), Thompson (1984) described the types of reductionism outlined by Ernst Mayr (1982).

According to Mayr (1982), *constitutive reductionism* is the position that the materials that constitute an event at one level of analysis are found at lower levels of analysis. Furthermore, none of the events and processes found at one level is in conflict with those found at another level. For example, behavior is composed of neurophysiological and biomechanical events and processes. Because behavior analysts prefer to define behavior in terms of environment-behavior relations, they may wish to add environmental terms to the list of materials of which behavior is constituted. Nonetheless, to say that behavior is composed of bodily events and processes is not particularly controversial.

Explanatory reductionism is the assertion that one cannot understand a whole until one has dissected it into its components... down to the lowest hierarchical level of integration" (Mayr, 1982, p. 60). The problem with this position, and the reason that behavior analysts should be skeptical of attempts at explanatory reduction, is that processes at higher levels of integration may act as units somewhat independently of the lower-level processes of which they are composed. In an extreme case, particle physics can provide little information about response rate on a fixed-ratio schedule. In less extreme cases, however, explanatory reductions are possible and may be useful. Mayr cites the example of the discovery by Watson and Crick of the structure of DNA, which made possible a fuller understanding of the function of genes. For present purposes, processes involved in alterations in synaptic efficacy (Stein, Xue, & Belluzzi, 1993, 1994, for example) have shed light on the process of reinforcement (Donahoe & Palmer, 1994).

The most troublesome reductionistic position is *theory reductionism*. According to theory reductionism, "theories and laws formulated in one field of science... can be shown to be special cases of theories and laws formulated in some other branch of science" (Mayr, 1982, p. 62). By this view, behavioral processes would be seen as special cases of processes at the neurobiological level (which would themselves be special cases of physico-chemical processes, etc.). Theory reductionism does not apply to behavioral concepts, however, because, as Mayr points out, such a position "confuses *processes* and *concepts*" (p. 62). Mayr writes:

> As Beckner (1974) has pointed out, such biological processes as meiosis, gastrulation, and predation are also chemical and physical processes, but they are only biological concepts and cannot be reduced to physico-chemical concepts. Furthermore, any adapted structure is the result of selection but this is again a concept that cannot be expressed in strictly physico-chemical terms. (p. 62)

By this view, even an elementary concept in behavior analysis, e.g., a discriminated operant, is composed of a collection of neurophysiological processes, knowledge of which may help illuminate how the brain participates in this behavior. But the discriminated operant has an identity, a functional character that is not shared with any particular neurophysiological concept. Thus, behavioral concepts cannot be derived from neurophysiological ones because behavioral concepts do not exist at the neurophysiological level.

It is this feature of processes in the two domains that provides force for Skinner's (1974) claim that the physiologist of the future...

> ...will be able to show how an organism is changed when exposed to con-
> tingencies of reinforcement and why the changed organism then behaves in a
> different way, possibly at a much later date. What he discovers cannot inval-
> idate the laws of a science of behavior, but it will make the picture of human
> action more complete. (p. 237)

This bears a striking similarity to Mayr's (1982) words about genetics:

> To be sure, the chemical nature of a number of black boxes in the classical genetic
> theory was filled in [by the discovery of DNA, RNA, etc.], but this did not affect
> in any way the nature of the theory of transmission genetics. (p. 62)

In summary, most behavior analysts may be called constitutive reduc-
tionists, because they readily agree that behavior is composed of bodily
processes. They may reject theory reductionism on the grounds that even
a thorough examination of processes at the physiological level will not
give rise to the orderly behavioral concepts they investigate. Explanatory
reductionism is more difficult to assess from a behavior-analytic perspective. On the one hand, there is sufficient order in the relations between
environment and behavior studied by behavior analysts to build a science of behavior independent of neurophysiology. On the other hand, as
Skinner pointed out repeatedly, there are gaps in those relations, and it is
likely that an understanding of the neurophysiological events that participate in behavior will allow some of those gaps to be filled. Assuming that
explanatory reductions are possible, it is useful to ask what explanatory
reductions would be like. What kinds of data would be needed at both
behavioral and neural levels to draw the necessary connections between
the two sets of phenomena?

In fact, Skinner (1938) himself sketched an outline for what would
be needed at the neural level. In *Behavior of Organisms*, he proposed that
a neurobiological understanding that progresses beyond the conceptual
nervous system would be one that:

> ...completes its local references and devises techniques for the *direct* obser-
> vation of synaptic and other processes. The network is to be carefully traced
> and its various parts described in physico-chemical terms.... Factual material
> has also begun to accumulate, and it may be assumed that a science of the
> nervous system will some day start from the direct observation of neural pro-
> cesses and frame its concepts and laws accordingly. It is with such a science that
> the neurological point of view must be concerned if it is to offer a convincing
> "explanation" of behavior. (p. 422)

Skinner (1938) went on the stress that "a rigorous description at the
level of behavior is necessary for the demonstration of a neurological cor-
relate" (p. 422), and that both behavioral and neurological facts "must be
quantitatively described and shown to correspond in all their properties"

(p. 422) before an explanatory reduction can be completed. It is a purpose of this chapter to show that rigorous descriptions of phenomena at both levels are available and correspondences have been established in some cases. Examples will be presented in order to examine what these tentative explanatory reductions look like. First, however, reasons behaviorists are often wary of such an endeavor will be presented.

Why Do Behaviorists Mistrust Neurobiological Reductionism?

There are many good reasons to exercise caution when attempting to reduce behavioral to neurobiological phenomena. Perhaps most important is the scientific status of *behavior* itself. In some of Skinner's earliest writings (1931) he asserted that the reflex is best understood as a correlation between classes of stimuli and classes of responses. This was asserted, in part, in opposition to identifying reflexes with a presumed underlying nervous system that mediates them. This was a tremendous advance in behavioral theory; now laws of the reflex (and other classes of behavior) are generally given the status of causal laws apart from the tissues that allow them to act. This is a core tenet of behaviorism: Behavior is an important subject of investigation in its own right, and it is unnecessary to relate the facts of behavior to facts at any other level in order to establish their importance.

Also in the first half of the 20th century, Lashley's (1929/1963) *Brain Mechanisms and Intelligence,* reported the results of experiments on the effects of brain lesions on learning and performance in rats. The most important and lasting contributions of that work were Lashley's Laws of Equipotentiality and of Mass Action. The former law states that any part of the cortex may carry out a given learning function; if part of the cortex is damaged, another part may take over. The Law of Mass Action states that the magnitude of the behavioral deficits produced by a brain lesion is proportional to the amount of brain tissue damaged. Although in several cases Lashley found evidence of localization of function, it was the repeated failure to find lasting deficits following localized lesions that, by default, provided support for an analysis of behavior in its own right, without reference to brain processes. In his introduction to Lashley (1929/1963) Hebb wrote:

> The stock-in-trade of physiological behavior theory had been synaptic resistances, detailed localizations of cortical function, and new paths from point to point in the cortex for new habits. Now, suddenly, it appeared from Lashley's work that such ideas were fantasy, not science. In these circumstances the

positivistic coup d'etat becomes more intelligible. Neither of the main movers, Tolman and Skinner, adopted his position because of Lashley, but one hardly doubts that their success in carrying others along with them owed much to work that made the ideas of physiological theory more than slightly ridiculous. (p. vi)

Another impediment to a behavior analyst's appreciation of neuroscience is its current close association with cognitive psychology, as reflected in the increasingly ubiquitous phrase, "cognitive neuroscience" (Gazzaniga, 1995). This connection of "cognitive" with "neuroscience" is a relatively recent development in cognitive psychology. The cognitive revolution (Gardner, 1987) was well under way before the development of the technology that allowed the moment-to-moment recording of brain activities that could be correlated with presumed cognitive activities. Nevertheless, neuroscience has strengthened cognitive psychology greatly in recent years, and will continue to do so both because of such technology and because cognitive psychology appears to provide clear directions for research in neuroscience, directions that are not as clearly provided by behavior-analytic theory. This is mostly due to a cultural bias toward conceiving of the brain as the agent of behavior. As such, both cognitivists and neuroscientists share the goal of describing the structure of the brain, although cognitivists typically use less direct methods (see Morris, this volume). This shared bias enhances the acceptability of cognitive psychology in general. Thus, many neuroscientists are searching for the mental processes identified in cognitive psychology, rather than characterizing the processes that participate in and allow the establishment of environment-behavior relations. It will be argued later that the involvement of behavior analysts in neuroscience may help establish the utility of the latter approach. A third impediment for behavior analysts was provided by Uttal (1998) who provides a convincing case that a completely reductionistic understanding of behavioral phenomena may be impossible. Two key ideas are: (a) that the number of neurons and their connections in the brain (the combinatorial explosion) is a practical problem that makes the precise relation of behavioral events to brain events impossible, and (b) that the molar outcomes or activities of the brain may relate to the activities of its fundamental neuronal units in a manner described by chaos theory, i.e., deterministic processes at the neuronal (or subneuronal) level give rise to apparently random activity at the molar level. The problem in the former case is that the technology has not been developed to solve the problem of the combinatorial explosion. The problem in the latter case is, even if the molar order in brain activity, i.e., the attractors can be discerned, the small interactions and uncertainties that may make the brain a chaotic system cannot be recovered. These and many other instructive arguments led Uttal to propose that neuroreductionism may not be possible, and that a more positivistic, behavioristic approach to theory is necessary in neuroscience.

Uttal (1998) did not argue that neuroscience should not continue, nor that its facts would not be useful in understanding behavior. His arguments mostly concerned the difficulties faced in reducing higher cognitive activities, such as consciousness, to brain events. He did not say that processes that underlie learning cannot be known to a useful extent. He does prescribe caution in this endeavor, however. A complete reduction, such as the kind implied by theory reductionism, is probably impossible. That does not mean that useful knowledge about the relations of brain processes to behavior (i.e., explanatory reductions) have not been discovered and will not continue to be discovered.

Finally, a healthy mistrust of explanations of behavior that go beyond the reliable and general functional relations that constitute the principles of behavior is strengthened by the proven success of the experimental analysis of behavior. A science of behavior largely free of references to unseen mediators was conceived and developed by researchers who recognized the problems inherent in theory reductionism. Many people are convinced that no problem in psychology is resistant to such an approach. The success of this nonmediational approach supports the behavior analyst's skepticism of neuroscience; order at the behavioral level suggests that references to physiological levels of explanation be entertained with caution. This skepticism may prove to be an important asset for any behavior analysts doing research in behavioral neuroscience. Such caution , however, does not necessitate rejection of neuroscience. Neuroscience may be usefully analyzed, critiqued, and informed by a perspective that employs such skepticism.

What follows are examples of neuroscience applied to behavioral problems. These examples are intended to show that a useful understanding of the participation of the brain in behavior may be viewed as simply an empirical issue. In considering these examples, interesting and important conceptual issues and complications will arise that both guide skepticism concerning this endeavor and provide new questions to consider as behaviorists.

Pavlovian Conditioning in Invertebrates

Research with invertebrates provides the nearest approximation to Skinner's (1938) vision of an explanatory reduction. For example, classical conditioning of the siphon and gill withdrawal reflex of the mollusk *Aplysia californica* has been shown. Carew, Walters, and Kandel (1981) presented a weak tactile stimulus (the conditioned stimulus, or CS) to the siphon, followed 30 s later by a shock (unconditioned stimulus, or US) to the tail, which elicited strong siphon withdrawal. Initially, a short-duration withdrawal response to the CS was obtained; as conditioning proceeded, the withdrawal response lengthened in duration. This short-term change in response duration did not occur in unpaired control, random control, or no-conditioning control groups. When the US was discontinued, the duration of the response to the CS shortened again. Differential conditioning (obtained by presenting CSs on different sites of the mantle skin) has also been obtained (Carew, Hawkins, & Kandel, 1983). Thus, a form of classical conditioning can be observed in *Aplysia* (for an alternative account of this phenomenon, see Schreurs, 1989).

Subsequent experiments sought the neural mechanisms underlying this conditioning. This requires the identification of the neuronal pathways that transduce and convey the effects of the CS and US, finding where these pathways converge, assessing whether changes at the points of convergence are critical for conditioning, and working out the inter and intracellular changes produced by CS and US pairing. Hawkins and colleagues (Hawkins, Abrams, Carew, & Kandel, 1983) accomplished this task by first dissecting the nervous system from the *Aplysia*, except for the tail and its sensory neurons. Using this reduced preparation, they conducted studies in which tail shock was preceded (or not, in unpaired, control neurons) by spike activity induced by brief, intracellular electrical stimulation of the sensory neuron that conducts the stimulation from the siphon skin. The excitatory postsynaptic potential from the siphon sensory neuron was enhanced by tail shock only in subjects in which these events were explicitly paired. The result was that the sensory-motor connection was facilitated, resulting in an enhanced response to the CS in conditioned neurons, an effect referred to as *activity-dependent presynaptic facilitation* (ADPF; Glanzman, 1995).

The mechanisms underlying classical conditioning have also been investigated in another mollusk, *Hermissenda crassicornis*. This mollusk responds to the stimulus produced by rotating its substrate (the US) by clinging to the substrate, observed as a contraction of its foot (the unconditioned response, or UR). Its initial response to a light (the CS) is a lengthening of the foot, but when a light is repeatedly paired with the rotation US, a contraction of the foot in response to light (the conditioned response, or CR) is conditioned (Lederhendler, Gart, & Alkon, 1986). Several changes in the *Hermissenda*'s nervous system have been correlated with and are necessary for this conditioning. In particular, conditioning appears to strengthen synaptic connections between photoreceptors that transduce the light CS and postsynaptic cells (Frysztak & Crow, 1994).

There are several implications of these findings with invertebrates. The most striking is that the neural mechanisms of classical conditioning may differ, sometimes substantially so, in different animals and different preparations. In *Aplysia*, a presynaptic effect contributes to conditioning, whereas for *Hermissenda*, a change in synaptic strength is involved. Conditioning in these animals obeys similar rules of contiguity and association, nevertheless different neural processes underlie this learning. The conditioning in these animals may be called *behaviorally homogeneous* and *neurobiologically heterogeneous*. That is, based on their similarities at the behavioral level they may be considered instances of the same phenomenon (conditioned reflexes), but at the neurobiological level they differ. This finding underscores the importance of explanations at the behavioral level because regardless of the neurology involved the responses were predicted and controlled by the concepts of conditioning. Behavioral analysis alone, however, cannot specify what the underlying neural mechanisms of behavior are, because even the simplest kinds of conditioning may involve different neural mechanisms. Neurobiological analyses may suggest subclassifications within behaviorally homogeneous classes; the differences in the neural mechanisms of conditioning in the two mollusks are probably responsible for the subtle differences in the two responses, e.g., in the dynamics of acquisition and extinction, of changes in CR strength with repeated elicitation, etc. These differences do not require discarding the behavioral classification, but they do suggest a basis for finer distinctions between topographically similar responses.

Finally, it should be noted that despite the relative simplicity of these organisms and their nervous systems, considerable disagreement remains over details of the nervous system plasticity involved in these conditioning phenomena. Nevertheless, the independent identification and measurement of events at behavioral and neural levels in these well understood behavioral systems provides fairly clear examples of what an explanatory reduction of conditioning might look like. Tentative explanations are currently being elaborated for other conditioning models, including the nictitating membrane reflex conditioning in the rabbit (which focuses on CS-US convergence in cerebellar deep nuclei; Thompson & Krupa, 1994) and conditioning using shock as the US in rats (which focuses on CS-US convergence in the amygdala; Ledoux, 1995). These tentative explanatory reductions have been successful by meeting Skinner's (1938) requirements, including well established and understood behavioral phenomena, precise, independent measurement of events at the neural level, and demonstrations of their correspondence and interdependence.

Working Memory in Monkeys

The goal of the research described above is to account for long lasting changes in behavior wrought by conditioning procedures. Other research has focused on local changes in already conditioned behavior produced by changes in stimuli, that is, stimulus control. An intriguing example of brain research of this type is provided by Goldman-Rakic and colleagues (for reviews see Goldman-Rakic, 1995a, 1995b, 1999). In these studies, monkeys were taught using a variation of the delayed-matching-to-sample task to, initially, fix their gaze on a central location of a view screen. A stimulus was then presented for 0.5 s in one of 8 locations distributed along a circle equidistant from the center fixation point. After a delay, during which monkeys maintained their gaze on the center point, the screen went blank, and to earn an apple juice reinforcer, the monkey had to shift its gaze in the direction of the previously presented sample. Monkeys learned this task readily. Recordings of single cells in the prefrontal cortex of the monkeys engaged in this task showed that the rate of firing specific neurons increased only during the delay period. Accurate responding at the end of the delay was highly correlated with the level of cellular activity at the end of the delay; if the neuron fired at a high rate the monkey responded correctly, but as the firing rate fell off, so did the accuracy of the response. Goldman-Rakic (1995b) referred to such cells as *memory fields*, analogous to the receptive fields of sensory neurons. These were defined as "maximal firing of a neuron to the representation of a target in one or a few locations of the visual field, with the same neuron always coding the same location" (Goldman-Rakic, 1995b, p. 478). (It should be noted that Goldman-Rakic (1999) has not asserted that the memory field of a stimulus resides in a single cell; rather, the cell from which the specific activity is recorded is more likely a representative of a group of cells that have this function.)

The activity of these neurons was equated with the working memory of the recently presented sample (Goldman-Rakic, 1995a, 1995b). This was supported by several additional observations. The increase in neuronal activity was restricted to the delay period; it was not elicited directly by the presentation of the sample stimulus (other cells do show sample-specific activity, however), and it did not necessarily spill over into the response period (other cells are active during the matching response). It was also, apparently, not simply neural activity preparatory to a particular response, e.g., waiting to look to the upper right. This was shown in studies in which monkeys were trained to look either in the same direction as the recently presented sample or, on alternate trials signaled by a different stimulus used as the fixation point, to look in the opposite direction (an *antisaccade*; Funahashi, Chafee, & Goldman-Rakic, 1993). Following a given sample stimulus, the same neuron was active during the delay regardless of the direction of the eventual response. In another study (Wilson, Scalaidhe, & Goldman-Rakic, 1993), gazing responses in the same direction were reinforced following presentation of either a spatial or a pattern sample stimulus. Despite the fact that identical saccades were reinforced, different neurons were active during delays following different stimuli. These results are all consistent with the notion that these neurons hold the working memory of recently presented stimuli until it is time to respond.

The working-memory interpretation of these results highlights the differences in the goals of a behavioral versus a cognitive neuroscience. For the behaviorist, there are two sets of observed facts to be related; the relations between recently presented events and behavior that are selected by the contingencies of the delayed-matching-to-sample procedure, and the sequences of neuronal activity that are also selected by the contingencies. Contingencies of reinforcement are the common factor in this endeavor, serving to organize the system so that behavioral and brain events are related to each other; activity of neurons in the prefrontal cortex allows monkeys to respond to recently presented stimuli. Contingencies of reinforcement retain the central role in the analysis, as they always do in radical behaviorist theories. For the cognitivist, behavioral relations are the manifestation of the mental processes that can be inferred from them, and the brain activity is the material basis for the mental process. Contingencies of reinforcement engage the mental process, which through its neuronal substrate governs the behavior. The mental processes retain the central role in the analysis, as they always do in cognitive theories.

These basic differences in the goals of behaviorists and cognitivists studying the brain result in different interpretations of the same findings. For example, according to Goldman-Rakic (1995a), the antisaccade effect shows that:

> ... monkeys are capable of holding "in mind" two sequentially presented items
> of information—the color of the fixation point and the location of a spatial cue—
> and of transforming the direction of response from left to right (or the reverse)
> based on a mental synthesis of that information. (p. 75)

The data of Funahashi et al. (1993), however, show only the delay-specific activity of the prefrontal neurons; they show neither neuronal activity related to the different fixation points nor the site where the response direction is transformed based on the two items of information. A behaviorist would point out that this is an instance of conditional stimulus control, and that neither the behavioral nor the brain results compel one to postulate mental processes of synthesis or transformation. As the same stimulus can participate in more than one environment-behavior relation depending on the context in which it occurs, the same brain activity may participate in more than one environment-behavior relation depending on the context. A similar logic may be applied to the different stimulus/same response findings of Wilson et al. (1993).

For a behaviorist, of critical importance is the *origin* of the function of memory-field neurons. Are neurons destined by their location to serve such a function or are they recruited to play this role through contact with contingencies of reinforcement requiring remembering over short intervals? More likely, the location of these neurons makes them ready candidates for recruitment by contingencies of reinforcement. Finding that the function of these neurons emerges from contact with contingencies would lend support to a more behavioral interpretation of the role of these neurons.

Implications of the Applications of Reductionism

Invertebrate classical conditioning exemplifies an explanatory relation between nervous system events and behavioral events. Researchers identified the transduction pathways for the CS and the US, determined the location of their convergence, identified details of the cellular changes produced by concurrent activity of those pathways, and showed that those changes were necessary for conditioning to be observed. Because observation of events at both levels could occur at approximately the same time, the result of the research is approximately what Skinner (1938) would have recognized as meeting the requirements of a successful explanatory reduction. The logic and methodology involved in establishing such reductions are similar for other simple forms of classical conditioning (and have been successfully applied in other cases). One might assume that further explanatory reductions of this type simply require someone to apply these techniques to other paradigms.

The memory-field studies of Goldman-Rakic and colleagues cited previously also show correlations between precisely measured brain events and behavior under control of reinforcement contingencies. The activity of the prefrontal lobe neurons identified in this research explains discriminative control by recently presented stimuli in the sense that the lingering activity during the delay differentiates the function of the presentation of the comparison stimuli at the end of the delay. Discriminative control by recently presented stimuli is temporally limited because the activity of these neurons fades with time. Remaining questions, e.g., the question of how such neurons are recruited, may simply suggest more research.

Positive effects of neuroscience on behavior analysis

What is a behavior analyst to do with findings such as these? First, it should be acknowledged that these examples of behavioral neuroscience research are not representative of the field in general. In Skinner's (1938) terms, the references are not completed at the behavioral or the brain level, in much neuroscience research. For example, a thriving area of neuroscience investigation concerns the effects of stress. Even a brief review of this area reveals myriad ways in which stress is induced and its effects are assessed, a lack of uniformity in the effects of stress on the body and brain, and little idea how altered brain activity leads to specific changes in animal behavior (Akil, Campeau, Cullinan, Lechan, Toni, Watson, & Moore, 1990; Selye, 1936). This does not mean that this research is not important, it just means that explanatory reductions of the effects of stress on behavior have not been accomplished. A goal of the current chapter was to present relatively *clear* examples of reductive explanations of behavior, with the hope of interesting students of behavior analysis in behavioral neuroscience, and perhaps convincing some of them that this is a field to which they may contribute. Before closing this chapter, then, it is important to ask what may be gained from such a collaboration.

First, Skinner (1974) called on neuroscientists to fill in the temporal gaps that separate prior experience from current behavior. Although many behavior analysts feel no compelling need to fill these gaps—past and present are related in an orderly fashion whether or not the brain events that participate in the relations are known—others view it as critical to the long-term success of behavior analysis. Donahoe and Palmer (1994) and Donahoe (this volume), for example, have compared the social ramifications of the identification in the brain of the retention mechanisms of operant conditioning to the identification of genes as the retention mechanism of natural selection. They suggested that the increase in the acceptance of Darwin's theory that followed the rediscovery of genes may occur as well for Skinner's concept of the operant once its retention mechanisms have been identified. Such a discovery may establish the reality of the operant for some theorists in a way that behavior analysis alone has not accomplished.

Second, neuroscience allows one to address questions that are incompletely answered by behavior analysis, the sorts of questions implied by Skinner (1974) when he wrote that "a step is missing"(p. 237) in behavior analysis. Nonreductive explanations of behavioral phenomena emerge from behavior analyses, without reference to "events taking place somewhere else, at some other level of observation, described in different terms, and measured, if at all, in different dimensions" (Skinner, 1950, p.193). For example, behavior analysts have elucidated the variables responsible for the reliable finding that unsignaled delays to reinforcement reduce response rates on schedules of reinforcement. Delayed reinforcers strengthen behavior other than the measured operant, either adventitiously or because the unmeasured behavior affords the animal rapid access to the reinforcer (Schaal, Shahan, Kovera, & Reilly, 1998; Sizemore & Lattal, 1977). Signaling the delay reduces or eliminates this effect because the delay signal, presented immediately after a response, functions as a conditioned reinforcer (Lattal, 1984; Schaal, Schuh, & Branch, 1992). Thus, behavioral research alone has established the fundamental importance of immediacy to the process of reinforcement, and is thus able to explain these effects in a nonreductive manner. A question lingers, however: *Why* are immediate reinforcers so much more effective than delayed ones? For most purposes, it is enough for behavior analysts to know *that* they are. But a critical part of the answer to this question, the missing step, concerns an animal's physiology. In the case of delayed reinforcement, there is evidence that the physiological events that allow reinforcement to occur, that characterize how the organism is changed by reinforcement, themselves only occur under conditions that are constrained temporally (Stein, 1997). Such questions, concerning the nature of the brain's participation in behavioral functional relations, linger behind every successful behavioral analysis. Answers to them constitute the explanatory reductions that have been the focus of this chapter.

Third, behavioral neuroscience may help behavior analysts solve some persistent puzzles of behavior. Knowledge of the cellular mechanisms of reinforcement, for example, has been brought to bear on the classic argument over whether classical and operant conditioning are distinct forms of learning. Donahoe, Palmer, & Burgos (1997) and Donahoe (this volume) argue that a unified theory, in which reinforcement in both classical and operant paradigms acts by strengthening S-R relations, is consistent with what is known currently regarding the mechanisms underlying the effects of reinforcement. Interestingly, Donahoe et al. drew heavily on a neuronal analogue of operant conditioning of Stein and colleagues (Stein et al., 1993, 1994), yet Stein (1997) argued that his data suggest that operant conditioning is distinct from classical conditioning. Although the disagreement continues, the attempt to square interpretations of behavior with what is known about neural mechanisms introduces an interesting, and perhaps important, constraint on behavioral theory. One wonders how the molar/molecular debate (cf. Lattal & Laipple, this volume) would evolve if similarly constrained by the neural mechanisms of reinforcement (or, conversely, how research into the neural mechanisms of reinforcement would be altered by data showing that aggregates of behavior extended in time appear to act as units).

Finally, and maybe most importantly, behavioral neuroscience is already well on the way toward characterizing alterations in the brain that are responsible for disorders such as some kinds of mental retardation, autism, Alzheimer's Disease, Parkinson's Disease, and many others. Behavior analysis owes a great deal of its vigor within psychology to its success in treating behavior problems using behavioral technologies. Most of these behavior problems may be characterized as constraints on the effectiveness of typical or normally occurring contingencies of reinforcement. These typical contingencies are sufficient to produce behavior change in persons without the disorders, but not for those affected by the disorder. For example, the primary constraint in Alzheimer's Disease appears to be diminished discriminative stimulus control by events in the recent and distant past, with the result that memory deficits are common in such persons. A behavior analyst who recognizes such constraints is in a better position to design procedures that help people overcome them, at least in a limited sense. A behavior analyst is also in an excellent position to clarify the behavioral relations that are altered in persons with these disorders, which is a necessary component of a reductive explanation of them.

Positive effects of behavior analysis on neuroscience

So, what can behavior analysts provide for neuroscientists interested in behavior? The most obvious answer is that the concepts and methodologies that have emerged from a science of behavior that eschews references to inner mediators has proven successful, and as such it is in a position to provide a program for neurobehavioral research. The success of a behavioristic approach already has been demonstrated in the neuroscience of drug abuse, where the identification of abused drugs as unconditioned stimuli, reinforcers, and discriminative stimuli, has set the stage for fruitful neurophysiological investigation (Lejuez, Schaal, & O'Donnell, 1998). For example, behavior analysts provided some of the first unambiguous evidence of the reinforcing effects of abused drugs (e.g., cocaine; Pickens & Thompson, 1968), which was critical to the investigation of both the special characteristics of drugs as reinforcers (e.g., their general adherence to behavioral economics models of reinforcer value; Bickel, DeGrandpre, Higgins, & Hughes, 1990) and the processes in the brain that participate in these effects (e.g., dopamine release in the nucleus accumbens coincident with drug-reinforced behavior; see Di Chiara, 1995).

The concept of positive reinforcement is applied creatively to a variety of problems in neuroscience. For example, Carlson (2001; p. 531) has speculated that the persistence of delusional thoughts in persons with schizophrenia may indicate that brain mechanisms that typically underlie reinforcement become active at inappropriate times. If they become active when a person is thinking delusionally, is it not possible for the thoughts to be reinforced adventitiously? This interesting speculation exploits both a basic behavioral principle and a behavioral approach to private events (delusional thoughts) that is consistent with radical behaviorism. It also accomplishes something that is rarely attempted in the neuroscience of psychological disorders. That is, Carlson attempted to bridge the gap between a brain abnormality that is presumed to be involved in a psychological disorder and the behavior that is diagnostic of the disorder. This gap-bridging exercise is the favored strategy in behavioral pharmacology, where the effects of alterations in brain function wrought by drugs are characterized in terms of the changes in the behavioral relations that control behavior in the absence of the drugs (i.e., behavioral mechanisms of drug action; Branch & Schaal, 1990; Thompson & Schuster, 1968).

A fundamental feature of the behavior-analytic approach is to locate the causes of behavior in the environment. This environmentalism may remedy a common bias in neuroscience (and cognitive) theorizing, which is to view causation as unidirectional, from brain to behavior. An alternative, more realistic approach, amenable to behavior analysis, is to view causation as interactive, that is, not just brain-to-behavior, but also behavior-to-brain. This may be an implication of an approach that is always attentive to the origins of behavior in the relations between an organism and its environment. This interactive approach has ample support in the neuroscience literature (e.g., the classic experiments on visual development in cats by Held & Hein, 1963; for a review of demonstrations of experience altering brain development see Greenough, Black, & Wallace, 1987).

A stunning example was provided by Tessel, Schroeder, Loupe, and Stodgell (1995). They treated rat pups with 6-hydroxydopamine (6-OHDA), which depleted levels of dopamine and its metabolites by about 90% in rats sacrificed as adults. Prior to sacrifice, some of the rats were trained on a response-number-discrimination task in which rats pressed different side levers depending on how many center-lever presses preceded introduction of the side levers into the chamber. Lesioned rats learned this task about as well as nonlesioned rats. When the trained rats were sacrificed it was discovered that, not only had dopamine levels returned to those of nonlesioned rats, they increased above those levels. Prior to this study, 6-OHDA was a standard means of reducing or eliminating dopamine in the brain, and it was assumed that such lesions were permanent. Tessel et al. not only revealed their impermanence, but also attributed this recovery to exposure to contingencies of reinforcement. The implications of these findings are still under investigation, but they suggest a potential role for behavioral treatments of dopamine-deficiency-related brain disorders. They also show clearly that the brain is as much influenced by behavior as behavior is influenced by the brain.

Finally, a behavior-analytic approach to neuroscience would remove constraints on neuroscience that are imposed by cognitive theory. The information processing model is currently the guiding idea behind most of this research. It extends even to the simplest behavioral paradigm, where neuronal changes due to classical conditioning are viewed as long-term memory formation and storage. It appears that, with few exceptions, this assumption is simply not questioned. Models based on neuroscience research differ little from the input-output models of cognitive psychology, except that many of the boxes lying between input and output are labeled with known brain structures and activity. This is an improvement over purely mental models, but it should be made clear that the brain need not be conceived as encoding, processing, storing, and retrieving information. An alternative conception, one that is more consistent with the functional approach of behavior analysts, is that the brain carries out the subbehavioral activity that makes the more molar concept, behavior, possible. This approach views brain events as necessary for functional relations to be observed, but not sufficient. It requires that brain tissues respond differentially to external and internal events, that the coactivity of these differentially sensitive tissues results, under the right circumstances (e.g., reinforcement), in changes in the interactivity of the tissues, and that changes in the combined activity of these tissues lead to changes in behavior. It also requires that behavior always be seen as something that whole animals do, as opposed to something that brains do using whole animals.

On first reflection, this conceptual alternative may not be compelling to most neuroscientists. Cognitive theory appears to provide an explicit statement of the goals of neuroscience; locate and describe the mental structures and processes proposed in cognitive theories of learning and behavior. Thus, researchers look for the engram that stores the conditioning experience, the working memory that connects recent stimulus to current matching response, the location and nature of the image that is retrieved in an act of imagining, etc. It may seem that behavior analysis provides no such explicit goal. Although the cognitive psychologist can tell the neuroscientist what brain processes *are*, the behavior analyst appears only to be able to tell the neuroscientist what brain processes *are for*. In a cognitive neuroscience, the cognitive concepts that explain phenomena at a psychological level also name the correlated brain activity (e.g., working memory). In a behavioristic neuroscience, behavioral concepts may not be applied to the brain processes that make the phenomena possible. The discriminated operant is an outcome of orchestrated brain processes, but it is only a behavioral concept. There may be no particular brain event that can be named, discriminated operant.

The behavioral approach, however, removes constraints imposed by cognitive theory. Neuroscientists are not told what to look for, but that does not mean that a behavior-analytic neuroscience would be without direction. As noted earlier, the goal is to illuminate more completely what the two sets of regularities are, and to work out the details of their correspondence. This is not a familiar sort of reductionism, but it is a kind of reductionism nonetheless. As discussed with respect to delays between environmental events and behavior, as seen in delayed reinforcement and delayed-matching-to-sample, behavior analysis can pinpoint some problems that apparently require a fuller understanding of the neurophysiology involved. Some students trained in behavior analysis will have to conduct neuroscience research and publish it in neuroscience journals to show that a behavioral neuroscience free of mental concepts is possible. The time may be ripe for a truly behavioral neuroscience, one that respects the reality of the behavioral functional relation, that views events at each level as thoroughly interactive, and that is free of the constraints imposed by the information processing model. It is heartening that there are some neuroscientists who seem to agree that behaviorism can play a role in neuroscience in the future (Thompson, 1994; Uttal, 1998).

References

Akil, H., Campeau, S., Cullinan, W. E., Lechan, R. M., Toni, R., Watson, S. J., & Moore, R. Y. (1990). Neuroendocrine systems I: Overview—thyroid and adrenal axes. In M. J. Zigmond, F. E. Bloom, S. C. Landis, J. L. Roberts, & L. R. Squire (Eds.), *Fundamental Neuroscience*. Academic Press, San Diego, CA, pp. 1127–1150.

Bickel, W. K., DeGrandpre, R. J., Higgins, S. T., & Hughes, J. R. (1990). Behavioral economics of drug self-administration: I. Functional equivalence of response requirement and unit dose. *Life Science*, 47, 1501–1510.

Branch, M. N., & Schaal, D. W. (1990). The role of theory in behavioral pharmacology. In Thompson, T., Dews, P. B. & Barrett, J. E. (Eds.) *Advances in Behavioral Pharmacology, Vol. 7* (pp. 171–196). Orlando: Academic Press.

Carew, T. J., Hawkins, R. D., & Kandel, E. R. (1983). Differential classical conditioning of a defensive withdrawal reflex in Aplysia californica. *Science*, 219, 397–400.

Carew, T. J., Walters, E. T., Kandel, E. R. (1981). Classical conditioning in a simple withdrawal reflex in Aplysia californica. *Journal of Neuroscience*, 1, 1426–37.

Carlson, N. R. (2001). *Physiology of Behavior, 7th Ed.* Needham Heights, MA: Allyn & Bacon.

Di Chiara, G. (1995). The role of dopamine in drug abuse viewed from the perspective of its role in motivation. *Drug and Alcohol Dependence, 38,* 95–137.

Donahoe, J. W., & Palmer, D. C. (1994). *Learning and complex behavior.* Needham Heights, MA: Allyn & Bacon.

Donahoe, J. W., Palmer, D. C., & Burgos, J. E. (1997). The S-R issue: Its status in behavior analysis and in Donahoe & Palmer's *Learning and Complex Behavior. Journal of the Experimental Analysis of Behavior, 67,* 246–253.

Frysztak, R. J., & Crow, T. (1994). Enhancement of type B and A photoreceptor inhibitory synaptic in conditioned *Hermissenda. Journal of Neuroscience, 14,* 1245–1250.

Funahashi, S., Chafee, M. V., Goldman-Rakic, P. S. (1993). Prefrontal neuronal activity in rhesus monkeys performing a delayed anti-saccade task. *Nature, 365,* 753–756.

Gardner, H. (1987). *The Mind's New Science : A History of the Cognitive Revolution.* Basic Books:

Gazzaniga, M. S. (1995). *The Cognitive Neurosciences.* MIT Press: Cambridge, MA.

Glanzman, D. L. (1995). The cellular basis of classical conditioning in Aplysia californica—it's less simple than you think. *Trends in the Neurosciences, 18,* 30–36.

Goldman-Rakic P. S. (1995a). Architecture of the prefrontal cortex and the central executive. *Annals of the New York Academy of Sciences, 769,* 71–83.

Goldman-Rakic, P. S. (1995b). Cellular basis of working memory. *Neuron, 14,* 477–485.

Goldman-Rakic, P. S. (1999). The physiological approach: functional architecture of working memory and disordered cognition in schizophrenia. *Biological Psychiatry, 46,* 650–661.

Greenough, W. T., Black, J. E., & Wallace, C. S. (1987). Experience and brain development. *Child Development, 58,* 539–559.

Hawkins, R. D., Abrams, T. W., Carew, T. J., & Kandel, E. R. (1983). A cellular mechanism of classical conditioning in Aplysia: Activity-dependent amplification of presynaptic facilitation. *Science, 219,* 400–405.

Held, R., & Hein, A. V. (1963). Movement-produced stimulation in the development of visually-guided behavior. *Journal of Comparative and Physiological Psychology, 56,* 872–876.

Lashley, K. (1963). *Brain mechanisms and intelligence: a quantitative study of injuries to the brain.* New York: Hafner Publications. (Original work published 1929)

Lattal, K. A. (1984). Signal functions in delayed reinforcement. *Journal of the Experimental Analysis of Behavior, 42,* 239–253.

Lederhendler, I., Gart, S., & Alkon, D. L. (1986). Classical conditioning of *Hermissenda*: Origin of a new response. *Journal of Neuroscience, 6,* 1325–1331.

Ledoux, J. (1995). Emotion: Clues from the brain. *Annual Review of Psychology, 46,* 209–235.

Lejuez, C. W., Schaal, D. W., & O'Donnell, J. (1998). Behavioral pharmacology and the treatment of substance abuse. In J. J. Plaud & G. H. Eifert (Eds), *From Behavior Theory to Behavior Therapy* (pp. 116–135). Needham Heights, MA: Allyn & Bacon.

Malcolm, N. (1977). *Memory and Mind.* Cornell University Press: Ithaca, NY.

Marr, M. J. (1990). Behavioral pharmacology: Issues of reductionism and causality. In J. E. Barrett, T. Thompson, & P. B. Dews (Eds.), *Advances in behavioral pharmacology* (Vol. 7, pp. 1–12). Hillsdale, NJ: Erlbaum.

Mayr, E. (1982). The Growth of Biological Thought. Cambridge, MA: Belknap Press.

Pickens, R., & Thompson, T. (1968). Cocaine-reinforced behavior in rats: Effects of reinforcement magnitude and fixed-ratio size. *Journal of Pharmacology and Experimental Therapeutics, 161,* 122–129.

Schaal, D. W., Shahan, T. A., Kovera, C. A., & Reilly, M. P. (1998). Mechanisms underlying the effects of unsignaled delayed reinforcement on key pecking of pigeons under variable-interval schedules. *Journal of the Experimental Analysis of Behavior, 69,* 103–122.

Schaal, D. W., Schuh, K. J., & Branch, M. N. (1992). Key pecking of pigeons under variable-interval schedules of briefly signaled delayed reinforcement: Effects of variable-interval value. *Journal of the Experimental Analysis of Behavior, 58*, 277–286.

Schreurs, B. G. (1989). Classical conditioning of model systems: A behavioral review. *Psychobiology, 17*, 145–155.

Selye, H. (1936). A syndrome produced by diverse nocuous agents. *Nature, 138*, 22.

Sizemore, O. J., & Lattal, K. A. (1977). Dependency, temporal contiguity, and response-independent reinforcement. *Journal of the Experimental Analysis of Behavior, 27*, 119–125.

Skinner, B. F. (1931). The concept of the reflex in the description of behavior. *Journal of General Psychology, 5*, 427–458.

Skinner, B. F. (1938). *The behavior of organisms*. New York: Appleton-Century-Crofts.

Skinner, B. F. (1950). Are theories of learning necessary? *Psychological Review, 57*, 193–216.

Skinner, B. F. (1974). *About Behavorism*. Random House: New York.

Stein, L. (1997). Biological substrates of operant conditioning and the operant-respondent distinction. *Journal of the Experimental Analysis of Behavior, 67*, 246–253.

Stein, L., Xue, B. G., & Belluzzi, J. D. (1993). A cellular analogue of operant conditioning. *Journal of the Experimental Analysis of Behavior, 60*, 41–53.

Stein, L., Xue, B. G., & Belluzzi, J. D. (1994). In vitro reinforcement of hippocampal bursting: A search for Skinner's atoms of behavior. *Journal of the Experimental Analysis of Behavior, 61*, 155–168.

Tessel, R. E., Schroeder, S. R., Loupe, P. S., & Stodgell, C. J. (1995). Reversal of 6HD-induced neonatal brain catecholamine depletion after operant training. *Pharmacology, Biochemistry, & Behavior, 51*, 861–867.

Thompson, R. F. (1994). Behaviorism and neuroscience. *Psychological Review, 101*, 259–265.

Thompson, R. F., & Krupa, D. J. (1994). Organization of memory traces in the mammalian brain. *Annual Review of Neuroscience, 17*, 519–549.

Thompson, T. (1984). Behavioral mechanisms of drug dependence. In T. Thompson, P. B. Dews, & J. E. Barrett (Eds.), *Advances in Behavioral Pharmacology* (Vol. 4, pp. 1–45). Orlando, FL: Academic Press.

Thompson, T., & Schuster, C. R. (1968). *Behavioral Pharmacology*. Englewoord Cliffs, NJ: Prentice-Hall.

Uttal, W. R. (1998). *Toward a New Behaviorism: The Case Against Perceptual Reductionism*. Lawrence Erlbaum: Mahwah, NJ.

Wilson, F. A., Scalaidhe, S. P., Goldman-Rakic, P. S. (1993). Dissociation of object and spatial processing domains in primate prefrontal cortex. *Science, 260*, 1955–1958.

6

Selectionism

John W. Donahoe

The goals of this chapter are threefold: (a) to characterize selectionism as a general approach to understanding complex phenomena as products of relatively simple processes acting over time, (b) to identify conceptual impediments to the acceptance of selection by reinforcement as the central process by which complex behavior emerges, and (c) to outline a program for a new modern synthesis for the selection of complex behavior through reinforcement that parallels the early history of evolution through natural selection.

Selection: the Wellspring of Complexity

A selection process consists of three interrelated steps: variation, selection, and retention. Variation provides the raw material upon which selection operates. It is the source of whatever novelty arises from repeated cycles of the three-step process because selection acts only on preexisting entities. Variation itself is undirected: The factors that affect variation are uncorrelated with those that implement selection (Campbell, 1974; although cf. Neuringer, this volume). Selection by the environment favors (or disfavors) some variants over others, and confers to the process whatever direction it appears to display. Selection processes are not directed in a teleological sense, however. The future does not

John W. Donahoe • Department of Psychology, University of Massachusetts at Amherst, Amherst, MA 01003-7710.

draw the present toward itself, but rather the past pushes the present into the future. The trajectory of selection depends utterly on the environment. If environmental contingencies are constant or change gradually, behavior appears to be adapted to the environment: to display foresight and purpose. This illusion is shattered when environmental contingencies change abruptly. Selection processes prepare us to behave in accordance with past contingencies, not future contingencies except insofar as they mirror the past. The third step, retention, permits favored variations to endure long enough to add to the variation upon which future selections act. Without retention, selections cannot accumulate and the possibility of complexity is precluded. Note that complexity is a possible, but not a necessary, outcome of the three-step selection process. (For discussions of the implications of selectionism for behavior, see Catania, 1995, Donahoe & Wessells, 1980, Donahoe & Palmer, 1994, Palmer & Donahoe, 1992, Skinner, 1966, and Staddon & Ettinger, 1989. For more general philosophical treatments, see Dennett, 1995; Hull, 1973; Mayr, 1988; and Sober, 1984.)

Two aspects of a selection process are emphasized here. First, the selecting factors are external to the objects of selection. That is, the environment does the selecting, not the organism. With respect to the selection of behavior, the environment and the organism are partners embraced in an eternal dance, but the environment is always in the lead. The organism is not autonomous. Of course, the organism may influence the course of selection indirectly through the effects of its behavior on the environmental contingencies encountered in the future. However, self control—in any scientifically meaningful sense—first requires acknowledgment of the primacy of environmental control. Paradoxically, the more one reconciles oneself to the primacy of the environment, the more one may truly achieve self-control.

The second aspect of selection is the interdependence of its three steps. As an illustration, consider the relation between variation and retention in the selection of behavior. At birth, the pool of behavioral variation consists of the retained effects of selection by the ancestral environment (e.g., reflexive relations between the environment and behavior) as they are affected by momentary variations in the contemporaneous environment. Following birth, the pool of behavioral variation is rapidly enriched by the retained effects of past selections by the individual environment; i.e., selection by reinforcement. If the contingencies of reinforcement are somewhat variable (i.e., if somewhat different operants are selected in similar environments), the pool of environment-behavior relations enlarges (see Neuringer, this volume). In contrast, if the environment selects only a small number of environment-behavior relations, variation diminishes and, with it, the possibility of complexity (e.g., Schwartz, 1980).

Selectionism has triumphed in biology. Darwin's principle of natural selection stands at the heart of accounts of the emergence of complexity from molecules to men. In psychology, however, the situation is different. Among the disciplines that claim behavior as their subject matter, only behavior analysis regards a single principle—the principle of reinforcement—as the central insight into phenomena from conditioning to cognition (e.g., Donahoe & Palmer, 1994) For behavior analysis, the consequences of behavior determine the fate of behavior, whether simple or complex. Some consequences increase the likelihood of a given behavior in an environment, and are termed reinforcers. Other consequences decrease its likelihood, and are termed punishers. A great deal of progress has been made toward formulating a principle of reinforcement that can accommodate a wide range of observations at many levels of measurement (e.g., Baum, 1974; Donahoe, Burgos, & Palmer, 1993: Herrnstein, 1970; Premack, 1959; Rescorla & Wagner, 1972; Timberlake & Allison, 1974; Timberlake & Wozny, 1979; Staddon, 1983). Nevertheless, few psychologists share the behavior-analytic view that reinforcement is fundamental to the emergence of complex human behavior.

Why has a single selection principle triumphed in biology, but languished in psychology? For clues to the answer, it is instructive to examine the events that led to the acceptance of selectionism in biology. Perhaps, comparable circumstances are necessary for the ascendance of selection by reinforcement in psychology.

Parallels with Evolutionary Biology

Natural selection is now accepted as the unifying principle of biology, but this consensus was reached only slowly, and remains controversial within the extrascientific community to this day. Within biology, most of Darwin's contemporaries accepted the general notion of evolution even before the publication of *On the Origin of Species* in 1859. That is, they accepted the general proposition that complex species were somehow related to their progenitors. Many of these same biologists, however, rejected natural selection as the overriding explanatory principle. Most believed that natural selection played a role in the production of small changes—varieties within species—but not in what were regarded as qualitative changes between species. Different plumage of pigeons might result from natural selection, but not the larger differences between species, say between reptiles and birds. The boundaries between different species—types, kinds, or essences—were regarded as unbridgeable by natural selection (Carpenter, 1860).

For students of behavior, the conceptual counterpart of evolution is individual development. The idea of development—that the child gives rise to the adult—is incontrovertible. Development of the individual is readily appreciated because, in contrast to the time scale of evolution, it may be detected within the lifetime of a single observer. Psychology, however, faces difficulties that were not encountered by the biologist in the analysis of evolution: Past selections leave no physical record that is readily observable at the behavioral scale of measurement, i.e., there are no behavioral fossils. What endure are such subtle relics as changes in behavior that emerge during extinction (cf. Epstein, 1983) or changes in synaptic efficacies among neurons. And, the latter are legacies that have little, if any, identifiable counterpart at the behavioral level. To observe synaptic changes requires a sophisticated technology that has only recently become available. This state of affairs—together with the intermittency of observations of the entire history of reinforcement of any complex behavior—encourages appeals to developmental discontinuities, to stages of development. Stages are the conceptual equivalents of special acts of creation and are hallmarks of many developmental theories (e.g., Piaget, 1953). Will more complete observations at the behavioral and neural levels reveal that the selecting effect of the environment no more requires the postulation of distinct stages of development than natural selection requires separate acts of creation? I suspect so. Darwin's comment on the incompleteness of the fossil record applies with equal force to the developmental record, "the more important objections relate to questions on which we are confessedly ignorant; nor do we know how ignorant we are" (Darwin, 1859/1969, p. 466).

Natural Selection

As noted, the biological community rapidly embraced the notion of evolution, but rejected natural selection as the driving force of evolution. Even Wallace, the coformulator of the principle of natural selection, resisted its application to that most complex creature, man: "Neither natural selection nor the more general theory of evolution can give any account whatever of the origin of sensation or conscious life..." (Wallace, 1869, p. 391). Darwin himself was careful in his early writings to minimize the implications of natural selection for human evolution. The reluctance to apply selectionism to humans was rooted in ideology, not science, as most philosophers and historians of biology agree.

Even the rediscovery of Mendel's experimental work on inheritance was not sufficient for the acceptance of natural selection. Prior to Mendel, Darwin had proposed a so-called blending theory of heredity in which the characteristics of offspring were intermediate between those of its parents. The Scots engineer Fleeming Jenkin (1867) argued that Darwin's own theory did not meet the requirements of natural selection—rare changes would be overwhelmed by the blending process. Mendel's results were crucial because they implied a particulate theory of genetics in which rare changes would not be obliterated. Mendel's work, however, was not immediately interpreted to support natural selection as the chief engine of complexity. Instead, the discovery of mutations, which critically enhance the variation upon which selection operates, was initially taken to mean that evolution was the result of many special acts of creation (mutations). In addition to Mendel's particulate theory of genetics, something else was needed before the full implications of natural selection could be accepted. The final piece of the puzzle was provided by population genetics. Population genetics is a set of quantitative methods that precisely trace gene flow over time (Fisher, 1930; Haldane, 1931; Wright, 1939). The integration of these methods with experimental work in genetics (e.g., Dobzhansky, 1937; Mayr, 1942) provided a means by which natural selection could be implemented and through which the emergence of complex species could be understood. This integration is known as the *modern synthesis* in evolutionary biology.

Impediments to Selectionism

What were the ideological impediments to the acceptance of selectionism in biology? Two philosophical precommitments of creationists are generally recognized: essentialism and teleology (Donahoe, 1983). Each of these factors is examined in turn because they now conjoin to resist selection by reinforcement as the central insight into the emergence of complexity in individual behavior.

Essentialism

Essentialism, in the evolutionary context, was the view that individual variability within a species masked an unchanging entity, or essence, that was the nature of that species. Different pigeons might vary in their appearance, but all pigeons were assumed to be expressions of a common, invariant "pigeoness." For the essentialist, the unobservable entity—the species prototype—was what was real. Individual differences merely obscured the true objects of study, the species. More generally, essentialism is the view that the variability inherent in observation is an imperfect reflection of an immutable underlying true reality. Essentialism may be traced to Plato's allegory of the cave. Plato likened efforts to understand the true nature of things to the task confronting an observer who attempts to infer the characteristics of objects casting shadows on a cave wall from the shadows alone. The observer detects only the shadows, not the objects casting the shadows. For the selectionist, the allegory of the cave is fundamentally misconceived. There can be no invariant objects—no essences—because selection processes do not produce static entities. The contingencies of selection imposed by a variable environment are themselves somewhat variable with the consequence that the products of selection processes are inescapably variable. Selection processes constrain the range of variation to a degree that depends on the variation in contingencies (Palmer & Donahoe, 1992; Skinner, 1935). Returning to the allegory of the cave, there are no objects, there are no essences.

The following are essentialist statements from Darwin's contemporaries. With appropriate substitutions of wording, e.g., complex behavior for complex structure, these statements are redolent of the current debate between behavior analysis and normative psychology concerning the role of selection by reinforcement. (In normative psychology, behavior is viewed as an imperfect reflection of unobservable entities—associations, attitudes, cognitions, and the like—that are the true objects of study. These events, however, are inferences from behavior and are not themselves amenable to direct experimental analysis.) The naturalist Wollaston said of the complex structures of living organisms, "Such cases bespeak thought, imagination, and judgment, all and each of the highest stamp, and are utterly inexplicable on any ... principle of selection" (Wollaston, 1860, p. 133). Sedgwick, a geologist, commented: "What is it that enables us to anticipate the future, to act wisely with reference to a future good? ... These faculties, and many others of like kind, are a part of ourselves quite as much as our organs of sense" (Sedgwick, 1860, p. 164–165). Or, "How unscientific to trust to an uncertain chance for existence, (rather) than ... a principle of adaptive creation" (Anonymous, 1860, p. 224). The Biologist Agassiz (1874) held that, "individual differences are 'individual peculiarities,' in no way connected with the essential features of the species" (p. 94). Agissiz proposed to discover these essential features through what he called "intuition." (The appeal to intuition is reminiscent of the view of some linguists that insights into the nature of language can be achieved through *linguistic intuition*.) As a final example of essentialism among Darwin's contemporaries, "Self-consciousness [and] reason [require] a representative faculty. ... Brutes have only the presentative faculty. The faculties of men and those of other animals differ in kind" (Mivart, 1871, p. 362–363.).

Contrast these essentialist statements with those of the modern biologist Mayr (1976):"Averages are merely statistical abstractions; only the individuals of which the populations are composed have reality" (p. 28). Or, in the words of one of Darwin's contemporary supporters, "The thing *species* does not exist; the term expresses an abstraction" (Lewes, 1860, p. 143). For the selectionist, terms such as *species* in evolutionary biology and *association* or *cognition* in normative psychology are instrumental fictions (i.e., they are intended to be theoretically useful, but entail no existential claim). (See the contrast between nominalism and realism in Palmer & Donahoe, 1992; see also Marr, this volume.) To wit, the term *species* might designate the modal features of a group of individual organisms of common ancestry and, as such, facilitate communication among evolutionary theorists. Consider also the term *association*. If a learner responds reliably in the presence of a particular stimulus on a number of occasions, the mean latency of the response may be computed. For some purposes, the mean latency may be useful; e.g., for predicting whether a given learner will generally respond faster than another. If, however, the mean value is taken as a measure of an entity that is said to exist within the learner—an association—then the theorist has reified the statistical abstraction. That is, the theorist has conferred existential status upon an abstraction and transformed it into a material or concrete entity: an essence. This error of reification is compounded when the theorist then speaks of the association as causing the behavior from which the entity was inferred: a further error of circular reasoning.

Within contemporary psychology, numerous instances of essentialist thinking are found. For Chomsky and his followers, variability in verbal behavior is thought to obscure underlying universal, language-specific rules (cf. Pinker, 1994). On this view, verbal behavior cannot be selected by the impoverished stimuli provided by the environment. Instead, verbal behavior is seen as the product of a Language-Acquisition Device—an organ of the mind—whose characteristics are inferred from verbal behavior and whose origins are uncertain. There are many difficulties with this proposal (see Catania, this volume; Palmer, 1986, 2000; Palmer & Donahoe, 1992), but the essentialist core of the position is illuminated by comparing Chomsky's views with those of Max Müller, a linguist who was Darwin's contemporary.

> When the evolutionists contend that the development of the mind of man out of the mind of an animal is a mere question of time, [I am] inclined to treat the idea with impatience. Animals must be animals as long as they lack the

faculty of abstracting general ideas. . . . Mr. Darwin's fallacy lurks in the very word 'development' for the admission of this insensible gradation would elim-inate the difference between ape and man. . . . In fact it would do away with the possibility of all definite knowledge. . . . Animals do not possess rational language *because they are not man* [italics added]. (Müller, 1872, p. 145)

From their shared essentialist conceptions of language, some present day linguists deny selection by reinforcement and assert natural selection whereas their predecessors denied natural selection and asserted creation-ism. What unites these linguists across the centuries is their common re-jection of selectionism—natural selection in Müller's case and selection by reinforcement in Chomsky's. They have mortgaged their souls to Plato and Kant (Dennett, 1995; cf. Weimer, 1973).

From the outset, behavior analysis was explicit about the variable products of selection by reinforcement as shown in the generic nature of the concepts of stimulus and response (Skinner, 1935). Typically, responding to a somewhat variable set of stimuli with a somewhat variable topography of responses satisfies a given reinforcement contingency. For example, a pigeon might respond to various aspects of the location, shape, or color of the key while striking the key with the beak or other body parts, all of which were followed by a reinforcer. A given reinforcement contingency generally selects a range of environment-behavior relations that differ from one moment to the next and from one organism to the other (cf. Catania, this volume; Reynolds, 1961). Invariant entities—essences—are not produced by selection processes, whether natural selection or reinforcement. (See Palmer & Donahoe, 1992 for a discussion of this issue.)

Teleology

The second ideological impediment to selectionism in biology was teleology. Teleological explanations appeal to events that could occur, if at all, only after the events that they are said to explain. Teleological expla-nations are inherently essentialist because they postulate the existence of causes that, by definition, cannot exist at the time they are called upon; i.e., before the events they are said to cause. Thus, teleological explanations are essentialist. In biology, an illustration of teleology would be an appeal to a future need to breath on land as the cause of the evolution of lungs in fish. This account requires the fish to know while in water what could be known only later on land. Darwin's critics decried his efforts to understand com-plexity as the emergent product of what they regarded as the overly simple process of natural selection. Said one critic: "Their whole occupation is to trace every fact to some immediate antecedent cause; and they are so anx-ious to establish regularity of sequence and uniformity of law, that they cannot bear the idea of a Creator stepping in" (*The Patriot*, 1863, p. 594). And another, "Forces which are not directed—so-called blind forces—can never, so far as I can see, produce order" (von Baer, 1873, as cited by Hull, 1973, p. 421). The biologist Huxley, Darwin's ardent supporter, replied that appeals to design "worked not only negative, but positive ill, by discouraging inquiry . . . " (Huxley, 1908, p. 182), a theme echoed in Skinner's much later critique of pseudoexplanations in normative psychology (Skinner, 1950). The biologist Weismann (1909) summarized the import of Darwin's principle of selection as follows: "Natural selection solved the riddle, how it is possible to produce adaptiveness without the intervention of a goal-determining force" (p. 4–5).

Modern psychology does not appeal to the deity as a goal-determining force, of course. In a selectionist approach to explanation, such locutions are regarded with suspicion lest they conceal a kernel that is not susceptible to the selecting effects of the environment. Natural selection transforms ancestral contingencies into the appearance of design; selection by reinforcement transforms individual contingencies into the appearance of intention.

Although teleology's siren call is most apparent in accounts of complex behavior, traces remain in some modern treatments of even simple behavior. An influential account of Pavlovian conditioning (Rescorla & Wagner, 1972) holds that behavioral change (i.e., learning) requires a discrepancy between the asymptotic associative strength supportable by a given reinforcer and the net associative strength of all contemporary stimuli that have been paired with that reinforcer. This inference is based on the finding that environmental and behavioral events that precede a putative reinforcing stimulus are unaffected when they are accompanied by another stimulus that was previously paired with the same reinforcer. As an example, suppose that a light was previously paired with food and a tone later accompanied the light when both stimuli were paired with food. If the tone is subsequently presented alone, it does not evoke salivation (c.f. Kamin, 1968, 1969). Prior pairing of the light with food is said to *block* conditioning to the tone. The phenomenon of blocking is among the most important in modern experimental work. This theoretical formulation of blocking, however, is problematic. Leaving aside the essentialist character of association, the theory postulates the existence at the outset of conditioning of an entity that can exist (if at all) only at the end of conditioning, namely, the *asymptotic* associative value. Unlike the net associative strength of all contemporary stimuli, which reflects the learner's experience with events in the past, the asymptotic associative value refers to an event that is in the future. For present behavior to be a function of asymptotic associative value, the organism must know from the outset of learning the ultimate strength of association sustainable by the reinforcer. In fact, this formulation requires universal foreknowledge of the asymptotic association strength sustainable by all reinforcers that might ever be encountered (Donahoe, 1984). From whence might such foreknowledge arise, from natural selection? And, if so, foreknowledge must exist for all possible conditioned reinforcers as well. For a selectionist account to be viable, the events that promote conditioning must be physical events that occur in the organism's past or present. In conditioning, these events are restricted to the sensory and behavioral consequences of the reinforcing stimulus and whatever other events are contemporaneous with the reinforcer. The concept of asymptotic association value may provide a useful summary term for the theorist in a description of learning, but its physical counterpart is not available to the learner at the outset of the conditioning process. As indicated shortly, discrepancy may be defined without recourse to teleological and essentialist concepts such as asymptotic associative value (see Donahoe, Crowley, Millard, & Stickney, 1982; Donahoe et al., 1993; Stickney & Donahoe, 1983).

A Possible Counterargument

Let us consider a possible counterargument to the claim that normative psychology and creationism share a deep philosophical kinship. The counterargument runs as follows: Behavior analysis and normative psychology are fundamentally different enterprises. They are so different that it is inappropriate to evaluate them by common epistemological criteria (see Morris, this volume, for further discussion of the relation between behavior analysis and normative psychology). According to this view, reinforcement theory seeks to identify functional relations between observed environmental and behavioral events whereas psychology seeks to characterize abstractly (i.e. in a purely logico-mathematical form) the structures and processes that underlie these relations. This purported counterargument recapitulates the *two-spheres* position in the 19th-century debate between selectionism and creationism about the origin of species (Ellegård, 1958). The two spheres were science and religion (cf. Galuska, this volume). Each was accorded primacy within its respective domain: matter in the first case and spirit, or mind, in the second. Although the modern version in normative psychology bears a fundamental similarity to the two-spheres attempt to reconcile science and religion, few psychologists would accept the explicit dualism of this version of the counterargument.

A more subtle version of the two-spheres counterargument holds that behavior analysis and normative psychology are incommensurate because they seek answers to different kinds of questions, differences in biology that are analogous to the *why* questions addressed by evolution and the *how* questions addressed by physiology. In this distinction, the evolutionist seeks to identify *why* (i.e., the selective pressures) a lizard's scale became a bird's feather whereas the physiologist seeks to determine how (the physiochemical mechanisms) the change came about. This more sophisticated version of the counterargument also fails to capture the distinction between behavior analysis and normative psychology. Behavior analysis seeks to answer both *how* and *why* questions by recourse to experimental analysis of events in the physical world (observable environmental and behavioral events); psychology, like religion, seeks its answers in the realm of inferred processes. The underlying entities of normative psychology are formalisms that are not defined in ways that permit them to be readily mapped onto the physical world (cf. MacCorquodale & Meehl, 1948). Indeed, some psychologists regard the liberation of theoretical constructs from physiology as one of the most important advances in the field (Mandler, 1981). Note, it is *not* the process of inference per se that is questioned—inference is the starting point of much experimental analysis—but only inferences about entities that cannot, in principle, be subjected to direct experimental analysis.

Evolutionists and physiologists regard the answers to both *why* and *how* questions as informed by selectionist thinking. As an example, consider the neurochemist inquiring into the biosynthetic pathway of a neurotransmitter, a *how* question. Even at the molecular level of analysis, the work is guided by selectionism. Natural selection leads neurochemists to anticipate that biosynthesis will terminate at the earliest possible step in the reaction chain after the target compound has been produced. Termination at the earliest step prevents the synthesis of unnecessary compounds whose metabolic costs would reduce fitness: the answer to a *why* question. If biosynthesis were found to terminate at a later step in the reaction chain, neurochemists would not reject natural selection. Instead, they would suspect the existence of a previously unrecognized compound that shared a portion of its biosynthetic pathway with the target compound. In short, natural selection is a unifying theme in biology that guides answers to both *why* and *how* questions. *Why* and *how* questions are directed at different parts of the same physical world, both of which are illuminated by selectionist thinking, not at two qualitatively different spheres.

Mayr summarized his analysis of the conflict between Darwinian selection and creationism thus: "No typologist [i.e., essentialist] has ever understood natural selection, because he cannot possibly understand it." (Mayr, 1976, p. 173); "No two ways of looking at nature could be more different" (Mayr, 1976, p. 28). If Mayr's pessimistic verdict applies to the present differences between behavior analysis and normative psychology, little can be gained from the present exploration of the parallels between psychology and creationism. One may hope for the redemption of normative psychology, however, because it can draw upon the Darwinian example of the triumph of selectionism over essentialism and teleology.

A number of signs suggest that normative psychology is evolving in directions consistent with selectionist thinking. First, an intensive analysis of the individual case is becoming more common in psychology, which represents a return to an earlier psychophysical tradition (cf. Uttal, 1999). Selection by reinforcement operates on a population of environment-behavior relations of a *single* organism, not a population of *different* organisms, which is the province of natural selection. Normative psychology has most often taken variation between individuals as its reference population, but this is inappropriate for a science of behavior (cf. Sidman, 1960). The cautions of the cognitive psychologist Hintzman (1980) concerning individual differences in memory illustrate one of the earliest encouraging trends in this direction within normative psychology (see also Neisser, 1982). Second, the logical and experimental pitfalls encountered when structures and processes are inferred from behavioral observations alone are becoming apparent in normative psychology. As but one example, behavioral findings from memory experiments have been variously inferred to indicate that experience is stored as propositions (verbal statements) or as images (perceptions). Many experiments attempted to identify the nature of what was stored, but they met with little success. Anderson's and Townsend's separate refinements of Skinner's (1950) reservations about identifying underlying processes from behavioral observations make this point (Anderson, 1978; Townsend, 1972), as does Hintzman's more general critique of cognitivism (Hintzman, 1993). Problems with identifying processes are particularly troubling because they undermine the falsifiability criterion; i.e., that scientific statements are potentially refutable by evidence. Third, normative psychology increasingly appeals to structures in the real nervous system, not merely instrumental fictions. The increasing appeal to neuroscience in the analysis of complex behavior, as in some instances of cognitive neuroscience, is evidence of this trend (e.g., Gazzaniga, 2000). Appeals to the real nervous system do not guarantee a selectionist approach, of course. Neuroscientists are members of a mentalistic culture and, as such, some recapitulate the errors of Darwin's contemporary critics (cf. Ellegård, 1958, p. 8). A final reason for guarded optimism is that static views of behavioral processes are being replaced by dynamic conceptions (e.g., Galbicka, 1992; Rumelhart & McClelland, 1986). Dynamic conceptions are less prone to essentialist explanations because there are no static entities to serve as surrogates for essences.

The future of normative psychology is much less promising if it persists in the pursuit of explanations that rely on essentialist inferred processes. Although history may applaud contemporary psychology for directing experimental attention toward complex behavior, very little of its theoretical content will endure. In this scenario, normative psychology will make a contribution much like that of Gestalt psychology: Gestalt psychology directed mainstream science toward important and overlooked phenomena, but its specific theoretical proposals are of historical interest only. Encouraging psychology to confront the complexities of human behavior is an important contribution, but much more can be achieved if the analysis and interpretation of complex behavior is informed by the Darwinian example. The modern synthesis in evolutionary biology took over 70 years from the publication of Darwin's *On the origin of species* in 1859 to Dobzhansky's *Genetics and the origin of species* in 1937. Will the acceptance of reinforcement as the central insight into complex behavior be similarly delayed, and what must occur for selectionism to triumph in psychology? The final section addresses these questions.

Toward a New Modern Synthesis

To review, the conjunction of three factors resulted in the triumph of selectionism in biology: (a) formulation of a functional principle of selection (natural selection), (b) identification of biological mechanisms that implemented the functional principle (genetics), and (c) development of quantitative methods that traced selection over time (population genetics). (See Table 1). What circumstances obtain in present day psychology?

Table 1. Historical parallels between the conditions necessary for the acceptance of selectionism in evolutionary biology and in psychology

Requirements for the acceptance of selection	In evolutionary biology	In psychology
Functional statement of a principle of selection	Natural selection	Selection by reinforcement
Biological mechanisms of selection	Mendelian genetics	Neuroscience (synaptic plasticity)
Quantitative procedures for tracing selection	Population genetics	Computer simulation (neural networks)

Principle of Behavioral Selection

A functional principle of selection by reinforcement is at hand. In the first half of the 20th century, experimental analysis identified one of two critical conditions: spatio-temporal *contiguity* with the reinforcer. Whether stimulus-reinforcer relations are studied with the Pavlovian procedure or response-reinforcer relations with the operant procedure, the selected events must occur close together in space and time (Catania, 1971; Grice, 1948). (Several challenges to contiguity remain, however, notably taste aversion in the respondent procedure; e.g., Domjan, 1980; and conditioning with long delays in the operant procedure; e.g., Lattal & Gleeson, 1990.) In the last half of the century, the second condition was identified: discrepancy. As defined at the behavioral level, a discrepancy occurs when the putative reinforcing stimulus evokes a *change* in ongoing behavior. The two factors of contiguity and discrepancy have been integrated into a functional principle of reinforcement that can be stated as follows: If a stimulus produces a change in behavior, that stimulus functions as a reinforcer, and whatever stimuli immediately precede or accompany the change acquire control of whatever responses immediately precede or accompany the change (Donahoe et al., 1982; Donahoe et al., 1993; cf. Rescorla & Wagner, 1972). This principle applies with equal force to the Pavlovian, or classical, procedure and the operant, or instrumental, procedure. In the classical procedure, the selected stimulus is the conditioned stimulus (in context) and the selected response is the response evoked by the reinforcing stimulus. Thus, a tone followed by food comes to control salivation. In the operant procedure, another response—the operant—joins the stimulus and response that are selected in the classical procedure. Thus, sight of the lever comes to control lever pressing in addition to salivation when pressing is followed by food. Because of the response-reinforcer contingency that defines the operant procedure, the operant occurs in temporal proximity to the reinforcing stimulus and its evoked response; i.e., to the behavioral discrepancy. In both procedures, food functions as a reinforcer to select environment-behavior relations because food produces a behavioral discrepancy, namely, a change in salivation. As a result, the operant as well as the reinforcer-evoked response is captured by the conditioning process. This account is consistent with Skinner's view that the operant contingency is fundamentally superstitious: Operants need not cause reinforcers to be selected; they need only accompany them (Skinner, 1948).

The foregoing statement of the reinforcement principle provides a basis for unified reinforcement theory (URT). This theory is unified in the sense that it applies equally to conditioning in the Pavlovian and operant procedures. URT is also consistent with Skinner's analysis of punishment

(Estes & Skinner, 1941). The account of punishment exploits the implication of URT that conditioning generally proceeds more rapidly for Pavlovian evoked responses than for operants: The evoked response, which occasions the discrepancy, occurs closer in time to the discrepancy than to the operant. That is, because the operant necessarily comes before the reinforcing stimulus by some time interval, the operant is temporally more removed from the discrepancy than the evoked response (see Donahoe & Palmer, 1994, p. 60 and Donahoe et al., 1993, for details). The more rapid conditioning of the evoked response leads to the prediction that a stimulus that evokes behavioral change functions as a punisher when the evoked response is incompatible with the operant. On this account, lever pressing that has been reinforced by food weakens when it is followed by shock because shock evokes escape responses that become conditioned to the sight of the lever and compete with lever pressing (Schoenfeld, 1969; cf. Bersh, Whitehouse, & Mauro, 1982). The operant, however, does not decline in strength as it would with an extinction contingency in which the operant occurs but is no longer reinforced. The punishing stimulus does not directly weaken the operant but, instead, conditions escape responses that interfere with the operant and thereby prevent its further occurrence. The suppression of lever pressing eliminates further pairings of lever pressing with food and thereby precludes the possibility of extinction. When the punishing contingency is removed, the operant may recover much of its strength after escape responses have extinguished.

Another implication of URT is that when reinforcer-evoked responses are compatible with the operant, the operant strengthens especially rapidly. Thus, food-reinforced pecking by pigeons is readily acquired because pecking both precedes the reinforcing stimulus and is also evoked by it. The observation that pecking reflects both the operant contingency in the location toward which the peck is directed and the reinforcer-elicited response in the topography of the peck is consistent with this account (Jenkins & Moore, 1973).

Finally, URT implies that aversive stimuli that would normally function as punishers can serve as reinforcers under some circumstances. To wit, if the operant is compatible with the responses evoked by the aversive stimulus, then the operant may be strengthened by the aversive stimulus. In confirmation of this prediction, when shock is intermittently made contingent on escape responses, escape responses continue indefinitely—and, consequently, so do presentations of the aversive stimulus (Burns & Donahoe, 1984). The aversive stimulus of shock evokes escape responses and, therefore, shock functions as a reinforcer for operants of similar topography when shock is contingent upon their occurrence. (See Morse & Kelleher, 1977, for a summary of the initial work in this area.)

Unified reinforcement theory, and other moment-to-moment accounts of reinforcement, can be reconciled with reinforcement principles that describe molar relations between variables, such as between responses and reinforcers in the matching relation (e.g., Baum, 1973, 1974; Herrnstein, 1970; but see Davison & Baum, 2000). In the matching relation, the relative frequency of an operant approximates the relative frequency of reinforcement for that operant. It has been shown that dynamic (i.e., moment-to-moment) accounts of reinforcement may yield this molar relation as their cumulative product under some circumstances (e.g., Shimp, 1969; Staddon, Hinson, & Kram, 1981; see also Donahoe, 1977). Thus, moment-to-moment accounts of reinforcement need not be inconsistent with the molar relations between variables found after prolonged exposure to the contingencies of reinforcement.

Biological Mechanisms of Selection by Reinforcement

A functional principle of natural selection is important for understanding evolution apart from the genetic mechanisms that implement it. Similarly, a principle of reinforcement based on behavioral observations is critical to understanding complex behavior apart from its biological mechanisms. Nevertheless, if the Darwinian parallel holds, the general acceptance of reinforcement as the central insight into complex behavior may depend upon identifying the mechanisms that implement it. Note that the motivation for seeking the biological mechanisms of reinforcement is pragmatic, not epistemological. That is, an understanding of reinforcement based only on behavioral observations may be logically sufficient, but politically unpersuasive (cf. Schaal on reductionism, this volume).

Behavioral justifications also exist for seeking knowledge of the biological mechanisms of reinforcement. Some stimuli evoke behavioral changes (thus satisfying the definition of a behavioral discrepancy), but do not function as reinforcers. For example, an increase in the ambient light level causes the pupil to dilate, but a tone paired with the increase in light does not come to control dilation. In contrast, electric shock evokes papillary dilation and does function as a reinforcer under otherwise comparable conditions (e.g., Gerall & Obrist, 1962; see Donahoe & Wessells, 1980, pp. 114–115 for other examples). Thus, the production of a behavioral discrepancy is not invariably an occasion for reinforcement. Conversely, some stimuli produce no readily apparent behavioral change (thus not satisfying the discrepancy requirement), but nonetheless function as reinforcers. For example, many conditioned reinforcers evoke little responding but, nevertheless, such reinforcers play a critical role in the acquisition of complex behavior. Thus, reinforcer-evoked responses do not always provide a reliable measure of the ability of a stimulus to function as a reinforcer. Finally, a purely operational definition of reinforcers as stimuli that increase the probability of the behavior on which they are contingent encounters difficulties in its generality. A stimulus that functions as a reinforcer for one response may not function as a reinforcer for a different response (e.g., Shettleworth, 1972); a stimulus that functions as a reinforcer for one organism may not function as a reinforcer for other members of the same species because of differences in their experiences (as in blocking); and a stimulus that functions as a reinforcer at one time may not function as a reinforcer at a different time for the same organism (as in variations in the state of deprivation) (cf. Meehl, 1950; Michael, 1993). An operational approach can be expanded to include reinforcement history and state variables among its prerequisites, but the foregoing cases suggest that a comprehensive theoretical treatment of reinforcement will draw upon the experimental analysis of neuroscience as well as behavior.

When behavior analysis began in the early 1900s, neuroscience was more a promise than a reality. Consequently, neuroscience could contribute little to understanding selection by reinforcement (see Skinner, 1938; Thorndike, 1903; see also Donahoe, 1999). The present state of affairs is different, however. Behavioral research has now identified the events that appear critical for reinforcement and new technologies in neuroscience increasingly permit the neural, cellular, and genetic accompaniments of reinforcement to be experimentally analyzed (for some examples, see Schaal, this volume). Although Skinner viewed the experimental analysis of behavior as "a rigorous, extensive, and rapidly advancing branch of biology" (Skinner, 1974, p. 255), he was equally clear that neuroscience was a different branch of biology. Although the two fields are independent enterprises, they are also interdependent in the same sense as other biological subdisciplines; e.g., neuroscience and biophysics. Under the working hypothesis that the acceptance of selection by reinforcement will parallel the acceptance of natural selection, what follows is a brief overview of the biological mechanisms of reinforcement. Special emphasis is given to the relation between these mechanisms and findings from the behavioral analysis of reinforcement.

Behavioral research has demonstrated that the environmental guidance of behavior is extremely flexible: almost any environmental event can control almost any behavior. How do the biological mechanisms of reinforcement accommodate this fact? Neuroscience indicates that reinforcement at the cellular level is dependent on compounds called *neuromodulators*. Axons from the cells that liberate neuromodulators project widely throughout the brain. Thus, neuromodulators can alter many synaptic efficacies simultaneously and permit almost any sensory input to control almost any motor output.

Unconditioned reinforcers, such as food, stimulate receptors that ultimately cause cells in the midbrain to liberate a neuromodulator (dopamine). Behavioral research indicates that reinforcers select environment-behavior relations only when these events occur close together in time: the contiguity requirement (Catania, 1971; Grice, 1948). When a presynaptic neuron fires—ultimately, because of the occurrence of an environmental stimulus—it liberates a transmitter (glutamate) that stimulates two types of receptors on a postsynaptic neuron—fast receptors and slow receptors. If fast receptors are sufficiently stimulated, the postsynaptic neuron fires. In addition, short lasting structural changes ("tags") are produced in the stimulated fast receptors. Further, if the fast receptors are stimulated for a sufficient duration, slow receptors also become engaged. Finally, if the reinforcer-instigated neuromodulator is present at about the same time that the slow receptors are engaged, a series of intracellular events take place that produce long-lasting structural changes in the tagged fast receptors. These changes cause fast receptors to undergo long-lasting increases in their sensitivity to the neurotransmitter liberated by the presynaptic neuron. (For experimental support for the preceding statements regarding the cellular mechanisms of reinforcement, see Frey, 1997; Stein & Belluzzi, 1989; Stein, Xue, & Belluzzi, 1993). This increased sensitivity is known as *long-term potentiation*. The net outcome of the process is that the neuromodulator potentiates multiple synapses between coactive neurons along the neural pathways that mediate reinforced environment-behavior relations. In this way, stimuli that precede the reinforced response come to control behavior.

In addition to the contiguity requirement, the discrepancy requirement established by behavioral research also has its neural counterpart: Reinforcing stimuli, including conditioned reinforcers, increase the release of the neuromodulator from cells in the midbrain only if those cells have not been activated recently. To illustrate, the ingestion of food normally increases the firing of these midbrain cells. If food, however, is preceded by a stimulus such as a light that has been previously paired with food, food no longer causes the liberation of the neuromodulator. Hence, food is rendered ineffective as a reinforcer under these conditions. Instead, the light now produces an increase in firing of the neuromodulator cells and, hence, functions as a conditioned reinforcer (Schultz, 1997). The inability of food to increase the firing of dopamine-producing neurons is responsible for the behavioral phenomenon of blocking (cf. Donahoe, 1997). Much remains before the neural mechanisms of reinforcement are fully known, but the correspondence between the contiguity and discrepancy requirements identified by behavioral research and the cellular requirements identified by neuroscientific research indicates that a comprehensive account of reinforcement is approaching.

Quantitative Means for Tracing Behavioral Selection Finally, what progress is being made in the development of quantitative techniques to trace the effects of selection by reinforcement? Are there methods in the offing that do for reinforcement what population genetics did for natural selection? The implications of natural selection and reinforcement can be illuminated by other than quantitative means, but if the Darwinian parallel holds, purely verbal accounts will not be fully persuasive, even within the scientific community. In addition, both behavior analysis and neuroscience increasingly appreciate that exploring the cumulative effects of basic processes may be too complex to pursue through experimental analysis alone. Complex behavior is the result of a complex history of reinforcement that is often impossible to duplicate in the laboratory. The difficulties are particularly formidable with nonlinear processes, such as occur in the nervous system: With nonlinear processes, two systems that behave identically under the same circumstances do not necessarily react identically when exposed to the same future circumstances (e.g., Smolensky, 1986). To model the effects of selection by reinforcement, a promising technique uses computer simulations of networks of neuron-like units. These simulations employ learning algorithms to modify the strengths of connections between units in a manner that is consistent with behavior analysis and neuroscience (e.g., Donahoe et al., 1993; Donahoe & Palmer, 1994; Donahoe, Palmer, & Burgos, 1997). To model the effects of natural selection on neural networks, a related type of computer simulation employs genetic algorithms to develop architectures of neural networks in a manner that is consistent with genetics and developmental neurobiology (e.g., Burgos, 1997).

The figure provides an overview of a comprehensive selectionist approach to the interpretation of complex behavior by means of computer simulation. The process begins with stimulation by simulated *environment inputs* to a *network architecture* (an artificial neural network). The network architecture is a product of a simulated *genetic algorithm*. The genetic algorithm simulates the effects of natural selection and neurodevelopmental processes on the *differential reproduction* of network architecture. The environmental input to the network architecture activates a *learning algorithm*. The learning algorithm then modifies the strengths of connections between units in the neural network, thereby simulating selection by reinforcement. An *environmental algorithm* specifies the stimuli that provide inputs to the network architecture (*the fading function*), the response topography that is required for reinforcement (*the shaping function*), and the consequences that occur for various topographies of response (*the reinforcement function*).

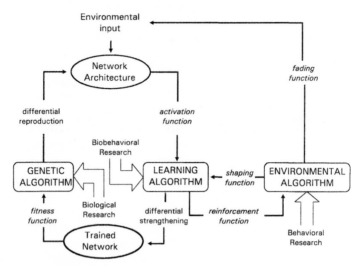

Figure 1. Overview of a comprehensive selectionist approach to the interpretation of complex behavior using computer simulations. The process begins with the stimulation by the simulated environment of inputs to a network architecture (an artificial neural network). The network architecture is a product of a genetic algorithm. The genetic algorithm simulates the effects of natural selection and neurodevelopmental processes on network architecture. A learning algorithm them modifies the strengths of connections between units in the neural network, thereby simulating selection by reinforcement. An environmental algorithm specifies the stimuli that provide inputs to the artificial neural network (the fading function), the response topography that is required for reinforcement (the shaping function), and the consequences that occur for various topographies of response (the reinforcement function). After the strengths of connections have been modified by the learning alorithm, a population of trained networks is formed. These networks differ from one another in their performance subsequent to the simulated contingencies of selection. The differences in performance are reflected in differences in the "fitness" of the networks. Repeated cycles of the selection process simulate successive "generations" of natural selection and selection by reinforcement. (See Donahoe, 1997.)

After the connections have been *differentially strengthened* by the learning algorithm, a population of *trained networks* is formed. These networks differ from one another in their performance following the simulated contingencies of selection. The differences in performance result in differences in the *fitness* of the networks to the contingencies. Repeated cycles of the selection process simulate successive generations of natural selection and selection by reinforcement. (See Donahoe, 1997.)

As with experimental analysis, the interpretation of selection processes can be carried out at different scales of measurement. Simulations can model the selection of environment-behavior relations at the behavioral level (Hutchison, 1997), and at the biobehavioral level—the selection of synaptic efficacies that mediate operants (e.g., Donahoe & Palmer, 1994; Donahoe et al., 1993). Similarly, simulations can model the synaptic level (e.g., Hasselmo & Wyble, 1997) or the neurochemical level (e.g., Smolen, Baxter, & Byrne, 2000). Whatever the level of the simulation, quantitative techniques must be constrained by findings from independent experimental analyses (see arrows in the figure indicating the influence of behavioral, biobehavioral and biological research). For example, within a neural network, a given unit (the analog of a neuron) cannot have direct excitatory effects on some units and inhibitory effects on others: A single neuron in the nervous system does not liberate both excitatory and inhibitory neurotransmitters. The need to be constrained by findings from experimental analysis distinguishes biobehaviorally acceptable quantitative methods from superficially similar methods in normative psychology such as parallel distributed processing (Rumelhart & McClelland, 1986). These latter simulations are primarily constrained by logical and mathematical considerations), not by experimental science (cf. Donahoe & Palmer, 1989). Ultimately, quantitative methods that draw upon experimental analyses from different scales of measurement must be integrated to provide a comprehensive theoretical account as depicted in the figure (see also Donahoe & Dorsel, 1997).

Conclusions

Selectionism holds that complex phenomena are products of a three-step process acting over time. First, variation occurs in the phenomena that are subject to selection. Then, selection unequally favors some of these variations. Finally, retention of the selected variations allows them to contribute to the pool of variation upon which later selection operates. The products of selection are themselves necessarily variable because variations in the contingencies of selection are inevitable. In principle, then, the product of a selection process cannot be a constant entity, or essence. Essentialism regards variations in phenomena as merely perturbations of an underlying, unchanging entity. Because of this inherent difference in their views of the nature of phenomena, selectionism and essentialism are fundamentally irreconcilable.

In evolutionary biology, selectionism won the day after an almost 100-year struggle against two philosophical obstacles: essentialism and teleology. In normative psychology, camouflaged forms of essentialism persist in the guise of entities such as associations, attitudes, cognitions, linguistic rules, and the like. Experimental observations are seen as imperfect reflections of underlying relatively fixed structures or processes whose characteristics can be inferred from the variable observations. By contrast, behavior analysis accepts the variation in observations as irreducible—even under circumstances that meet the rigorous demands of experimental analysis—and seeks to induce principles that accommodate variation. Chief among these principles is a principle of reinforcement, which describes the processes that select behavior. Behavior analysis views a well-conceived principle of reinforcement as playing the same role in the understanding of complex behavior that natural selection already plays in understanding the evolution of complex organisms.

The triumph of selectionism in biology was principally due to the formulation by Darwin of the principle of natural selection. However, a functional statement of the principle of natural selection was not sufficient for its acceptance. General acceptance awaited the discovery of the biological mechanisms that implemented natural selection and the development of quantitative procedures that traced its implications. The conjoining of these enterprises is known as the *modern synthesis*. Behavior analysis, critically supplemented by experimental findings from studies conducted within the conceptual framework of associationist psychology, appears to have identified a powerful functional statement of the principle of reinforcement. Although this functional statement may be logically sufficient to provide an account of the emergence of complex behavior, it may not be adequate for the acceptance of selectionism in psychology. If the fate of selectionism in psychology parallels its course in evolutionary biology, the biological mechanisms of reinforcement must be discovered and suitable quantitative techniques must be devised before most will find the account persuasive. The rate of progress in both of these enterprises encourages the belief that a new modern synthesis is emerging over the horizon.

References

Agassiz, L. (1874). Evolution and permanence of type. *Atlantic Monthly, 33*, 92–101.

Anderson, J. R. (1978). Arguments concerning representations for mental imagery. *Psychological Review, 85*, 249–277.

Anonymous. (1860). Editorial. *Eclectic Review, 3*, 224. (as cited in Ellegård, 1958)

Baum, W. M. (1973). The correlation-based law of effect. *Journal of the Experimental Analysis of Behavior, 20*, 137–153.

Baum, W. M. (1974). On two types of deviations from the matching law. *Journal of the Experimental Analysis of Behavior, 22*, 231–242.

Bersh, P. J., Whitehouse, W. G., & Mauro, B. C. (1982). Pavlovian processes and response competition as determinants of avoidance response-prevention effects. *Learning and Motivation, 13*, 113–134.

Burgos, J. E. (1997). Evolving artificial neural networks in Pavlovian environments. In J. W. Donahoe and V. P. Dorsel (Eds.), *Neural-network models of cognition: Biobehavioral foundations* (pp. 58–79). Amsterdam: Elsevier Science Press.

Burns, R., & Donahoe, J. W. (1984). Unified reinforcement principle: Shock as reinforcer. Paper presented at the annual meeting of the Psychonomic Society, San Antonio, TX. (described in Donahoe & Palmer, 1994)

Campbell, D. T. (1974). Evolutionary epistemology. In P. A. Schlipp (Ed.), *The philosophy of Karl Popper* (Vol. 14–1, pp. 413–463). LaSalle, IL: Open Court Publishing.

Carpenter, W. B. (1860). Review. *National Review*. (as cited in Hull, 1973)

Catania, A. C. (1971). Reinforcement schedules: The role of responses preceding the one that produces the reinforcer. *Journal of the Experimental Analysis of Behavior, 15*, 271–287.

Catania, A. C. (1995). Selection in behavior and biology. In J. T. Todd & E. K. Morris (Eds.), Modern perspective on B. F. Skinner and contemporary behaviorism (pp. 185–194). Westport, CT: Greenwood Press.

Darwin, C. (1859/1964). *On the origin of species. A facsimile of the first edition.* Cambridge, Harvard University Press.

Davison, M. & Baum, W. M. (2000). Choice in a variable environment: Every reinforcer counts. *Journal of the Experimental Analysis of Behavior, 74*, 1–24.

Dennett, D. C. (1995). *Darwin's dangerous idea: Evolution and the meanings of life.* New York: Simon & Schuster.

Dobzhansky, T. (1937). *Genetics and the origin of species.* New York: Columbia University Press.

Domjan, M. (1980). Ingestional aversion learning: Unique and general processes. In J. S. Rosenblatt & M. Busnel (Eds.), *Advances in the study of behavior* (Vol. 11), New York: Academic.

Donahoe, J. W. (1977). Some implications of a relational principle of reinforcement. *Journal of the Experimental Analysis of Behavior,27*, 341–350. 1980).

Donahoe, J. W. (1983). A plausible analogy?: Reinforcement theory : Cognitive psychology :: Natural selection : Special creationism. Invited address presented at the annual meeting of the American Psychological Association, Anaheim, CA.

Donahoe, J. W. (1984). Commentary: Skinner—The Darwin of ontogeny? *The Behavioral and Brain Sciences, 7*, 287–288.

Donahoe, J. W. (1997). Selection networks: Simulation of plasticity through reinforcement learning. In J. W. Donahoe & V. P. Dorsel (Eds.), *Neural-network approaches to cognition: Biobehavioral foundations.* Amsterdam, Netherlands: Elsevier Science Press.

Donahoe, J. W. (1999). Edward L. Thorndike: The selectionist connectionist. *Journal of the Experimental Analysis of Behavior, 72*, 451–454.

Donahoe, J. W., Burgos, J. E., & Palmer, D. C. (1993). Selectionist approach to reinforcement. *Journal of the Experimental Analysis of Behavior, 60*, 17–40.

Donahoe, J. W., Crowley, M. A., Millard, W. J., & Stickney, K. J. (1982). A unified principle of reinforcement: Some implications for matching. In M. L. Commons, R. J. Herrnstein, & H.Rachlin (Eds.), *Quantitative Analyses of Behavior. II. Matching and maximizing accounts* (Vol. 2, pp. 493–521). New York: Ballinger.

Donahoe, J. W., &. Dorsel V. P. (Eds.). (1997). *Neural-network approaches to cognition: Biobehavioral foundations.* Amsterdam, Netherlands: Elsevier Science Press.

Donahoe, J. W., & Palmer, D. C. (1989). The interpretation of complex human behavior: Some reactions to Parallel Distributed Processing, edited by J. L. McClelland, D. E. Rumelhart, and the PDP Research Group. *Journal of the Experimental Analysis of Behavior, 51*, 399–416.

Donahoe, J. W., & Palmer, D. C. (1994). *Learning and complex behavior.* Boston: Allyn & Bacon.

Donahoe, J. W., Palmer, D. C., & Burgos, J. E. (1997). The S-R issue in behavior analysis and in Donahoe and Palmer's *Learning and complex behavior. Journal of the Experimental Analysis of Behavior, 67*, 193–211.

Donahoe, J. W., & Wessells, M.G. (1980). *Learning, language, and memory.* New York: Harper & Row.

Ellegård, A. (1958). *Darwin and the general reader: The reception of Darwin's theory of evolution in the British periodical press, 1859–1872.* Stockholm: Almqvist & Wiksell.

Epstein, R. (1983). Resurgence of previously reinforced behavior during extinction. *Behavior Analysis Letters, 3*, 391–397.

Estes, W. K., & Skinner, B. F. (1941). Some quantitative properties of anxiety. *Journal of Experimental Psychology, 29*, 390–400.

Fisher, R. A. (1930). *The genetical theory of natural selection.* Oxford: Clarendon Press.

Frey, U. (1997). Cellular mechanisms of long-term potentiation: Late maintenance. In J. W. Donahoe & V. P. Dorsel (Eds.), *Neural-network approaches to cognition: Biobehavioral foundations* (pp. 105–105–128). Amsterdam, Netherlands: Elsevier Science Press.

Galbicka, G. (1992). The dynamics of behavior. *Journal of the Experimental Analysis of Behavior, 57*, 243–248.

Gazzaniga, M. S. (2000). *Cognitive neuroscience.* Malden, MA: Blackwell Publishers.

Gerall, A. A., & Obrist, G. A. (1962). Classical conditioning of the papillary dilation response of normal and curarized cats. *Journal of Comparative and Physiological Psychology, 55*, 486–491.

Grice, G. R. (1948). The relation of secondary reinforcement to delayed reward in visual discrimination learning. *Journal of Experimental Psychology, 38*, 1–16.

Haldane, J. B. S. (1931). A re-examination of Darwinism. (as cited in Haldane, 1966)

Haldane. J.B. S. (1966), *The causes of evolution.* Ithaca, NY: Cornell University Press.

Hasselmo, M. E., & Wyble, B. P. (1997). Free recall and recognition in a network model of the hippocampus: Simulating effects of scopolamine on human memory function. *Behavioral Brain Research, 89*, 1–34.

Herrnstein, R. J. (1970). On the law of effect. *Journal of the Experimental Analysis of Behavior, 13*, 243–266.

Hintzman, D. L. (1980). Simpson's paradox and the analysis of memory retrieval. *Psychological Review, 87*, 398–410.

Hintzman, D. L. (1993). Twenty-five years of learning and memory: Was the cognitive revolution a mistake? In D. L. Meyer & S. Kornblum (Eds.), *Attention and performance 14: Synergies in experimental psychology, artificial intelligence, and cognitive neuroscience* (pp. 359–391). Cambridge, MA: MIT Press.

Hull, D. L. (1973). *Darwin and his critics: The reception of Darwin's theory of evolution by the scientific community.* Cambridge, MA: Harvard University Press.

Hutchison, W. R. (1997). We also need complete behavioral models. *Journal of the Experimental Analysis of Behavior, 67*, 224–228.

Huxley, T. H. (1908). *Lectures and essays.* London. (as cited in Ellegård, 1958)

Jenkin, F. (1867). Review. *The North British Review.* (as cited in Hull, 1973)

Jenkins, H. M., & Moore, B. R. (1973). The form of the auto-shaped response with food or water reinforcers. *Journal of the Experimental Analysis of Behavior, 20*, 163–181.

Kamin, L. J. (1968). Attention-like processes in classical conditioning. In M. R. Jones (Ed.), *Miami symposium on the prediction of behavior* (pp. 9–31). Miami, FL: University of Miami Press.

Kamin, L. J. (1969). Predictability, surprise, attention and conditioning. In B. A. Campbell & R. M. Church (Eds.), *Punishment and aversive behavior* (pp. 279–296). New York: Appleton-Century-Crofts.

Lattal, K. A., & Gleeson, S. (1990). Response acquisition with delayed reinforcement. *Journal of Experimental Psychology: Animal Behavior Processes, 16*, 27–39.

Lewes, G. H. (1860). *Cornhill Magazine, 1*, 443. (as cited in Hull, 1973)

MacCorquodale, K., & Meehl, P. E. (1948). On a distinction between hypothetical constructs and intervening variables. *Psychological Review, 55*, 95–107.

Mandler, G. (1981). What is cognitive psychology? What isn't? Invited address, *Division of Philosophical Psychology, American Psychological Association*, Los Angeles, CA.

Mayr, E. R. (1942). *Systematics and the origin of species.* New York: Columbia University Press.

Mayr, E. R. (1976). Typological versus population thinking. In E. Mayr (Ed).), *Evolution and the diversity of life (pp. 26–29).* Cambridge: Belknap Press.

Mayr, E. R. (1982). *The growth of biological thought: Diversity, evolution, and inheritance.* Cambridge, MA: Harvard University Press.

Mayr, E. R. (1988). *Toward a new philosophy of biology.* Cambridge, MA: Harvard University Press.

Meehl, P. E. (1950). On the circularity of the law of effect. *Psychological Bulletin, 47,* 1950, 52–75.

Michael, J. (1993). Establishing operations. *Behavior Analyst, 16,* 191–206.

Mivart, St.-G. J. (1871). Darwin's descent of man. *Quarterly Review, 131,* 47–90. (as cited in Hull, 1973)

Morse, W. H., & Kelleher, R. T. (1977). Determinants of reinforcement and punishment. In W. K. Honig & J. E. R. Staddon (Eds.), *Handbook of operant behavior* (pp. 174–200). Englewood Cliffs, NJ: Prentice-Hall.

Müller, M. (1872). Report of lecture. *Nature, 7,* 145.

Neisser, U. (1982). *Memory observed.* New York: W. H. Freeman.

Palmer, D. C. (1986). Chomsky's nativism: A critical review. In P. N. Chase & L. J. Parrott (Eds.), *Psychological aspects of language* (pp. 49–60). Springfield, IL: Charles Thomas.

Palmer, D. C. (2000). Chomsky's nativism reconsidered. *Analysis of Verbal Behavior, 17,* 51–56.

Palmer, D. C., & Donahoe, J. W. (1992). Essentialism and selectionism in cognitive science and behavior analysis. *American Psychologist, 47,* 1344–1358.

Patriot. (1863). Editorial, Sept. 10, p. 594. (as cited in Ellegård, 1958)

Piaget, J. (1953). *The origins of intelligence in the child.* London: Routledge & Kegan.

Pinker, S. (1994). *The language instinct.* New York: William Morrow.

Premack, D. (1959). Toward empirical behavioral laws: I. Positive reinforcement. *Psychological Review, 66,* 219–233.

Rescorla, R. A., & Wagner, A. R. (1972). A theory of Pavlovian conditioning: Variations in the effectiveness of reinforcement and nonreinforcement. In A. H. Black & W. F. Prokasy (Eds.), *Classical conditioning II* (pp. 64–99). New York: Appleton-Century-Crofts.

Reynolds, G. (1961). Attention in the pigeon. *Journal of the Experimental Analysis of Behavior, 4,* 203–208.

Rumelhart, D. E., & McClelland, J. L. (1986). PDP models and general issues in cognitive science. In D. E. Rumelhart, J. L. McClelland, & The PDP Research Group (Eds.), *Parallel distributed processing* (Vol. 1). Cambridge, MA: MIT Press.

Schoenfeld, W. N. (1969). "Avoidance" in behavior theory. *Journal of the Experimental Analysis of Behavior, 12,* 669–674.

Schultz, W. (1997). Adaptive dopaminergic neurons report value of environmental stimuli. In J. W. Donahoe & V. P. Dorsel (Eds.), *Neural-network models of cognition: Biobehavioral foundations* (pp. 317–335). Amsterdam: Elsevier Science Press.

Schwartz, B. (1980). Development of complex, stereotyped behavior in pigeons. *Journal of the Experimental Analysis of Behavior, 33,* 153–166.

Sedgwick, A. (1860). Objections to Mr. Darwin's theory of the origin of species. *The Spectator, April 7.* (as cited in Hull, 1973)

Shettleworth, S. J. (1972). Constraints on learning. In D. S. Lehrman, R. A. Hinde, & E. Shaw (Eds.), *Advances in the study of behavior* (pp. 175–198). New York: Academic Press.

Shimp, C. P. (1969). Optimal behavior in free-operant experiments. *Psychological Review, 76,* 97–112.

Sidman, M. (1960). *Tactics of scientific research: Evaluating experimental data in psychology.* New York: Basic Books.

Skinner, B. F. (1935). The generic nature of the concepts of stimulus and response. *Journal of General Psychology, 12,* 40–65.

Skinner, B. F. (1938). *Behavior of organisms.* New York: Appleton-Century-Crofts.

Skinner, B. F. (1948). "Superstition" in the pigeon. *Journal of Experimental Psychology, 38,* 168–172.

Skinner, B. F. (1950). Are theories of learning necessary?*Psychological* Review, *57,* 193–216.

Skinner, B. F. (1966). The ontogeny and phylogeny of behavior, *Science, 153,* 1203–1213.

Skinner, B. F. (1974). *About behaviorism.* New York: Random House.

Smolen, P., Baxter, D. A., & Byrne, H. (2000). Modeling transcriptional control of gene networks—methods, recent results, and future directions. *Bulletin of Mathematical Biology, 62,* 247–292.

Smolensky, P. (1986). Neural and conceptual interpretations of PDP models. In J. L. McClelland, D. E. Rumelhart, & The PDP Research Group (Eds.), *Parallel distributed processing* (Vol. 2, pp. 390–431). Cambridge, MA: MIT Press.

Sober, E. (1984). *The nature of selection: Evolutionary theory in philosophical focus.* Cambridge, MA: MIT Press.

Staddon, J. E. R. (1983). *Adaptive behavior and learning.* Cambridge: Cambridge University Press.

Staddon, J. E. R., & Ettinger, R. H. (1989). *Learning: Introduction to principles of adaptive behavior.* New York: Harcourt, Brace, Jovanovich.

Staddon, J. E. R., Hinson, J. M., & Kram, R. (1981). Optimal choice. *Journal of the Experimental Analysis of Behavior, 35,* pp. 397–412.

Stein, L., & Belluzzi, J. D. (1989). Cellular investigations of behavioral reinforcement. *Neuroscience & Biobehavioral Reviews, 13,* 69–80.

Stein, L., Xue, B. G., & Belluzzi, J. D. (1993). A cellular analogue of operant conditioning. *Journal of the Experimental Analysis of Behavior, 60,* 41–53.

Stickney, K., & Donahoe, J. W. (1983). Attenuation of blocking by a change in US locus. *Animal Learning & Behavior, 11,* 60–66.

Thorndike, E. L. (1903). *Elements of psychology.* New York: A. G. Seiler.

Timberlake, W., & Allison, J. (1974). Response deprivation: An empirical approach to instrumental performance. *Psychological Review, 81,* 146–164.

Timberlake, W., & Wozny, M. (1979). Reversibility of reinforcers between eating and running by schedule changes: A comparison of hypotheses and models. *Animal Learning & Behavior, 7,* 461–469.

Townsend, J. T. (1972). Some results on the identifiability of serial and parallel processes. *British Journal of Mathematical and Statistical Psychology, 25,* 168–199.

Uttal, W. R. (1999). *The war between mentalism and behaviorism: On the accessibility of mental processes.* Boston: Houghton-Mifflin.

von Baer, K. E. (1873). The controversy over Darwinism. *Augsburger Allegemeine Zeitung, 130,* 1986–1988. (as cited in Hull, 1973)

Wallace, A. R. (1869). Review. *Quarterly Review, 126,* 391–393. (From A. Ellegård, 1958.)

Weimer, W. B. (1973). Psycholinguistics and Plato's paradoxes of the *Meno. American Psychologist, 28,* 15–33.

Weismann, A. (1909). The selection theory. In A. C. Seward (Ed.), *Darwin and modern science* (pp. 1–12). Cambridge, MA: Cambridge University Press.

Wollaston, T. V. (1860). Review of the Origin of Species. *Annals and Magazine of Natural History, 5,* 132–143.

Wright, S. (1939). *Statistical genetics in relation to evolution.* Paris: Hermann.

7

Humanism and Skinner's Radical Behaviorism

J. E. R. Staddon

"Science" and "humanities" are usually placed in opposition. The contributions of the humanities are in areas that are not usually thought of as scientific, such as morality and values, aesthetics, and an understanding of ultimate purposes. But, like his eminent younger colleague E. O. Wilson, B. F. Skinner recognized no dividing line. Science in general, and radical behaviorism in particular, provide all the knowledge needed, he argued, to guide society into a happy and, above all, long-term, future. His confidence is widely shared. Most middle-class parents, most psychotherapists and educators, the majority of political and social theorists, whether behavior analytically inclined or not, all now share Skinner's confident belief that what they do is grounded in science.[1] They acknowledge traditional practices, but doubt they have much to learn from them. They believe that all questions are at bottom scientific questions. Science, in principle, embraces all knowledge. This view, it is not unfair to say, has become the religion of the educated elite.

---

[1] To define *science* would take a book, which could not be conclusive no matter how long or well-written. For present purposes, I will simply define science as knowledge that is susceptible to intersubjective (i.e., third-party) verification, leaving open whether "verification" is "falsification" or something else. By this means I hope to exclude "private" events and personal revelations from the choir invisible.

J. E. R. Staddon • Department of Psychological and Brain Sciences, Duke University, Durham, NC 27708-0086.

How true is this "scientific imperialism"? How did Skinner's radical behaviorism advance it, and by what means did he bridge the gap between the "why" questions of human existence, not traditionally deemed scientific, and the "how" questions that have always been the accepted province of science?

Skinner's conceptual tools for tackling these problems were his philosophical analyses of truth, free will, and value from a point of view that has recently returned to fashion, evolutionary epistemology. In this chapter I examine radical behaviorism's version of evolutionary epistemology to see how successful it is in spanning what used to be considered an unbridgeable gap. I believe that it fails. The gap remains unbridgeable, and for a pretty obvious reason. A reason that implies there will be areas forever closed to science, hence open to whatever other systems of belief—religious, humanistic, philosophical—people may choose to aid them in making decisions that can never, even in principle, be based on scientific proof (see Galuska, this volume).

The Darwinian Metaphor

In a paper entitled "The phylogeny and ontogeny of behavior" (Skinner, 1966; see also 1981) Skinner turned to a view of reinforcement different from the "strengthening" metaphor he had inherited from Thorndike. According to Darwin, nature acts to favor certain individuals for survival and reproduction, that is, to *select* individuals. She does not, as was previously believed, actively strengthen their adaptive characteristics. In the same way, argued Skinner, reinforcement does not directly strengthen behavior, as older views implied. Instead reinforcement *selects* behavior in a quasi-Darwinian fashion. Just as adaptation in nature can be traced to selection rather than direct environmental action, so (he claimed) adaptation to contingencies of reinforcement reflects the selective action of reinforcement.

The basic idea of evolution by natural selection is that some process creates a set of variants: individual organisms that differ in various ways. Some of these variants are more successful than others in giving rise to progeny. If the critical differences between successful and unsuccessful individuals are heritable, that is, if they are passed on without undue dilution, then the next generation will be that much fitter than the one that went before. Darwin's insight was to see that across geological time these small generational changes might accumulate not just to modify a species but, eventually, to differentiate one from another, to create new species.

When he first heard Darwin's idea, T. H. Huxley is reported to have exclaimed "How extremely stupid not to have thought of that!"—because it is a very simple idea that, once understood, is immediately persuasive to most people. One can see the actual reproducing units, the *phenotypes*. Scientists know more and more about the heritable characteristics, the *genotypes*, that are associated with different phenotypes and about the processes of *development* that translate a fixed genotype into a range of possible phenotypes. And people can see in the way that each organism interacts with its environment, in its ecological niche, just why it is that more fit animals are in fact more successful. Faster horses do better than slower because they are less subject to predation, sharper claws are better to catch prey, lighter bones are better for flying and so on. People can see, in short, what selective factors are at work.

All of these features are much attenuated when the Darwinian idea is applied to reinforcement learning (but see Donahoe, this volume; and Glenn, this volume). What is the behavioral analogue to the genotype, for example? To the phenotype? How can one compare a set of activities extending over time, a repertoire, to the tangible phenotypes that are the units of natural selection? And what, in the selection of behavior, corresponds to differential reproduction? To heritability? What corresponds to selective factors in a niche? And where are the masses of facts—about geographical distribution, about the relations between development and descent, about the structure of the geological record, about "affinities of organic beings" and how they are explainable by descent with modification—that Darwin used so persuasively to support his theory? These uncertainties are why the parallel between learning and evolution is a metaphor, not a fact.[2]

The Darwinian metaphor includes both variation and selection. But Skinner largely ignored behavioral variation, placing all emphasis on the selective effects of reinforcement. He made no attempt to specify the mechanisms of variation. Indeed, in his famous simile "Operant conditioning shapes behavior as a sculptor shapes a lump of clay" (Skinner, 1953, p. 91) he implies that "moment-to-moment variation is small in magnitude, and essentially random . . . in direction" (Staddon & Simmelhag, 1971, p. 31). Like Darwin, Skinner was a gradualist. But unlike Darwin, who was well aware of the existence of large and often directional phenotypic

---

[2] This is also why I believe that Richard Dawkins' (1976) idea of a *meme* (e.g., Dennett, 1996; Blackmore, 1999; but see Aunger, 2001) is largely empty. A meme is an idea or a fashion or an invention—anything that can be culturally transmitted. Scientists, however, do not know either what is selected (the meme equivalent of a gene) or why it is selected (the meme equivalent of adaptiveness). One consequence is that the concept is circular: memes that spread are fitter than those that do not; fitter memes are those that spread. Memes, for Dawkins, and operants, for Skinner have a similar conceptual status in the Darwinian metaphor. But the operant is at least traceable to the action of reinforcement, a partially understood process, whereas the selective factors acting on memes are still a matter for conjecture.

changes from generation to generation, Skinner never seriously considered the possibility that variation might follow principles of its own at least as orderly and important as those he himself had proposed for the mechanism of selection (cf. Neuringer, this volume).

Evolutionary Epistemology

Skinner's commitment to the Darwinian metaphor implies allegiance to what has come to be known as *evolutionary epistemology*, the notion that knowledge is entirely a product of evolutionary history. Truth is what worked in evolution. Evolutionary epistemology is thus a variant of *pragmatism*, the philosophy proposed by Harvard philosopher and logician Charles Sanders Peirce and promoted by psychologist-philosopher William James (see Lattal & Laipple, this volume). For all varieties of pragmatism, truth equals functional utility. Truth is what works. Evolutionary epistemology adds the phylogenetic dimension: what works, yes, but not just during one's lifetime, also during the lifetimes of one's ancestors.

Natural selection is contingent, that is, it depends on both chance and necessity in Jacques Monod's (1971) memorable phrase, on the vagaries of variation and the steady push of selection. Nothing is certain, not logic, not the hand in front of one's face not the tree seen through the window. Truth is not absolute. Everything apparently known is the outcome of millions of years of natural selection, and thousands of years of cultural selection. Thus, people believe in logic not because logic is true in some essential, Platonic sense, but because those individuals and cultures that failed to believe in logic lost out in the struggle to reproduce. Something is said to be true not because it really is, but simply because it has survived in a quasi-Darwinian struggle for intellectual existence. As in Skinner's version of the pigeon in the "superstition" experiment, one may believe in superstitions if the right variant (idea) fails to occur. If no one has the idea that the earth circles the sun, rather than the other way around, the consequences of that idea cannot be tested and it cannot prevail and, like Skinner's pigeon, people will misbelieve. If the correct idea does not occur, it cannot be selected, so that what occurs will not accurately represent the world. A consistent evolutionary epistemologist would go on (as D. T. Campbell, 1975, did) to contend that value systems and religious beliefs have also survived a Darwinian history and should on that account be granted some degree of truth. This step, however, was not taken by Skinner.

Evolutionary epistemology is not nihilistic. Although it denies access to absolute truth, the existence of some more or less stable "external reality" within which natural selection can take place is tacitly assumed. There has to be something that does the selecting, and the assumption is that that something has fixed properties. This belief in a fixed external reality, however, is, and must be, a *belief*, not something provable as fact.[3] It is nevertheless a belief that can be justified in several ways. First, it is (I would argue) essential to the normal activities of science. Absent any belief in reality, the usual scientific tests lose their power to convince. After all, if the laws of nature can change capriciously from day to day, why should any test be decisive? Second, if there is no truth, contentious issues of fact will be decided by politics or force: "... the idea that there is no such thing as objective truth ... [is] closely linked with authoritarian and totalitarian ideas,"(pp. 4–5) wrote Popper (1962), paraphrasing Bertrand Russell.

Unworried by this invitation to rule by tyranny and the arts of persuasion, some thinkers nevertheless have proposed that the idea of truth should be abandoned. In its place they propose locutions such as relatively permanent beliefs or consensually agreed beliefs. These substitutes miss the point, which is that for evolutionary epistemology the truth of any proposition is relative to the challenges it has successfully met. Thus, an unquestioned belief is likely to be less true than one that has emerged unscathed from numerous tests. On the other hand, a longstanding belief, even if it has not been—or can not be—explicitly tested, is more likely to be true than something one just thought of: *veritas temporis filia*. Persistence and consensus , however, are only indirectly related to truth, as evolutionary epistemology views it.

There are a few beliefs, like the laws of logic or arithmetic, the belief that the chair I am sitting in is real, and so on, that survive every conceivable test. Such beliefs are the best kind of truth available. When one asks of some new proposition "Is it true?" all that is meant is "Will it be as resistant to disproof as the laws of logic?" In effect, those beliefs that are most resistant to disproof become the standard by which the truth of others is judged. To the extent that it espouses a kind of evolutionary pragmatism, the epistemology of radical behaviorism is hard to fault.

Truth is Falsehood

Radical behaviorism's epistemology can be seriously misread, however. Radical behaviorism is congenial to some humanist fans of the "postmodern aesthetic" (Andresen, 1991) and there are indeed similarities

[3] To acknowledge that belief in a stable (if largely unknowable) external world is both unprovable and necessary to almost any epistemology is just another way of acknowledging the force of David Hume's argument against induction. That the sun will rise tomorrow cannot be proven, but it must be believed, and many other things like it, if science is to proceed.

between the views of Skinner and Skinnerians and proposals of social constructionists and relativists such as Foucault, Derrida and Latour (see, for example, Latour, 1993; Smith, 1997, and Hayes, 1993; see Marr, this volume, and Zuriff, 1998, for a critique; and Shimp, 2001, for an attempt at rapprochement). All are skeptical of rationalism, objectivity and the idea of an independent, external reality. How true is this attack on . . . truth?

The attack on the idea of truth seems to the naïve eye self-refuting: Is it *true* that there is no such thing as truth? This proposition is either true or false. If it is true, then the proposition is false. If the proposition is false, it can be ignored. Case closed. Like famous paradoxes "'All politicians lie' said the senator"—the proposition has no truth value. Relativists disagree and mostly decline to debate the issue.

One who has accepted the challenge is crypto-behaviorist Herrnstein Smith (1997) in her book *Belief and Resistance*. The book is persuasive; a reviewer commented "I highly recommend it . . . [it] is short and written in a clear, vigorous style, and it elucidates clearly the postmodern claims about objectivity and 'the social construction of knowledge'". (Akin, 1999, p. 61) Herrnstein Smith gets to the point in the chapter "Unloading the self-refutation charge." If she is granted that no proposition, no empirical proposition at any rate, is *certainly* true or false, the issue then becomes, What does it mean for one theory or proposition to be better or worse than another? Herrnstein Smith argues that "the common and unshakable conviction that differences of 'better' and 'worse' must be objective" (pp. 77–78) is a fallacy.

> The supposed relativist [says] that her point is, precisely, that theories . . . can be and are evaluated in *other* non-"objective" ways. Not all theories are equal because they . . . can be, and commonly will be, found better or worse than others in relation to measures such as applicability, coherence, connectability and so forth. These measures are not objective in the classic sense, since they depend on matters of perspective, interpretation and judgment, and will vary under different conditions." (pp. 77–78)

Herrnstein Smith seems to be saying that some theories are better than others, but the criteria by which these judgements are made are not themselves absolute. They vary depending on perspective, interpretation, and so on. This view does not differ from a sophisticated pragmatism: that (the belief in) the truth of a proposition is relative to the tests it has undergone. And no historian of science, and few working scientists, would deny that test criteria are far from immutable. They differ from school to school and evolve as a discipline develops. Ebbinghaus came to his conclusions without the aid of statistics, for example; now they are mandatory. Pasteur's clinical studies were not double-blind, now the practice is universal; and so on. If this evolution of criteria is postmodernist social construction of knowledge it is also just common practice in science and does not differ philosophically from a nuanced pragmatism.

Is Herrnstein Smith's relativism then nothing more than a sort of literary pragmatism? Not really. Relativism fails to provide any *reason* for testing an idea in scientific (empirical, logical) ways. If there is no "reality" what is the point of testing an hypothesis? Does a scientist test merely to "overcome an opponent in argument" in the style that Francis Bacon condemned many years ago? Is it just a matter of public relations or politics all the way down? Occasionally (I admit with some reluctance) the answer is "yes." Galileo notoriously commented that his experiments were often to convince others, because he himself was already convinced. Physics is not all of science, however, and Galileo's view is not typical.[4] Scientists justify their desire for test by a core belief that relativism lacks: that there is a unique reality behind our contingent views of it. Relativists are correct that belief in such a reality is a matter of faith. It cannot be proved. Without it, however, science reverts either to scholasticism, the medieval mindset that truth should be decided by argument without recourse to facts; to advertising—persuasion by any means possible; or, as we are reminded by *1984* and the sorry history of the 20th century, to the totalitarian idea that truth is established by the power to coerce. Science is different. It is not just politics and public relations nor does it compel belief by force.

Truth as a Consequence: The Genetic Fallacy

Relativism is also subject to a more subtle error, an updated version of something long recognized in philosophy as the *genetic fallacy*: confusion of the reasons for a belief with the reasons for its truth. As will be seen, Skinner was subject to a similar fallacy in his discussion of personal responsibility.

Passionate Democrats tend to think ill of a Republican president, for example, just because they are Democrats and the President is not. They may be right nonetheless. The source of their belief has no necessary bearing on its truth. Neutral observers, however, may find their party affiliation an insufficient reason to agree with their evaluation. Some reasons for belief are generally persuasive because they are seen as having a bearing on its truth; others are not, because they do not. Closer to home, the problem also can be illustrated by analysis of operant conditioning in animals. There is an old Columbia *Jester* cartoon from the heyday of Skinnerian influence

---

[4] Although the dramatically counter-intuitive demonstrations that gain attention in some parts of social psychology and memory research (on eyewitness testimony, for example) often look uncomfortably like advertising stunts rather than real investigative research.

that shows a rat pressing a lever in a Skinner box. "Boy have I got this guy conditioned!" the rat explains to his companion, "Every time I press the lever he gives me a pellet!" The relativist, and the Skinnerian, would contend that the rat is mistaken, because they know that his behavior is simply a consequence of a certain history of reinforcement. In other words, they argue that because they know the process by which the behavior came about, the belief has no truth value. It is "contingent" in Herrnstein Smith's (1997) terms.

Human beings, however, with a more comprehensive world-view than the rat, know that his belief is in fact largely correct. The apparatus, if not the experimenter, is indeed "conditioned" to present a pellet every time the bar is pressed. And the way the rat knows this is via its history of reinforcement. In short, not only does knowing the process not invalidate this particular belief, it is the reason and justification for the belief. It is only in this rather benign sense that science is socially constructed. It by no means justifies the statement (a commonplace in postmodernism) that

> It has thus become increasingly apparent that physical "reality", no less than social "reality", is at bottom a social and linguistic construct; that scientific "knowledge", far from being objective, reflects and encodes the dominant ideologies and power relations of the culture that produced it ... (Sokal, 1996)[5]

Truth-value and reinforcement history are not antithetical, one is the product of the other. That does not mean that beliefs will always be correct. An extraterrestrial who bears the same relation to humans as they do to the rat would no doubt find humans often subject to superstitions. Not always, however; nor would he be immune from the perspective of a still higher being. In short, some beliefs are better than others because they are truer. And they are known to be truer because they pass (or have passed) (scientific) tests better. That is what (scientific) truth means.

The extraordinary thing is that Skinner (1976), apparently unaware that he was contradicting himself, probably would have agreed: "The truth of a statement of fact is limited to the sources of the behavior of the speaker. ... A scientific law is ... limited by the repertoires of the scientists involved" (p. 136). When truth is defined in this way, however, there is no contradiction between tracing a belief to a particular reinforcement history and evaluating it as true or false. Some histories, those that involve a sufficient "repertoire" of test and evaluation, tend to lead to true beliefs; others

---

[5] This quote is not in fact from a social constructionist, but from a paper by New York physicist Alan Sokal that has become perhaps the most famous academic hoax of the twentieth century. Sokal's article, which was full of nonsense physics laced with constructionist cant like this, was assumed to be a serious contribution and was published in a leading humanist journal.

lead to beliefs that are either false or of unknown truth value. Joe Sixpack may believe the end of the world is nigh because he drank too much and had a hallucination; astronomer Janet Jeans may believe the same thing because she just measured the speed of an approaching asteroid. Both beliefs are products of particular histories. Some histories, however, are better than others.

Indeed, one can turn the social constructionist argument back on itself. Bauerlein (2001), in an unconsciously behavioristic analysis, has beautifully punctured the epistemological claims of social constructionism by pointing out that it does not even pretend to be a philosophy, because no practitioner acknowledges that it is open to question:

> To believe that knowledge is a construct, that truth, evidence, fact, and inference all fall under the category of local interpretation, and that interpretations are more or less right by virtue of the interests they satisfy is a professional habit, not an intellectual thesis.

If social constructionism is not philosophy, then what is it? Why, a (pure) social construction, of course: "One can prove the institutional nature of social constructionism by noting how easy it is to question" (Bauerlein). After describing some of the ad hominem attacks on the opposition that have become routine in this field, Bauerlein comments:

> This polarizing, personalizing rhetoric indicates that social constructionism has an institutional basis, not a philosophical, moral, or political one.... Herein lies the secret of constructionism's success: the critical method that follows from constructionist premises has proven eminently conducive to the exigencies of teaching, lecturing, and publishing. In a word, it is the school of thought most congenial to current professional workplace conditions of scholars in the humanities.

In short, the social constructionists are hoist by their own petard: The social constructionist dogma exists not because it is true, but because it satisfies the social reinforcement contingencies of a careerist professoriate.

In the next section, I will show how the philosophical errors of radical behaviorism contributed to Skinner's scientific imperialism. With the calm certainty of a religious convert, Skinner unhesitatingly prescribed behavioral remedies for all society's ills.

Ethics

A complete ethical system has two ingredients: some definition of good and bad; some means of discouraging bad behavior and encouraging good. Skinner offered several bases for values, none wholly satisfactory. His methods for promoting good behavior were supposedly based on the science of operant conditioning. I have discussed elsewhere the legitimacy of his extrapolations from the laboratory (Staddon, 2001). The present discussion is restricted to the concept of personal responsibility, which Skinner wrongly believed inimical to the idea of behavioral control, and to his views on values and on the special contribution that radical behaviorism could make to the debate.

Personal Responsibility

Skinner objected to the concept of personal responsibility because he thought it incompatible with the scientific approach to behavior. He cut the Gordian knot of the free-will problem by means of a two-part argument. Almost as an aside, he contrasted the idea that a person's behavior is his own achievement with the idea of determinism. Then he established the fact of determinism:

> In what we may call the prescientific view, a person's behavior is at least to some extent his own achievement... he is to be given credit for his successes and blamed for his failures. In the scientific view... a person's behavior is determined by a genetic endowment traceable to the evolutionary history of the species and by the environmental circumstances to which as an individual he has been exposed. Neither view can be proved, but it is in the nature of scientific inquiry that the evidence should shift in favor of the second. (Skinner, 1971, p. 96)

This passage promotes a false opposition between the process by which a behavior comes about: "In the scientific view... a person's behavior is determined by... the environmental circumstances to which... he has been exposed" and the status of that behavior as responsible or not: "a person's behavior is... his own achievement... he is to be given credit for his successes and blamed for his failures." This opposition is yet another version of the genetic fallacy. It is like the relativists' false opposition between the truth of a belief and the process by which one arrives at the belief. Here also, the two opposed concepts, determinism and autonomy (free will), are not in fact contradictory. Understanding the causal chain that led to an act need not diminish the autonomy of the actor any more than understanding the causes of a belief diminishes its truth. The claim that free will is compatible with causal determinism is known as *compatibilism*, and it is held by many, if not all, philosophers.

Perhaps because Skinner failed to understand the genetic fallacy, he embraced an odd notion of personal responsibility: that autonomous equals uncaused. He attacked a straw autonomous man, who represented his idea of free will:

> Two features of autonomous man are particularly troublesome. In the tradi-
> tional view, a person is free. He is autonomous in the sense that his behavior
> is uncaused. He can therefore be held responsible for what he does and justly
> punished if he offends. That view, together with its associated practices, must
> be re-examined when a scientific analysis reveals unsuspected controlling rela-
> tions between behavior and environment. (Skinner, 1971, p. 17)

Only the individual totally uninfluenced by his environment is totally autonomous, argued Skinner. Because no such individual exists, the idea of
free will must be abandoned. Reflection shows, however, that this idea is
untenable if not absurd: "The last thing anyone would call free are actions
based on random choices, unconnected to preferences and unforeseeable
by the agent himself" Levin (1997, p. 319) wrote, in a thoughtful discussion of this issue. Where did Skinner get the idea that personal freedom is
equivalent to absence of causation? He cited no source in Skinner's (1971)
Beyond Freedom and Dignity and I can find none.[6]

Perhaps Skinner's opposition between freedom and predictability is
persuasive to some because it conflates subject and object. Freedom is an
entirely subjective concept: Men are free if they feel free. If they choose so as
to satisfy their desires, they do not feel—and are not—unfree. Even though
desires themselves are largely outside a person's own control, the way they
attain them, through operant behavior, is not. Predictability, on the other
hand, whether by oneself (predicting one's own behavior) or by others, is
an objective property. It simply has little or no bearing on the feeling of
freedom. The husband whose behavior is completely predictable by his
wife is no less free than the husband whose wife is constantly surprised.
What is more, it could be argued, an individual who cannot predict his
own behavior is likely to feel less free, less autonomous, than someone
who better knows himself. So, if anything, the feeling of freedom is more
likely to coexist with predictability than with caprice.

Assuming that they attach some value to the "feeling of freedom"
good behaviorists would go on and ask, "What are the environmental
conditions that cause men to give expression to this feeling: When do men
feel free?" This, of course, is precisely the subject matter of the literatures
of freedom and dignity that Skinner dismisses with faint praise.

Skinner (1971) does not agree: "Some traditional theories could conceivably be said to define freedom as the absence of aversive control, but

---

[6] John Malone (personal communication, 2001) has suggested "Surely [Skinner] meant that
'free' means determined by remote causes. Doesn't free will mean only less influenced by
immediate contingencies and more by remote ones (character, etc)?" Well, maybe, but that
represents a much more complex position that would probably undercut the argument
Skinner wanted to make. And it isn't what he said.

the emphasis has been on how that condition *feels*" (p. 32). Freedom *is* a feeling, of course, and when his guard was down Skinner himself said things like individuals should "enjoy the greatest sense of freedom" and the like. Moreover, aversive control is not always perceived as a limitation on freedom. One learns to skate in part by avoiding painful contact with the ice. This, however, is not usually perceived as a limitation on freedom. Freedom is sometimes the recognition of necessity. The fact is that Skinner has confused determinism, which is an objective property of the observer in relation to what is observed, with freedom, which is a subjective property of the observed.

If not the absence of causation what then is personal responsibility? Why, just sensitivity to reward and punishment, as I have argued elsewhere (Staddon, 1995, 2001). This is a view of responsibility perfectly congenial to behaviorism and indeed one that Skinner himself espoused in other places (cf. Chiesa, this volume; Galuska, this volume).

Values: The Naturalistic Fallacy

Skinner (1971) devoted an entire chapter in *Beyond Freedom and Dignity* to values. He was well aware that people would look to his philosophy for a guide to "the good." He was also aware that values are a no-go area for science. Skinner said:

> Questions of this sort...are said...to involve "value judgments"—to raise questions...not about what man can do but about what he ought to do. It is usually implied that the answers are out of the reach of science....It would be a mistake for the behavioral scientist to agree. (p. 97)

Is he right?

Skinner (1971) offered three definitions for "good." In one place he equated good with positive reinforcement and bad with punishment: "...the only good things are positive reinforcers, and the only bad things are negative reinforcers" (p. 99, p. 102). This point of view was recently defended by Hocutt (2000) who argued that human psychobiology should provide us with an objective way to estimate the value of actions. As it stands, however, it provides no independent guide to "the good" because it does not yet define what is reinforcing. Unfortunately the set of all possible reinforcers, for a pigeon much less a human being, cannot be specified in advance (although Hocutt believed it may be in the future). And, of course, there are many things that are reinforcing to some people that others, and perhaps even the people themselves, would regard as undesirable. The seven deadly sins are all pretty reinforcing, after all and few people would agree with "If it feels good, do it!" as an adequate moral guide.

Skinner (1971) offered a second solution to the values problem: that the words good and bad can be defined in terms of community practice: "Behavior is called good or bad . . . according to the way in which it is usually reinforced by others" (p. 104). This says little more than good acts are what people call good, and bad acts are what they call bad, which is often true, but does not solve the problem, for at least three reasons. First, one culture may reinforce what another punishes, and vice versa. Polygamy is permitted in Saudi Arabia, but not in Connecticut, or even in Utah. Prostitution is legal in The Netherlands, but not in New York; and so on. Second, the kind of character that is honest is not generally admired only when dishonesty would be punished; truthful only when a lie would be detected. Virtue is more than mere prudence. And finally, Skinner's definition of virtue would exclude people like Socrates, Jesus and Mahatma Gandhi, who defied the law and the rules of the dominant class. They were punished for behavior most would call good. Hence good cannot be just behavior that is not punished by society.

Nothing that Skinner said refutes the general philosophical point that even the most careful observation of how people actually behave fails to discover any rule that will permit deducing all and only things that they all call good. The hypothesis that what ought[7] to be can be inferred from what is was termed by G. E. Moore the *naturalistic fallacy*. There is a vast literature on the problem of whether or not values can be derived through reason from facts. With a few exceptions, the philosophical consensus is that the endeavor is, and must be, a failure.

The Evolutionary Escape Hatch

Skinner (1971) offered a third solution to the naturalistic fallacy: "The ultimate sources [of values] are to be found in the evolution of the species and the evolution of the culture" (p. 157). In other words, survival of the culture or the species is offered as a superordinate value from which all others can be deduced. This is the only ultimate value Skinner explicitly defended in his utopian writings. It is hard to quarrel with this position in the abstract. Few would defend a belief or custom that is bound to cause the downfall of the culture that gives rise to it.[8] The problem with survival as a value is that it provides little or no practical guidance in difficult cases. It is precisely as true, and as helpful, as the advice to a young investor "buy

---

[7] Throughout I use the word *ought* in the moral sense—what is right action—not in the practical sense—what ought I to do to attain this or that objective.

[8] Of course, the view that "survival" is *the* primary value is not itself provable. It offers no escape from the naturalistic fallacy.

low, sell high". Well, yes, but... What *is* "low"? What *will* conduce to the survival of the race?

The latter may seem less problematic than the former, but a little thought shows that it is not. For example, cultures addicted to alcohol and tobacco are presumably less fit in the Darwinian sense than cultures not so addicted. This, however, is not at all obvious. There may be hidden benefits to one or the other that cannot now be foreseen. The Puritan consensus used to be that alcohol is an unmitigated evil. The social benefits associated with moderate drinking were assumed to be outweighed by its many other bad effects. Yet alcohol ingestion is a custom common to the majority of cultures and now, it turns, out there may even be health benefits to moderate drinking. So the evolutionary balance sheet on alcohol is not yet closed. "Well," one may respond, "alcohol may be controversial, but smoking is certainly bad." This, however, is not so clear either. Some smokers (by no means all) die from lung cancer and emphysema, usually in unpleasant ways (not that dying is ever a walk in the park). Such deaths are unquestionably bad. Smoking-induced illnesses, however, generally do not kill until their victims reach their fifties and sixties, after their productive life is almost over and before they become a burden to their children and society. It is an evolutionary truism that life history is determined by adaptive considerations. Perhaps a society that encourages smoking, which yields a generally short but productive life, will be more successful in the long run than one that discourages smoking and has to put up with a lot of unproductive old people. Perhaps a callous suggestion, but not one that can be dismissed out of hand.[9]

What about other cherished values that most people accept as obvious, like the principle of equality. Most people in developed countries assume that hierarchy is bad and democracy is good. The most known stable (i.e., evolutionarily successful) societies, however, were not democratic, but hierarchical. The ancient Egyptian culture survived substantially unchanged for thousands of years. The Greeks, the inventors of democracy, survived as a culture only for two centuries, and were defeated by the highly undemocratic Romans, who lasted three or four times as long. The oldest extant democracy is less than 300 years old. In the animal kingdom, the ants and

---

[9] Indeed, because these words were first written, news reports have appeared of a study sponsored by the Philip Morris company for the Czech Republic which shows that in a socialist economy, where the state must pay pension, health-care and housing expenses, a population of smokers will cost less because the reduced pension and housing costs more than compensate for the increased medical costs. The benefit amounts to $1227 per cadaver, says the *New York Times* (*Death Benefit*, July 29, 2001). Whether reduced financial cost corresponds to evolutionary advantage is of course not known. In any event, the study was called "callous" by critics.

bees, with built-in hierarchies, have outlasted countless more egalitarian species. The attempt to base values on evolutionary success soon raises questions about traditional beliefs, albeit in an inconclusive way. (See J. Q. Wilson, 2000, for an accessible account of some of these issues.)

The problem with survival of the culture as a value is that it requires perfect knowledge of the future if it is to be a general guide. Although some customs are maladaptive under all imaginable circumstances, others are more contingent. The problem is that most of the prescriptions of traditional morality fall in the latter class. People simply do not know, belief by belief, custom by custom, whether their culture would be better off in the long run with or without them.

Certainly some cultures will survive longer than others. It seems likely, moreover, that the ones that survive will have many beliefs that were in fact essential to their survival. The importance of at least some of those beliefs, however, could not have been foreseen, even in principle. The idea that all that conduces to the survival of society can be known is a weak version of the idea that human history is inherently predictable. This belief, which was advanced most persuasively by Karl Marx, was termed *historicism* by Karl Popper and was conclusively refuted by him (e.g., Popper, 1950). It is the fatal flaw in Skinner's belief, and E. O. Wilson's (1998) claim, that the fact of evolution allows all morality to be reduced to science. Scientific imperialism is simply false and the argument that demolishes it also provides a rational basis for faith, although not for any faith in particular.

In short, Skinner's approach to the problem of value is fundamentally inconsistent.[10] He vacillated between a "final-cause" evolutionary viewpoint and several versions of proximal causation: values are just reinforcers: and reinforcers just *are*, or they can be derived via conditioned reinforcement from a few primaries, or they are whatever the community decides. Each of these solutions has its difficulties, but no matter: Skinner was not really interested in the problem of values, because he knew what

---

[10] Ayn Rand, the founder of the libertarian philosophy of objectivism, was not herself a subtle philosopher, but was keenly aware of error in others. She took an even harsher view of *Beyond Freedom and Dignity*: "The book itself is like Boris Karloff's embodiment of Frankenstein's monster: a corpse patched with nuts, bolts and screws from the junkyard of philosophy (Pragmatism, Social Darwinism, Positivism, Linguistic Analysis, with some nails by Hume, threads by Russell, and glue by the *New York Post*). The book's voice, like Karloff's, is an emission of inarticulate, moaning growls—directed at a special enemy: 'Autonomous Man'" (From Rand, 1985, Ch. 13, internet version). *Beyond Freedom and Dignity* was equally offensive to left and right on the political spectrum. Leftist Noam Chomsky's (1972) lengthy diatribe, though less well-known than his (1959) denunciation of *Verbal Behavior*, is no less acerbic than Rand's attack from the right wing. It would be a mistake, however, to think that Skinner's ability to offend the extremes either places him in the middle ground—or makes him right.

he believed. For him, the real task was implementation: "To confuse and delay the improvement of cultural practices by quibbling about the word *improve* is itself not a useful practice" (Skinner, 1961/1955, p. 6)

Conclusion

Skinner committed radical behaviorism to an evolutionary epistemology that is in effect a generalized version of Peirce's pragmatism (see Lattal & Laipple, this volume). Skinner extended the "successful working" of pragmatism from the life of the individual to the evolution of the race: Those actions not traceable to personal reinforcement must be instincts traceable to natural selection.

Evolutionary epistemology is not free of unprovable assumptions, however. It cannot provide a comprehensive naturalistic ethics nor can it do without some belief in reality. To seek for laws of nature is to assume, implicitly, that they exist and that they do not change from day to day. Understanding Nature and her laws must necessarily be imperfect, because the process of selection, natural selection or the selective process termed *reinforcement*, is always limited by the range of behavioral or genetic variation: "A scientific law is . . . limited by the repertoires of the scientists involved" (Skinner, 1976, p. 136). Evolutionary epistemology and Skinner both assume that an external world exists. They are no friend to the relativism encouraged by some of Skinner's comments and embraced with enthusiasm by a few adherents of radical behaviorism (see also Marr, this volume).

Skinner made related errors in his approach to the idea of truth and the concept of personal autonomy. His fundamentally pragmatic view was that the truth of an idea is relative to the tests it has undergone. He mistakenly inferred from this that tracing a belief to its reinforcement history drained it of truth value. If a belief, a behavior, is determined, it cannot be true, argued Skinner. Some histories, however, are better than others and some beliefs are therefore truer than others. The fact a belief can be traced to a chain of causes and effects has no necessary bearing on its truth. Much the same is true of the idea of personal autonomy. The fact that behavior is determined has no necessary bearing on feelings of freedom or on one's autonomy. Both of these errors are forms of the genetic fallacy.

Skinner wrongly believed that radical behaviorism provides a way around the naturalistic fallacy. He claimed he could derive what ought to be from what is, ethics from science. He tried three approaches to defining "the good." Good is what people call good; good is what is reinforcing; and good is what conduces to the survival of the culture. There are obvious problems with the first two and the third leads to a conclusion different from Skinner's. He assumed, wrongly, that what is good for the culture can be discovered by the methods of science. Evolution, however, is inherently unpredictable. Some practices whose benefits cannot be proved may nevertheless turn out to be good for the survival of a culture. Others that seem good may turn out to be bad. Consequently the evolutionary argument implies that a successful culture will believe some things that cannot be proved. It also reveals that what those things will be cannot be known in advance.

Acknowledgments

I thank Mark Cleaveland, John Malone and Clive Wynne for comments on an earlier version of the MS. Thanks also to NIMH for research support over many years.

References

Akin, E. (1999). Review of *Belief and Resistance*, by B. Herrnstein Smith *Quarterly Review of Biology, 74*, 61.

Andresen, J. (1991). Skinner and Chomsky 30 years later or: The return of the repressed. *The Behavior Analyst, 14*, 49–60.

Aunger, R. (Ed.) (2001). *Darwinizing culture: The status of memetics as a science*. Oxford, UK: Oxford University Press.

Bauerlein, M. (2001). Social constructionism: Philosophy for the academic workplace. *Partisan Review*, 2 May. http://www.partisanreview.org/archive/2001/2/bauerlein.html

Blackmore, S. (1999). *The meme machine*. Oxford, UK: Oxford University Press.

Chomsky, N. (1959). A review of B. F. Skinner's *Verbal Behavior. Language, 35*, 26–58.

Chomsky, N. (1972). Psychology and ideology. *Cognition, 1*, 11–46.

Campbell, D. T. (1975). On the conflicts between biological and social evolution and between psychology and moral tradition. *American Psychologist, 30*, 1103–1126.

Dawkins, R. (1976). *The selfish gene*. Oxford, UK: Oxford University Press.

Dennett, D. C. (1996). *Darwin's dangerous idea: Evolution and the meanings of life*. New York: Simon & Schuster.

Hayes, L. J. (1993). Reality and truth. In S. C. Hayes, L. J. Hayes, H. W. Reese & T. R. Sarbin (Eds.) *Varieties of scientific contextualism*. Reno, NV: Context Press.

Hocutt, M. (2000). *Grounded ethics: The empirical bases for normative judgments*. New Brunswick, NJ: Transaction Publishers.

Latour, B. (1993). *We have never been modern*. Cambridge, MA: Harvard University Press.

Levin, M. (1997). *Why race matters: Race differences and what they mean*. Westport, CT: Praeger.

Monod, J. (1971). *Chance and Necessity; an essay on the natural philosophy of modern biology*. New York: Knopf.

Popper, K. R. (1950). *The open society and its enemies*. Princeton NJ: Princeton University Press.

Popper, K. R. (1962). *Conjectures and refutations: The growth of scientific knowledge*. New York: Basic Books.

Rand, A. (1985). *Philosophy: Who needs it?* New York: New American Library.

Shimp, C. P. (2001). Behavior as a social construction. *Behavioural Processes, 54,* 11–32.

Skinner, B. F. (1953). *Science and human behavior.* New York: Macmillan.

Skinner, B. F. (1961). Freedom and the control of men. In *Cumulative record,* pp. 3–18. (Original work published 1955)

Skinner, B. F. (1966). The phylogeny and ontogeny of behavior. *Science, 153,* 1205–1213.

Skinner, B. F. (1971). *Beyond Freedom and Dignity.* New York: Knopf.

Skinner, B. F. (1976). *About behaviorism.* New York: Vintage Books.

Skinner, B. F. (1981). Selection by consequences. *Science, 213,* 501–504.

Smith, B. H. (1997). *Belief and resistance; Dynamics of contemporary intellectual controversy.* Cambridge, MA: Harvard University Press.

Sokal, A. D. (1996). Transgressing the boundaries: Towards a transformative hermeneutics of quantum gravity. *Social Text, 46/47,* 217–252 (spring/summer). See also http://www.physics.nyu.edu/faculty/sokal/lingua_franca_v4/lingua_franca_v4.html.

Staddon, J. (1995). On responsibility and punishment. *The Atlantic Monthly,* Feb., 88–94.

Staddon, J. E. R., & Simmelhag, V. (1971). The "superstition" experiment: A reexamination of its implications for the principles of adaptive behavior. *Psychological Review, 78,* 3–43.

Staddon, J. E. R. (2001). *The new behaviorism: Mind, mechanism and society.* Philadelphia, PA: Psychology Press.

Wilson, E. O. (1998). *Consilience: The unity of knowledge.* New York: Alfred Knopf.

Wilson, J. Q. (2000). Democracy for all? *Commentary,* March (Internet edition).

Zuriff, G. (1998). Against metaphysical social constructionism in psychology. *Behavior & Philosophy, 26,* 5–28.

8

Concepts and Theories
RELATION TO SCIENTIFIC CATEGORIES

Emilio Ribes-Iñesta

The nature of scientific theory has been an exclusive domain of philosophy. Nevertheless, scientific concepts and theories may be conceived as conventional stimulus objects or entities with which individual scientists constantly interact. In the case of psychology, it seems especially necessary to examine the assumptions and characteristics of theories and concepts, because, as Wittgenstein (1953) pointed out:

> The confusion and barrenness of psychology is not to be explained by calling it a "young science"; its state is not comparable with that of physics, for instance, in its beginnings. (Rather with that of certain branches of mathematics. Set theory.) For in psychology there are experimental methods and *conceptual confusion*. (As in the other case conceptual confusion and methods of proof.) (p. 232)

In agreement with Wittgenstein, I think that psychologists have paid little attention to the nature of the concepts they use, to the assumptions that underlie their theories, and the ways such concepts are applied in the study of behavior. Conceptual analysis of the language used in behavior theories should be, at least, of equal concern to the empirical analysis of behavior and to experimental and quantitative methods and procedures.

I will discuss how a behavioral model of scientific theories may deal with concepts (Ribes, 1993, 1994a; Ribes, Moreno, & Padilla, 1996), but first

Emilio Ribes-Iñesta • University of Guadalajara, Centro de Estudios e Investigaciones en Comportaminto, Zapopan, Mexico 45030.

I will address some of the functional properties of concepts and theories. This discussion is based on the contributions of the English philosopher Gilbert Ryle to the analysis of language, scientific theories and statements, and the nature of psychological concepts.

Scientific language, although based on the practices of ordinary language, is mainly denotative and descriptive. Consequently, scientific theories are special systems for building technical uses for words and expressions denotating and describing the conceptual objects and properties under analysis. The construction of a theory not only involves the identification of empirical referents, but also the definition of how words are used in relation to the properties and features of those referents to yield concepts. To do so, the function of concepts and expressions in scientific language is acknowledged in terms of the logical role they play regarding phenomena and events being refered to, described by, or defined by a theory. These logical boundaries delimiting the use or function of words as concepts are called 'categories'. Every scientific theory, explicity or implicitly, embraces categories that fulfill its goals in classifying, explaining, predicting, defining, representing, and so on. The functions of concepts and expressions are determined by the categories delineated by a theory.

On Words, Concepts and Statements

Definitions

I will base my analysis of concepts upon what has been labeled "the philosophy of ordinary language." Ryle (1964) observed that the philosophical analysis of ordinary language is

> interested in the informal logic of the employment of expressions, the nature of the logical howlers that people do or might commit if they strung their words together in certain ways, or, more positively, in the logical force that expressions have as components of theories and as pivots of concrete arguments. That is why, in our discussions, we argue *with* expressions and *about* expressions in one and the same breath. (p. 40)

As Austin (1961) put it, "... ordinary language is *not* the last word: in principle it can everywhere be supplemented and improved upon and superseded. Only remember, it *is* the *first* word" (p. 185).

Concepts are identified by words, but are not identical to words. Concepts have to do with the functions of words, that is, the context of *use* or application of words (and terms) for all those who share the same linguistic *usages*. A *usage* is a custom, fashion, or vogue, while *use* involves the techniques of doing something. A usage always presupposes a use. Words have many meanings and the meaning of any particular word depends on the expressions, that is, the context in which it is included. Otherwise, words have only potential meanings, most of which are usually listed in dictionaries. When words are used in expressions, they can be appropiate or inappropiate. Therefore, expressions, as a result of the words included, may be properly used or misused.

When concepts are analyzed, an inquiry is made about the use of words as part of expressions. Ryle (1964) commented that in the investigation of the meaning of a word "the inquiry is an inquiry not into the other features or properties of the word [. . .], but only into what is done with it or with anything else with which we do the same thing" (p. 28). Traditionally, the verb 'to mean' stood for a relation between an idea or expression and some other entity. The meaning of an idea or expression was taken to be an entity that had that expression for its name. Nevertheless, when dealing with the use of words and expressions, psychologists are not dealing with the concepts or ideas corresponding to such words or expressions. They are dealing with procedures and techniques for handling and employing words as expressions.

Concepts imply that one has to learn to use expressions and words, and that this learning involves doing certain things with them, but not other things, as well as when to do those things and when not to. So to speak, using words as concepts not only implies learning to manage and to employ words and expressions, but also learning to not mismanage and misemploy them. Among the things that are learned are what, according to Ryle (1964), are vaguely called "rules of logic." From this perpective, concepts cannot be absurd or meaningless, but they can be misemployed when a certain expression is used absurdly. To manage and to employ words and expressions as concepts implies knowing how to operate, that is, knowing the ways or techniques of saying things properly. Mathematical concepts and expressions, for example, are a mixture of ordinary words and special symbols that are used as generalized abbreviations of technical descriptions of properties and relations. These properties and relations may be applied to empirical phenomena (ultimately denotated by natural language concepts and expressions) or to symbolic objects as numbers and geometric dimensions, among other things.

When words and expressions are appropriately used as concepts, one might say that they are employed in correspondence to the logical categories to which they pertain. Words and expressions can function as different concepts to the extent that they can correspond to different categories.

Categories can be thought of as the criteria describing the uses and misuses of words and expressions in relation to certain contexts of application. Because of this, certain categories may or not be included in a particular theory, depending on the kind of concepts the theory uses in reference to an empirical or symbolic domain. Once included, categories determine the functions and scope of a given theory. A concept is properly used when it corresponds to the use criteria related to a significance boundary line.

On Category Mistakes

A concept used as belonging to a different category, following Ryle (1949), constitutes a "category mistake." A category mistake occurs when words, functioning as concepts, represent facts of a certain kind as if they belonged to one logical category (or range of categories), when they actually belong to another. An example of a category mistake would be to consider that the expression "Let's cheer for general satisfaction" is of the same type that "Let's cheer for General De Gaulle." Ryle (1962) described category mistakes as litigations rather than competitions between lines of thought:

> Sometimes thinkers are at loggerheads with one another, not because their propositions do conflict, but because ... the two sides are, at certain points, hinging their arguments upon concepts of different categories, though they suppose themselves to be hinging them upon different concepts of the same category, and viceversa. (p. 11)

Two kinds of category mistakes may occur. In one, concepts belonging to different categories are used as equivalent. This kind of category mistake is usual when nouns are confounded with entities ("table" as contrasted to "pain") and verbs are confused with actions ("to run" as contrasted to "to think"). Many verbs denote actions that may be identified as specific movements and their effects, e.g., eating, walking, talking, cleaning, brushing, etc. Nevertheless, other verbs, although they may imply actions, do not denote actions as such. These verbs, instead, denote functions, outcomes, or circumstances of actions, e.g., perceiving, relaxing, observing, escaping, or avoiding. Verbs always involve actions, but they do not necessarily describe actions. Verbs denote actions only when they refer to *ostensible* and *specific* kinds of behavior or movement.

Psychology is replete with examples of this kind of mistake, in which it is assumed that the application of a verb corresponds to a specific, identifiable kind of action. There are many verbs that in ordinary expressions entail activities, but do not describe particular kinds of actions and that psychologists use as if such verbs actually describe special actions. *To think* illustrates this kind of mistake. Although the verb *to think* implies that one speaks, reads, writes and other things, none of these actions by themselves are *thinking*. *Thinking* involves doing and saying things, but *thinking* is not identical with any of such actions (Ribes, 1992). Some psychologists assume that, because *thinking* is not separately observable from those actions during which the words are applied, *thinking* must be a kind of hidden, unseen additional parallel activity determining the doing and saying being observed. As a consequence of this kind of mistake, special theories are formulated to account for the characteristics, locus and workings of such unseen actions.

The second type of category mistake occurs when concepts belonging to a category are used as if they belonged to a different category. An example of this kind of category mistake is reification: replacing a subject matter by its metaphor (Turbayne, 1962). An example of reification is when the universe and living bodies are identified with a machine. Psychology is replete with such reifications. Modern cognitive psychology, for example, has used the computer model of information processing as an analogue for human behavior in dealing generally with learning and knowledge. Instead of studying actual behavior, however, most cognitivists become concerned with the workings of the complex computer-like mechanisms presumably responsible for the individual's performance when solving problems. The metaphor has become the subject matter and actual behavior is neglected.

Theories and Technical Language

The word 'theory' has different meanings. Scientific theories may include assumptions, postulates, definitions, explanations, and many other conceptual ingredients. It is important to distinguish between constructing a theory and applying a theory. Theorizing may be understood in either of these two senses. The routine operation of activities considered by a theory does not qualify as theorizing. Ryle (1949) compared building a theory with traveling and having a theory with being at one's destination. In the case of building theories, theories are the final product or outcome of a number of operations largely unknown, that are not necessarily mirrored by the formal or discursive presentation of the theory. In the case of applying theories, the theories direct the activities and discourse in the inquiry about something.

Scientific theories, in contrast to ordinary language, involve the use of technical terms. Nontechnical terms in ordinary language have multiple meanings. Technical terms, on the other hand, are usually employed as words with unequivocal meanings. Technical terms are coined in different ways. They may consist of words specially created to designate an object, phenomenon, or operation (e.g., the name of a chemical element). Technical terms also may make metaphorical use of ordinary words or of other semitechnical or technical terms (e.g., the concept of reinforcement suggesting the strengthening of an entity). In still other instances, technical terms may be words from ordinary language that are constrained in their use through special definitions (e.g., concepts such as speed, distance, etc.). In any case, technical terms are often considered to be more precise and hard-meaning than nontechnical terms typical of ordinary language.

Nevertheless, general and scientific technical terms do not differ in their functions from nontechnical terms. Technical terms do not have any essential or necessary meaning in relation to things or ideas. As noted already, the meaning of words as concepts is not fixed, but also depends on the criteria that regulate their employment or application. The difference between technical and nontechnical terms are the criteria that regulate their use. Ryle (1962) stated that:

> We have no such manuals in which to look up the codes which fix the roles of the concepts of a science, or the concepts of untechnical life. We have to read the unwritten codes of their conduct out of their conduct and we have no works of reference to tell us whether we have misread . . . The special terms of a science are more or less heavy with the burthen of the theory of that science. The technical terms of genetics are theory-laden, laden, that is, not just with theoretical luggage of some sort or other, but with the luggage of genetic theory. Their meanings change with changes in the theory. Knowing their meanings requires some grasp of the theory. (p. 90)

Some Category Mistakes in Behavior Analysis

Having developed the way that I use the words "concept," "categories," and "theories", I shall examine two kinds of misuses of concepts, that is, category mistakes, that are frequent in behavior analysis. I shall illustrate both kinds of misuses examining the concept of *reinforcement* as it is used in operant theory. One category mistake is that reinforcement is used differently from the rules that prescribe its use. This is a definitional category mistake. Here, reinforcement as a concept is identified only with one of the components of the definition, either the presentation of a consequence, or the occurrence of a high frequency of responding. A second category mistake is that in which the concept of reinforcement is used as if it had different logical functions in the theory. In this mistake, reinforcement is used as a causal concept when, in fact, the definition and application of the concept corresponds to a dispositional category.

Technical Definitions of Reinforcement

The term reinforcement was coined by Pavlov (1927), who assumed that contiguity between a so-called "neutral" stimulus and a "natural" stimulus strengthened the temporal association between the stimuli and particular activities. Skinner adopted the term and used it to describe the strengthening of an operant class, as measured by an increase in the rate of responding. Reinforcement was used as a metaphor suggesting a parame-chanical effect of a stimulus following a response on the capacity of future emission of that response (Skinner, 1938). When the reflex reserve concept was abandoned, the strength of an operant class was directly equated with its rate of response and not with the rate of the consequence (Ferster & Skinner, 1957).

Two procedural operations (not categories) anchored the meaning and, hence, the conceptual use of the term reinforcement. One of these operations was manipulative: the scheduling or occurrence of a stimulus (the reinforcer). The other was one of measurement: recording and counting the occurrence of a specified response in time. The first was the presentation or occurrence of a stimulus following a particular response. The second was an increase in the frequency of that particular response in the time interval between the presentation of two reinforcing stimuli (so called if the response increment occurred). Reinforcement (and the ancillary terms "reinforcing" and "reinforcer") was to be applied when a predetermined response increased in frequency after being followed by a consequent stimulus according to a rule of delivery, labeled a reinforcement schedule (Ferster & Skinner, 1957).

The definition of reinforcement established which responses could be classified as instances of an operant and which stimuli could be classified as reinforcers. If a particular response increased in frequency after a given stimulus followed it, then the response could be considered as a member of an operant class and the stimulus that followed the response could be identified as a reinforcer. If the response increased in frequency without any identifiable consequent stimulus, or if the consequent stimulus did not increase response frequency, then the concept of reinforcement was disallowed.

Violations of the Definition of Reinforcement

The concept of reinforcement, however, also has been applied when the conditions that prescribe its use are not satisfied or are different from those initially prescribing its application. The concept of reinforcement has been used to describe response effects other than increases in the rate of responding, and in reference to situations in which high response rates are observed, but no consequent stimulus is identified. The former misuse consists of applying the concept of reinforcement only in terms of the presentation of a stimulus following the selected response, while the second misuse consists of using the concept when a high rate (or duration) of response is observed without any identifiable stimulus being presented. In both cases, the concept, which defines a relation, is incorrectly used by reducing the relation to only one of its members, either the stimulus presentation or the behavioral effect.

Examples of the first type of misuse are the decrease observed in wheel running compared to baseline when the behavior was reinforced under a fixed-interval schedule (Skinner & Morse, 1958), the nonoccurrence of a predetermined response, such as lever-pressing, when differential reinforcement of low rates is scheduled (Wilson & Keller, 1953), the occurrence of a relatively stereotyped pattern of responding in each interreinforcement interval when the stimulus is provided independently of responding (Skinner, 1948), and the occurrence of single responses fulfilling accuracy requirements, as in matching-to-sample situations in humans, and verbal behavior in general (Goldiamond, 1966; Skinner, 1957).

Examples of the second kind of mis-application are the occurrence of high-rate behavior (Premack, Schaeffer, & Hundt, 1964) or spatial preferences (Blough, 1971) in the absence of or in opposition to any identifiable consequence. In Premack et al., a high-rate response (running) was identified as a reinforcer in terms of its effects on drinking, when drinking was required to produce access to running. Running is not an stimulus, but in Premack's (1959) analysis, a rate differential between two responses constitutes the sufficient condition for reinforcement. In Blough's study, on the other hand, inaccuracy in discrimination functions was interpreted in terms of the interference of spatial preferences, conceived as a source of competing reinforcement. In similar situations where high rates of responding are observed in the absence of a conspicuous consequence, reinforcement is traced to a hypothetical history (Skinner, 1953).

All these cases are examples of applying the concept of reinforcement under conditions where the criteria defining its use are ignored or even contradicted. Argument is not raised regarding the explanatory power of the concept. The argument is only that these mis-applications lead to category mistakes regarding the role that the concept of reinforcement should play in describing operations and phenomena related to behavior. Although the concept of reinforcement could be changed in such a way to encompass ways of understanding strengthening other than measuring rate or frequency of behavior, this change would require changes in other theoretical concepts, such as the definition of a response, the varied functions of antecedent stimuli, and the relation between frequency and topographical and physical dimensions of behavior. Another possibility, however, is to abandon the concept of reinforcement in the context of a theory that also abandons the notion of strengthening behavior. This possibility requires a theory that is not based on changes in the frequency of repetitive "particles" of behavior (the responses) as its unit of analysis.

Reinforcement as a Dispositional Category

Concepts have different logical functions in a theory, depending on the kind of events they are used to describe. Ryle (1949) distinguished between *dispositional categories* and *occurrence categories*. Concepts and expressions in each of these categories have different logical functions as explanatory and descriptive tools in a theory. Dispositional categories are collections of occurrences, either simultaneous (within a situation) or successive (as trends of events in time). Dispositional categories are related to events and happenings, but not as single, discrete, episodic occurrences. Although occurrence categories are related with statements that describe incidents and happenings,

> ... dispositional statements are neither reports of observed or observable states of affairs, not yet reports of unobserved or unobservable states of affairs. They narrate no incidents. Their jobs, however, are intimately connected with narratives of incidents, for, if they are true, they are satisfied by narrated incidents. (Ryle, 1949, p. 125).

Dispositional categories are related to collections of happenings. Happenings are relevant insofar as they are parts or instances of a collection.

Occurrence and dispositional statements play different theoretical roles in regard to the formulation of laws and explanations. Dispositional statements are statements about individuals having a certain capacity, tendency or propensity, or being subject to a certain liability. Dispositional statements are not laws because they mention particular individuals in particular circumstances. Dispositional statements, however, are law-like by being partly variable and open. They are the kind of statements that precede a law, and they can also be deduced from laws. Nonetheless, dispositional statements are not laws. Dispositional statements are predictive, and law statements are explanatory.

Returning to the issue of reinforcement, the concept of reinforcement seems to fit the kind of statements that describe collections of events without narrating particular incidents. The term reinforcement is used to describe the increased tendency to respond in a certain way after a particular stimulus (normally water or food) has been presented consistently after particular responses have occurred. From this perspective, reinforcement is a dispositional concept. Statements describing reinforcement as an effect, the presentation of reinforcing stimuli, and the reinforcing properties of a given stimulus, cannot be considered law statements. Statements about reinforcement are statements describing generic happenings: the tendency of a collection of responses in time to covary with the repeated presentation of similar stimuli. There are no attempts to explain why such generic happenings may occur.

Reinforcement is considered the fundamental law or principle accounting for operant behavior. To the extent that the concept of reinforcement describes the joint occurrence of generic happenings, however, responses and reinforcers (or key pecks and feeder openings), the concept seems to belong to a dispositional category. The concept of reinforcement, then, becomes circular and reflexive when it is used as an explanation because it does not justify how, when and why the generic covariation described may take place. The occurrence or nonoccurrence of the covariation of response and stimulus happenings becomes an issue to be identified and accounted for only empirically in every possible case. No laws can be formulated based on the concept of reinforcement because reinforcement principles only state correlations between operations and outcomes.

When the concept of reinforcement is used only to *describe* an operation and its effect on response frequency, the criticism of circularity cannot be applied. When, however, it is used as an explanation, it is circular (components of the definition are mutually replaceable) and reflexive (the explans and the explanandum are the same).

The concept of reinforcement is circular for two reasons. First, because one set of the generic happenings occurs as an artifact of the operations set up by the investigator. For example, the occurrence of food presentations is procedurally interlocked with the occurrence of number and timing of responses such that a predetermined correlation will result. Second, because the concept is applied only if the two generic happenings occur at the same time. That is, reinforcement is said to occur if and only if the increased rate of key pecks and food presentations take place together. The food presentations, then, are said to reinforce responses producing or being correlated with them.

The concept of reinforcement is reflexive because one of the two terms included in the definition, the consequence, becomes independent and self-explanatory of the phenomenon being defined. Schoenfeld (1966) noted this perverse logical relation between the concepts of the operant and reinforcement. The operant is defined as a class of covariations or a covariation of classes of stimuli and responses. The stimuli that define the class or covariation are those that follow the response and increase its future frequency, that is, reinforcing stimuli. Because the strength of the operant as a class is *accounted for* by the action of the reinforcer, however, reinforcement, as a functional relation, only describes the previously defined covariation. The reinforcer is one of the two elements included in the definition of any operant, but at the same time it is assumed to be responsible for the changes in the structure and functional properties of the class of which it is member. The reinforcer is *explanans* and *explanandum*. The logical implications of this analysis for theoretical proposals such as the law of effect and the matching law are obvious.

Categories, Theories and the Function of Concepts

Theories prescribe the roles to be played by concepts. The application of a theory consists of using concepts in accord with the roles given to terms in that theory. When concepts are misused, they lose their meaning, giving rise to three possibilities: 1. Concepts are replaced, creating new roles for terms previously not prescribed by the theory. 2. Theoretical arguments and premises are modified to provide logical support for the new conceptual uses of the same terms. 3. The theoretical statements involving such misuses become meaningless. When the uses of concepts change, the theory in which they are used changes in one way or another by changing the concepts or the rules prescribing the roles to be played by these concepts. Otherwise, the theory itself becomes contradictory or ambiguous and, therefore, useless.

The roles played by concepts in a theory depend on the category to which they belong. Categories delineate the functions of concepts. In this sense, categories constitute the logical domain or geography in which a concept can be applied or used. In ordinary language the logical nature of categories varies with the circumstances and social criteria in which words and expressions are used. In scientific language, the logical nature of categories depends on the domain for which a theory was constructed, and to which the theory is applied. There are no universal functions of scientific concepts, nor general categories setting up the logical boundaries for using particular types of concepts. Theoretical categories, like concept meanings, are heterogeneous and their characteristics depend on the particular science they serve and the way that science conceives its subject matter.

The specificity and heterogeneity of categories lead me to propose a classification of categories that is relevant only to psychology, and, even more, only to those theoretical approaches within psychology based on experimental methods as the fundamental validity criteria. Therefore, even when this classification might be employed to examine the functional structure of theories in any empirical science, I prefer to be cautious and to restrict its scope to only the above-specified kinds of theorizing in psychology.

My view is that theoretical categories consist of samples or types of "acting collective language" (Bentley, 1935). The various theoretical categories are related to the things and events that constitute the empirical content to be studied, to those members of the same specialized linguistic (scientific) community, and to the individual scientist interacting with her subject matter and her linguistic community.

Categories shape the diversity of functional contents of a scientific theory, and they constitute the logical geography of the theory. A logical geography represents the boundaries of possible practices of a discipline. Each type of category represents a specific and distinctive content, for which they rule the functional roles of linguistic applications of a theory to different boundary lines. Four types of categories may be identified: taxonomic, operational, measurement, and representational. Figure 1 describes these categories in a particular theory, as exemplified by various types of behavior or learning theory. The arrows suggest the tentative formal interactions between categories.

This figure depicts the formal relations between the different types of categories within the theory. Scientists manipulate the events and objects abstracted by concepts related to facts and processes, and they receive in return the effect of these manipulations in the form of data and evidence, that in turn feed the theory as it is formally communicated to other peers in the community. Taxonomic categories rule the criteria for concepts concerned with the facts that constitute the subject matter of the theory. These facts are the theoretical representations of events, things and actions in ordinary language. Hanson (1971, 1977) asserted that *facts* are those three-dimensional, objective conditions that a subject matter must satisfy to qualify as intelligible and treatable through the lenses of a particular theory. According to this view, "... facts emerge as the possibilities that the world has to *be* described in an available language, possibilities that will be everywhere so theory laden as descriptions themselves have revealed to be" (Hanson,

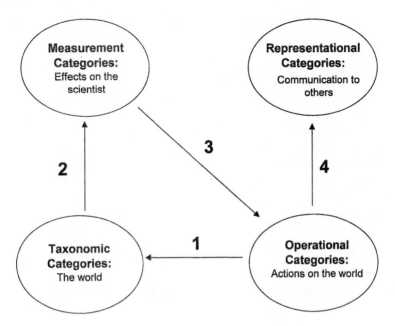

Figure 1.

1971, p. 20). Facts are abstractions from events and things, according to the criteria of a given theory. The facts of a theory and the things and happenings of ordinary language are concepts belonging to different categories. Concepts about facts are not technical translations of concepts about ordinary happenings and things. Taxonomic categories consider and classify the facts *of the theory*, by pointing to the properties that *relevant* events must satisfy. Taxonomic categories are built and used to interact with the subject matter of interest and its content in the form of events, actions, effects, processes, and so on. Processes, due to their descriptive inclusiveness, constitute the kind of concepts employed as explanatory devices and are the basic ingredients of law statements. Taxonomic categories represent the world to be studied by the scientist.

Operational categories are those practices involved in the scientist's actions when observing, recording, and manipulating events that constitute the world under study. Operational categories partially correspond to what has been generically labeled "the scientific method." Operational categories involve all those concepts dealing with the actions of inquiry on the events of "reality." These actions include activities concerned with the production and recording of *facts*. Facts are the direct outcome of experimentation, recording, and observation of certain properties of objects and events. Concepts describing operations, in this context, are directed towards the facts considered by the theory. The validity of operational categories depends on the outcomes (facts) obtained from their application. Although theoretically ruled operations usually produce the facts required by the theory, unexpected facts may arise. Operational categories, from this perspective, may work as sources of theoretical change. Although entailing the development and application of procedures, operational categories are not identical to those procedures. Operational categories consist of the criteria and rules to formulate concepts that give support to the search and application of meaningful operations as procedures. Operational categories, at the same time, specify the boundaries of replicability of the scientist's actions regarding the production of facts and their communication to the members of the same linguistic community.

Measurement categories are concerned with the "return" action of scientists' operations on objects and events. Measurement categories "visualize" how the return actions of reality to operations affect the scientist's behavior. This feature of measurement categories emphazises that identifying and interpreting changes in reality is a two-way process, an interaction between the scientist's operations and the reciprocal actions of reality on the assumptions and statements of the scientist about its properties and workings. There is a close interaction between the way a scientist measures facts and relations between facts and the theories about measuring and its techniques. Measuring, as a conceptual enterprise, is not merely "printing" facts and their properties on a record, nor a disturbing intrusion on the "natural" existence of facts and their relations. Measurement categories do not deal with the procedures of recording, but rather with their outcomes in the form of *data*. Data are the result of a conceptual selection of properties and relations about facts. Data are the aspects of facts that are relevant to the theory, and are the *evidence* that support the theory.

Representational categories are concerned with the conceptual presentation and the social communication of the theory and the data generated in its support. An example of a representational category is the concept of "strength," and the mechanical metaphor associated with such terms as reinforcement, chaining and so on. Representational categories do not overlap with the other types of categories. In fact, representational categories consist of conceptual relations that are different from those concepts rooted in the observational properties of facts and data. Representational concepts and descriptions of phenomena are, and have to be, different. Representational categories are the basis for scientific communication and for teaching science. Normal science, as described by Kuhn (1970) rests on representational categories. These categories are related to what Fleck (1986) called the "thinking collective." Representations are social institutions (interindividual practices) that function as allegories, presenting and explaining empirical fields in the form of a well-structured and justified fiction. Representations are not the phenomena, but they provide a collective understanding and description of the phenomena. Representational categories are not necessarily bound to a particular field of empirical phenomena or to a particular theory. Representations provide visual substance to the contents and internal logics of a variety of particular theories. Models, as metaphors, have been the representational category *par excellence*. Nevertheless, as Turbayne (1962) convincingly demonstrated in the case of Cartesian and Newtonian mechanics, representational categories may entail a risk: that the empirical content of a theory gets replaced by its allegory. This is a most dangerous instance of category mistake: that of replacing the person by the mask.

Conclusions

It is possible to conduct a functional analysis of theories by weighting the roles that each kind of category play in the conceptual structure and functions of a particular theory. Each of the categories that has been examined (taxonomic, operational, measurement, and representational) plays a specific role in any given scientific theory and, to that extent, its logical properties have to fit in the particular kind of interactions involved in the relation between the scientist, the world, and the professional community. A well-structured theory is one that is balanced among the four types of categories, and in which none assumes the role corresponding to another of the categories. An unbalanced theory is in danger of reducing the different categorical functions (descriptive, heuristic, explanatory, manipulatory, communicative) down to that exclusive of the dominant category. Representational dominance in psychoanalytic theory, and operational dominance in operant theory, are examples of categorial imbalance in psychological theories.

Ribes, Moreno, and Padilla (1996) proposed a tentative set of interactions among the four types of categories in psychological theories, as a result of actual practices. We suggested that representational categories are not *directly* affected by the other categories, but do affect taxonomic and measurement categories. Other interactions assume the influence of taxonomic on measurement categories, and reciprocal influences between operational and taxonomic categories and between measurement and operational categories. This functional architecture suggests why a fundamental set of taxonomic, operational, and measurement categories like those of operant theory may share different, and even incompatible, representational categories, but at the same time these latter categories may facilitate the emergence of specific taxonomic and measurement categories. The relative independence of representational categories also would help in understanding what has been called "resistance to scientific change," because theoretical models seem to be relatively autonomous and "immune," in some sense, to the interactions among taxonomic, operational, and measurement categories. The changes in definitions, procedural and recording methods, and the evidence criteria for data do not necessarily modify the models and assumptions on which the original categories were based.

In the case of behavioral science, operant theory exemplifies an unbalanced theory, because it is dominated by operational categories over the other types of categories, and also supplants logical criteria corresponding to taxonomic and measurement criteria to those of operational categories. The reasons for this distorted formulation and evolution of the theory are multiple and varied, and I have discussed some of them (Ribes, 1994b; 1999). I agree with Smith (1992) who suggests that, from its outset, operant psychology was infused with a technological orientation. This technological orientation assumed, among other things, that scientific inquiry could discover the laws in nature through obtaining orderly data (according to Cartesian and Newtonian criteria). The replicability of data was the fundamental criterion of validity. Concepts should be constructed as descriptions of the operations used to produce and measure such ordered and reliable data. The imbalance of the theory towards operational categories is shown by the fact that taxonomic categories are simply operational categories describing different observational criteria to classify behavioral phenomena. The distinctions between emitted and elicited behavior (i.e., operant vs.respondent), between private and public behavior, and between rule-governed and contingency-shaped behavior, are all based on criteria describing the operational restrictions in observing behavior. Because of this, the three taxonomic distinctions are questionable and logically weak. In the absence of robust taxonomic categories, operant theory has been supplemented by a diversity of representational categories that, contrary to the metaphoric nature of allegories and models, do not transfer similarities from one concept to another. Current representational categories seem to identify behavioral phenomena with the models and allegories built for phenomena in other sciences. Unfortunately, today, behavior has become the subject matter of ecological, econometric, evolutionary, mechanistic and equivalence logics models. Behavior is studied to explore its fit to the properties and functions of phenomena studied by other disciplines. Because of the technological emphasis on control and replicability, behavior, paradoxically, has been theoretically lost.

References

Austin, J. L. (1961). *Philosophical papers*. Oxford: Oxford University Press.
Bentley, A. F. (1935). *Behavior, knowledge, fact*. Bloomington, IN : Principia Press.
Blough, P. (1971). The visual acuity of the pigeon for distant targets. *Journal of the Experimental Analysis of Behavior, 15,* 57–67.
Ferster, C. B. & Skinner, B. F. (1957). *Schedules of reinforcement*. New York: Appleton Century Crofts.
Fleck, L. (1986). *La génesis y el desarrollo de un hecho científico*. Madrid: Alianza Universidad.
Goldiamond, I. (1966). Perception, language and conceptualization rules. In B. Kleinmuntz (Ed.), *Problem solving: Research, method and theory* (pp. 183–224). New York: J. Wiley.
Hanson, N. R. (1971). *Observation and explanation: A guide to philosophy of science*. New York: Harper & Row Publishers. (Spanish translation, 1977: *Patrones de descubrimiento*. Observación y explicación. Madrid: Alianza Universidad).
Kuhn. T. S. (1970). *The structure of scientific revolutions*. Chicago: The University of Chicago Press.
Pavlov, I. P. (1927, English translation). *Conditioned reflexes*. Oxford: Oxford University Press.
Premack, D. (1959). Toward empirical behavior laws. I. Positive reinforcement. *Psychological Review, 66,* 219–233.
Premack, D., Schaeffer, R. W., & Hundt, A. (1964). Reinforcement of drinking by running: Effect of fixed ratio and reinforcement time. *Journal of the Experimental Analysis of Behavior, 7,* 91–96.
Ribes, E. (1992). Some thoughts on thinking and its motivation. In S. C. Hayes & L. J. Hayes (Eds.), *Understanding verbal relations* (pp. 211–224). Reno: Context Press.
Ribes, E. (1993). La práctica de la investigación científica y la noción de juego de lenguaje. *Acta Comportamentalia, 1,* 63–82.
Ribes, E. (1994a). The behavioral dimensions of scientific work. *Mexican Journal of Behavior Analysis, 20,* 169–194.
Ribes, E. (1994b). Skinner y la psicología: Lo que hizo, lo que no hizo y lo que nos corresponde hacer. In E. Ribes (Ed.), *B. F. Skinner: In memoriam* (pp. 139–174). Guadalajara: Universidad de Guadalajara.
Ribes, E. (1999). *Teoría del condicionamiento y lenguaje: Un análisis histórico y conceptual*. México: Taurus.
Ribes, E., Moreno, R., & Padilla, A. (1996). Un análisis funcional de la práctica científica: extensiones de un modelo psicológico. *Acta Comportamentalia, 4,* 205–235.
Ryle, G. (1949). *The concept of mind*. New York: Barnes & Noble.
Ryle, G. (1962). *Dilemmas*. Cambridge: Cambridge University Press.
Ryle, G. (1964). Ordinary language. In V. C. Chappell (Ed.), *Ordinary language*. New York: Dover.
Schoenfeld, W. N. (1966). Some old work for modern conditioning theory. *Conditional Reflex, 1,* 219–233.
Skinner, B. F. (1938). *The behavior of organisms*. New York: Appleton Century Crofts.
Skinner, B. F. (1948). 'Superstition' in the pigeon. *Journal of Experimental Psychology, 38,* 168–172.

Skinner, B. F. (1953). *Science and human behavior*. New York: MacMillan.

Skinner, B. F. (1957). *Verbal behavior*. New York: Appleton Century Crofts.

Skinner, B. F. & Morse, W. H. (1958). Fixed-interval reinforcement of running in a wheel. *Journal of the Experimental Analysis of Behavior, 1,* 371–379.

Smith, L. (1992). On prediction and control. B. F. Skinner and the technological ideal of science. *American Psychologist, 47,* 216–223.

Turbayne, C. M. (1962). *The myth of metaphor*. New Haven: Yale University Press.

Wilson, M. P. & Keller, F. S. (1953). On the selective reinforcement of spaced responses. *Journal of Comparative and Physiological Psychology, 46,* 190–193.

Wittgenstein, L. (1953). *Philosophical investigations*. Oxford: Basil & Blackwell.

II

Interpretations

9

Cognition

David C. Palmer

The behavioral approach to cognition is a kind of atomic theory. Phenomena commonly called "cognitive," such as recall, problem solving, composition, planning, and imagining, are typically complex behavioral events that are compounds of elementary or atomic operants. For example, a long division problem can be solved by a series of one-digit multiplication and subtraction calculations along with various ordering operations. The compound usually serves some adaptive purpose, and over repeated instances can itself emerge as a kind of behavioral molecule—the solution to a brain teaser can be dashed off after it has been worked out a few times—but more commonly such compounds are unique; they are seldom repeated exactly when people solve problems, recall an episode, or plan their day. In any case, it is the first instance of a phenomenon that poses a special challenge to science. From a behavioral perspective, such phenomena are best analyzed at the level of the elementary operant, appealing only to principles of behavior that have emerged from experimental science. The behaviorist's task is to show how such behavioral atoms can combine to produce complex human behavior. Although some examples, such as solving long division problems, may be formulaic, others, such as recalling what one ate for dinner Sunday night, are not. The challenge is formidable. The experimental analysis of even a single operant requires considerable effort, and the study of the relations between two competing operants has kept researchers busy for decades. How much more difficult must be the study of unique mosaics of many operants!

David C. Palmer • Department of Psychology, Smith College, Northampton, MA 01063.

Nevertheless, the topic is essential to an understanding of human behavior, and however incomplete the account, behavior analysis must advance its case, for alternative approaches are influential. In this essay, my goal is to clarify the conceptual foundation of the behavioral approach to cognition, not to attempt to summarize that approach or to review the literature. I begin by identifying a fundamental assumption that distinguishes the behavioral approach from competing paradigms. I then submit several examples of human behavior that seem to call for special treatment; at the level of observations, behavior does not seem to be related in an orderly way to environmental antecedents or consequences, but seems to emerge from within the individual. I suggest that this lack of order inevitably arises when there are gaps in the data, and that for cognitive behavior such gaps are common. I then present an example of a behavioral interpretation in which order is restored to the data by referring to plausible unobserved variables that fill in the gaps. Next I discuss the role of such tentative interpretations in science and claim that they are not peripheral , but central to the understanding of nature. I conclude by characterizing a behavioral program for analyzing cognitive phenomena and argue that, in contrast to the fruits of other paradigms, the results of such a program offer a genuine explanation for such phenomena.

The Assumption of Uniformity

Because of the complexity of cognitive phenomena and the difficulty of collecting reliable data, any account of cognition must be tentative and cautious, a circumstance that has encouraged a profusion of competing models and theories. To regard them as equally plausible would lead to paralysis or aimlessness. When I was a boy, I sometimes wondered if there were a black void behind my back. I would try to test this proposal by turning around suddenly, but I was never fast enough; the world would be set perfectly in place just as if it had always been there. I have never been able to refute this curious hypothesis, but of course I never took it seriously. Not only did it require considerable machinery for which I had no evidence, I realized that there were countless alternative hypotheses of equal merit: Perhaps the world behind me was populated by unicorns, griffins, and other fabulous creatures, or by a phalanx of angry elementary school teachers. The conventional assumption that the world behind my back was of the same stuff as the world in front of my eyes was simple, adequate, and required no imaginary stage managers.

The behavioral approach to cognition assumes an analogous kind of uniformity: Behavioral phenomena do not obey one set of principles when they are observed and a second set when they are not. The topic of cognition embraces phenomena that are challenging to study because some of them cannot ordinarily be directly measured or even observed, and it is tempting to populate this hidden domain with conceptual unicorns that have no counterpart among observable phenomena. The behaviorist, however, doggedly assumes that this landscape is composed merely of behavioral phenomena governed by the same principles that govern observable behavior. Thus cognitive phenomena are interpreted as complexes of elementary discriminated operants, some of which may be covert.

This assumption of uniformity sets the behavioral approach apart from all other paradigms in the domain of cognition. Like every assumption in science, it might be wrong, in which case all that follows from it will be of uncertain value. The assumption, however, is both parsimonious and practical: Until it is shown to be inadequate, it forestalls the need to entertain countless alternative mechanisms that one might invent. Moreover, the assumption has exalted precedents. Over 300 years ago Isaac Newton (1687/1952) listed four rules that guided his interpretation of natural phenomena:

1. We are to admit no more causes of natural things than such as are sufficient to explain them.
2. To the same natural effects we must, as far as possible, assign the same causes.
3. The qualities found to belong to all bodies within the compass of our experiments should be assumed to be true of all bodies.
4. In experimental philosophy we are to look upon principles inferred by general induction as accurate or very nearly true, notwithstanding any contrary hypothesis that may be imagined, until such time as evidence accrues from which they may either be made more accurate or liable to exception. (pp. 270–271, passim)

These points are just an elegant expression of the criterion of parsimony and the assumption of uniformity. A glance at the history of science suggests that Newton's rules have been widely honored. An understanding of all nature, from the interactions of subatomic particles to the origin of the universe, rests on the assumption that the principles that emerge in the laboratory can be extended to domains where experimental control is impossible. Geologists, following Charles Lyell, Darwin's mentor, enshrined the assumption in a technical term, *uniformitarianism*, because most understanding of geological phenomena requires it. Inspired by such distinguished examples, one may ask where the assumption leads in the domain of cognitive phenomena.

The Problem

When, in the presence of certain stimuli, a particular behavior is commonly followed by a reinforcer, behavior analysts speak of a three-term contingency. Investigation of the relations among the terms has revealed general principles that form the nucleus of operant theory (but see Ribes, this volume). An analysis of such contingencies facilitates a plausible and straightforward interpretation of much human behavior. When a child responds "144" to the question, "What is 12 times 12?" one naturally infers that the question has been encountered in school and that the appropriate response has been reinforced. There are two reasons why one is unlikely to cavil with this assumption. First, the inferred history is plausible; a parent or teacher may even be able to point to a relevant flash card or worksheet. Second, the performance is analogous to paradigmatic discrimination experiments, such as one in which a pigeon pecks a key under differential control of a green light. A great range of other adaptive human behavior yields to comparable interpretations. Naming objects, identifying faces, navigating through familiar terrain, following a recipe, operating machinery, reciting poetry, swatting pesky insects, and countless other commonplace behaviors can be assumed to have arisen over the course of an appropriate history of exposure to three-term contingencies. Furthermore, one can plausibly assume that programs of gradually changing contingencies have shaped the highly differentiated behavior of the skilled athlete, artist, craftsman, and technician. The three-term contingency is a powerful interpretive tool because such contingencies have been thoroughly analyzed experimentally, they are ubiquitous, and their scope of application is apparently limitless. Moreover, the three-term contingency is a fundamental unit of analysis: Order emerges, even over lapses of space and time, without our invoking mediating events such as physiological processes and anatomical structures.

Not all human behavior, however, is interpreted so simply. Consider the following cases:

1. Appropriate behavior sometimes occurs on occasions in which critical features or relations have never been encountered. For example, it is unlikely that an educated adult has encountered the particular question, "What is 542 plus 20?" yet few would fail to reply, "562." Although such a performance is commonplace, it cannot be

explained by simply pointing to the reinforcement of that response to the question on an earlier occasion. An act of "mental arithmetic" seems to be required.

2. Sometimes only one response is reinforced in a particular setting, but when that setting recurs, an entirely different response is emitted. Suppose, for example, you ask a friend on two consecutive days, "What is today's date?" Even if you were to lavishly reinforce the first response, "June 30th," and took care to hold constant every detail of the immediate setting, along with all relevant motivational variables, it would be surprising if the friend did not emit a different response, "July 1st," on the second day. Must one not appeal to a "mental calendar," rather than a history of reinforcement?

3. Some behavior seems to be under control of future events or hypothetical events that are not represented in the current setting. For example, I might pass up a rich dessert, citing its expected effect on my waistline, or do calisthenics, pointing to its expected effect on my blood pressure. All examples of self-control illustrate the apparent control of behavior by future events. More generally, people resolve all ethical dilemmas apparently by comparing the projected outcomes of our various alternatives (see Chiesa, this volume; Galuska, this volume). How can the future affect present behavior, unless expectations, plans, or intentions are invoked?

4. Some behavior seems to occur in a stream, often hidden from view and seemingly independent of context, a stream that cannot be easily broken into discrete three-term units. People dip into that stream when they ask, "What are you thinking about?" The answers to such questions usually are accepted, although the subject may be suspected of lying. In neither case, however, is there much doubt that there really is such a stream of hidden behavior that is the proper subject of the question.

5. Some behavior seems to be controlled, not by antecedent events, but by stored "memories." When I ask, "What color is Steve's new van?" the answer appears to be a response to a retrieved image, or perhaps has been directly retrieved from some storage vault where information about objects in experience is kept.

6. Verbal behavior is richly structured, but the variables controlling this structure are obscure. I ask, "Where are you going?" but seldom "Where you are going?" One can characterize this structure with grammatical rules that do not apply to nonverbal behavior, and it is tempting to suppose that humans are equipped with a special "faculty" that organizes verbal behavior according to these rules.

These examples are commonplace. They have in common the feature that appropriate behavior seems to come out of nowhere. At least when presented as anecdotes, there is no order or predictability at the level of what can be observed. A common response is to assume that order arises from within the individual and will appear at another level of analysis, the physiological level, or perhaps a hypothetical cognitive level. Cognitive maps, schemas, lexicons, encoding and retrieval mechanisms, intentional fields, storage registers, and other hypothetical constructs are invoked to impose order on the data. Unfortunately each such concept introduces a qualitatively new element that itself requires explanation or justification. That is, each new term must ultimately be paid for in the coin of physical, biological, or behavioral events. Like the improvident debtor who pays off one credit card by drawing down the balance of a second, such devices provide only temporary satisfaction, for the overall explanatory burden has been increased, not reduced.

In contrast, the behaviorist insists that each of the above examples is actually a web of orderly *behavioral* phenomena; the lack of order is an illusion arising from our observing only a portion of the performance. As an analogy, suppose one were to touch up a videotape of a ping-pong match by excising or painting out the ball. The remaining performance— two people waving paddles in the air, apparently without effect—would be baffling to the naive observer, not to say ridiculous. Psychologists are in much the same position when trying to interpret complex behavior when some of it is hidden from view. They see fragments of behavior that occur seemingly independent of controlling variables. The behaviorist asserts that if all behavioral and contextual variables could be evaluated, this illusion would disappear. This claim, however, naturally raises a troublesome question: If relevant variables controlling human behavior are commonly unobserved, is not science helpless? Is there no alternative to invoking hypothetical constructs? To answer this question, I must digress and address what it is that science can offer.

The Two Purposes of Science

Science serves two purposes. First, it underlies human mastery of nature: The experimental analysis of nature leads to the discovery of principles that can be exploited by technology; thus science can take credit for most medical, material, and technical progress, and it promises much more to come. Second, science helps one make sense of the world: It often provides elegant and satisfying explanations for the order observed in natural phenomena. Why are there two tides a day, and not one? Why do all the planets orbit in a common plane? How does a monarch butterfly, with its insignificant brain, navigate from its birthplace in Canada to a tiny wintering colony in Mexico? One may have no interest in controlling tides, planets, or butterflies, but one is fascinated by such puzzles and the answers that science provides. One, would hate to be without the tangible benefits of science—antibiotics, computers, and compact disk players—but one would hate even more to be plunged into the intellectual midnight of the distant past when nature was seen as the slave of goblins and spirits.

The two functions of science require different levels of control. As an analogy, consider a card trick requiring sleight of hand. To perform the trick may require extraordinary finesse and precision, but to understand how it is done requires none. Likewise, the mastery of nature requires precise control of every relevant variable. If a geneticist is cloning a sheep, a few misplaced DNA bases or a few extra hydrogen ions in the soup can spell ruin; if an engineer is manufacturing a microchip, slack of a few microns in the apparatus can make all the difference between success and failure. To resolve a puzzle about a natural phenomenon requires neither control nor precision; scientists only need to discover one path that nature might have taken to produce the phenomenon at hand, and if this account invokes only familiar scientific principles and plausible events, they will be satisfied. Hurricanes, volcanoes, tides, mountain formation, and the genesis of planets do not lend themselves to experimental control, but most people feel satisfied by current scientific interpretations of these things, however tentative and incomplete they might be.

Evolutionary biology supplies many such examples. Natural selection explains an extraordinary range of cunning biological adaptations, and the evolutionary account is so elegant and so general that many people find it deeply satisfying. Interpretation of any particular adaptation, however, is usually based on scanty evidence. The bombardier beetle's noxious emissions may be explained by appealing to millennia of differential predation in which the most unpleasant beetles were avoided in favor of easier prey. The extraordinary camouflage of the walking stick is explained in a similar way: Those individuals most difficult to detect were more likely to pass on their traits than other members of the group. Such accounts are commonly speculative. For supporting evidence, evolutionary biologists seldom have more than scattered fossil remains, some field observations, a few suggestive anatomical details, perhaps some genetic data, in addition to only general information about changes in prevailing contingencies of survival over evolutionary time. In some cases the evolutionary biologist can offer no more than a plausible scenario, with no direct evidence at all. Nevertheless, evolutionary explanations are satisfying, because they show one path that nature might have taken to produce the remarkable interrelation between an organism and its environment, and the explanations appeal only to easily demonstrated contingencies such as variability among offspring and differential reproduction iterated over generations.

It is important to note that any particular evolutionary account might be utterly wrong; most such accounts are fleshed out with plausible inferences, not empirical observations. For the purpose of resolving a puzzle about nature, it does not matter, for what is at stake is not the accuracy of the account , but the adequacy of the analytical tools. As long as the tools are adequate, evolutionary biologists don't much care whether every detail is correct. Perhaps there are three different ways in which a magician might pull a rabbit out of a hat. One only needs to know of one way to be satisfied that the performance is not outside the compass of understanding of how the world works. Similarly, evolutionary interpretations, however tentative, serve to displace appeals to unknown or mysterious forces.

Scientific interpretations from the fields of geology, cosmology, evolutionary biology, and meteorology all share the virtue of displacing occult theories by showing that established scientific principles are sufficient to account for puzzling phenomena. In the face of incomplete data, such accounts are tentative, but the greater part of what passes for scientific understanding of the world is of this tentative sort. Only a handful of natural phenomena has been submitted, or is ever likely to be submitted, to controlled experimentation. Experimental analysis has an exalted status among scientists, and deservedly so, for it underlies the mastery of nature; but perhaps its most important service is that it provides a necessary foundation for effective scientific interpretation. It is not laboratory demonstrations, but interpretations of nature that are all encompassing, or nearly so, and it is they that stir the blood.

Scientists distinguish, then, between the experimental analysis of nature and the interpretation of nature. Experimental analysis underlies human mastery of nature and requires the observation, measurement, and control of all relevant variables. Scientific discovery and understanding of general principles of nature arise entirely from experimental analyses. Interpretation is the extension of these principles to domains where observation and experimental control of all important variables is impossible or impractical , but where incomplete data are available.

Scientific understanding of cognition is of this tentative sort. No one, behaviorist, cognitive scientist, nor neuroscientist, is in a position to offer a definitive account, except in very restricted domains, for such phenomena typically exemplify the interaction of many variables. Some of these variables are unobserved, outcomes may depend upon unknown histories, and attempts to measure relevant variables are likely to distort the behavior under study. Perhaps the best one can do is to lift the shroud of mystery from such phenomena. Our purpose, then, is to offer plausible interpretations of behavior commonly called "cognitive," interpretations that rest only upon principles that have been established independently of the phenomena to be explained.

An Example

Let me offer an example, chosen because everyone is likely to agree on how appropriate behavior actually emerges; it is only superficially puzzling. (For other examples of the present approach, in several cognitive domains, see Donahoe & Palmer, 1994; Palmer, 1991; 1998.) Suppose we ask someone, "What is the tenth letter after F?" Most adults answer this question correctly, after a pause, but it is fair to assume that the question is novel. If we restrict our consideration to just those responses that can be observed, the behavior of announcing the answer is puzzling. The response is adaptive, in the sense that it is scheduled for reinforcement, but it appears to be evoked by variables (the context, the question) that have not been encountered before. We cannot simply point to a history of reinforcement for correct responding to the question, as I can with "What is 12 × 12?" we explain this apparent anomaly by arguing that the subject has engaged covertly in precurrent behavior, that is, some sort of related behavior that potentiates the target response. Specifically, we note that the question is similar enough in both intonation and wording to other questions that the subject has encountered that the mere posing of the question signals a negative reinforcement contingency in which an aversive condition can be escaped only by emitting a particular target response. Unfortunately, the target response, "P," is not the prepotent response under prevailing conditions. We must appeal to a history in which the subject has learned to respond to questions for which no immediate response is strong by emitting collateral behavior that produces supplementary stimuli that, together with contextual variables, are sufficient to occasion the target response. The subject has undoubtedly learned to identify the Nth item in an array by arranging the items in order and counting to N. In the present case, we suspect that the subject has, among other behavior, emitted two intraverbal chains: counting to ten and reciting the alphabet. This precurrent behavior might be conspicuous, but more commonly it is below the threshold of observability to an onlooker. (Indeed, before announcing the answer, most subjects move their ten fingers, one by one, apparently pacing a covert recital of the alphabet past F.) The response "P" must be assumed to be a low-probability response to the question, "What is the tenth letter after F?" but it is a high-probability response to the intraverbal chain, "-L-M-N-O-". Thus the response is surprising in relation to observable variables, but is unremarkable if one considers plausible mediating behavior. Readers who have troubled to answer the question have undoubtedly found themselves doing something of this sort, or something equivalent.

This behavior-analytic account is an example of an interpretation, analogous, for example, to evolutionary accounts of bipedal locomotion in primates. It controls no variables and cites no experimental data. It shows, however, how a superficially puzzling example of behavior can be understood as the product of a plausible history and familiar principles, such as generalization, reinforcement, and chaining. The plausibility of the account, however, rests on an appeal to covert mediating behavior. Can behavior analysts justify resorting to variables that cannot be observed or measured? Is this not cousin to the discredited but popular habit of inventing hypothetical mechanisms to explain behavior? One must make a distinction here between covert behavior and the internal representations and other machinery commonly invoked to explain complex behavior.

The Threshold of Observability

In the laboratory, behavior is defined as any activity of the organism that can be shown to vary in orderly ways with the manipulation of antecedent and consequent events. The orderliness of these relations serves as a criterion for determining the analytical units in a science of behavior (Skinner, 1935; 1938). More generally, then, behavior must be any activity of the organism that *does* change in an orderly way with such variables, whether behavior analysts are in a position to demonstrate that order or not. The status of behavior is independent of the observer: Some behavior is out of reach of experimental manipulations, but it must be assumed that the principles governing the behavior do not change simply because it has moved out of reach.

Whether a particular response can be observed is not a property of the response itself; rather, it depends upon the vantage point, the faculties, and the tools of the observer. A perfunctory "Hello" might be perfectly clear in a quiet room, indistinct in a noisy one, and wholly inaudible across a quadrangle. For the hard of hearing, amplification might be required even under the most favorable conditions. For the stone deaf, the response could be detected only by transducing it instrumentally into another modality such as a flickering light or a speech spectrogram.

The same considerations, suitably modified, apply to the bellowing of a drill sergeant, the whispering of a school child, and the indistinct muttering of a disgruntled employee. Each response will be observable under some conditions and unobservable under others. Some behavior, such as covert speech, is observable only to the subject himself, while other behavior, such as minute muscle twitches and vascular contractions, may be observable, even to the subject himself, only with instrumental transduction. Perhaps some behavior is beyond detection with current tools , but will yield to future technology. The threshold of observability can be defined as that set of conditions under which the response is just detectable. Which side of that boundary the response lies on a particular occasion will determine whether or not it is deemed observable. It is simply a fact that, for a given observer at a given time, some portion of the behavior of a subject lies below this threshold of observability.

Behavior analysts can consider observability to be a continuum, and because the boundary between the overt and covert is an arbitrary and variable point along that continuum, it can be assumed that the laws of observed behavior hold for the unobserved (cf. Skinner, 1953). This is not to deny that different response systems may be subject to different constraints; rather, the claim is that observability itself does not usefully define two different categories of behavior, because it is determined by the vantage point of the observer and is not a property of the behavior itself. It is possible of course that some classes of covert behavior do have special properties—there might indeed be a black void behind my back—but such a claim cannot be put to experimental test, and it has no more status than any other untestable speculation.

Because experimental analysis requires the manipulation of observable variables, speculations about covert behavior play no role in the experimental analysis of behavior. Rather, they serve the second function of science: They help one understand the world. Complex human behavior, particularly phenomena commonly called cognitive—language, memory, planning, problem solving—is one of the most challenging frontiers of science, and the ability to interpret it runs far ahead of the ability to experimentally analyze and control it. The account of the subject reciting letters of the alphabet is just a plausible possibility that is consistent with experience, but of course this does not meet the standards of a controlled experiment. I have shown, however, how adaptive behavior might have arisen by exploiting only terms of a behavioral analysis. No new terms have been invented. To the extent that behavior analysts can point out ways that the known principles of behavior might account for all cognitive phenomena, behavior analysis can offer a parsimonious, consistent, and intellectually satisfying account of human experience.

The Illusory Power of More Permissive Paradigms

To recapitulate, behavior analysis interprets cognition as behavior, as the confluence of observed and unobserved events interacting according to established behavioral principles. This might seem self-evident except that it stands in contrast to a more permissive paradigm. Normative cognitive science also endorses experimental analysis and acknowledges that the principles of behavior play some role in human behavior; however, it appeals as well to other things: (a) hypothetical constructs such as intentions, expectations, beliefs, images, and representations, (b) structures such as memory stores and the lexicon, and (c) control processes such as encoding, storage, retrieval and elaboration.That is to say, it is not constrained by the assumption of uniformity. One might argue that because cognitive science embraces principles of behavior and much else besides, it is a superset of behavior analysis and is necessarily the more powerful paradigm. The force of this conclusion depends entirely on the merits of the additional terms permitted under the cognitive paradigm. Give a man a 5/8-inch socket wrench and ask him to remove the spark plug from his lawnmower. Make the same request of a second man, but give him the key to a warehouse full of tools. Which man will fetch the plug first? Extra tools are a liability if they are not to the purpose. In practice, cognitive scientists have devoted nearly all of their effort to exploiting the additional terms. In all the prodigious literature of cognitive science, the basic principles of behavior are scarcely mentioned at all.

One might argue that an appeal to covert mediating behavior is nothing short of an endorsement, half a century late, of the practices of mainstream cognitive science, that a supposed covert recitation of the alphabet is no more scientifically respectable than an appeal to representations, encoding, storage, retrieval, schemas, intentions, and so on; all are hypothetical intervening variables. To argue so is to miss an important distinction: Covert responses are not representations. The interpretive tools of the behaviorist are constrained by an independent experimental analysis; no explanatory concept can be invoked that has not been analyzed in the laboratory under experimental control, and the terms must interact according to empirical principles. Consequently, such terms are not free to carry whatever burden the example requires. A covert response, for example, must change in strength in orderly ways, it must be plausible with respect to the prevailing contingencies, and there must be a plausible history that would predict such a response. As a unit of behavior, it must have the dimensions of behavior and cannot have special ad hoc properties. Mediating behavior that is not constrained in these ways can carry no explanatory burden at all. It is true that most cognitive metaphors can be interpreted as having some behavioral dimensions; a partial translation is usually possible. It is a hallmark, however, of the cognitive science paradigm that it regards itself as liberated from the methodological and conceptual constraints of behaviorism. From the present perspective, that is an odd quality to celebrate.

A Refinement of Terms

I have argued that the distinction between experimental analysis and interpretation clarifies what science can offer in the domain of cognition. Furthermore, I have claimed that interpretation is not merely a poor cousin to experimental analysis; rather each enterprise contributes crucially to one of two purposes of science, and with respect to understanding cognitive phenomena, interpretation plays a dominant role. If it is to carry a burden this heavy, however, I must be clear about what I mean by interpretation. How does it differ from related terms, such as hypothesis, inference, and speculation? Under what conditions should one engage in interpretation rather than experimental analysis, and what are the risks of doing so?

Skinner (1988) defined interpretation as

> the use of scientific terms and principles in talking about facts about which too little is known to make prediction and control possible ... Plate tectonics is an example. It is not philosophy but an interpretation of the state of the crust of the earth, using physical principles governing the behavior of material under high temperatures and pressures established under the conditions of the laboratory, where prediction and control are possible. (pp. 207–208)

As Skinner's (1988) example makes clear, an interpretation can be considered a kind of hypothesis, in the sense of a provisional explanation of a phenomenon in the light of a scientific theory, but the term hypothesis is more commonly applied in science to a tentative prediction about the effect of some variable than to a plausible explanation of facts at hand (cf. Moore, this volume; Ribes, this volume). Scientific interpretations, however, share an important property with hypotheses: They help guide and organize research.

An inference is a statement about behavior or its controlling variables that follows from or can be derived from a given state of affairs. If I observe a high-school senior correctly determine the difference between two 3-digit numbers without a pencil, with a suitable latency, and with a fixed expression, I infer that he has done the problem "in his head." In some cases, such inferences provide all of the content of the interpretation; in others, they serve only as parts of the interpretation; in still others, they may play no role at all; the latter term is broader than the former. An interpretation is only a possible scenario that might account for a state of affairs, not a necessary one. A particular evolutionary account of a biological adaptation may be just one of several equally plausible alternatives. There may be no reason to prefer one interpretation to another, but interpretations all serve the purpose of showing that a phenomenon *can* be attributed to natural causes. To the extent that an interpretation consists only of plausible inferences, it will be particularly persuasive. An interpretation that includes no element of inference is still preferred to an alternative account that appeals to principles that have no empirical foundation.

Interpretation differs from mere speculation in that the latter is unconstrained by experimental analysis. Speculation may play a helpful role, so long as it is identified as such. It may be a useful exercise to suggest, for example, that children learn language so reliably because they are endowed with a language acquisition device. Discussion of such a proposal can help clarify what is known and what remains to be shown. To the extent that such speculations appeal to principles or phenomena that do not have empirical foundations, however, they do not solve the puzzles in question.

Although scientific interpretation has been exalted in this essay, its limitations must be acknowledged. Interpretations do not explain how nature works, but, rather, how it might work; they are just plausible scenarios, not facts about the world. Interpretations are only the extension of established principles to domains outside the laboratory and cannot discover anything new. Consequently they should not be advanced when empirical study is possible. Interpretation should be reserved for only those phenomena of which experimental control is impractical, unethical, or impossible. Because interpretation can be done from one's armchair, and experimentation is hard work, the appeal of interpretation may seduce potential researchers and actually interfere with the progress of science. There is an additional and perhaps more serious danger: A plausible interpretation of a puzzling phenomenon tends to satisfy scientific curiosity even when it is wrong. In such a case, it dulls the tendency to investigate the matter further. Unfortunately, the plausibility of an interpretation can only be evaluated by an expert in the basic science: Does it in fact follow from empirical principles, and is it consistent with available facts? Natural phenomena that resist experimental control can invite many competing accounts. Because few are in a position to evaluate them, a superficial account may be widely acclaimed and retard the acceptance of a more cogent interpretation. Such risks cannot be avoided, and the influence of a scientific interpretation will depend in part on the vigor of the paradigm in which the interpretation is embedded.

A Strategy for Understanding Cognition

An appropriate strategy for understanding cognitive phenomena includes two parallel endeavors. First is the unabashed behavioral interpretation of the entire landscape of human behavior, showing how every aspect of it might be accounted for by basic processes, thus laying claim to the domain; second is experimental analysis guided by those interpretations. The two endeavors can be thought of as analogous to a connect-the-dots picture puzzle. In this case, the puzzle includes the entire panorama of cognitive phenomena. Interpretation provides the dots; that is, it provides a skeleton or outline of what a complete account might look like. Experimental analysis connects the dots, here and there, wherever controlled observation is possible. Each line added by experimental analysis is recognizable only in the context of the interpretive outline.

As suggested by this analogy, the experimental analysis of cognition would be guided and inspired by the interpretive framework. In the absence of the framework, the empirical work—a line here, a line there—would seem pointless and random. For example, several studies have confirmed the functional independence of verbal operants, such as tacts, mands, and intraverbals (Chase, Johnson, & Sulzer-Azaroff, 1985; Lamarre & Holland, 1985; Lee, 1981; Sundberg, Endicott, & Eigenheer, 2000). This empirical work is significant in the context of Skinner's interpretation of verbal behavior, which predicted such effects (Skinner, 1957). Outside of that context, the studies would seem isolated and unrelated to other verbal phenomena. Thus, even though a complete experimental analysis of cognition may be out of reach, experimental details will accumulate over time that, together with the interpretive framework, will provide a mosaic of increasing texture.

One need not be dispirited by the modesty of this goal. The role of natural selection in the origin of adaptive complexity in nature was once appreciated by only a relative handful of ardent partisans, but it continued to gather support incrementally as the principle was shown to be able to integrate nearly every new experimental observation and field datum that emerged over the next century. Now, of course, the importance of natural selection is not seriously questioned in scientific circles, even though its role has been demonstrated in only a small proportion of biological adaptations. To the extent that complex human behavior really is the product of selection contingencies, behavioral interpretations will accumulate support in an analogous way.

One might evaluate this optimism by considering what has already been accomplished, and to what effect. Skinner devoted much of the latter half of his career to a comprehensive interpretation of complex behavior, much of which would be embraced by the term cognition, and there are few topics that he did address, at least in passing. Of course, Skinner has not been alone in offering interpretations of complexity; there is a substantial and growing literature of similar work. It is fair to say, however, that the compass of Skinner's work is unusually wide, and that he remains the most influential single behaviorist. Therefore he serves as a useful test case: Has all this interpretation been fruitful? Has it led to a growing appreciation of the power and parsimony of the behaviorist's position analogous to the increasing influence of evolutionary biology?

A cursory glance at the field of cognition would suggest a resounding "No." In the hundreds of empirical studies and conceptual analyses on cognitive phenomena published every year in mainstream journals of psychology and philosophy, Skinner and behavior analysis are usually represented, if at all, only in caricature. The patent failure of Skinner's approach is often cited, usually to help justify an alternative approach. Even authors who find themselves drawn to compatible positions take pains to argue that there are fundamental differences (e.g., McClelland & Rumelhart, 1986; Snow, 1996; see also Morris, this volume), apparently lest the reader dismiss their claims out of hand. Of course, much of this animus can be dismissed as merely recycled dogma: There is seldom evidence that the dismissal of Skinner's work is based on familiarity with it. A few prominent critics (e.g., Chomsky, 1959, 1971; Dennett, 1978) tend to be cited as authoritative to the neglect of primary sources. Nevertheless, this state of affairs must count as evidence against my suggestion of the potential influence of behavioral interpretations.

If science proceeded by acclamation, the popularity of competing paradigms would be discouraging indeed, but the circumstances that make a position popular need not ensure its survival; the earth was once overrun with trilobites, but today they are just fossil curiosities. A more cogent criterion is whether Skinner's interpretive exercises have contributed to a self-perpetuating and growing field of inquiry that is to some extent nourished by such interpretations, and here the evidence is unambiguously affirmative. For several decades, Skinner's interpretations of cognitive phenomena were admired by a handful of people but ignored by everyone else. They gradually, however, began to guide experimental work and to inspire refined interpretations, much of which would be difficult to evaluate if not for the framework that Skinner provided. Although this publication steam is small relative to that of mainstream psychology, in relation to its origins it is enormous.

The behavioral approach to cognition is progressing steadily. At present it is by no means as influential as traditional approaches, but in the evolution of science it has two important advantages that will ensure that it prevails: It is parsimonious, and it stands on a foundation of independent empirical principles. It offers a genuine explanation of complex behavior.

What Does it Mean to Explain Something?

In this chapter I have attempted to describe and justify the behavioral approach to understanding phenomena for which there is only incomplete data. I have argued that in the face of such gaps, all paradigms must resort to interpretation, and that interpretation plays a central role in science. Behavior analysis is distinctive in that its interpretations invoke only established principles that have arisen from a vigorous experimental science, and it is therefore especially well placed to offer cogent interpretations. Moreover, by restricting its interpretive terms in this way, behavior analysis offers actual explanations for cognitive phenomena. When a puzzling phenomenon has been interpreted in terms of principles that have an independent justification, the mystery shrouding that phenomenon has been resolved and it can reasonably be claimed that the phenomenon is explained. In contrast, the seductive metaphors of cognitive science raise as many questions as they answer. As Machado, Lourenço, and Silva (2000) have asked of one such metaphor:

> If we say that a rat navigates a maze efficiently because it scans with the mind's eye a stored representation of the maze, a cognitive map, and then admit that there is literally no mind's eye, literally no internal action of scanning, literally no map, at least in the sense that we usually conceive of eyes, scanning actions, and maps, then how does our account *explain* the rat's behavior? (p. 30)

Not only should psychologists like explanations to rest on independent principles, they should like them to be smoothly integrated with the rest of biology. In particular, they should like them to be compatible with what is known about physiology and evolutionary biology, for otherwise, an account carries the extra burden of accommodating any discrepancies. Here too a behavioral account satisfies, for plausible neural mechanisms of behavioral processes have been identified, and the adaptive significance of such processes is conspicuous (Donahoe & Palmer, 1994). In contrast, metaphors do not have physical foundations or evolutionary origins. Only when they have been translated into biological or behavioral terms will it be possible to evaluate them by these criteria.

I have argued that the work commonly assigned to hypothetical cognitive constructs—mental arithmetic, problem solving, recall, planning ahead, and so on—can be accomplished by mosaics of elementary operants, some of which are commonly below the threshold of observability. This claim cannot be proven, of course, but it follows from the behavior-analytic assumption of uniformity, that what lies beyond the field of view obeys the same principles as what lies within it. Because experimental analysis requires the observation, measurement, and control of relevant variables, the plausibility of the claim rests rather on offering cogent interpretations of cognitive phenomena. Interpretations are not without risks, but they can provide a hazy picture of the domain of interest and integrate fragmentary empirical work. Although such accounts are necessarily tentative, they can serve one of the main purposes of science—to offer plausible explanations of complex phenomena in terms that are rooted in experimental analysis and integrated with other biological sciences.

References

Chase, P. N., Johnson, K. R., & Sulzer-Azaroff, B. (1985). Verbal relations within instruction: Are there subclasses of the intraverbal? *Journal of the Experimental Analysis of Behavior, 43,* 301–313.

Chomsky, N. (1959). Review of *Verbal Behavior* by B. F. Skinner. *Language, 35,* 26–58.

Chomsky, N. (1971, December 30). The case against B. F. Skinner. *The New York Review of Books, 17,* 18–24.

Dennett, D. (1978). *Brainstorms.* New York: Bradford Books.

Donahoe, J. W. & Palmer, D. C. (1994). *Learning and complex behavior,* Boston: Allyn & Bacon.

Lamarre, J., & Holland, J. G. (1985). The functional independence of mands and tacts. *Journal of the Experimental Analysis of Behavior, 43,* 5–19.

Lee, V. L. (1981). Prepositional phrases spoken and heard. *Journal of the Experimental Analysis of Behavior, 35,* 227–242.

Machado, A., Lourenço, O., & Silva, F. J. (2000). Facts, concepts, and theories: The shape of psychology's epistemic triangle. *Behavior and Philosophy, 28,* 1–40.

McClelland, J. L. Rumelhart, D. E. & the PDP Research Group (Eds.) (1986). *Parallel distributed processing.* Cambridge, MA: MIT Press.

Newton, I. (1952). *Mathematical principles of natural philosophy.* Chicago: Encyclopedia Britannica Press. (Original work published 1687)

Palmer, D. C. (1991). A behavioral interpretation of memory. In L. J. Hayes & P. N. Chase (Eds.) *Dialogues on verbal behavior* (pp. 261–279). Reno, NV: Context Press.

Palmer, D. C. (1998). The speaker as listener: The interpretation of structural regularities in verbal behavior. *The Analysis of Verbal Behavior, 15,* 3–16.

Skinner, B. F. (1935). The generic nature of the concepts of stimulus and response. *Journal of General Psychology, 12,* 40–65.

Skinner, B. F. (1938). *The behavior of organisms.* New York: Appleton-Century-Crofts.

Skinner, B. F. (1953). *Science and human behavior.* New York: Macmillan. Skinner, B. F. (1957). *Verbal behavior.* New York: Appleton- Century-Crofts.

Skinner, B. F. (1988). Reply to Stalker and Ziff. In A. C. Catania & S. Harnad (Eds.), *The selection of behavior: The operant behaviorism of B. F. Skinner: Comments and Consequences* (pp. 207–208). Cambridge: Cambridge University Press.

Snow, C. E. (1996). Toward a rational empiricism: Why interactionism is not behaviorism any more than biology is genetics. In M. L. Rice (Ed.), *Toward a genetics of language* (pp. 377–396). Mahwah, NJ: Erlbaum.

Sundberg, M. L., Endicott, K., & Eigenheer, P. (2000). Using intraverbal prompts to establish tacts for children with autism. *The Analysis of Verbal Behavior, 17,* 89–104.

10

Privacy

Howard Rachlin

Let me start by distinguishing between two kinds of privacy. First, there is the privacy I have when I am sitting alone in a room writing. My behavior in that room is known to me alone; it is private as opposed to public behavior. It is what legal scholars mean when they talk about the right to privacy. Let us call this Privacy A. I have no quarrel with Privacy A. Of course there is another sense in which we use the term, private behavior—to refer to behavior that no one else could *possibly* see because it is covert rather than overt—because it is going on inside my head. Let us call this kind of privacy, Privacy B. If I were to behave privately, in the sense of Privacy B, in a crowded, well-lit room, none of the people in that room could possibly observe that behavior. I have no quarrel with Privacy B either. Of course there are all sorts of events going on inside my head, neural events, hormonal events, physiological events. I can even talk to myself, possibly picture things to myself and possibly introspect about those words and pictures. My quarrel is with the notion that these private events (as opposed to the reports of them) are kinds of events that are properly studied by psychologists.

Some psychologists would argue that physiological or introspective events are the *only* kinds of events properly studied by psychologists. Some people, including some modern philosophers of psychology, believe that psychology's main job is to make sense of introspections. Others see behavioral observation and measurement only as a sign or indication of

---

Howard Rachlin • Department of Psychology, State University of New York At Stony Brook, Stony Brook, NY 11974-2500.

the psychologically fundamental physiological events within the nervous system. Modern cognitive neuroscience is of this persuasion. A cognitive model, for them, is just a stand-in for eventual physiological reification. Those of us who call ourselves behaviorists accept neither of these notions. Certainly no one who, like myself, considers himself a Skinnerian behaviorist would accept either of them. I call the kind of behaviorism espoused here *teleological behaviorism* (Rachlin, 1992, 1994, 2000). Teleological behaviorism is based on Skinner's ideas, but departs from them in its rejection of internal events (internal stimuli, responses and reinforcers) and in its use of mental terms to describe temporally extended behavioral patterns.

The following quotation is from a memoir I (Rachlin, 1995) wrote for The National Academy of Sciences about Skinner:

> What then is Skinner's lasting contribution? Not, I think, his utopian vision of a self-experimental society, nor the educational technology, nor a highly successful mode of psychological therapy based on behavioral consequences, nor the Skinner box and a host of other useful inventions, nor his contribution to pharmacological testing, nor the journals and societies based on his work, nor the individuals he has influenced, nor the fact that he has put his stamp indelibly on the face of American psychology, although all of these flow from his central conception. That conception and Skinner's most lasting contribution is in my opinion more philosophical than psychological. It is nothing less than a new way to look at life; in other words (words to which he would strenuously object) a new way to conceive of the soul.
>
> I should not, however, call his vision of the soul entirely new. The ancient Greeks, Aristotle in particular, conceived of souls as modes of living, as patterns of overt behavior of organisms, more or less complicated depending on species and individuals within species. Psychology for them was the identification and manipulation (the prediction and control) of these patterns of behavior, including one's own. To Skinner we owe the renaissance of this conception. (p. 67)

The great advantage of behaviorism is its emphasis on publicly observable events. To hypothesize intrinsically private events that are at the same time psychological events is to give up authority as psychologists to either the object of study (the subject) or to the physiologist. What does it mean in practical terms to give up authority? It means to give up prediction and control. If a person can predict and control her own behavior better than a behaviorist can it is only because she has *more* data than the behaviorist does; she has Privacy A. But she does not have *better* data than the behaviorist does; she does not have Privacy B in addition. The behaviorist's data are at least as good as, probably better than, those of the subject (because they are observed directly rather than by reflection).

Behaviorists prior to Skinner frequently began by denying or at least ignoring the existence of psychologically meaningful private events. Watson of the behaviorist manifesto, Hull before the days of r_g-s_g's, Tolman before cognitive maps (when he called himself a molar behaviorist), denied the place of Privacy B within psychology. Skinner's commentary on Pavlov, recently re-published in the *Journal of The Experimental Analysis of Behavior* (Skinner, 1999) cites Pavlov's focus on the nervous system as the point where he went wrong. As their behavioristic theories were challenged, however, these behaviorists responded by retreating to the interior of the organism—by postulating Privacy B in one or another form. It is my contention that such a retreat by behaviorists is a sign of inadequacy in their theories. When they invoke intrinsically private events (such as internal stimuli, responses, and reinforcers) to explain behavior, behaviorists necessarily compete with physiological, cognitive and introspective psychologists on *their* grounds. The interior mechanisms of cognitive and physiological psychology are much more subtle—and the interior states posited by the introspectionists are much more meaningful—than the interior mechanisms and states postulated by the behaviorists. So behaviorists, when they venture into the interior of the organism, come off looking simplistic, crude, and irrelevant to central human concerns. As an illustration consider the phenomenon of avoidance.

Avoidance

In the typical signaled avoidance procedure a rat is put in a chamber with a light that can go on or off, a lever that can be pressed, and a grid floor. Every minute or so the light goes on for 10 seconds, the rat is briefly shocked through the grid floor, and the light goes out. However if, during the 10 seconds that the light is on, the rat presses the lever, the light immediately goes out, and the rat is not shocked. In other words, pressing the lever in the presence of the light avoids the shock. After repeated exposure to these contingencies some rats learn to press the lever when the light goes on thus avoiding the shock. Question: What reinforces the lever press? This is a difficult question to answer because when the rat presses the lever shock does *not* occur. How can the nonoccurrence of an event reinforce a response? The standard answer is that, before the rat learns to press the lever, shock makes the light itself aversive (by classical conditioning); then, the lever press is reinforced by reduction in aversiveness (or fear) when the light goes off (by instrumental conditioning). In other words, according to this explanation (called two-factor theory), by escaping from the light the rat incidentally avoids the shock.

The problem with two-factor theory, from a behavioral viewpoint, is that the light's aversiveness and its reduction is unobserved; it is internal to the rat. Of course, the mere fact that an explanation of a phenomenon relies on internal events does not automatically make it wrong. Nevertheless, two-factor theory is wrong. Evidence indicates that the light, in and of itself, does not become aversive. Rats learn to press the lever when lever presses avoid the shock but do not turn off the light and they do not learn to press the lever when lever presses turn off the light but do not avoid the shock (Kamin, 1956). Rats also learn to avoid shock when the light is dispensed with entirely (Sidman, 1953; Herrnstein & Hineline, 1966); in these procedures shocks come at fixed or variable intervals and lever presses produce fixed or variable shock-free periods. To explain avoidance with these procedures, two-factor theory must invent multiple internal clocks, the readings of which become more and more aversive as shock approaches. Then, the reinforcer of the lever press is the (internal) reduction of aversiveness (or fear) when a clock is reset.

These versions of two-factor theory are quite ingenious and it will always be possible to hypothesize internal reinforcement when no immediate external reinforcement exists. A more parsimonious explanation of avoidance, however, notes that every avoidance situation, by definition, programs a negative correlation over time between rate of avoidance responding (*overt* behavior) and rate of aversive stimulation (environmental consequences). It is this negative correlation as a whole that reinforces avoidance responding (Herrnstein, 1969). This is the best explanation we have of avoidance and it does not rely on events supposed to occur inside the organism (Privacy B).

The second we admit the essential privacy of psychological events is the second we give up the very quality that raises behaviorism above all other psychologies—its reliance on publicly observable events. Herrnstein (1969) explains avoidance, not with the methods and concepts of the cognitivists, the physiologists, the introspectionists, but with ours—with behavioral methods and behavioral concepts—public behavior—behavior that engages the external environment—behavior that can be reinforced—behavior that can serve as a signal to other organisms. What *does* reinforce avoidance? The answer, as Herrnstein and Hineline (1966) argued, lies in a molar concept of behavior and reinforcement. It is the *rate* of avoidance responses, taken as a whole, that is reinforced. It is the contingency between the rate of responding over time and the rate of reinforcement over time that determines the properties of avoidance behavior. No single avoidance response is reinforced. A single avoidance response has no meaning in the Herrnstein-Hineline conception. It is impossible, in that conception, to assemble the determinants of avoidance—stimulus, response and reinforcement—at any given moment. The important factor is the relation among these variables over time.

Thus we are left with two explanations for avoidance:

1. We can say that avoidance is reinforced by fear reduction or aversiveness reduction (where aversiveness is conceived as an internal, Privacy B, event). This explanation allows us to preserve the momentary contiguity of response and reinforcer at the cost of abandoning any behavioral understanding of the reinforcer.
2. We can say that the reinforcement of avoidance lies in the negative contingency between rate of responding and rate of aversive stimulation. Here we give up contiguity, but gain observability.

Explanation 1 sends us into the organism on a search for the cognitive, physiological and introspective correlates of fear. Behaviorists are not qualified to pursue this search (and even those who are qualified have not succeeded). Explanation 2 sends us into the environment on a search for the functional correlates of avoidance. For this search, the behaviorist *is* equipped. And, in this search, the behaviorist has been successful.

Explanation 2 requires the abandonment of a billiard-ball concept of causation—a concept that was abandoned even by physics ever since gravity was explained without a series of hooks and chains. If bodies can act over a spatial distance why can't they act over a temporal distance? If a single response is not apparently reinforced, the behaviorist should be looking for the reinforcer not *deeply* inside the organism but *widely* into the organism's temporally extended environment.

Prior to Skinner, behaviorists (like Pavlov) felt the need to find an immediate stimulus for every response. Where the stimulus did not apparently exist in the environment, they invented one inside the organism.[1] This is what justified them in their physiology. Skinner showed that responding could be understood without reference to an immediate stimulus and consequently rejected physiological explanation of behavior. The next step would have been to abandon the search for a reinforcement of each individual response and to look for reinforcers of operants, more widely defined. Skinner did not take this step. He believed that if a response did not have an immediate stimulus it must have an immediate reinforcer. And he speculated (Skinner, 1953) that the reinforcer might be internal: "The reinforcing effect is carried by private as well as public stimuli" (p. 272); "With the exception of physical restraint all the variables that one may

[1] Rowland Stout (1996), one of the few contemporary behaviorist philosophers, calls this tendency "The Internal Shift."

manipulate in self-control [discriminative stimulus, response, and reinforcement] are available at the private level" (p. 275). Those behaviorists who have followed these speculations have become essentially cognitive and physiological psychologists (and as such are doing valuable and important work). But there is another way to follow Skinner—to go to where he was pointing instead of to where he was—to take the next step—to renounce Privacy B (even in cases, such as avoidance, where individual responding is not apparently reinforced) and to look for contingencies of reinforcement in the wider environment.

This is the program of teleological behaviorism—not only to explain avoidance but to explain the whole vocabulary of emotional and mental concepts—fear itself, pain, hope, expectancy, intention, imagination, and even cognition—in terms of temporally extended correlations between behavior and reinforcement. When you do this, not only does the reinforcement of avoidance become clear, but so does that of the whole mental vocabulary. The remainder of this article will try to show how this might be done.

Behaviorists have tended either to deny that mental terms refer to real entities or to concede that such entities exist, but to deny any interest in them—to leave their study to introspectionists, cognitivists, or physiologists. The reaction of most people (scientists and nonscientists alike) to these tactics is to conclude that behaviorists are not psychologists and the result has been to marginalize behaviorism within academic psychology.

The cognitive psychologist George Miller (1962) is correct to define psychology as the science of mental life. But it is also true that behavioral psychology is the *fundamental* science of mental life. The cognitive psychologist believes that he is studying the mind itself (mind/body = carburetor/automobile) while the behaviorist is studying only its behavioral effects. But the teleological behaviorist believes that she is studying the mind itself (mind/body = acceleration/automobile) while the cognitivist is studying only the mechanism behind it. Mental life is life of the whole organism—widely understood. It is we behaviorists who are the proper scientists of mental life. Mental life is too important to leave to the cognitivists or physiologists or introspectionists.

This is not just a semantic issue. Studying the mind is not just a more popular label for what behaviorists would be doing anyway ("You want mental life? *We'll* give you mental life.") Rather, it determines the research we do. A behaviorist who rejects Privacy-B explanations will do different sorts of experiments from one who accepts Privacy-B explanations. The remainder of this article contains two examples of an approach to behavior that rejects Privacy-B explanations: one is in the well-researched area of *self-control*; the other is on the topic of *imagination*—not usually considered to be amenable to behavioral analysis.

Self-Control

An alcoholic must make repeated choices between drinking and not drinking. Every time he passes a bar, attends a party, goes to a restaurant with friends, a choice has to be made. When the alcoholic chooses to drink, the reinforcer is clear and distinct, but what reinforces his choice on those occasions when he chooses not to drink? Good health, social acceptance, better relations with family, better job performance, might be cited. These reinforcers, however, are meaningless at any given moment and do not follow from any individual act of drink refusal. It has been argued that such reinforcers are delayed rather than immediate (Ainslie, 1992). They are certainly delayed, but they differ from the sorts of reinforcers studied in the laboratory in delay-of-reinforcement experiments. When, in the laboratory, a pigeon chooses a larger delayed reinforcer over a smaller immediate reinforcer, a key is pecked, a delay period follows, and then the reinforcer is obtained. But if an alcoholic refuses a single drink at a party he does not wake up one morning, three weeks later, a healthier, happier person. Such reinforcers depend not on any single drink refusal but on a *pattern* of drink refusals over some considerable time. A single drink refusal is never reinforced, not now, not ever.

To discover the reinforcer of the alcoholic's drink refusal you have to refrain from gratuitously hypothesizing reinforcers inside the alcoholic (little blasts of internal satisfaction as it were) summing up to counteract the value of the drink. One needs to step back and, just as with avoidance behavior, look for the correlation between overt actions and environmental consequences. In this case there is a negative correlation between drinking and health, or social acceptance, or earnings over time. Each drink is not punished—either immediately or with a delay. (This is why drinking is so difficult to control.) Rather, over time, drinking reduces the value of many activities. To decrease drinking, this negative correlation needs to gain control over the alcoholic's behavior (Rachlin, 2000).

As a more mundane example of a self-control problem, consider the following: You are driving from New York to California. Let us assume that you like both classical and popular music so you take along 10 compact discs of each kind. Now you get into the car and start to drive. The following is the order of your preferences: (a) an hour-long symphony; (b) a 3-minute popular song. The choice seems to be obvious—you should play a symphony. The problem is that the first 3-minutes of the symphony is the lowest valued of all the alternatives. In fact, any random 3-minute section of any of the symphonies is less valued than any of the popular songs. Although a symphony is highly valued, its value cannot be determined by adding up the values of 20 successive 3-minute sections. You can see this if you think how you would feel if you listened to 57 minutes of the symphony and found the final 3 minutes missing from the disk. You would not be 57/60 as happy as you would have been had you listened to the whole thing. You would likely be very unhappy. We do enjoy long activities while they are going on, but that enjoyment depends on the pattern being completed.

So what do you do in this case? You could play one popular song and then listen to the symphony (like the alcoholic who has one "last drink" before quitting). Unless you quickly tired of the popular songs, however, you would be in the same spot after listening to that one song as you were before. Then you could listen to another song, and another—reaching California without ever playing a symphony—and so (by hypothesis) having a less enjoyable trip. This problem is mirrored by the conflict between watching TV and reading a novel, between doing crossword puzzles and writing this article, between smoking a cigarette, having a drink, eating a rich meal, and not doing these activities. Such conflicts may be characterized more precisely as follows:

> There exists a normally long-duration activity lasting T time units and a normally short-duration activity lasting t time units, where $T = nt$. A self-control problem exists when the value of the longer activity is greater than that of an equal time (T) spent at the shorter activity ($V_T > nV_t$), but the value of the shorter activity is greater than that of an equal time (t) spent at the longer activity ($V_t > V_{T/n}$).

Laboratory research on self-control would then be directed at methods of getting humans and nonhumans to choose the longer-duration activity in situations of this kind.

Teleological behaviorism says to the applied behavior analyst: "When small behavioral units (individual responses) resist behavioral analysis—that is, when individual responses have no clear reinforcing consequences—do not yield to the temptation to invent consequences inside the organism (internal "satisfaction" and the like) but take a step backward, and look for reinforcers in the long-term patterns into which the smaller units fit."[2]

---

[2] This teleological viewpoint may be taken with respect to verbal as well as nonverbal behavior. It implies that words may not ordinarily be reinforced outside of their verbal context. In Skinner's (1957) terms, all words may be intraverbals. The (nonverbal) value of verbal behavior may emerge only at the level of extended discourse. For example, the high value (for me) of writing this chapter lies in the chapter as a whole and not in the words, or even the sentences, paragraphs, etc. that make it up. This is of course what makes writing a problem of self control.

Imagination

As an example of the utility of the behavioristic conception of terms, almost always considered to be mental, consider *imagination*. It would seem as if imagination is the paradigm of a Privacy B event. What else *could* it be? Again, though, let us try not to be dazzled by this mentalistic word into hypothesizing internal events. Instead of thinking of imagination as having an image inside one's head, think instead, as Skinner suggests, how the word is used in everyday speech, how imagination functions in peoples' lives. This question hardly ever occurs to the cognitivist, still less to the physiologist or introspectionist. Nevertheless, regardless of one's psychological orientation, imagining something depends in some way on sensing or perceiving it.[3] So, before discussing imagination from a behavioral viewpoint we have to get straight what we mean by *sensation*.

Consider this question: "What is the difference between two awake individuals, one of them stone deaf, who are both sitting immobile in a room in which a record-player is playing a Mozart string quartet?"[4] The answer has to be: "One individual is hearing the quartet and the other is not." Differences in psychological orientation emerge when we ask the further question: "What does it mean to hear something?" For the behaviorist, a hearing person discriminates between one sound and another and between sounds and nonsounds while a deaf person does not make this discrimination. But then what does it mean to discriminate or fail to discriminate in this way? A person who can hear behaves differently in the presence of sounds and nonsounds while a person who cannot hear behaves in the same way in the presence of sounds and nonsounds. For a hearing person there is a nonzero correlation between sounds and overt behavior, but for the deaf person there is a zero correlation between sounds and behavior. The hearing and deaf people of Gray's question are doing the same thing at this moment but this moment is just one point in two ongoing correlations—a zero correlation and a nonzero correlation. These may overlap at several points—in fact they have to overlap (two nonparallel lines must cross).

To say that the hearing and deaf people in Gray's question are doing the same thing is like saying that a high-school physics student is doing the same thing as Einstein when they both write $E = mc^2$ on the blackboard.

---

[3] According to Aristotle (*De Anima* 429a), imagination is "...a motion produced by the activity of sense."

[4] This is based on a question put to me by the physiologist Jeff Gray, quoted by Staddon (2001, p. 177). Gray believed the question to be unanswerable by a behaviorist.

Of course they are doing the same thing in a trivial sense. But in any psychologically meaningful sense they are doing different things. For psychologists other than teleological behaviorists the essential difference between the hearing person and the deaf person or between the high-school student and Einstein lies in some Privacy-B event going on inside their heads while they are writing the equation. For the teleological behaviorist, on the other hand, the difference lies in the temporally extended pattern of acts to which the present act belongs. This pattern is of course different for hearing and deaf people and for Einstein and the high-school student. And, given this difference in pattern, it does not matter, for the teleological behaviorist, what internal mechanism was responsible. You could open up the deaf person's head and find her brain to be perfectly normal while the hearing person's brain was just a lump of jello. The bottom line is whether the person can hear or not, and that distinction is based entirely on behavioral variables: discriminative stimuli; overt behavior; environmental consequences.

What does all this have to do with imagination? The answer is that imagination depends on sensation. A behavioral conception of what it is to imagine something is to behave in the absence of that thing as you would normally do in its presence.[5] If you generally behave one way in the presence of and another way in the absence of red lights you are discriminating between red lights and other things. But if, on occasion, you behave in the absence of a red light as you normally would in its presence you are, on that occasion, imagining a red light.

Suppose a driver typically drives in the left lane (the passing lane) of the road. When a truck comes roaring up from behind, the driver's typical reaction is to swerve suddenly to the right. Each time this happens (in its typical form) swerving may be conceived as a discriminative act. Given this habit, a driver who swerved in the absence of a truck would be imagining a truck—the stimulus is missing. This is what Aristotle meant when he said, "Imagination is impossible without sensation." (*De Anima*, 428b) Imagination is acting not dreaming; vividness of imagination is not vividness of interior image but of overt behavior. Suppose two people in a room are asked to imagine an uncaged lion in the room with them. One closes his eyes, adopts a dreamy expression, and says, "Yes, I see it.

---

[5] Skinner (1953) says, "One...has to explain how an image can occur when the thing is not present...A study of behavior point[s] to variables that lead the organism to see X in the absence of X" (p. 278). The difference between Skinner's conception and the present one is that, for Skinner, seeing X in the absence of X is a covert response. Skinner never explains what the difference could be between a covert response and a covert stimulus. In the present conception, seeing X in the absence of X is an overt response (in the context of a particular reinforcement history).

It has a mane and a tail, . . . etc." The other runs screaming from the room. According to the behavioral conception, the second person is truly imagining the lion. He is doing what he would do (presumably) if the lion were really there. The first might be imagining a picture of a lion, again doing what she would do if the picture were really there. In all cases, imagination implies action. If we speak of an "imaginative solution to a problem," for example, are we referring to an ordinary solution of the problem plus an image in the head or are we referring to an unusual aspect or a dimension of the solution? I think the reader will agree that the latter makes more sense.

In the present view, imagination is not a filler to glue a series of discrete events together. A rat pressing a lever at a certain rate on a Sidman shock avoidance schedule, for example, would, at many moments, be neither pressing the lever nor actually being shocked. Yet the Sidman avoidance contingency (the negative relation between rate of lever pressing and shock rate) still determines rate of lever pressing. No internal image of shocks between actual shocks or lever presses between actual lever presses need be postulated. Similarly, a driver who stops at a red light need not be imagining an accident. The red light is just a discriminative stimulus for stopping.

Imagination could enter into avoidance, however, when avoidance responding is brought under stimulus control. Imagine, for example, a rat pressing a lever under a multiple schedule where a red light signals a Sidman avoidance contingency and its absence signals extinction. The rat has learned to press the lever during the red light and not to press the lever during its absence. If, in the absence of the red light, the rat were to emit a sudden burst of responding, it could be said to be imagining the red light. If the burst were to have some actual effect—reduction of shock intensity at some future time, for example—it might be repeated and made part of a new behavioral pattern. Imagination thus may serve as a label (our label, not the rat's) for a certain kind of behavioral variability, a stepping stone from old to new behavioral patterns. From the original pattern, to the imaginative response, to the new pattern, the behavior analyst needs to account only for overt behavior, for the behavior of "the organism as a whole," to use Skinner's often repeated phrase.

Consider a borderline case. Suppose someone is standing near a road and a bus goes by. She follows the bus with her eyes until it is just a dot on the horizon. Some friends come along. The person points to the dot and says, "See that bus?" They say, "No, you're just imagining it." Is the person seeing it or just imagining it (or perhaps seeing the dot and imagining the bus)? The teleological behaviorist says that she is indeed seeing the bus because the bus is there. If it were not there (if, say, the person blinked and the bus were actually out of sight; the dot would be a bump in the road) the friends are right—the person was just imagining the bus. The important point is that the environmental object (the bus) and only that object makes the difference between sensation (or perception) and imagination. The person's behavior is the same in either case. In deciding the issue between the person and her friends what counts is: Is that dot a bus or not? The location, intensity, orientation, or even the existence of a Privacy-B image in one's head would be entirely irrelevant. The person as the observer would not know whether the object of her sensation was there or not—whether she were actually sensing it or just imagining it.[6]

Once this view of imagination is taken, its crucial function in everyday life becomes clear. The actress, Shirley MacLaine (no behaviorist, to say the least) tells the story of how she used to hate Hollywood parties. Finally she figured, "Hell, I'm an actress. I'm going to act as if I'm enjoying myself." Then of course she did enjoy herself. This is the function of imagination.

To repeat, when we imagine something we are behaving in the absence of some state of affairs as we would in its presence. Whenever we do something new in a given situation, we are imagining. The study of behavioral variability and its reinforcement (Neuringer, 1986; this volume) is the study of imagination. And, as I have found in my own research, imagination is a vital part of self-control in everyday life (Rachlin, 2000). Consider the alcoholic again. His rate of drinking is one quart per day. Now he wants to quit. He wants to go to zero quarts per day. One day, say New Year's day, he stops drinking. I think it will be clear that there are no reinforcers for this act, considered as an isolated act. Certainly there are no reinforcers on that first day of not drinking. The alcoholic is in great pain on that day. If, the next day, the alcoholic returns to drinking, the first day's abstinence would have been wasted. It will *never* be reinforced.

Aristotle's analogy for this situation was a soldier, in the midst of a rout in battle, turning and making a stand. Unless others join him, his act is wasted. Analogously, unless an individual act of self-control is joined by other acts in a behavioral pattern, it is wasted. In other words, the original act of abstinence, although not reinforced *as such*, may be reinforced as part of a pattern of acts. If we look for the cause of the first drink refusal deep inside the organism we might talk about internal willpower or determination. If we look widely rather than deeply, however, we can see the refusal

---

[6] But an actor on a stage knows that the object of his anger (say) is not there. He is just (temporarily) behaving as if it were, which is another way of saying he is imagining the object. A good imagination is not just an aid or tool in good acting. Rather, good acting is good imagining.

of the first drink as an act of imagination whose function is to bring about the very thing imagined.

The case of alcoholism is an extreme example. I would claim, though, that imagination functions not only in self-control, but every time we try something new—whenever we start behaving in a new pattern in a given situation. The first act in the pattern may be silly or pointless and never reinforced as such: the first day at a new school; going to one's first concert; learning a new sport; meeting a new person. It is only when a series of such acts are put together that they attain value.

In order to quit, the alcoholic has to behave, in the absence of a pattern of not drinking, as if that pattern already existed (just as the soldier in a rout who first turns and makes a stand acts as though others have already turned). What is imagined, in the alcoholic's very first drink refusal, is all those other days of abstinence. We cannot say that *quitting* has been reinforced in the past—because it hasn't. Perhaps the alcoholic has tried to quit 1,000 times before and failed 1,000 times. But we can say that, in areas other than drinking, *imagination* has been reinforced in the past— imagination, not as a picture in the head, but as a pattern of overt behavior. Imagination, thus conceived, is a vital part of self-control, as it is of every creative act.

Why use the term imagination at all? Why not just speak of situational behavioral variability? The answer is, because it is this sort of behavioral variability, not pictures in the head, that captures the function of imagination in peoples' everyday lives. Cognitivist studies of imagination as pictures in the head, valuable and interesting as they may be (for example, Shepard & Metzler, 1971), are studies of the mechanism behind imagination. Behavioral studies of imagination, however, are studies of the thing itself.

Conclusions

It may seem to the reader trained in traditional behavior analysis that, in refusing to posit internal reinforcers for acts comprising behavioral patterns, teleological behaviorism abandons any explanation of how such acts can be learned. How can patterns be shaped if there is no reinforcement for the very first act of change? I ask those readers to consider what characterizes reinforcement in the first place. The most defensible current theory of reinforcement is Premack's (1965) wholly behavioral theory in which all acts are arranged on a scale of value (determined by a choice test). Higher valued acts may then reinforce lower valued acts. A rat's eating reinforces its lever pressing because in a choice test with both freely available the rat spends more time eating than lever pressing. The self-control problem emerges when, for example, in a choice between one year of drinking and one year of abstinence, the alcoholic would choose abstinence while in a choice between one evening of drinking and one evening of abstinence the alcoholic would choose drinking. The reinforcer for the first evening of abstinence, according to this model, is the high value of the year-long pattern itself. The very first evening of abstinence is reinforced only when the longer pattern is formed. Otherwise it is not reinforced. An evening's abstinence is thus an act of imagination as we have defined it here. It is emitted in the first place to the extent that acts of imagination have been reinforced in the past—to the extent that individual unreinforced acts have in the past been put together into valuable patterns.[7]

This is the sort of reasoning that will keep behaviorists focused on behaviorism. It is speculative to be sure—but a lot less speculative than positing hypothetical internal stimuli, responses and reinforcers, and hoping that physiologists will eventually discover them.

In summary, it is only by abandoning Privacy B that we can find consistent behavioral explanations for such behavioral phenomena as avoidance. But a more important reason to abandon Privacy B is that it enables us to view mental life as *life*. And, as with the part of life that is *clearly* behavioral, it enables us to find reasons (that is, functions) for what we do.

---

[7] An extension of this theory (Rachlin, Battalio, Kagel, & Green, 1981) replaces Premack's value scale with a utility function, contingencies with constraints, and reinforcement with maximization of utility.

References

Ainslie, G. (1992). *Picoeconomics.* New York: Cambridge University Press.
Herrnstein, R. J. (1969). Method and theory in the study of avoidance. *Psychological Review, 76,* 46–69.
Herrnstein, R. J., & Hineline, P. N. (1966). Negative reinforcement as shock-frequency reduction. *Journal of the Experimental Analysis of Behavior, 9,* 421–430.
Kamin, L. J. (1956). The effects of termination of the CS and avoidance of the US on avoidance learning. *Journal of Comparative And Physiological Psychology, 49,* 420–424.
Miller, G. A. (1962). *Psychology: The science of mental life.* New York: Harper & Row.
Neuringer, A. (1986). Can people behave randomly?: The role of feedback. *Journal of Experimental Psychology: General, 115,* 62–75.
Premack, D. (1965). Reinforcement theory. In D. Levine (Ed.) *Nebraska symposium on motivation: 1965,* pp 123–179. Lincoln: University of Nebraska Press.
Rachlin, H. (1992). Teleological behaviorism. *American Psychologist, 47,* 1371–1382.
Rachlin, H. (1994). *Behavior and Mind.* New York: Oxford University Press.

Rachlin, H. (1995). Burrhus Frederic Skinner (1904–1990). *National Academy of Sciences Biographical Memoirs, 67.*

Rachlin, H. (2000). *The science of self-control.* Cambridge, MA: Harvard University Press.

Rachlin, H., Battalio, R., Kagel, J., & Green, L. (1981). Maximization theory in behavioral psychology. *Behavioral And Brain Sciences, 4,* 371–388.

Shepard, R. N., & Metzler, J. (1971). Mental rotation of three-dimensional objects. *Science, 171,* 701–703.

Sidman, M. (1953). Avoidance conditioning with brief shock and no exteroceptive warning signal. *Science, 118,* 157–158.

Skinner, B. F. (1953). *Science and human behavior.* New York: Macmillan.

Skinner, B. F. (1957). *Verbal behavior.* New York: Appleton-Century-Crofts.

Skinner, B. F. (1999). Some responses to the stimulus "Pavlov." *Journal of the Experimental Analysis of Behavior, 72,* 463–465.

Staddon, J. (2001). *The new behaviorism: Mind, mechanism, and society.* Philadelphia: The Psychology Press.

Stout, R. (1996). *Things that happen because they should: A teleological approach to action.* Oxford: Oxford University Press.

11

When We Speak of Intentions

Philip N. Hineline

"The road to hell is paved with good intentions." Surely people all find this a valid aphorism despite any skepticism regarding hell as a distinct geographical location. Even if one assumed that Hades were to be found at some particular place, this reference to a road and its paving would be recognized as purely metaphorical, and one would not confuse intentions with bricks or cobblestones. Nevertheless, most discussions of intention, as well as intentional statements themselves, are subtly susceptible to the kinds of distortion that can occur through metaphor. Behavior analysts have traditionally steered clear of that problem by eschewing intentional language. If intentions are mentioned at all, it typically is to reject them as "mental fictions." But important and interesting relations are at issue when people speak of intentions, and it may be enlightening to closely examine those ways of speaking and writing. Most pervasively, intentional language induces us to look within the actor for sources of action even though the identification of intentions is usually based upon external consequences of the relevant actions. It can be shown, however, that more subtle features in common patterns of speaking and writing can also obscure the events that intentional prose is actually about.

Metaphor as Illustrating Transfers of Function

A useful starting point for such an analysis is provided by Jaynes (1976), in addressing the common practice of describing mental events

Philip N. Hineline • Department of Psychology, Temple University, Philadelphia, PA 19122.

in spatial terms. Jaynes noted that metaphorical language often occurs when one is concerned with some particular aspect of a thing for which words are not available, or with some abstract phenomenon or relationship. He coined the term *metaphrand* as identifying that which is to be expressed—or in behavior-analytic terms, a metaphrand is the feature or relation that occasions a particular metaphorical statement. In phrasing patterned after that of algebra, Jaynes identified a *metaphier* as some similar, more familiar or concrete thing that is understood as operating upon the metaphrand (analogous to a multiplier operating upon a multiplicand). Again behavior-analytically, the metaphier is the familiar or concrete metaphorical statement itself, occasioned by some feature of the metaphrand. The metaphier also has its own set of features, which Jaynes called *paraphiers*. One or a few of these are the features that validate the metaphor. There typically are additional paraphiers, however, that arise from the "normal" or nonmetaphorical origin of the metaphier, and it is these that provide the richness of metaphorical language. When these additional characteristics of the paraphier "project back" into the metaphrand, they also change our understanding of the metaphrand—sometimes elaborating, sometimes distorting. Jaynes called these *paraphrands* of the metaphrand.

A specific example may clarify these terms and relations: If I say, "Snow blankets the ground," the metaphrand is some aspect of the snow, and "blanket" is the metaphier. Most likely, the paraphier that validates the metaphier is the feature of snow as a covering that softens and obliterates detail. Additional paraphiers of "blanket," which through the metaphorical process become paraphrands of snow, are those of protection during a period of dormancy and a suggestion of warmth. These are just fine, so long as they do not result in a person's going to sleep within a snowdrift. Of course, the directly sensed thermal properties of the snowdrift make this unlikely. When such countervailing features are lacking, however, inappropriate transfers of function may occur.

As a whimsical example of the kind of mischief these transfers might produce, consider the possibility of teaching someone to label lengths of lines with color names. With adequate practice, it should be possible to become precise in doing this, and the person could learn to see colors as a continuum from red, to orange, to yellow, to green, and then blue, with these labels being occasioned by lines of increasing length. But what if one then were to attempt a plane geometry that incorporated the relations of color mixture? Surely the result would be nonsense; derivations based upon such combinations would support nothing comparable to the Pythagorean theorem.

More plausible—indeed, familiar but seldom explicitly noticed—is the metaphor of *depth* as applied to emotional phenomena. A person who, when provoked acts quickly and violently and then promptly calms down, is not the one described as deeply angry. Intensely angry, yes, but not deeply so. The deeply angry person is the one who ponders the insult for days or weeks, perhaps not even retaliating. Thus, apparently the feature of such phenomena that occasions "depth" (i.e., the paraphier), is the property of being dispersed or extended in time, perhaps hidden because one can thus "look right through it." But does the depth of emotion mean that a neuroscientist should look for its correlates deep in the brain instead of near its surface—in the medulla instead of the cortex? In Jaynes's terms, to do that would be to act in accordance with a paraphrand of depth.

Similar, and more explicit, is the term, "internalization," as commonly applied to psychological process. When a child refrains from participating in serious mischief under the instigation of peers, and instead acts in relation to the likely long-term consequences of conforming or nonconforming, people are likely to speak of the child having "internalized values." Psychological theorists commonly accept this terminology, even though just what a "value" is remains vague, and how it might get translated into behavior is an unsolved problem. This is not a trivial issue when those attempting to facilitate or account for such behavior look within the individual instead of looking to the individual's history, which is where the origins of the child's circumspect behavior are more likely to be found.

Other Transfers of Function

Another slippery transfer of function between verbal patterns is embedded in traditional "language about language." How is it that it seems appropriate to speak or write about *using* words, when in most other domains, speaking of "using one's behavior" sounds odd? For example, if I describe my picking up a glass of water, it sounds odd to say, "I used a reach." To be sure, there are exceptions, and these may be informative: If I am playing tennis and I score a point by hitting a lob-shot instead of a backhand stroke, it sounds fairly normal to speak of "using a lob-shot" or "using a back-hand stroke" even though, just like reaching for a glass of water, hitting the ball back-handedly is an episodic bit of behavior. Intuitively, then, it seems that people speak of *using* a behavior pattern, instead of merely engaging in it, when there are two or more alternative behavior patterns that may be effective. This is not the whole story, though, for people do not speak of using a right-handed instead of a left-handed reach in lifting the glass of water. Nevertheless, in the case of "using words," a transfer of function often occurs, apparently resulting from the fact that "using" most typically applies to objects. That is, I might win a golf match by using a three-iron instead of a driver. And of course, it would be normal to ask where the three-iron is when I am not using it. In contrast, it seems peculiar to ask where my lob-shot was when I was not using it. But losing sight of the fact that words are bits of behavior, memory theorists often ask how words are stored and how that storage is organized, and in that context take spatial descriptions at face-value—going to sleep in the snow-drift, so to speak. Countervailing paraphiers, like the frigidity of snow, are lacking—indeed, there are additional relations that support this transfer of function because words as products of behavior (e.g., when written) have properties of things. Thus, in terms of Jaynes's analysis, the patterns of phrasing that apply to *things* appear to function as paraphiers of "using," when one is concerned with the uttering of words. Some of these patterns might be identified as *idioms*, that is, expressions "not readily analyzable from grammatical construction or from the meaning of component parts" (Funk & Wagnalls, 1960, p. 627); nevertheless, their paraphiers still can have distorting effects.

More obviously, the "language of things" also gets insinuated into discussions of un-thing-like phenomena simply by virtue of their being the main topic of discussion. That is, although psychological or behavioral scientists are appropriately concerned with what humans and other organisms do and the ways in which they do them, it is difficult to discuss those activities without organizing the discussion around nouns. Thus, as Woodworth (1921) noted long ago, remembering becomes "memory," thinking becomes "thought," and effective action becomes "intelligence." Although grammatically, the activity-based nouns could be replaced with gerunds and the manner of activity could be discussed in adverbial terms, it is nouns that fit the customary interpretive patterns (Hineline, 1980). Nouns, then—even psychological nouns—bring along the various paraphiers of "things." And, thus, discussing the intentionality of acts becomes discussion of intentions.

Things Acquiring Agency, or Agency Requiring Things

Relatedly, and of special relevance to the topic of intention, are the ways in which patterns of speech smuggle "thing-terms" in as part of the process of generating agency. First, as noted by Whorf a few decades ago (e.g. see Carroll, 1956), in English as well as in Indo-European languages generally, occurrences are not readily described as "just happening." Rather, they must be described as having an agent that makes them happen. Thus, people say "Lightning flashed" when the flash *is* the lightning. Furthermore, the agency often is characterized misdirectively, as in "I looked at the moon." Looking is not something I did to the moon; rather, I oriented my eyes in such a way that the moon could do something to me. If I look at, or even describe the moon, it will be unaffected by those actions that were occasioned by it.

Hand-in-glove with attributing agencies to happenings is the bipolar limitation of interpretive prose: noun—verb, cause—effect, independent variable—dependent variable (Hineline, 1986, 1990, 1992). This is significant as a limitation, because psychological/behavioral phenomena are inherently tripolar, involving: a) terms identified with the organism (e.g., its physiology, moods, and motivations), b) terms identified with its environment (both present and past) and c) terms focused upon what the organism does (its behavior). Statements interpreting behavior, then, almost always privilege either the organism or the environment, each to the denigration of the other. Attribution theorists within mainstream social psychology have noted this and have identified some interesting shifts of agency. One that is relevant here is illustrated by the following:

> I have carried out careful and detailed observations with myself as experimental subject, and have concluded that wine is stronger than beer.
> I have carried out similarly careful and detailed observations with myself as experimental subject, and have concluded that I am more allergic to tulips than to roses.

Note that in one case, implicit agency is in the beverage instead of the person, whereas in the other, implicit agency is in the susceptibility of the person instead of the potency of the flower. This difference occurs even though in each case there is a known physiological mechanism and an identified environmental variable. The potency of the beverage *is* my susceptibility to it, and my allergic sensitivity to the flower *is* its potency to make me sneeze. Nevertheless, a subtle shift of agency occurs, apparently depending upon whether everyone is affected similarly. While, the shift of agency has nothing to do with where the "real causes" are, it is reflected in antagonisms between psychological traditions. For organism-based theorists, thinking, perceiving, remembering and the like are construed as processes within the organism that underlie and thus account for behavior, whereas for the environment-based theorist, those activities are included as behavior to be explained.

"Agency" arises in one's asserting, implicitly or explicitly, *why* a happening occurred, or an occurrence happened (note how difficult it is here, to avoid the implicit reification of saying someTHING happened even though a happening is not a thing. Note also, that the occurrence *is* the happening). When applied to environment-behavior relations, the cause-effect language pattern also tends to be understood as implying contiguous push-type, reflexive relations. Even for the reflex this is a slight mischaracterization, for reflex relations such as pupillary constriction or the knee-jerk result from pulsing a system that was at equilibrium, and the observed effect is an active reaction leading to restoration of equilibrium, rather than a passive result of stimulation. Addressed to operant relations, push-type causal language introduces more serious distortion, for, as will be elaborated below, the effect of a reinforcing event differs in fundamental ways from a reaction to a push.

When We Speak of Causes

A more formal consideration of causation and agency might begin with (or at least include) Aristotle and the four types of causation that he identified (see also Moore, this volume). First, it should be noted that it is not clear the extent to which Aristotle gave causes thing-like status. I am unable to speak or read Greek, but presumably Sambursky (1974) did when selecting the passages to quote in his book illustrating the evolution of physical thought. In a relevant passage, Sambursky quotes Aristotle as introducing his enumeration by saying: "We must proceed to consider causes, their character and number," (p. 64) thus seeming to give thing-like character to causal relations. In closing that section, however, Sambursky quotes Aristotle as saying: "This, then, perhaps exhausts the number of ways in which the term, 'cause' is used" (p. 65). The latter, of course, is closer to my own preferred locution, "When we speak of cause," which avoids the distortion of treating causes as things. Similarly, Killeen (2001), calls them Aristotle's "four (be)causes," suggesting that the terms identify four ways in which phenomena are explained.

Rachlin (1994) has described in detail the four usages that Aristotle identified: a) formal, b) material, c) efficient, and d) final causation. The last two of these are the usages that I am concerned with as relating to intentional statements. Although Rachlin's "teleological behaviorism" does not correspond exactly with my own views on these issues, we share a focus upon the distinction between those two. Thus, from Sambursky's (1974) translations of Aristotle:

c) Efficient cause—"The primary source of the change or coming to rest." or "What makes of what is made, and causes change that is changed" (p. 65). Example: The man who gave advice is the cause of that advice.
d) Final cause— "... in the sense of the end or 'that for the sake of which' a thing is done" (p. 65).

Thus characterized, the notion of final cause seems incompatible with modern natural science, since the phrase, "for the sake of which," seems to invoke animism or autonomous agency. That is, a boulder rolling down hill is *an instance of* the distance between two centers of gravity tending to decrease, but having abandoned the animistic view of rocks one would not describe the boulder's motion as occurring "for the sake of" such minimization. One also would not make the boulder agent of its own motion. As Baum (1995) has argued, imputing agency within the locus of an occurrence is tantamount to removing the occurrence from the domain of natural science.

Behavior analysis explicitly places behavior, *per se*, among the phenomena of natural science, accounting for it directly in terms of its relations to other events, rather than treating it as product of inferred underlying processes that could be granted the special explanatory status constituting agency. This strategy has sometimes been characterized as "merely descriptive," as when Catania (1992) discussed "the vocabulary of reinforcement:"

> When a response becomes more likely because it has produced a stimulus, we say the response has been reinforced and we call the stimulus a reinforcer. If asked how we know that the stimulus was a reinforcer, we point to the increase in responding. If then asked why the increase occurred, we may say it did so because the response was reinforced ... Once we define a reinforcer by its effect on behavior, we create a problem of circular definition if we simultaneously defined the effect by the reinforcing stimulus.
>
> One solution is to recognize that the term *reinforcement* is descriptive rather than explanatory. It names a relation between responses and the environment; it does not explain the relation. (p. 72)

In my view, this concedes too much. First, its circularity becomes nontrivializing when the principle of reinforcement is systematically interrelated in a network with other kinds of relations as an integral part of behavior-analytic theory. More pertinent to the present concern, the reinforcement relation is found to occur in the behavior of a wide variety of organisms in a wide variety of circumstances. Furthermore, it is an instance of the even more general principle of selection by consequences, which Skinner (1981) illustrated as applying on phylogenic and cultural as well as ontogenetic levels, and which Dawkins (1981) discussed as arising as a combination of other extremely general characteristics—survival of the stable, fecundity, and longevity. Hence, just as it is explanatory to identify the boulder rolling downhill as an instance of gravitational attraction, it also is explanatory to identify instances of behavior as reinforced,

While behavior analysis places agency outside the behavior to be accounted for, this does not mean that it ignores the relations that occasioned Aristotle's "final cause" label. To the contrary, those relations closely resemble (although they are not identical with) some fundamental behavior-analytic concepts; those relations also are at issue when people commonly speak of intentions and in intentional language. The problems of (or with) intentions and discussions of intentionality concern how one can best speak of such relations minimizing the distortions that tend to arise from extraneous paraphrandic relations.

Intentions, Consequences, and Causal Relations

So, when do people speak of intentions or of intentional acts? One clue to this was supplied by a philosopher colleague who began a lecture by defining an intentional act as one in which the actor is "cognizant of possible disagreement" (D. Welker, personal communication, September, 1979). Initially taking "cognizant" at face value, implying verbal awareness or an ability to describe, I acknowledge that there are many situations in which people explicitly describe what they plan, hope, or expect to do, with implied adjustments to be made if they were to encounter opposition or non-success. The nature and the role of such descriptions have been discussed by Lana (1994) and Neuman (2002), both of whom assert that intentions, in this sense, are not causes (note that the aphorism at the beginning of this essay constitutes a similar assertion). Statements of intent are behavioral events in themselves, and are to be accounted for as such. To be sure, one repertoire can affect another. At one extreme, an overt statement of intent can be a commitment. Especially if made public, it increases the likelihood of actually doing what was described, either through contingencies involving others (Hayes et al., 1985), or through discriminations facilitated by the statement, as in cases whereby people speak of "self-reinforcement" (Catania, 1975). At the other extreme, one often is called upon to account for one's actions, and typically, it is explanations in terms of intent that have been selectively reinforced. As often as not, these intentional statements are generated after the fact— as when, after you execute a particularly flagrant maneuver in navigating your automobile through traffic, your passenger asks for justification. Your actions among the rapidly flowing events surely did not entail the logical deliberations implied by the subsequent justification. Many instances lie between these two extremes, they often are amenable to analyses as rule-governed behavior (e.g., Hayes, 1989), and most can be treated as relations between two or more repertoires. Nevertheless, these need not imply the special causal status that intentional statements seem to claim. Furthermore, if one is concerned with accounting for the intentional statement itself, rather than for its result, more general issues are involved.

My colleague's "possible disagreement" need not be confined to relations involving language, and it is these additional cases that enable me to address those more general issues of intentionality. To do this, the suggestions of awareness and rationality implied by the term, "cognizant" need to be eliminated (despite the wide acceptance of Descartes' "I think, therefore I am," it is problematic to treat cognizance as accounting for itself). One can address the issue by simply re-phrasing the criterion for an intentional act as one in which the actor's behavior is *sensitive to* possible disagreement, and note that the disagreement need not involve language. Thus, if I swing my arm in the vicinity of your head, the intentionality of my action would be revealed by what I did if you were to duck. Your evading the blow would constitute disagreement: Would I swing again? There are, of course, correlated characteristics that would aid the interpreter's discriminations—closed fist, aggressive posture, and the like, but the key feature to be discerned would be *whether the behavior was to be understood in relation to its consequences*. As Skinner (1974) asserted, "operant behavior is the very field of purpose and intention" (p. 55). This does not mean that "operant" and "intentional" are interchangeable, however, for coming from different interpretive traditions their usages involve differing assumed relations to agency, awareness and related issues. Also, the vernacular distinction between *voluntary* and *involuntary* actions often overlaps with that between *intentional* and *unintentional* ones, but the two distinctions are not identical, for a coerced action might be called intentional but not voluntary. One might also wonder whether "understood in relation to its consequences" concerns the interpreter's or the actor's understanding. The situation is least complicated if we attribute such understanding to the person interpreting the action: Schnaitter (1978) provides a concise illustration of how this "understanding" can be couched as behavior-analytic interpretation (Hineline, 1992, and Hineline & Wanchisen, 1989, provide more comprehensive but more complex accounts). If the interpreter and the actor are one and the same, and if the interpretation is not entirely post hoc, verbal behavior may have a role in the action itself, as noted just above for instances where we take "cognizant" at face value.

Re-framing the issue of intentional actions in terms of their relevant consequences enables us to discern interpretive confusions that may arise through a mis-match between, on the one hand, the ways in which the behavior of concern is organized, and on the other hand, the patterns in which people have commonly learned to talk about causal relations. That is, certain types of situations occasion speaking in causal terms; people learn to speak causally with respect to the relations that Aristotle identified as constituting efficient causation. There is a plethora of discriminanda for children and other members of the community to learn to say appropriately: "It pushes, . . . she hits, . . . they chop"—agent-action, cause-effect. Thus one finds interpretive language to be comprised predominantly of the patterns of efficient causation. Arising as paraphiers of "thing-as-agent" or "agent-as-thing," these patterns support the common practice of speaking of intentions as gratuitously reified entities that are invoked as having efficient-causal status. Beyond, and perhaps more important than the problems of reification, the verbal patterns of efficient causation yield distortion when they are occasioned by situations that are not organized in the bipolar pattern that is implied by the locutions of efficient causation. It may be helpful to delineate some of those situations, so as to clarify their mismatch with the efficient-causal pattern of intentional phrasing.

Mis-Matches Between Causal Language and its Phenomena

Ostensibly simple cases arise if I ask questions like: "Did you *intend* to leave the car unlocked?" or "Did you *intend* to go the long way around?" or "Did you *intend* to injure him?" In each case the clarifying question is not whether the person *had* a thing called *an intention*, but rather, whether the external events specified as characterizing the intention were the effective, functional consequence of the action or inaction. In accounting for the behavior patterns that might have prompted these questions, an Aristotelian would identify those specified events as final causes. Thus, for example, Braithwaite (1959) pointed out that in teleological (i.e. goal-directed or goal-intended) explanations "the idea of 'final cause' functions as 'efficient cause'" (p. 325). Killeen (2001) pithily observes that "Final causes were given a bad name (*teleology*) because they were treated as errant formal, material, or efficient causes" (p. 137). Braithwaite's and Killeen's analyses do not draw upon language patterns as in the present discussion, however.

A behavior analyst would identify the same functional consequences as probably reinforcing the behavior. The difference is not merely one of labels, however, for the behavior analyst would be appealing to *past* consequences, thus invoking a likely account of how such behavior had come to occur, without appealing to a presently attendant event. The unlocked car had proved more convenient to use; "the long way around" had afforded the more pleasurable scenery, and injuring someone had preserved one's own safety. Interpretations such as these are likely to seem non-explanatory to a person who understands causal relations only through the efficient-causal patterns of ordinary interpretive language. Such a person will hear the statement as a flawed efficient-causal explanation, with the episodes identified as accounting for the behavior having occurred *after* instead of before the actions that are at issue. Actual "mishearing" of this kind can be discerned when critics of behavioral interpretation sometimes ask how reinforcement can account for a person's action, when, by definition, it occurs after the action. Behavior analysts sometimes reply to such criticism by couching the answer in a way that does not explicitly challenge the critics' assumptions, by proposing that similar actions were followed by those consequences in the past, and that generalization accounts for the subsequent behavior (e.g., Hineline & Wanchisen, 1989).

An alternative reply is to clarify the departure from efficient causation, characterizing the behavior as constituted of classes of actions and classes of consequences, which together comprise an ongoing entity that is extended in time. Glenn and Field (1994) have discussed this at length, noting the similarity between operants as temporally distributed aggregates of behavior and species as temporally distributed aggregates of organisms, with membership in an operant class or a species being understood in terms of common origins. Lacking that extended interpretive rubric, however, the aforementioned critics will find that the locally relevant events do not fit the efficient cause-effect pattern. In their view, this apparent problem is to be solved by converting the adverbial "intentionally" to "intention," thus providing an entity that can be granted agency in explanation. An "expectation" is typically invoked as well, smuggling in past events as bases for the intention without acknowledging them. Despite these gratuitous additions, the interpretation in terms of intention or expectation (or both), achieves an apparent simplicity by yielding to the patterns, and yielding the paraphiers, of cause-effect, agent-action language.

Similar confusions arise from applying the implicit push-type logic of efficient causal statements to highly variable behavior patterns. Specifically, it sometimes is asserted that reinforcement cannot account for novelty of behavior, for by their very newness, novel responses cannot have previously been reinforced. In the behavior analyst's functional analyses, however, topographical variability may be largely irrelevant to the specification of the behavior of concern. That is, operant behavior often is adequately specified in terms of its consequences without reference to the specific form of the behavior or to the physical mechanics that it entails. Thus the phrase, "opening the door," is occasioned by a functional class that includes variants of behavior that may be extremely disparate in form—reaching, grasping and turning, nudging with one's hip, asking a friend to do it, gesturing—all of which are aggregated on the basis of a common class of consequences. Furthermore, as Neuringer has demonstrated, variability itself is a property of behavior that can be selected through reinforcement (e.g., Neuringer, 1993; Neuringer, Deiss, & Olson, 2000; Neuringer, this volume). To understand this interpretation, however, one must recognize that the selective process is not localizable to an instant where cause produces effect. Instead, the process is intrinsically extended in time, involving multiple instances of the consequence as well as multiple and/or temporally extended patterns of behavior.

Even if one recognizes selection as a distinct type of natural process not requiring an agent, the patterns of conventional causal language make it difficult to discuss that process in a nondistorting way. This is evident in the phrase, *selection pressure* that is often invoked in discussions of evolutionary process. Stringent contingencies of selection are an important feature affecting the rate and degree of evolutionary change, but that stringency is fundamentally *unlike* the efficient-causal relation that the term "pressure" suggests. The subtle ubiquity of this kind of problem can be discerned in locutions involving the term "produce" in this context. While it is appropriate to say, "the farmer produced more productive cows through selective breeding," it would be subtly distorting to say that it was the selective process that produced the more productive cows. Rather, the development of more productive cows was *an instance* of selective process. That is, to the extent that the term "produce" implies the pattern of efficient causation, neither the effects upon an individual organism's behavior of past response-consequent relations, nor the effects of differential opportunities to reproduce, of members of an evolving breed of cattle, fits the implied configuration. This comparison—"the farmer produced" vs. "differential opportunity to replicate was an instance of"—may seem to draw a distinction that is too subtle to be practical, and indeed it probably is unrealistic to abandon the "selection produced" locution. Still, communication is improved by being alert to subtle constraints and distortions as well as to the ones that become evident when they are the apparent bases for vehement disagreements.

If I speak of what I or someone else intends to do, I often am not identifying a brief episodic act, but rather, an extended pattern of behavior—going to town, writing an article, cooking a meal. Such extended behavior patterns are typically identified by their terminating events—arrival in town, completed article, palatable food—and the interpretive patterns accounting for them entail the same issues and relations just discussed in accounting for brief actions with functional consequences. But sometimes the extended pattern has no clear end point, or it might be characterized as "an end in itself," as in taking a vacation or listening to a symphony. For these cases, component patterns within the action—staying late in bed, wearing a pair of headphones—may be understood in terms of the larger action of which they are a part. As I understand it, in Aristotelian terms the identification of the relation between the component and the larger pattern qualifies as identifying a final causal relation. Here, the intention as applying to the larger pattern is rather like the gratuitous agency of "lightning flashed." If I say he slept late *because* he was taking a vacation, I am interpreting the component pattern in terms of its place in the larger one. Identifying his sleeping late as part of being on vacation, instead of as a failure to set the alarm, could be rephrased in terms of whether sleeping late was intentional or not. If that rephrasing is in a variant of "intention produced sleeping," a final-causal relation has been transmogrified into the Procrustean pattern of efficient-causal language.

Addressed in behavior-analytic terms, the local action as part of a larger pattern can be directly understood as directly involving the issue of multiple scales. Sometimes the larger unit can be deconstructed into components according to established principles, as in cases where the constituent parts comprise a behavioral chain whereby each action is occasioned by one stimulus and is subsequently reinforced by the onset of another stimulus that occasions the next action. The deconstruction may involve different causal modes at different scales—as in the example supplied above, whereby the farmer produced more productive cows (efficient cause), through a process that, analyzed at a smaller scale, was organized as selection by consequences, which does not fit the efficient-causal pattern. In other cases, two or more independently acquired repertoires may get selected and fused into a single unit when they occur together and produce a common consequence, through a process that Andronis and his colleagues have identified under the term, *contingency-adduction* (Andronis, 1983; Andronis, Layng, & Goldiamond, 1997; Layng & Andronis, 1984; Johnson & Layng, 1992). The specific configurations of the component repertoires will arise through their mutually coordinating roles in the larger unit. In still other cases, the observation by Morris, Higgins, and Bickel (1982) may be most apt: " ... if one fails to find an immediate stimulus that controls a response, perhaps the response is only an element of a larger functional unit which is controlled by currently operating variables not immediately attendant to that element" (pp. 119–120). Still more abstractly, one behavior pattern may be understood mainly through its membership in a higher-order class—as, for example, when events arising directly from one imitative act may affect a person's subsequent imitating of other kinds of behavior in other circumstances. In most of these, the simple, bipolar, push-type efficient cause-effect locution implied by "intentions produce actions" is not well matched with the phenomena of concern. For these as well as the forgoing cases, an interpretive language with minimal paraphrandic distortion would enable a behavior analyst to easily say, as suggested above, that the process of concern is *an instance of* selection by consequences and thus explained in the sense of belonging to a set of orderly phenomena having great generality.

Legal Intent and Responsibility

The context of legal responsibility is a domain in which discussions of intention are especially salient. Whole books and countless legal opinions have addressed the problems of discerning a person's intent and the implications thereof, and a brief discussion here cannot pretend to supplant those learned writings. Nevertheless, lest it be concluded that in omitting intentional terms from its explanations behavior analytic interpretation becomes irrelevant to legal affairs (see Chiesa, this volume, and Galuska, this volume, for additional discussions of legal affairs from a behavior-analytic viewpoint), discussions of a few additional observations are in order: First, discussions of legal intent, and of the related assignment of responsibility, appear to be mainly concerned with whether to punish. Second, discussions of punishment easily become muddled by the conflation of two fundamentally different meanings of that term. By one meaning, punishment applies to a person, and is justified by invoking the concepts of intent and responsibility. By the other meaning, punishment applies to the person's behavior, and those terms are indirectly relevant at best. Within the legal professions this distinction is sometimes recognized by differentiating between "the administering of justice" and "deterrence." The concept of intentionality, however, remains embedded in discussions of both kinds of issues, contributing to their conflation. Third, keeping the concepts of intent and responsibility separate from the meaning of punishment as a consequence that reduces the likelihood of specified behavior, enables a pragmatic reformulation of the issues (see also Lattal and Laipple, this volume). It is then a relatively straightforward matter to take into account research that has identified the characteristics of punishment that make it more effective or less so.

Punishment of the Person is expressed in phrases such as "An eye for an eye," or in statements to the effect that "Having been punished, the person has paid her debt to society." Implicitly if not explicitly, each of these concerns retribution, or more plainly stated, vengeance. Such phrases are silent about what the person is likely to do in the future. Behavior analysis has had little to say about vengeant behavior, perhaps because such behavior would be ethically problematic to study in experiments. Nevertheless, contemporary events as well as records of human history make amply clear that vengeant behavior does occur and its determinants need to be understood. Interestingly, as applied to punishment this focus would concern the behavior of those who implement punishment procedures, more than that of people on the receiving end.

Punishment defined in relation to a person's behavior and not as applied to the person, is the meaning traditionally advocated by behavior analysts. Behavior analysts have asserted that this is what punishment *should* mean, or at least that this is, unequivocally, what the term identifies within behavioral practices and interpretations. Understood in this way, the susceptibility of behavior to punishment is seen as a fundamental and adaptive property that contributes to the wellbeing of the behaving individual. In brief, sensitivity of behavior to some consequences whereby that behavior becomes less likely in the future is extremely important; if burning my hand were to have no effect upon my subsequent likelihood of touching hot stoves, I would be in big trouble. It follows that studying processes of punishment is important to understanding when it will, and *when it will not* be effective. At the same time, advocating the study of punishment for those reasons *is not the same as advocating punishment as the practice of choice* in practical situations. Despite all these considerations, to recommend a punishment procedure even as a last resort, for example, in dealing with a person's seriously self-destructive behavior, is to risk being misunderstood as advocating vengeance upon that already unfortunate person. As members of the vernacular community, scientists, teachers, lawyers, and judges all speak an everyday language in which the two meanings of punishment continue to be conflated. Thus, suggestions of "vengeance" are problematic paraphiers of the term, "punishment."

Putting the punishment issue aside, an additional kind of misunderstanding tends to arise regarding behavior analysis in legal contexts. That is, the behavior analyst's environment-based account of behavior is mistaken as implying that "anything goes"—that accounting for people's behavior in terms of their past histories excuses them from responsibility for their actions. To the contrary, just like more conventional citizens, a behavior analyst views some kinds of behavior as completely unacceptable, and views other behavior as inappropriate, to be made as unlikely as possible, and so forth. In deciding what to do about these, however, a behavior analyst appeals to what is known about the maintenance of potentially punishable behavior, and about the effectiveness or ineffectiveness of the feasible arrangements for punishing. The key question is whether those arrangements are likely to reduce the likelihood that the same or other individuals will subsequently engage in that act or similar acts. Thus, instead of looking for evidence of intentionality, a behavior analyst focuses directly upon how the behavior of concern might be understood in terms of its consequences. Instead of asking "Who had the motive for the crime?" The behavior analyst would ask, "For whom would the result of the crime constitute a reinforcer, and how so?" People's contingencies of reinforcement are more amenable to analysis and investigation than are their inferred internal states.

Although behavior analysts favor invoking reinforcement contingencies whenever possible, a focus on punishment as functional consequence of behavior, combined with a principled understanding of the features that make its effect on subsequent behavior less or more effective, can inform the decisions that implement legal/cultural practice. Nevertheless, while this alternative approach may clarify issues that are obscured by concerns with intentions and responsibility, it cannot eliminate all dilemmas. Thus, if a woman arranged for her husband to be shot, it would make a difference to a behavior analyst (as well as to a traditional jurist), if the husband had been assaulting her repeatedly despite court orders, her appeals to social service agencies, and the like. Her behavior would be interpreted as a product of powerful negative reinforcement contingencies without available alternative repertoires. In contrast, if the major discernable consequence of the husband's death were the widow's receipt of the proceeds from a large insurance policy, a behavior analyst would offer a quite different recommendation. Recommendations in each case, while not simple, would be informed by explicit focus upon the likelihood of that individual subsequently repeating a comparable act, and upon the likelihood of others behaving imitatively in similar circumstances. Even if one is less ambivalent about the relevant people's circumstances, though, a behaviorally informed analysis may simply demonstrate the intractability of a problem rather than yielding a straightforward solution. For example, behavioral research has shown that a most important determinant of the effectiveness of punishment is whether an alternative, socially acceptable, reinforced and unpunished repertoire is available. Knowing this to be true does not yield an obvious method for changing the behavior of a person who lacks conventionally marketable skills, but makes thousands of dollars per week selling addictive drugs. Relatedly, it is well established that to be maximally effective in suppressing behavior, punishment has to be swift, certain, and relatively intense. Still, most people would prefer not to live in a country where the police were enabled to deliver swift and certain punishment, because that entails unacceptable risk of the punishing events impinging upon (the behavior and life-circumstances of) innocent people.

Nevertheless, addressed to issues of social importance, behavior-analytic focus upon behavior and its consequences, without appeals to intent and responsibility, has promise for cutting across traditional dichotomies that impede more effective social practices. It has been aptly observed that "political conservatives fail to understand compassion, while political liberals fail to understand contingencies." In contrast, a behavior-analytic approach occupies a principled middle ground between those two extremes. Response-independent delivery of rewards (as in "the welfare state") is recognized as destructive, while it is also recognized that contingencies of reinforcement must take an individual's currently available repertoires as a starting point for change. Even the concept of human rights bears constructive reexamination if one replaces the appeals to autonomous intentions with serious consideration of behavior as selected by consequences. Thus considered, rights are best concerned not with possession of things, but with being enabled to produce things for oneself (Skinner, 1978).

Conclusions

There is a difference between the stance of taking seriously what is at issue when people speak or write of intentions or of intentional behavior, and that of accepting at face value the assumptions implied by those prose patterns. This essay does adopt the former stance, provisionally identifying intentional behavior as behavior specified in terms of what it might produce or prevent—which is to say, its relevant consequences. It follows from this, however, that the latter stance is to be challenged. The assumptions implied by intentional prose typically lead people to accept the notion of intentions as entities or internal states that cause actions. Specifying behavior in intentional terms is thus misdirective, inducing us to look within the actor for sources of an action rather than to the related, especially past consequences of actions in that class. The main focus of the present essay has been to examine how it is that these misdirections come to occur. Rather than appealing to mechanisms or to logic that would risk adopting the assumptions of intentional language while attempting to examine it, the focus here has been directly upon characteristics of explanatory prose, specifically the characteristics that induce the kinds of prose patterns that include intentional phrasing. These characteristics are most clear when they occur in explicitly metaphorical statements, sometimes enriching and sometimes distorting or constraining descriptions. The distorting effects can sometimes be understood as arising through the language of efficient causation applied to the patterns that Aristotle identified as final causation. Distorting characteristics can be so subtle as to be unnoticed when, for example, they simply make it briefer and easier to specify behavior in "intentional shorthand," rather than terms of the functional relations that clearly define the behavior and indicate how it comes to occur and be maintained. Constraining effects occur when the bipolarity cause-effect or agent-action pattern of efficient causation is invoked with respect to the inherently tri-polar relations of context, organism, and behavior. These latter effects often can be discerned in disagreements between interpretive viewpoints such as the behavior-analytic, which entails environment-behavior locutions, and contrasting interpretations that entail mainly organism-behavior locutions.

References

Andronis, P. T. (1983). *Symbolic aggression by pigeons.* Dissertation: The University of Chicago, Chicago, IL.
Andronis, P. T., Layng, T. V. J., & Goldiamond, I. (1997). Contingency adduction of "symbolic aggression" by pigeons. *The Analysis of Verbal Behavior, 14,* 5–17.
Baum, W. M. (1995). Radical behaviorism and the concept of agency. *Behaviorology, 3,* 93–106.
Braithwaite, R. B. (1959). *Scientific explanation: A study of the function of theory, probability, and law in science.* Cambridge, England: Cambridge University Press.
Carroll, J. B. (Ed.) (1956). *Language, thought and reality: Selected Writings of Benjamin Lee Whorf.* Cambridge: MIT Press.
Catania, A. C. (1975). The myth of self-reinforcement. *Behaviorism, 3,* 192–199.
Catania, A. C. (1992). *Learning (third edition).* Inglewood Cliffs, NJ: Prentice-Hall.
Dawkins, R. (1981). Selfish genes and selfish memes. In D. R. Hofstadter & D. C. Dennet (Eds.), *The mind's I: Fantasies and reflections on self and soul* (pp. 124–144). New York: Basic Books.
Funk & Wagnalls (1960). *Standard dictionary of the English language: International edition.* New York: Funk & Wagnalls.
Glenn, S. S. & Field, D. P. (1994). Functions of the environment in behavioral evolution. *The Behavior Analyst, 17,* 241–259.
Hayes, S. C. (Ed.) (1989). *Rule-governed behavior: Cognition, contingencies and instructional control.* New York: Plenum.
Hayes, S. C., Rosenfarb, I., Wulfert, E., Munt, E. D., Korn, Z., & Zettle, R. D. (1985). Self-reinforcement effects: An artifact of social standard setting? *Journal of Applied Behavior Analysis, 18,* 201–214.
Hineline, P. N. (1980). The language of behavior analysis: Its community, its functions, and its limitations. *Behaviorism, 8,* 67–86.
Hineline, P. N. (1986). Re-tuning the operant-respondent distinction. In T. Thompson & M. D. Zeiler (Eds.), *Analysis and integration of behavioral units: A festschrift in honor of Kenneth MacCorquodale* (pp. 55–79). Hillsdale, NJ: Erlbaum

Hineline, P. N. (1990). The Origins of Environment-Based Psychological Theory. *Journal of the Experimental Analysis of Behavior, 53*, 305–320.

Hineline, P. N. (1992). A Self-interpretive behavior analysis. *American Psychologist, 47*, 1274–1286.

Hineline, P. N., & Wanchisen, B. A. (1989). Correlated hypothesizing and the distinction between contingency-shaped and rule-governed behavior. In S. G. Hayes (Ed.), *Rule-governed behavior: Cognition, contingencies and instructional control* (pp. 221–268). New York: Plenum.

Jaynes, J. (1976). *The origins of consciousness in the breakdown of the bicameral mind.* Boston: Houghton Mifflin.

Johnson, K. R., & Layng, T. V. J. (1992). Breaking the structuralist barrier: Literacy and numeracy with fluency. *American Psychologist, 47*, 1475–1490.

Killeen, P. R. (2001). The four causes of behavior. *Current Directions in Psychological Science, 10*, 136–145.

Lana, R. E. (1994). Social history and the behavioral repertoire. *Journal of the Experimental Analysis of Behavior, 62*, 315–322.

Layng, T. V. J., & Andronis, P. T. (1984). Toward a functional analysis of delusional speech and hallucinatory behavior. *The Behavior Analyst, 7*, 139–156.

Morris. E. K., Higgins, S. T., & Bickel, W. K. (1982). Comments on cognitive science in the experimental analysis of behavior. *The Behavior Analyst, 5*, 109–125.

Neuman, P. (2002). An intentional interpretive perspective. Unpublished manuscript.

Neuringer, A. J. (1993). Reinforced variation and selection. *Animal Learning and Behavior, 21*, 83–91.

Neuringer, A. J., Deiss, C., & Olson, G. (2000). Reinforced variability and operant learning. *Journal of Experimental Psychology: Animal Behavior Processes, 26*, 98–111.

Rachlin, H. (1994). *Behavior and mind: The roots of modern psychology.* New York: Oxford University Press.

Sambursky, S. (1974). *Physical thought: From the presocratics to the quantum physicists.* London: Hutchinson.

Schnaitter, R. (1978). Private causes. *Behaviorism, 6*, 1–12.

Skinner, B. F. (1978). The ethics of helping people. In: Skinner, B. F. *Reflections on behaviorism and society* (pp. 33–47). Englewood Cliffs, NJ: Prentice-Hall.

Skinner, B. F. (1974). *About Behaviorism.* New York: Knopf.

Skinner, B. F. (1981). Selection by consequences. *Science, 213*, 501–504.

Woodworth, R. S. (1921). *Psychology* (revised edition). New York: Holt.

12

Operant Contingencies and the Origin of Cultures

Sigrid S. Glenn

Writers from a variety of disciplines recognize that culture is composed of or depends on behavior, but is also somehow more than an unorganized collection of behavioral events. Biologist Bonner (1980) defined culture as "behavior transmitted from one individual to another by teaching and learning" (p. 17). Cultural anthropologist Harris (1964) stated, "human behavior constitutes the cultural field of inquiry" (p. 20). However, human responses *are definitely not* cultural things," (Harris, p. 22) but rather are the empirical events to which scientific operations must be applied to arrive at cultural classifications. Behavior analyst Baum (2000) stated, "culture consists of behavior and ... cultural change constitutes an evolutionary process" (p. 182).

In this paper I take as a starting point that cultures are nothing more than learned behavior and its physical products, in the same sense as living organisms are nothing more than chemical elements. But the origins and evolution of biological phenomena cannot be explained without recourse to principles in addition to the laws describing physical and chemical processes. Nor can learned behavior be explained without recourse to principles in addition to those of biological evolution. In the same vein, an explanation of the origin and evolution of cultures requires going beyond the evolutionary and behavioral principles that account for species

Sigrid S. Glenn • Department of Behavior Analysis, University of North Texas, Denton, Texas 76205.

characteristics and the learned behavior of individual organisms. Analysis at another level is required, but where to begin?

Skinner (1981) provided a clue when he pointed out that, in addition to natural selection and operant selection, human behavior was also due to "the special contingencies maintained by an evolved social environment" (p. 502). One interpretation of Skinner's statement is that the contingencies of an evolved social environment function differently than the contingencies maintained by the nonsocial environment. In responding to commentary on his article, however, Skinner (1988) made clear that he was proposing "no new behavioral process," (p. 38) but rather "a different *kind* of selection" (p. 38). In short, the behavior acquired by each individual during his or her lifetime is explained by behavioral level processes, whether the concrete particulars of the behavior-environment contingencies are material or social, and whether they are human-made or the products of other natural processes. The particulars of the behavior-environment relations that come to exist in cultures (i.e., the particulars of an evolved social environment), however, require "a third kind of selection" (Skinner, 1981, p. 502) to explain their existence.

Skinner's suggestion that three different kinds of selection bear directly or indirectly on human behavior has led to behavior-analytic examinations of selectionist perspectives as they pertain to learned behavior and to cultural evolution (e.g., Baum, 2000; Catania, 1995; Donahoe, 1984, this volume; Glenn, 1991; Glenn, Ellis, & Greenspoon, 1992). From the present perspective, the ultimate value of selectionist theories is their success in accounting for complexity without appealing to prior design.

Selectionist Approaches to the Evolution of Complexity

In organic evolutionary theory, organisms having complex structures and functions are said to be traceable to single-celled ancestors of the distant past. Organismic complexity, like all complexity in selectionist theories, is said to result from repeated rounds of selection acting on phenomena resulting from earlier rounds of selection. In many cases, complexity of structure and function increases over time. It does so when complexity adds value to the fit between individuals in a lineage undergoing selection and the selecting environment. It should be noted that *more complex* does not connote *better adapted* or *more evolved* because single-celled organisms currently existing are as much the result of evolution via selection as organisms (e.g., humans) composed of many parts with complex interrelated functions.

Anything more than casual understanding of any selection process requires consideration of two related issues: how the selection process works and the nature of the phenomena playing various roles in the process. There is a voluminous literature, and a variety of perspectives, on the units of selection in organic evolution. What varies and how are these variations observed? What is selected? What does it mean to be selected? What is retained as a result of variation and differential selection? How and where does retention take place? How are the levels of organization within a domain related to one another historically or conceptually (e.g., how do genes relate to organisms, regarding both ontogeny and evolutionary history?)? How can the phenomena of interest be classified so that broadly applicable scientific principles can be formulated? To complicate matters, theories comprise answers to such questions only in the context of answers to other questions.

Consider the relation between the concepts of variation and selection. Evolution by selection requires variation among entities *that are part of a changing (evolving) unit* of some kind. Retention of what is selected can be observed only at the level of this more inclusive unit. In biology, species are generally viewed as the larger unit where the results of selection are seen. A species is a unit that changes over time (evolves) as selection continues. The level of organization at which the relevant variation should be examined is a matter of debate. Traditionally, biologists have viewed organisms (of a particular species) as the biological units that vary and thereby differentially interact with their environments, resulting in retention of some organismic trait values over others in that species. Some biologists (e.g., Dawkins, 1976) point out that genes are what replicate and retain characteristics in a species; therefore, genes are the variants that constitute the units of selection. Others (e.g., Wilson, 1980) suggest that at least some *groups* of organisms function as a biological unit that can be selected.

According to Hull (1980), failure to resolve the unit of selection problem in evolutionary biology is due to different writers' exclusive focus on only one of two related subprocesses of selection: replication and interaction. In natural selection, these subprocesses can be (and often are) carried out by differing classes of biological entities. For example, genes are *replicators* and account for the retention of organismic characteristics in a species. More inclusive entities such as organisms and colonies often play the role of *interactor* in organic selection, because they are the cohesive wholes that interact differentially with their environments. Their differential interaction results in differential replication of genes in organic lineages. A *lineage* of genes/organisms is the entity that evolves. It is "an entity that changes indefinitely through time as a result of replication and [differential] interaction" (Hull, p. 327). A generic definition of selection is "a process in which the differential extinction and proliferation of interactors cause the differential perpetuation of the relevant replicators [i.e., the recipes for trait characteristics that better fit the current environment] that produced them" (Hull, p. 338). The results of selection processes are seen in the evolution of lineages. The general problem in selectionist accounts, then, is one of identifying units of replication that retain in the lineage the recipe for the units of interaction that differentially fit the world outside themselves.

Hull, Langman, and Glenn (2001) developed a general account of selection by applying Hull's terminology to organic selection, operant selection, and somatic selection of antibodies in the immune system. In the case of operant selection, operant instances or acts, belonging to a particular operant (lineage), were viewed as units of interaction that fit differentially with their selecting environment (behavioral consequences). As in the case of organic selection, operant interactors (instances or acts) stand in a hierarchical relation to their replicators (neural components of operant acts; see Donahoe, this volume) .

In the remainder of this paper, I apply the general concepts of replicators, interactors, and lineages (Hull, 1980) to the problem of explaining the origin of cultural-level phenomena built up from operant behavior in social environments. My goal is to demonstrate that evolutionary processes are of the same kind, whatever the domains, but that new phenomena result from the interplay of those processes with phenomena already existing. Specifically, I will suggest preliminary answers to the following questions: How could cultural lineages have arisen from the behavior of individual organisms? What constitutes a cultural lineage? What is the nature of the units playing the roles of replication and interaction at the cultural level? And finally, I will briefly touch on the role of verbal behavior or language in the origin of cultures.

Contingencies of Reinforcement and the Formation of Culturo-Behavioral Lineages

In considering the origin of cultures, it is necessary to avoid using human cultures as they currently exist as a starting point. That would be comparable to using observations of human organisms to develop a theory of the origin of living things (and, indeed, is apparently how preDarwinian accounts were formulated). The environment in which human cultures originated was different from today's world because human cultures have virtually created much of today's world. It seems likely that the story began sometime during the history of our ancestor species. Although no species other than our own appear to have participated in anything like modern human cultures, there is some evidence that extinct hominid species, including those considered ancestral to Homo sapiens, participated in rudimentary cultures (White, 1982). This suggests that cultural phenomena antedate language. Do elements of human cultures antedate hominid species themselves? Unless culture is *defined* so that it excludes elements of human cultures seen among living nonhumans, the answer is likely to be affirmative.

Bonner (1980) cited numerous examples of transmission of learned behavior across individuals within and between generations in many different species. There is always the issue of exactly what is learned by the receiver in cultural transmission. Topography? Stimulus function? Spatial orientation? Some combination of these? From a behavior-analytic perspective, that which is learned may include any or all of these and the question regarding any particular behavior is an empirical one. For present purposes I focus on questions regarding the processes by which learned behavior is transmitted. Is it explicitly taught? Is it acquired by imitation? If so, is the learner's imitating proclivity the result of natural selection, learning history, or both, in some combination? Even if there is phylogenic proclivity to imitate the learned actions of conspecifics, must the imitated act produce reinforcing consequences (automatic or contrived) to be maintained in the learner's repertoire? If not, then should one not expect any and all imitations to occur repeatedly once they appear in an organism's behavior stream? If imitated variations were not affected by behavioral consequences, then would they not be as likely to *reduce* the likelihood of reinforcement as to *increase it*? If reduction of primary reinforcers works against survival, would not imitation of novel topographies, responses to novel stimuli, etc., be (on average) as detrimental as they were useful to survival?

An often-cited example of the rapid transmission of learned behavior across nonhuman repertoires may provide some guidance in answering such questions. Japanese scientists studied intensively over several years a troop of macaque monkeys living on an island (Kawamura, 1959). The scientists laid out sweet potatoes on the beach to entice the monkeys to come near so they could be better observed. The monkeys often rubbed the sandy potatoes against their bodies before eating, presumably brushing off much of the sand. A juvenile female, Imo, was observed one day to dip potatoes in a brook before eating them. It is unclear whether Imo rubbed the potato while it was in the water or simply dipped the potato in the water in the first recorded instance of potato washing. Theretofore, no monkey had been observed dipping potatoes in water before eating them. Within 3 years, 11 monkeys had acquired the behavior. Within 5 years,

"6 adult males and 5 adult females, that is 18.1% [had] acquired sweet potato washing behavior, and 15 of 19 monkeys, aged between two and seven (10 males and 9 females), that is, 78.9% acquired also the behavior" (Kawai, 1965, p. 3). In general, younger monkeys acquired the behavior first and older monkeys took longer, some never acquiring the behavior at all. Monkeys born 6 years or longer after the first observed potato washing "accepted [sweet potato washing] as a normal feeding behavior and learned it without any resistance at all" (Kawai, p. 8). Harris (1989) called this potato washing by the troop of Japanese macaques a "rudimentary culture" (pp. 62–64), because learned behavior was transmitted across organisms that were interacting with each other.

From the present perspective, a better designation for the observed potato washing behavior would be *preculture*. The minimal requirements for designating a phenomenon as *precultural* are these: (a) an operant lineage (class) of behavioral instances must originate in the repertoire of at least one organism; (b) instances of that operant must have a stimulus function with respect to the behavior of conspecifics; and (c) contingencies of reinforcement must be repeated in successive repertoires to establish a lineage of learned behavior that replicates across organismic boundaries. Such a lineage is designated here as a *culturo-behavioral lineage*. These characteristics of precultural phenomena will be expanded upon in the next three sections.

Operant Lineage Requirement

A single instance of learned behavior will rarely be sufficient as the starting point for cultural transmission. Behavioral variants are no doubt occurring all the time, but cultural transmission would be highly improbable if instances of novel behavior typically occurred only once. Furthermore, if a novel act did not make a [useful] difference, repetition in another repertoire would be useless if not actually detrimental. To become part of a cultural process, a behavioral variant must first be established in the repertoire of at least one organism. How could the potato washing operant have come to exist in Imo's repertoire? The question needs to be asked in two parts: (a) What could have accounted for the first instance of Imo's potato washing behavior? (b) What could have accounted for repetition of the behavior?

Observers reporting the phenomenon do not provide much information, so one must consider reasonable possibilities. Imo had been observed often to eat potatoes from which she rubbed the sand. Imo's potato rubbing was operant—a lineage of repeated acts selected by the consequence of more-potato-less-sand taste. The first instance of Imo's potato washing may have been adventitious (and may or may not have been observed by the scientists). She may have played in or near the water while eating and accidentally dropped the potato in the water before eating the first washed potato. Alternatively, an operant of removing mud or sap from her hands or other parts of her body by rubbing them in the brook may have been acquired previously. The behavior of washing the potato would then be an instance of response generalization. Another way to view Imo's first instance of potato-washing would be as a kind of *adduction*—the combining of acts from two independently acquired operants, with the result of an otherwise unavailable consequence (e.g., Andronis, 1983; Epstein, 1985). In this case, the presence of water where hands had been dipped and a dirty potato that ordinarily evoked rubbing resulted in rubbing the potato while dipping it in the water.

The point is that instances of novel behavior have many sources, but those sources all involve variations or combinations of previously acquired environment-behavior relations. The variation may be in the topography, in the conditions under which a topography occurs, or a combination thereof. In recounting the potato washing of Imo's troop, writers often collapse all of these possibilities into vague statements such as, "Imo got the idea of washing the potatoes," which effectively remove any need to consider the historical and current conditions that must have been necessary for the behavioral variant to occur.

Whatever the historical and current circumstances giving rise to the first instance of Imo's potato washing, one can reasonably assume that Imo's washed potato had even less sand than those she had rubbed against her body. Presumably, the consequence of less-sand/more-potato taste increased the likelihood that the act would occur again—whatever the source of its first occurrence. As a result of the contingency between potato washing and tasty meal, an operant lineage of potato washing arose and survived in Imo's repertoire.

The importance of the behavioral consequences of a novel act, leading to the emergence of a behavioral lineage in a repertoire, is easily overlooked in accounts of cultural transmission. But if Imo's act of dipping the potato had resulted in a potato that tasted just like the ones she rubbed against her body hair, it is unlikely that she would have continued dipping potatoes. For a novel behavior to make a difference, either its consequences must differ from those of previously learned behavior, or it must produce the previous consequences more expeditiously. Potato washing is more costly than potato rubbing: often one has to take the potato to the water rather than stand or sit where one is, rub the sand off, and eat.

Stimulus Function of Behavior for Conspecifics

The second prerequisite for cultural-level phenomena is that there is a necessary relation between behavior acquired *sui generis* by one organism and behavior similar in topography or stimulus control appearing later in the repertoire of another organism. Imo's potato washing subsequently was observed in increasing numbers of Imo's troop within a fairly short time. It seems unlikely that Imo instructed her conspecifics in potato washing, so I presume that one or more troop members saw Imo dip the potatoes before eating them. They may have seen Imo do this once or many times before one of them dipped his or her potato the first time. Thus, Imo's behavior functioned as a stimulus for the behavior of conspecifics.

The relation between the dipping acts of Imo and the dipping of a second monkey who observed Imo's potato washing qualifies as a stimulus-control relation, specifically, *imitation*. In imitation the activity of one organism has the stimulus function of evoking a similar topography (or controlling relation) in the behavior stream of a second organism. This is complicated by the fact that imitative behavior can occur some time after the act that is imitated (Meltzoff, 1988), but little is known regarding the importance of particular kinds of behavioral histories for the occurrence of such delayed imitation. Imitation in nonhumans has been experimentally analyzed (e.g., Curio & Vieth, 1978) and there is experimental evidence to support the contention that human inheritance includes a strong propensity to imitate observed actions (Meltzoff & Moore, 1977). Such inheritance would enhance fitness so long as the inherited propensity for imitative acts was accompanied by *susceptibility of those acts to operant selection*. In other words, imitative acts as first instances are a great way for variants to appear in novice repertoires—so long as they are subsequently susceptible to differential selection by operant contingencies.

Instances of the recurring behavior that constitute an operant lineage can function as cultural-level replicators only if they evoke behavior that is novel in the repertoire of a learner. Contrary to Dawkins' claim, cultural replicators cannot propagate themselves by "leaping from brain to brain" (Dawkins, 1976, p. 206). Transmission can occur only via events that can be observed by participating organisms. The behavior of conspecifics (verbal and nonverbal) and the relation of that behavior to environmental events are the events so observed. Thus, *cultural-level* replicators are not events in the brains of organisms, but events (verbal or nonverbal) in the behavior streams of organisms. More specifically, they are operant acts, because they must be susceptible to differential selection at the behavioral level to be very useful at the cultural level.

So, a necessary element for the origin of culture is the replication of operant behavior across successive repertoires *in which the behavior of earlier learners functions as part of the behavioral environment of later learners.* The other monkeys did what Imo was doing (or did). As part of the environment of her peers, Imo's potato washing had an evocative function and the evoked imitative acts produced their own consequences, which accounted for operant lineages of potato washing in successor repertoires.

Learning in which the behavior of conspecifics functions as part of the behavioral environment of the learner is sometimes called *social learning* and distinguished from *individual learning.* As has been pointed out, however, "It is always individuals who learn" (Galef, 1988, p. 12). The inclination to view social learning and individual learning as fundamentally different rests on a failure to distinguish between process and content (cf. Glenn & Malagodi, 1991). It is likely that the same behavioral and biological processes account for learning accomplished by individual organisms, whether the environmental events that enter into the behavioral contingencies include the behavior of other organisms or not. Social learning is distinguished by the content of the learner's environment and not by the processes accounting for the learning.

Replication of Operant Contingencies in Culturo-Behavioral Lineages

Discussion in this chapter, so far, has focused on behavioral level entities (acts and lineages of acts) in the repertoires of individual organisms, and the functional relations between the acts of one organism (as stimulating environment) and the acts of another organism (as learner). The third prerequisite for the emergence of cultural level phenomena forms the bridge between behavioral things and cultural things. I have previously labeled these bridging phenomena culturo-behavioral lineages.

In the origin of cultures, culturo-behavioral lineages play a role similar to that played by biochemical lineages of replicating molecules in the origin of the organic world. Operant behavior is the element required for the emergence of culturo-behavioral lineages. The repetitions of a novel behavior acquired by one learner and the stimulus function of that behavior for other learners are necessary, but not sufficient for the emergence of culturo-behavioral lineages. There also must be repetition of the behavioral *contingencies* maintaining the originally learned behavior. As in the case of Imo's behavior, it is not only important that the novel behavior was imitated by a second learner, but also that the second learner's imitative act produces consequences sufficient to maintain its *continuing recurrence.* Maintenance of the second learner's potato washing would have approximately doubled the number of potato washing acts available as evocative events in the environments of other monkeys. This could more than double the likelihood that a third monkey would imitate, because the probability of imitation could increase as a function of the number of different monkeys seen to be washing potatoes. Variations in the consequences (as variations in the acts themselves) can occur as the behavioral contingencies are replicated in successive repertoires. In fact, variations in any or all elements of the replicating behavioral contingencies would contribute greatly to the variation needed for rapid evolution sometimes seen in cultures.

Readers may note some similarity in the present perspective and the concept of memes, introduced by Dawkins (1976) and richly elaborated by Blackmore (1999; see also Staddon, this volume, for a critique of memes). There are two main differences. First, for Dawkins and for Blackmore cultural replicators (memes) seem always to involve imitation. Although the example under discussion up to this point does involve lineages of imitated acts, there are other ways that cultural transmission can occur (for example, by verbal description). Second, both Dawkins and Blackmore are vague about what counts as a meme; memes include thoughts, ideas, and information as well as acts. As stated earlier, however, only overt behavior can function as part of the behavioral environment of a conspecific. Whatever may have been going on in Imo's brain, nothing leaped from her brain to the brain of another monkey. Only her potato washing was available as part of the environment of her troop members. Her potato washing was the cultural replicator. (Note: The inclination to locate cultural replicators in the brains of behavers seems to turn on a failure to recognize learned behavior as a kind of phenomenon requiring explanation at its own level of analysis. Reasons for the conceptual lacuna may be traced to more than simple disaffection toward behavioral theories. First, behavior itself is difficult for many people to conceptualize as a subject matter that extends beyond the boundaries of an organism's skin [see Lee, 1992] and involves patterns that exist over extended time [Hineline, 1992]. Second, the interactors in operant lineages [the single component or multicomponent acts that do or do not result in particular consequences] are here one minute and gone the next, and what is left is a changed organism. Replication in *behavioral* lineages may occur mainly at the level of neural events [see Donahoe & Palmer, 1994; Donahoe, this volume; Hull, Langman, & Glenn, 2001], but replication in *cultural* lineages must occur at the level of overt acts. These conceptual difficulties may contribute to the tendency to link organic selection to cultural selection without consideration of the behavioral selection processes that account for the behavior that plays a necessary role in cultural evolution.)

I have used the example of culturo-behavioral lineages in which transmission occurs via imitation because those are probably the least complex kind of culturo-behavioral lineage and the most likely to have appeared first in the history of cultural evolution. Imitation is not, however, the only way that behavior can be transmitted across operant repertoires. What some humans learn the hard way, others can learn by reading or hearing descriptions of the behavior (and, for maximum efficiency, descriptions of the conditions under which the behavior is to occur and the predicted consequences of that behavior.) Whatever the mode of transmission, that which must be replicated across repertoires in cultural transmission is not just learned acts, but learned behavior-environment relations that are subsequently selected by their reinforcing consequences. To repeat, the behavior of learners in cultural transmission (or the products of that behavior, such as printed words and machines) must, in turn, function as part of the behavioral environments of later learners. In the case of verbal instruction (spoken or written) the instruction reliably must result in listeners (readers) behaving in relation to their environment as described by the instruction. Thus, even in the more complex case where instruction replaces imitation, repetition of behavioral relations across repertoires requires replication of behavioral contingencies across repertoires. Such replication is the first step in the evolution of cultures. Replicating behavioral contingencies set the stage for the origin of cultural level selection.

Transition to Cultural Selection

Although social and nonsocial elements of the environment function the same way in behavioral selection processes, behavioral selection cannot by itself (or together with natural selection) account for the evolution of cultural complexity. The evolution of cultural complexity is made possible by the several roles that operant behavior plays in the ontogeny of individual repertoires and in the evolution of cultural phenomena.

Culturo-behavioral lineages are viewed here as the substantive link between behavioral and cultural processes. They are *proto*-cultural because no cultural-level processes are yet at work; and they are proto-*cultural* because without them there would be no cultural processes. The distinction between operant lineages and culturo-behavioral lineages rests on the fact that operant lineages are parts of the repertoires of individual organisms and they cease to exist when their host organism dies. A culturo-behavioral lineage exists so long as the operant lineages of any participant repertoires continue being replicated in the repertoires of other participants.

Cultures would not amount to much if the elements of culturo-behavioral lineages did not become parts of more complex cultural entities. The organic analogues of culturo-behavioral lineages are the first lineages of replicating molecules in the primeval soup. Primitive organic lineages were composed of chemicals that had the capacity to reproduce themselves. From those lineages, natural selection fashioned lineages of increasingly complex *interactors*—entities with interrelated components that interacted as *cohesive wholes* with their environments, resulting in differential replication of their components in subsequent interactors of the lineage. How might a similar transition have occurred in the evolution of cultures? Unless one locates the origin of cultures in the exceptionally creative minds of a few prehistoric humans, one must account for the origin of cultural phenomena and the evolution of cultural complexity in terms of the relations between the behavior of organisms and their environments.

Emergence of Cultural-Level Interactors

In the case of Imo and her conspecifics, an operant in Imo's repertoire was transmitted to repertoires of conspecifics and those operants were transmitted to more conspecifics (so long as behavioral contingencies maintaining the operants remained in effect.) The point of contact between Imo's operant lineage and the behavior of the first imitator could have been as brief as a single instance in which Imo was observed washing a potato. Whether the imitator first imitated the potato washing after one or after several observations of Imo's washing, once the imitative behavior occurred and was reinforced, Imo's behavior did not need to participate further in the contingencies that maintained the imitator's potato washing. This proto-cultural lineage bears little formal resemblance to the cultural phenomena of the everyday lives of readers of this book. But, then, lineages of biochemical replicators bear little resemblance to humans, and scientists are confident that the latter can be traced historically to the former. Replicating DNA made possible the evolution of organic complexity through natural selection. Culturo-behavioral lineages made possible the evolution of cultural complexity through selection of a third kind (Skinner, 1981).

If selection of a third kind works like phylogenic (natural) selection and ontogenic selection (reinforcement), then culturo-behavioral lineages can give rise to more inclusive cultural-level entities that eventually come to function as cultural-level *interactors*. The following hypothetical scenario develops further the theoretical perspective of this chapter by suggesting how cultural-level interactors could have arisen during human history. The scenario is based on guesses regarding likely behavioral content of human ancestors. The point of the scenario is *not* to suggest particular behavioral events that may have occurred, but rather to suggest the process by which the earliest cultural-level interactors may have emerged from operant contingencies and then been maintained by a third kind of selection.

Interlocking Behavioral Contingencies

Consider Deke and Sam as members of a species ancestral to our own who spend much of their time hunting animal prey. Being part of a species where sociality has been selected, they have a propensity for observing the behavior of conspecifics and such observation has played a role in the behavior they have acquired thus far. But consider that the hunting behavior of neither has a systematic effect on the behavior of the other, even if they happen to be hunting in close proximity to one another. Sam and Deke each have several operants in their repertoires that pertain to capturing prey animals. The first instances of some of these operants no doubt appeared in their repertoires after they observed more experienced conspecifics hunting, so the various acts of each are (a) elements in their individual repertoires and (b) elements in culturo-behavioral lineages extending into their ancestral repertoires. What is seen now is repetition, with variation, of acts that relate to their environment in ways that have been successful at capturing prey for several generations.

Imagine that Sam and Deke happen on a bevy of four small animals that do not scatter in different directions as they are approached by the predators. Instead they all run toward a hollow tree not observable at the moment by Sam or Deke, who pursue their prey. Sam happens to move to the right of the pack of prey and Deke to the left. When one of the prey sees Sam approaching from its right, it changes course and goes left. But when it sees Deke to the left it moves back to the right. Sam and Deke close in on the prey, whose actions in swinging from left to right have slowed their approach to the hollow tree, so they manage to kill all their prey and carry them back to their camp. Due to their joint, albeit unplanned and uncoordinated, actions Sam and Deke bring home more prey per capita than they would have, if the prey had run off in different directions and Sam and Deke each had been successful in nabbing one. As a result of these fortuitous events, Sam and Deke return with prey in both hands. If Sam and Deke happen to be members of a troop who share food with their troop, others benefit from their good fortune as well (and perhaps provide social reinforcement to the providers).

Consider what could happen if Sam became more likely to behave in response to the activities of Deke (as well as the movements of the prey) as a result of the foregoing experience. Over time, even if prey started off in different directions, the position of Deke as well as the movements of the prey could jointly control Sam's chasing. In these cases, Sam would move so as to force the prey in Deke's direction. If Deke were at some point to observe Sam's actions, then he might do the same. The consequences of *their interrelated behavior*—more food per hunt or higher probability of food per hunt—would be likely to maintain the new behavior-environment relations in the repertoire of each.

Experimental analysis of cooperative behavior has revealed that behavioral contingencies similar to those portrayed in the above scenario do support continuing cooperative behavior of the individuals involved. For example, Mithaug (1969) found that in a situation where cooperative (interdependent) behavior and independent behavior both produced the same reinforcer, subjects' preferences for cooperative behavior increased as the response requirement per reinforcer increased. Hake and Vukelich (1973) also found that cooperative (interdependent) behavior was more likely than independent production of reinforcers when the cooperative behavior entailed less effort. In general, research on cooperative behavior has found that such behavior is well maintained when payoffs for individuals behaving cooperatively meet or exceed payoffs for behaving independently. In short, individuals cooperate when interdependent behavior produces more reinforcement than independent behavior. Cooperative behavior can be viewed, then, as a form of maximization. Thus, Sam and Deke's behavior in participating in the interlocking contingencies was maintained by the reinforcers produced. The interlocking contingencies were a fortuitous side effect of the operant processes accounting for the behavior of each of them.

The point critical to the present theoretical perspective, however, is that food resulting from the interrelated behavior of Sam and Deke functions in selection processes at *two levels*. It supports the cooperative operants of the participating individuals (Sam and Deke), as did the reinforcers in the experimental studies cited above. And it also *selects the interlocking contingencies themselves* in which both Deke's and Sam's behavior participates. The operant processes that result in maximizing also result in the emergence of a cultural-level interactor that functions as a cohesive whole with respect to its selecting environment. These two levels of selection can be distinguished in terms of the entities functioning as cohesive wholes in the two selection processes. The units involved in behavioral selection (i.e., the operant activities of Sam and Deke) exist independently as parts of their separate repertoires. If a lion ate Sam, Sam's operant behavior could no longer participate in the interlocking contingencies, but Deke's repertoire could remain intact. The cultural-level unit in which his behavior participates can live on if someone else, say, Tom, has learned to do what Sam did in hunting episodes. If Tom's behavior replaces Sam's in the interlocking contingencies the lineage of cultural interactors continues to be replicated across hunting occasions with continuing opportunity to be selected (or not). As long as the cultural interactors result in consequences *that maintain the interlocking contingencies as a cohesive whole,* the cultural lineage continues to be susceptible to evolution by differential selection.

In this example, the cultural-level interactor comprises the interlocking behavioral contingencies that produce high quantities of food—food that has the dual function of maintaining the operant behavior of individual participants as well as maintaining the interlocking contingencies that can span the lives of many generations. This dual function provides the bridge to cultural selection processes, which eventually account for highly complex cultural entities. Skinner (1984) proposed a similar dual function for primary reinforcers providing a bridge between natural selection and operant reinforcement in the emergence of the phenomena of operant behavior.

Similarly, the earliest cultural consequences in the above scenarios were redundant with the operant consequences that maintained the behavior of participating individuals. Only as cultural evolution continued did different consequences come to maintain cultural lineages and the operant behavior that constitutes them, just as different consequences came to maintain gene lineages and operant lineages.

The relations between interlocking behavioral contingencies and their consequences have been designated as *metacontingencies* (Glenn, 1988, 1991) to distinguish them from their component operant contingencies although recognizing the part/whole relation between behavioral and cultural phenomena. In metacontingencies, interlocking behavioral contingencies function as a cohesive unit (a cultural-level interactor) in cultural selection processes. The selecting environment that results in evolution, maintenance, or disappearance of a lineage of cultural interactors eventually comes to have little or no consequent functions with respect to the behavior in the interlocking contingencies. Metacontingencies describe the process by which complex cultural entities evolve—entities such as universities, legislative bodies, churches, scientific laboratories, and other cultural units composed of many interrelated parts and interacting as a cohesive whole with their selecting environments. Cultural-level entities become more complex when the interlocking behavioral contingencies functioning as a cohesive whole come to involve more acts of more organisms; but those acts are themselves maintained by behavioral consequences embedded in the interlocking contingencies themselves.

To summarize, the primary role of operant behavior in cultural selection is that of cultural-level replicator. Repetitions of operant acts under control of the behavior of conspecifics are required for the emergence of culturo-behavioral lineages. When the behavior replicated in culturo-behavioral lineages participates in repetitions of interlocking behavioral contingencies, cultural-level selection becomes possible. Cultural-level selection is selection of interlocking behavioral contingencies, not just the behavior of individuals. In fact, different individuals may participate in the interlocking contingencies from one instance of their instantiation to the next. In the transition from operant behavior to cultures, events functioning as reinforcers for individual behavior in interlocking contingencies also functioned as cultural-level selectors for the interlocking contingencies as cultural-level units. These interlocking behavioral contingencies contain interrelated culturo-behavioral lineages and they outlive the repertoires of any of their participating organisms so long as they function adequately in the cultural selection contingencies.

Culture, Behavior, and Natural Selection

Maynard Smith (1994) characterized the increases in complexity during evolution of the organic world as resulting from a succession of processes that became possible only when a previous level of complexity had been reached—processes that, in turn, gave rise to a new level of complexity. Although he precisely delineates the transitions that purportedly led to increasingly complex organic phenomena from replicating molecules through insect societies, the transition from insect societies to human societies is said simply to be the result of language (Maynard Smith). From the present perspective the leap from insect societies to human societies collapses several evolutionary domains, each involving its own selection processes, into a single evolutionary domain: organic evolution. Positing language as arising from insect societies and giving rise to human societies may be fairly characterized as explanation of the sort "... and then a miracle occurs."

Some time ago I began trying to place operant behavior in a framework of increasingly complex phenomena from chemicals to cultures (Glenn, 1986). Having since then foraged in the literatures of behavior analysis, evolutionary biology, anthropology, and philosophies of science, and having benefited from Maynard Smith's (1994) depiction of the bootstrapping nature of evolution, I hope that Table 1 improves upon that earlier effort. I have collapsed Maynard Smith's elegant and detailed delineation of the early, formative, stages of organic evolution into a couple of cells, but the miracle has been replaced with a series of transitions that are proposed herein to have led from organic complexity to cultural complexity. The entries in bold italics indicate the part of the chronology that is pertinent to

Table 1.   Chronology of Processes and Products of Three Kinds of Selection. The origin of cultures is seen in the context of organic and behavioral selection processes. The left column lists several kinds of phenomena that played important roles in these evolutionary processes, in order of historical appearance on Earth. Each domain subsumes and builds on the phenomena that emerged during earlier periods. The right column shows elements of transition. These are the processes and conditions that arose from the previous domain and that gave rise to the next-emerging domain.

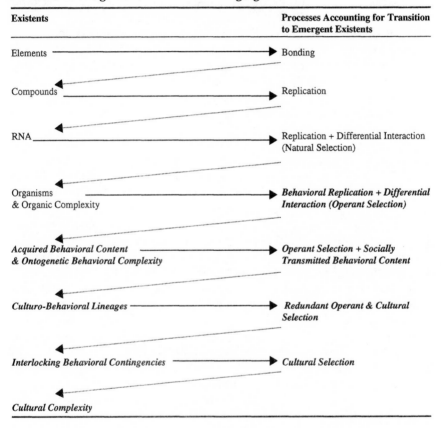

Existents	Processes Accounting for Transition to Emergent Existents
Elements	Bonding
Compounds	Replication
RNA	Replication + Differential Interaction (Natural Selection)
Organisms & Organic Complexity	*Behavioral Replication + Differential Interaction (Operant Selection)*
Acquired Behavioral Content & Ontogenetic Behavioral Complexity	*Operant Selection + Socially Transmitted Behavioral Content*
Culturo-Behavioral Lineages	*Redundant Operant & Cultural Selection*
Interlocking Behavioral Contingencies	*Cultural Selection*
Cultural Complexity	

the present topic. But the present story makes more sense if it is considered in the context of the broader framework.

To preclude misinterpretation of my thesis, I should make clear that I am *not* denying that natural selection as a causal process is relevant to the origin of human cultures. It is as relevant as chemical bonding is to the origin of organic complexity. But at times, the complex products of one domain can give rise to new processes, which in turn account for complexity in a new domain. In accounting for the complexity of human behavior, the behavioral processes that account for unique repertoires of individuals must be considered. In accounting for cultural complexity, processes that account for organic and operant evolution are a given. I have proposed, however, that additional processes are needed to account for the emergence and evolution of cultural-level units that cannot be accounted for entirely by natural selection and/or the operant selection of behavioral repertoires during ontogeny.

Little has been said here about the role of language in the evolution of cultures. The verbal behavior of humans, as well as the lineages of interlocking behavioral contingencies that constitute a linguistic community, have obviously been critical in the evolution of human cultures. The earliest cultural phenomena in proto-human histories may have predated language, however. The advantages of even rudimentary culturo-behavioral lineages (such as the potato washing lineage described above) for the survival of a species seem evident and the emergence of such lineages among our preverbal ancestors seems very likely. Because verbal behavior, by its very nature, involves interlocking behavioral contingencies (as first schematized by Skinner, 1957, pp. 38–39), the earliest speaker/listener episodes may have resulted from operant noises made by speakers and the functionally related behavior of listeners who were participating in interlocking behavioral contingencies that produced consequences sufficient to maintain the behavior of each participating organism *as well as* the interlocking contingencies themselves. Thus, rudimentary speaker/listener repertoires of individual organisms were derived from and supported the evolution of increasing cultural complexity as well as increasing complexity of neural organization in hominid lineages. These, in turn, may have resulted in survival of the populations in which such early verbal episodes arose. In any case, evolution of the culturo-behavioral phenomena of language has clearly been a factor in the rapid evolution of human cultures during an exceedingly brief period of Earth's history.

Acknowledgments

I am indebted to Marion Blute, Janet Ellis, David L. Hull, and Manish Vaidya for their valuable feedback on the written paper.

References

Andronis, P. (1983). *Symbolic aggression by pigeons: Contingency adduction*. Unpublished doctoral dissertation, University of Chicago.

Baum, W. M. (2000). Being concrete about culture and cultural evolution. In N. Thompson & F. Tonneau (Eds.), *Perspectives in Ethology* (Vol 13, pp. 181–212). New York: Kluwer Academic/Plenum.

Blackmore, S. (1999). *The meme machine.* Oxford: Oxford University Press.

Bonner, J. T. (1980). The evolution of culture in animals. Princeton, NJ: Princeton University Press.

Catania, A. C. (1995). Selection in behavior and biology. In J. T. Todd & E. K. Morris (Eds). Modern perspectives on B. F. Skinner and contemporary behaviorism (pp. 185–194). Westport, CT: Greenwood Press.

Curio, E. V. & Vieth, W. (1978). Cultural transmission of enemy recognition: One function of mobbing. *Science, 202,* 899–901.

Dawkins, R. (1976). *The selfish gene.* Oxford University Press.

Donahoe, J. W. (1984). Commentary: Skinner—The Darwin of ontogeny? *The Behavioral and Brain Sciences, 7,* 287–288.

Donahoe, J. W., & Palmer D. C. (1994). *Learning and complex behavior.* Boston: Allyn & Bacon.

Epstein, R. (1985). The spontaneous interconnection of three repertoires. *The Psychological Record, 1985, 35,* 131–141.

Galef, B. G., Jr. (1988). Imitation in animals: History, definition, and interpretation of data from the psychological laboratory. In T. R. Zentall & B. G. Galef, Jr. (Eds.) *Social learning: Psychological and biological perspectives.* Hillsdale, NJ: Lawrence Erlbaum.

Glenn, S. S. (1986). Behavior: A gene for the social sciences. Poster presented at American Psychological Association convention. Washington, D. C.

Glenn, S. S. (1988). Contingencies and metacontingencies: Toward a synthesis of behavior analysis and cultural materialism. *The Behavior Analyst, 11,* 161–179.

Glenn, S. S. & Malagodi, E. F. (1991). Process and content in behavioral and cultural phenomena. *Behavior and Social Issues, 1* (2), 1–14.

Glenn, S. S. (1991). Contingencies and metacontingencies: Relations among behavioral, cultural, and biological evolution, in P.A. Lamal (Ed). *Behavioral analysis of societies and cultural practices.* New York: Hemisphere Press (pp. 39–73).

Glenn, S. S., Ellis, J., & Greenspoon, J. (1992). On the revolutionary nature of the operant as a unit of behavioral selection. *American Psychologist, 47,* 1329–1336.

Hake, D. F., & Vukelich, R. (1973). Analysis of the control exerted by a complex cooperation procedure. *Journal of the Experimental Analysis of Behavior, 19,* 3–16.

Harris, M. (1964). *The nature of cultural things.* New York: Random House.

Harris, M. (1989). *Our kind.* New York: Harper & Row.

Hineline, P. N. (1992). A self-interpretive behavior analysis. *American Psychologist, 47,* 1274–1286.

Hull, D. L. (1980). Individuality and selection. *Annual Review of Ecology and Systematics, 11,* 311–332.

Hull, D. L., Langman, R. E., & Glenn, S. S. (2001). A general account of selection: Biology, immunology and behavior. *Behavioral and Brain Sciences, 24,* 511–528.

Kawai, M. (1965). Newly acquired pre-cultural behavior of the natural troop of Japanese monkeys on Koshima Islet. *Primates, 67,* 1–30.

Kawamura, S. (1959). The process of sub-culture propagation among Japanese macaques. *Primates, 2,* 43–60.

Lee, V. L. (1992). Transdermal interpretation of the subject matter of behavior analysis. *American Psychologist, 47,* 1337–43.

Mithaug, D. E. (1969). The development of cooperation in alternative task situations. *Journal of Experimental Child Psychology, 8,* 441–454.

Maynard Smith, J. (1994). The major transitions in evolution. In G. Cowan, D. Pines, & D. Meltzer (Eds). *Complexity: metaphors, models, and reality*. SFI Studies in the Sciences of Complexity, Proc. Vol. XIX, Addison-Wesley.

Meltzoff, A. N., & Moore, M. K. (1977). Imitation of facial and manual gestures by human neonates. *Science, 198,* 75–78.

Meltzoff, A. N. (1988). The human infant as Homo Imitans. In T. R. Zentall & B. G. Galef, Jr. (Eds.) *Social learning: Psychological and biological perspectives*. Hillsdale, NJ: Lawrence Erlbaum.

Skinner, B. F. (1957). *Verbal behavior*. Englewood Cliffs, NJ: Prentice-Hall.

Skinner, B. F. (1981). Selection by consequences. *Science, 213,* 501–504.

Skinner, B. F. (1984). The evolution of behavior. *Journal of the Experimental Analysis of Behavior, 41,* 217–221.

Skinner, B. F. (1988). BFS commentary in canonical papers of B. F. Skinner: Selection by consequences. In A. C. Catania & S. Harnad (Eds.), *The selection of behavior*. Cambridge: Cambridge University Press.

White, R. (1982). Rethinking the middle/upper paleolithic transition. *Current Anthropology, 23,* 169–192.

Wilson, D. S. (1980). *The natural selection of populations and communities*. Menlo Park, CA: Benjamin Cummings.

13

Implications of Determinism
PERSONAL RESPONSIBILITY AND THE VALUE OF SCIENCE

Mecca Chiesa

Determinism is the view that all natural phenomena are products of interrelated antecedent processes. It is a guiding assumption of scientific inquiry and there is no controversy in asserting that behaviorists subscribe to determinism in the same way as other scientists. Because human action takes place in the same physical universe as all other phenomena, behaviorists have no objection to determinism, and, for the behaviorist, determinism does nothing to undermine the richness, individuality, and complexity of the human experience. There are implications of determinism and of the use of the word *determined*, however, that need to be carefully considered and addressed.

Specifically when applied to human action, determinism, and thus behaviorism, conflicts with some fundamental concepts that many people rely on to explain behavior. The removal of these concepts from the explanatory sphere can evoke misunderstanding and even hostility in the form of attack by others, with behaviorism frequently the target of that hostility and those attacks. For many listeners the word *determined* connotes words like *controlled* and *controllable, unavoidable, inescapable, inevitable, predictable,* and other words evoking uncomfortable emotional reactions. Determinism also poses a problem for the assertion that individuals can and should be held accountable for their behavior. Wilson (1979) stated the problem this way:

> The main problems raised by determinism are usually taken to be the challenge
> it represents to the traditional conception of human free will and the related

Mecca Chiesa • Applied Social Science, University of Paisley, Paisley, Scotland, UK.

> institutions of moral blame and punishment. It is almost universally acknowl-
> edged to be morally unreasonable and unjust to blame or punish someone for
> behavior when the behavior in question was inevitable. (p. 243)

If determinism evokes uncomfortable reactions for other people, why are behaviorists not equally prone to such reactions? This chapter attempts to interpret the reactions of listeners who continue to resist the determinist principle in the realm of human behavior and to respond by emphasizing some of its more positive implications.

Determinism, for some listeners, implies predictability, which in its turn implies less-than-flattering expressions such as conventional, banal, boring, humdrum, and so on. This is a somewhat gloomy implication of determinism and so it is worth stating from the outset that predictability is not a given result of determinism. Furthermore, even when behavior can be predicted or explained scientifically, behaving persons become no less interesting than other equally explicable natural phenomena.

Where other listeners react negatively to an implied loss of self-control, behaviorists do not so react to determinism because their scientific practices allow them to seek out potentially controlling events, evaluate those events, and find ways of altering them. In the same way that other sciences provide means for solving problems in their own domains, the science of behavior analysis provides a set of practices that can be brought to bear when problems involve behavior.

Where other listeners are dismayed by the implication that people cannot be held responsible for their behavior, behaviorists accommodate determinism and accountability. The positive implication of determinism in the area of moral responsibility is that it can encourage compassion in judgements of behavior (one's own and that of others) by focusing attention on the offensiveness of *acts* rather than persons. Another positive consequence is that it may help to alleviate emotional reactions on the part of professionals who have to work with offenders, particularly where the offences in question are especially distressing to observers.

In dealing with determinism here, I will suggest that determinism does not inevitably involve loss and vulnerability and that it does not challenge the uniqueness and complexity of persons. In addition, I will show how determinism encourages respect for persons and compassion in the treatment of those whose behavior is less than desirable.

Philosophical Reactions to Determinism

Determinism began to pose serious problems for ethical conceptions of responsibility as evolutionary theory closed the gap between humans and other animals: "in our culture, the species barrier has commonly been seen as being also the boundary of the moral realm, and metaphysical doctrines have been built to protect this boundary" (Midgley, 1991, p. 6). As evidence accumulated in support of human evolution, the dominant religious accounts of ethics and responsibility that relied on the soul as the origin of human choice were undermined. According to Midgley, Darwin was distressed by the conclusion of his collaborator A. R. Wallace that "God must have added souls to emerging primate bodies by miraculous intervention during the course of evolution" (p. 7).

The soul was traditionally the seat of free will, and thus moral responsibility. It needed to be somehow reintroduced into the otherwise natural, biological process of evolution in order to maintain its role. Having been reintroduced, the soul continued to be held responsible for the moral or ethical realms of human conduct. The idea of an entity inhabiting an otherwise determined biological structure is also not uncommon among nonreligious thinkers who may call it other things such as the autonomous self or the free agent.

Secular attempts to justify holding persons morally responsible for their actions do so by exempting some features of human behavior from the determinist principle. Indeterminists do not generally deny the causal principle in the realm of inorganic nature, nor in most areas of organic nature where biology and biochemistry persuasively demonstrate causation in action. Newman, Reinecke, and Kurtz (1996) noted, however, that even authors with impressive scientific credentials and well-known skeptical allegiances, although agreeing that humanity is part of the natural world, nevertheless appeal to features of human behavior that give it special status—notably features called free will and choice. Even by some scientists, universal causation is often disputed in the area of human action.

The philosophical movement of compatibilism attempted to resolve the incompatibility between determinism and free will, arguing that free will was not possible without the concept of determinism and that the determinant of action was, simply, an entity called the person or self. According to compatibilism, the self is the agent, the determiner, the cause of action. In a curious linguistic move, the prime author of the compatibilist position translated free will into determinism in the following way: "The principle of free will says: 'I produce my volitions.' Determinism says: 'My volitions are produced by me.' Determinism is free will expressed in the passive voice" (Hobart, 1934, p. 7).

Although claiming to resolve the incompatibility between free will and determinism, compatibilists appealed to the same entity as indeterminists, an autonomous self, as the originator (cause) of action. Although theologians account for the soul by asserting that it is God-given, neither compatibilists nor indeterminists are concerned to provide an account of how the autonomous self comes to be. They simply assert its existence, assign causal status to it, and thus justify holding persons responsible for their behavior. The autonomous self is exempt from the laws of science that operate in the rest of nature. The self is thought of as an entity standing apart from behavior and credited (or blamed) for initiating, organizing and guiding behavior. In this traditional view, "what the person does is of secondary importance to what the person *is*. The person, the essential self, is both the organizer and initiator of behavior, with behavior standing in a dependent variable position to the self as independent variable" (Chiesa, 1994, p. 97).

By comparison, the starting point of a behavioral account of the self is the biological nature of organisms. Organisms, including complex, fully functioning adult humans, comprise a unique genetic endowment and a unique reinforcement history. From this it follows that the entity called the self comes to be that unique entity through interaction with the contexts to which it has been exposed (including other people and the verbal behavior of the culture), through the consequences of its own acts, through positive and aversive conditioning, and through its genetic susceptibility to reinforcing and punishing contingencies. Behavior is a product of interactions between many types of causal variables and the self, in a behavioral account, is the meeting place of these complex multiple causes. Behavior at any given moment is determined by how they come together. In this way, the behavioral concept of self places that entity in a dependent rather than independent variable position while continuing to accommodate concepts of uniqueness and complexity:

> A person is not an originating agent; he is a locus, a point at which many genetic and environmental conditions come together in a joint effect. As such, he remains unquestionably unique. No one else (unless he has an identical twin) has his genetic endowment, and without exception no one else has his personal history. Hence no one else will behave in precisely the same way. (Skinner, 1974, p. 168)

The behaviorist concept of self is not a mysterious, unexplained entity standing apart from, directing, and guiding behavior. The self (or person) is a consequence of many causal variables coming together in unique ways, and the sum of genetic and learning history referred to as me, you, him or her, is determined in the sense that the causal principle operative in other spheres of nature similarly applies (for elaborations of this position see Baer, 1976; Hineline, 1980; Skinner, 1972). Whereas this account may be taken to imply that the person has no active role in influencing events in the world, the implication does not play out in real life. The following section will discuss how the behavior of organisms (including those organisms referred to as persons) plays an important part in bringing about (causing) other events in the world.

Negative Reactions to Determinism

Determined and *determinism* are often taken to imply that things happen in the world *in spite of* people's actions. There is a lurking implication for some listeners that in a determinist scheme the person is outside of and unable to influence the causal web. Indeed, it was noted above that the behavioral account of self (or person) may seem to lead to precisely this conclusion.

Philosophers note that this reaction is actually a confusion of doctrines—a confusion of the doctrines of determinism and fatalism. Fatalism also views everything as caused, but it denies that human beings have any role in changing or influencing the course of events. Yet even the most casual of observations refutes fatalism: if my car has a problem and I call the garage, make an appointment to take the car there, and subsequently do take the car, the problem will be repaired (assuming the mechanics also engage in appropriate behavior). If I fail to behave in those ways, my car will not work properly. My actions bring about events in the world and are causally related to subsequent events. Similarly, if a student spends some time studying for an exam, that action will have a different outcome than if the student watches television or plays computer games without opening a textbook. It is true that lots of things will happen regardless of our behavior, but behavior itself changes the environment (that is the definition of the operant or operant class). So the behavior of an individual at any given time does affect subsequent events, including subsequent behavior, and thus the subsequent events are not due to some mysterious force called fate. Rather they can be causally traced to an individual's own prior actions.

In addition to the helplessness that is encouraged by fatalism and is reminiscent of the emotional state called despair, a variety of reactions often found in print refer to determinism and its implications in strong and emotional terminology. Writing on agency and responsibility in the *Times Literary Supplement*, the philosopher Strawson (1998), for example, outlined deterministic objections to compatibilism and referred to determinists as *pessimists* throughout the article. A pessimist is "one who habitually takes the worst view of things" (*Shorter Oxford English Dictionary*, 1988, p. 1563) which suggests that Strawson considers determinism to be the worst possible view of agency and responsibility. Reacting specifically to *Beyond Freedom and Dignity* (Skinner, 1971), Black (1973) referred to a managed (behavioral) environment as one

> ...arranged by skillful hidden manipulators, in which the very language of responsible action had been expunged by effective conditioning.... We might justifiably regard the end product as a dehumanization, in which men were no longer accorded the dignity of being treated as persons. A world of well-controlled bodies emitting physical movements in response to secret reinforcements, might perhaps seem hardly worth preserving. It may, after all, be better to be dead than bred—like cattle. (p. 132)

Clearly for Black such a managed environment conforms to Strawson's worst possible view of things and it is telling that his text is entitled *Some Aversive Responses to a Would-Be Reinforcer*.

Dennett (1984) referred to the behavioral notion of environmental control as "chilling": "it hints subliminally at the dark idea that the environment *wants* us to do this and that, and acting on the desire, *makes* us do what it wants" (p. 57). Although he pointed out that Skinner's interpretation of environmental control did *not* give agency in this sense to the environment, Dennett was describing the way people react to the determinist principle when presented with it. In another place he refers to "the illusory slide from causation to control that *feeds our fear* of determinism" (p. 59, italics added). Dennett went on to describe a variety of reactions that refer to inevitable control by other persons (personified objections), reactions that hint of terror or confusion at the prospect of the disappearing self, and reactions that hint of despair and the futility of deliberation.

Personified objections to determinism involve the listener inventing an agent who takes over control and manipulates the behaver secretly or against their will, who holds the behaver up to ridicule by others for being out of control, or who blocks them from doing the things they want to do. Dennett (1984) referred to one reaction as the invention of an Invisible Jailer; this response reasons that if I am not free to behave as I decide, want, or wish, then I must be in a kind of prison, because to be without freedom is to be imprisoned, and prison implies a jailer. There must therefore be an invisible jailer keeping me in this state.

He described another reaction as the invention of a Nefarious Neurosurgeon who arranges electrodes in a person's brain and controls them secretly. The Hideous Hypnotist and the Peremptory Puppeteer are also inventions in response to determinism: "what is particularly chilling about them is that unlike the Nefarious Neurosurgeon, they may leave no physical trace of their influence" (Dennett, 1984, p. 8). In relation to the Cosmic Child Whose Dolls We Are he wrote "without free will, we seem diminished, merely the playthings of external forces" (p. 291). Finally, he referred to the Malevolent Mindreader: "if only you could find a strategy of unpredictability that would be proof against (the malevolent mindreader's) calculations! Then you wouldn't be so impotent, so vulnerable in the game of Life" (p. 10).

In all the cases of personified objections described by Dennett (1984), the objector invents another human or quasi-human agent to replace the agent that is lost to determinism, and in each case the invented agent is a hideous character evoking fear and dread. Another reaction does not involve the invention of dreaded persons, but is also full of dread and awfulness—*The Disappearing Self*:

> that spooky sense one often gets when observing or learning about insects and other lower animals: all that bustling activity but *there's nobody home....* The ants and bees, and even the fish and the birds, are just "going through the motions." *They* don't understand or appreciate what they are up to, and no other comprehending selves are to be found in the neighborhood. This is the fear of the incredible Disappearing Self. (p. 13)

Determinism and its incompatibility with attempts to explain action with concepts such as free will or self-agency generates emotional responses because it seems to remove a crucial feature of the way people think about their actions. The reasoning seems to proceed in this manner: If I am not directing my actions, and if I am not prepared to invent another agent who is directing my actions, then that entity I think of as me or myself disappears and there is nothing to replace it. I become like the ants and wasps and busy bees going about the world without any awareness of what I am doing. For the listener that is an uncomfortable way—to use the words philosophers have used, a cold and chilling and despairing and pessimistic way—to think about their existence.

Such responses are not unusual in the history of scientific or philosophical analysis. The reactions to Darwin's demonstrations of natural selection are well known and it was noted above that some of Darwin's contemporaries (including A. R. Wallace) reintroduced the soul during the course of evolution so that a number of explanatory concepts lost to evolutionary theory could be preserved. In the same vein, secular philosophies (or freethinking as it used to be known) disrupted the stability of conceptual schemes that relied on extra human authority for both explanation and guidance. There are still people who charge secular philosophers with being unable to live by moral codes without this other authority to establish good and right conduct.

It seems that when scientific or philosophical analysis disturbs the stability of conceptual schemes it will be met with hostility and counterattack, and it is really no surprise that behaviorism, with its denial of free will and self-agency, should be subject to these reactions in the same way as other challenging explanatory systems have been. I would argue that the slide from causation to fatalism or from determinism to despair is often a consequence of not having been exposed to a science of behavior that *demonstrates* that human behavior is an important part of the causal web and that has led to practices allowing for analysis and management of controlling variables.

Strawson's reference to determinists as pessimists and Dennett's reference to people's fear of determinism suggest that most ordinary people find determinism at least emotionally unsatisfying and at worst terrifying. If that is really the case, then it is clear why many people avoid determinism and engage in elaborate escape behavior to remove determinism from their lives. How do behaviorists avoid the slide from determinism to despair or from determinism to fear and vulnerability that is characteristic of the reactions described above?

I consulted fellow behaviorists about their reactions to determinism and to the absence of self-agency and free will as explanatory constructs. Their responses, which are noted below as personal communications, indicate that determinism and a learning history with the science of behavior result in positive, compassionate, and optimistic approaches to life quite in contrast to the fear and dread of determinism expressed by Dennett and others.

Reconsidering the Negative Reactions to Determinism

Determinism and Predictability

One of the negative reactions to determinism noted above is the notion that because behavior is determined it is therefore predictable. For some listeners, *predictable* connotes monotonous, boring, tedious, or unexciting, and for those listeners the idea that their actions might be predictable is not necessarily flattering. Another reason to consider predictability and its relation to determinism is that, contrary to the assumption that prediction *follows from* determinism, determinism has only limited implications for prediction as systems, processes, or actions become more complex (J. Marr, personal communication, April 4, 2000).

Determinism and predictability are two different types of philosophical assertions. Determinism is a metaphysical position, a statement about how the world *is*. Predictability is an epistemological position that is dependent on determinism, but is also dependent on the amount of knowledge available about any given phenomenon. A popular example in the philosophical literature that is used to expose the distinction between determinism and predictability is the example of a marble rolling down a rocky path. There is no quarrel with an assertion that the physical forces acting on the marble and the materials implicated in its journey determine its course, but it does not follow from this that its course is predictable by an observer. If the marble was released at the top of a smooth wooden chute a physicist or engineer might be able to predict its velocity and the point at which it would land, but the complexity involved in the rocky path scenario makes it unlikely that the same observer could predict the marble's course and its landing place.

With increasing complexity, the behavior of organisms also becomes less predictable but not less determined. Sheldon (1982) used the following example to expose the distinction between determinism and predictability in cases of human behavior:

> ...a quantitative change from one single, simple reflex to a multiplicity of stimulus-response connections, produces a qualitative change in appearance, and behaviour turns into a *process* in the same way that a series of film stills is turned into movement and drama by the rapid motion of the movie projector. The stills are there all the time and are the invisible components that give rise to the perception of behaviour on the screen. Action and interaction become a *flow* of behaviour, or a *stream* of events. However, we need to remember that even streams have their component parts, right down to the individual molecules of hydrogen and oxygen that are their building blocks. (pp. 29–30)

These two examples show that in the real world predictability does not inevitably follow from determinism. It is worth noting in addition that behavior analysts have demonstrated that complexity and thus predictability is itself a product of contingencies of reinforcement. Page and Neuringer (1985; also see Neuringer, this volume), for example, arranged contingencies that generated highly variable response sequences in the behavior of pigeons, and Neuringer (1986) arranged contingencies in such a way that response sequences produced by humans gradually became indistinguishable in terms of predictability from computer-generated random number sequences. Even behavior that is variable to the point that it might almost be described as random can be shown to be determined by contingencies of reinforcement. Behavior, like the subject matter of other sciences, is complex; and the challenge for a behavior analyst is the same challenge faced by other scientists, to find the functional relations that exist within the subject matter. Meeting this challenge, however, rarely results in perfect or even near-perfect prediction.

For the listener who remains uncomfortable with the idea that even some of their behavior is predictable, it is worth pointing out that scientific accounts do not render the behaving person (or any other natural phenomenon) uninteresting, boring, or unexciting. Consider the performance of an accomplished ballet dancer, concert pianist, or public speaker; accepting that their performance is determined and even that the quality of their performance is predictable does nothing to lessen the visceral and intellectual pleasure to be gained by the observer.

More Control (Not Less)

Although some might find solace in Marr's determined but not predictable argument, others still find the apparent loss of control implied by determinism aversive. Dennett (1984, noted above) described the reaction that involves replacing the self-as-agent that is lost to determinism with a controlling and frightening person-like entity. Dennett also referred to the listener's sense of vulnerability and impotence when faced with the apparent loss of control by the self. Recognizing the difficulties involved in prediction that arise from complexity and armed with a scientific training, behaviorists react to this implication of determinism in a more optimistic manner.

D. Palmer (personal communication, February 25, 2000), for example, observed that a commitment to determinism and a learning history with the science of behavior challenges him to search for the controlling variables rather than resorting to free-choice as though that were explanatory. Confronted by a personal problem, and unable to rely on concepts such as self-agency or free will either to explain or guide behavior, a behaviorist instead relies on an expertise with contingency analysis and a training with the science to seek out and evaluate causal variables and observe the outcome of changing those variables.

Proponents of free will and self-determination imply that people can simply *decide* or *declare* or *choose* their way in and out of undesirable situations or uncomfortable reactions. But, like fatalism, this position does not stand up to even casual observation. If deciding or choosing in an autonomous manner was really available to people, there would be none of the confusion that everyone experiences in trying to account for and influence their own actions and reactions. Behavior analysts investigate self-management techniques experimentally. Self-management, however, is not actually managing an autonomous entity called the "self" that stands apart from behavior. Rather it is analyzing and managing contexts and consequences of behavior with a view to changing that behavior. It is called self-management because the behavior manager and the behaver in this case are located in the same physical space. The activities involved in seeking out and evaluating causal variables are part of a behavioral repertoire, and a given individual will be more or less competent at these activities depending on their training with the science. It is easy to appreciate how a listener who is denied self-agency as an explanatory construct, but who has no involvement or history with the principles and practices of behavior analysis, could be overwhelmed by what appears to be a complete loss of influence over the world around them or their own behavior. Behavior analysts need to emphasize the potential of the science for allowing persons to be more rather than less involved in planning, managing, and influencing events.

Blame and Moral Responsibility

Apart from emotional reactions to determinism involving fear, despair, and vulnerability, there is also the important issue of moral responsibility to be considered. This chapter opened by noting the problems determinism poses for assertions that people can and should be held morally accountable for their actions and by recognizing that determinism seems to threaten the culture's justification for doing this. Young (1991) summed up the implications of determinism for concepts such as morality and responsibility:

> The entire apparatus of moral decision-making, praise and blame, reward and punishment, seems to be premised on the assumption that in normal circumstances we are responsible for what we freely choose to do. Determinists maintain that there is a causal explanation for everything that happens in the universe, human behavior included. This seems to suggest that we do not freely choose to do anything, and this in turn appears to imply that we are not morally responsible for anything we do. (p. xiii)

To counter this reaction it might help to remove the word *moral* from the expression *moral responsibility* and consider what is meant by *responsibility*. Responsibility, liability, and accountability all mean that others will provide consequences for a person's behavior. An example that does not normally carry ethical overtones would be the consequences provided by a teacher when a student fails to submit an assignment or submits the assignment late. As a determinist, I fully appreciate that my student is not to blame. Given that the behavior (or lack of it) is determined by genetic endowment, learning history, and features of the current context, the student could do nothing other than fail to submit the assignment. Therefore, as a determinist, I do not make any "moral" judgements about the person or the behavior. Nevertheless, my student and I are involved in a complex set of contingencies (including statements delivered orally or in writing about what will follow from the nonsubmission of assignments) that require me to provide consequences for the failure to perform in specified ways. Although, as Wilson (1979) noted in an earlier quotation, it seems unreasonable to punish someone when the behavior was inevitable, it is not unreasonable or unjust to provide consequences for behavior. Young (1991) pointed out a situation in which consequences are provided by society even in a situation where a person is clearly not considered responsible: "we do take steps to protect ourselves against carriers of contagious diseases even though they aren't usually considered responsible for posing a threat to society" (pp. 540–541).

In situations where a person is to be considered responsible (where the culture is going to provide consequences) legal systems recognize the importance of learning history when they allow for what are called mitigating circumstances and what a behaviorist might call contextual variables to be taken into account. Courts request evaluations from psychiatrists, psychologists, social workers, and others when considering how to respond to acts that their society abhors. They frequently want to know something about the contingencies to which a transgressor has been exposed before deciding how to deal with the transgressor. Courts also differentiate consequences for the same act depending on the circumstances in which the act occurred. Some legal systems differentiate consequences for the act of ending the life of another person depending on whether the act occurred with or without prior planning. In the British legal system the act is called murder if it involved planning and is called manslaughter if no prior planning was involved. The act is the same in the sense that the behavior of one person brings about the death of another. The consequences imposed by the legal system, however, vary according to the circumstances in which the act took place.

Determinism requires rethinking the concepts of *blame* and *moral* responsibility, but does not require the culture to abandon consequences for behavior that is considered unethical (unacceptable). Just as my student and I are jointly involved in a complex set of contingencies that require me to provide consequences for the student's behavior, those who violate a society's code of conduct are involved with many others whose safety and other kinds of interests need to be protected: "Even if no-one deserves to be punished, and the usual forms that punishment takes have little to recommend them, we still need to protect the law-abiding from those who, because of their individual psychology or the sociology of their situation, break the laws" (Young, 1991, p. 541).

In relation to the kinds of behavior normally considered in the literature of ethics, stealing, harming other people, damaging their property and so on, Young (1991) notes that determinism continues to allow for the control of unacceptable behavior at the same time as it de-emphasizes *moral* responsibility and blame. If the metaphysical doctrine of determinism is accepted in the realm of human action, he argues: "Misbehavior won't be immoral behavior (because those who misbehave will not be able to do anything else). But it will still need to be controlled if the interests of those who don't pose a social problem are not to be subject to intolerable risk of being interfered with by miscreants" (Young, p. 540).

It is possible to accept that a person's behavior is determined to the same extent as all other natural phenomena and at the same time to recognize that a given community has a right, even a responsibility, to provide consequences in the interests of other persons within the community.

Compassion: Judging and Being Judged

Accepting determinism in the area of human action also may lead to compassion in judgements of one's own and others' behavior and to a greater level of respect for persons whose behavior is considered unacceptable than does the alternative view. Without requiring that the principle of accountability be abandoned, determinism encourages people to judge themselves and others less harshly than they might have been taught to by their culture: "The more I learn about learning histories and schedules of reinforcement and how antecedent conditions evoke behavior, the less inclined I am to judge anybody harshly, including myself" (J. Landis, personal communication, February 9, 2000).

Consider the kinds of judgements the free will or self-as-agent position might encourage. If an observer thought that a person could freely choose how to act, that observer might be encouraged to "blame" the actor for unacceptable behavior and thereby impose harsher consequences than a determinist might. If an observer really thought that there was an autonomous self directing and guiding behavior, and if a given behavior was considered repulsive, that observer would be correct to judge the self (or person) as repulsive because it was the self (or person) that generated the act. Interpreting the self as the sum of its history and current behavior, however, encourages an observer to judge the act rather than the actor as repulsive. Consequences are then rightly directed at the unacceptable act while other aspects of the offender's behavior (the self or person) can still be treated with compassion and respect. My student who fails to submit an assignment or submits the assignment late will have a penalty imposed for that act, but will otherwise be treated supportively and regarded with respect.

Determinism may be especially important for professionals who have to work with offenders. J. Landis (personal communication, Febrary 9,

2000) also noted the reaction of one of her professors who has to work with sexual offenders: "She says that it's impossible to work with them unless you can say to yourself that if you were that person, with those genes, and that learning history, you would have done the same things." Some kinds of offenses, perhaps including sexual offenses, evoke especially strong emotional reactions in observers, and professionals working with such offenders may be as prone to strong (perhaps even distressing) reactions as anyone else. Determinism serves to remind the observer that an offender's behavior was not of their choosing and this may help to alleviate the distress caused by particularly heinous acts.

The Value of Scientific Explanation

Skinner (1971) wrote: "to make a value judgement by calling something good or bad is to classify it in terms of its reinforcing effects" (p. 105). That which is good, which is valued, is that which is positively reinforcing, and to members of a behavioral community, scientific practices and the verbal behavior generated by them or extrapolated from them are good. Those things reinforce our behavior as individuals and as a community, and for many of us they have the additional effect of being exciting or stimulating in some way: "When I came to believe there was no Santa Claus, I felt disappointment. When I came to believe there was no God, I felt anxiety. However, when I came to believe there was no agency, I felt titillated. The same way I feel when I solve some difficult crossword puzzle or when I first came to understand evolution, or when I hear an explanation of plate tectonics" (J. Morrow, personal communication, 10 February, 2000). Given their learning history with the science, behaviorists react to determinism applied to human action in much the same way as scientists in other fields react to it applied to their subject matters; by valuing the opportunities for problem solving, understanding, explanation, and prediction inherent in the scientific method.

The complex repertoire called science is valued by behaviorists in Skinner's (1971) functional sense of the term *valued*. That is to say, behavior is influenced by reinforcers built into scientific activity. The details will differ for each person, but explanations that appeal to demonstrable functional relations affect subsequent behavior. Behavior analysts value explanations that have some scientific basis and take the view that scientific evidence, either explicitly demonstrated or extrapolated from data and reliable theoretical principles, should underpin accounts of behavior and treatments for behavior that is somehow maladaptive, uncomfortable, or inappropriate. Although determinism applied to human action appears to take something away from the culture—concepts of free will, self-determination, and self-as-agent—behaviorists do not see that as a loss because they have a learning history with a set of practices that, paradoxically, gives them more control over their lives and their worlds than those other prescientific concepts allow. As with other sciences, it also provides them with the means to find solutions to difficulties encountered in their own lives and in the lives of others and it has the additional positive consequence of encouraging them to judge behavior compassionately, their own and that of other people.

The challenge facing behavior analysts and other determinists is to convince the culture, both through verbal behavior and scientific demonstrations that behavior is an important part of the causal web, that human actions do bring about other events in the world, and that causation is reciprocal between the person and their context. Fatalism, vulnerability, and despair do not inevitably follow from determinism, and behaviorists do not fear determinism because of their learning histories with science. The responsibility for behaviorists and other determinists is to emphasize the positive consequences of determinism and to show the culture that the scientific approach is as valuable in interpreting human action as it is in interpreting other natural phenomena.

References

Baer, D. (1976). The organism as host. *Human Development, 19*, 87–98.

Black, M. (1973). Some aversive responses to a would-be reinforcer. In H. Wheeler (Ed.), *Beyond the punitive society* (pp. 125–134). London: Wildwood House.

Chiesa, M. (1994). *Radical behaviorism: The philosophy and the science.* Boston: Authors Cooperative.

Dennett, D. C. (1984). *Elbow room: The varieties of free will worth wanting.* Cambridge, MA: MIT Press.

Hineline, P. (1980). The language of behavior analysis: Its community, its functions, and its limitations. *Behaviorism, 8*, 67–86.

Hobart, R. E. (1934). Free will as involving determination and inconceivable without it. *Mind: A quarterly review, 43*, 1–27.

Midgley, M. (1991). The origin of ethics. In P. Singer (Ed.), *A companion to ethics* (pp. 3–13). Oxford: Blackwell.

Neuringer, A. (1986). Can people behave "randomly?": The role of feedback. *Journal of Experimental Psychology: General, 115(1)*, 62–75.

Newman, B., Reinecke, D. R., & Kurtz, A. L. (1996). Why be moral: Humanist and behavioral perspectives. *The Behavior Analyst, 19(2)*, 273–280.

Page, S., & Neuringer, A. (1985). Variability is an operant. *Journal of Experimental Psychology: Animal Behavior Processes, 11(3)*, 429–452.

Sheldon, B. (1982). *Behaviour modification: Theory, practice, and philosophy*. London: Tavistock.

Shorter Oxford English Dictionary (3rd ed.). (1988). London: Guild Publishing.

Skinner, B. F. (1972). A lecture on "having" a poem. In B. F. Skinner *Cumulative record: A selection of papers* (3rd ed.), (pp. 345–355). New York: Appleton-Century-Crofts.

Skinner, B. F. (1971). *Beyond Freedom and Dignity*. New York: Knopf.

Skinner, B. F. (1974). *About Behaviorism*. London: Jonathan Cape.

Strawson, G. (1998, June 26). Luck swallows everything: Can our sense of free will be true? *Times Literary Supplement*, 8–10.

Wilson, E. (1979). *The mental as physical*. London: Routledge.

Young, R. (1991). The implications of determinism. In P. Singer (Ed.), *A companion to ethics* (pp. 534–542). Oxford: Blackwell.

14

Advancing Behaviorism in a Judeo-Christian Culture
SUGGESTIONS FOR FINDING COMMON GROUND

Chad M. Galuska

The relationship between science and religion has been described as war-fare (Draper, 1874/1897; White, 1896/1960). This characterization is un-doubtedly too strong. Indeed, Gould (1999) has argued that it is false, fueled more by political agendas than historical fact. Nevertheless, it is undeniable that conflicts between science and religion have occurred, and often have been well publicized. The trial of Galileo in 1633 is perhaps the prime example of the persecution of science by a dogmatic theology. Three centuries later, opposition to Darwinian thought resulted in the media circus surrounding the *Scopes vs. Tennessee* (1925) trial. Today, fundamen-talist Christians in some parts of the United States continue to oppose the teaching of evolution in public schools, and new conflicts are emerging where science has outpaced the current system of ethics, such as in the case of human cloning.

Skirmishes aside, at the dawn of a new millennium science and religion coexist. Gould (1999) has conceptualized science and religion as occupying *nonoverlapping magisteria* (abbreviated NOMA). According to NOMA, sci-ence defines the natural world although ultimate questions about existence lie within the domain of religion. NOMA claims that science should not interfere within the domain of religion and vice-versa.

Chad M. Galuska • Department of Psychology, West Virginia University, Morguntown, WV 26506-6040.

NOMA can be seen in practice. The world's major religions have, for the most part, yielded authority to science on matters pertaining to the natural world. This was dramatically illustrated by the Roman Catholic Church's acceptance of evolution as factual in 1996. At the same time, many scientists are devoutly religious and from this vantage examine moral issues that are vital in promoting the well being of society. With respect to cloning, for example, religion cedes to science that it may be possible to clone a human, but science cannot decide if it is ethical to do so.

A practical problem with Gould's (1999) conceptualization of science and religion is that only deistic religions are compatible with NOMA. Deism purports that a supernatural deity (hereafter God) created the universe and set it in motion. Thereafter, God does not intervene in its workings (for an overview of deism, see Gould). Deism is incompatible with religions that assert the existence of a personal, intervening God. This incompatibility often is overlooked when discussing the nonconflicting subject matter of science and religion and will be discussed later in this chapter. This incompatibility notwithstanding, science and religion do coexist in areas of traditional science. For example, those of religious faith do not object to the laws of physics because they are deterministic and preclude supernatural intervention.

The debate between science and religion intensifies when studying people, however, precisely because science and religion appear to claim domain over the same subject matter. The resistance that biology faced when evolution was applied to humans is well known. Less chronicled is the debate between psychology and religion. It has been argued, for instance, that human behavior is not lawful, and therefore is not an appropriate subject matter for science (for analyses of such arguments see Chiesa, 1994; Grunbaum, 1953). Within psychology, the philosophy of behaviorism seems most at odds with the religious thought of the Judeo-Christian worldview.[1] Behaviorism often is seen as robbing humans of their special place in the universe, denying the existence of free will and moral responsibility, and rejecting notions of an intervening God. Perhaps because the behaviorist conceptualization of people runs counter to a culture dominated by Judeo-Christian thought, some have reacted to it negatively, using emotionally charged terms. For example, one critic labeled *Beyond*

---

[1] The scope of this chapter is limited to Judeo-Christianity because the Judeo-Christian faith is the most common religion in the Western culture, and seems to be the most relevant to this discussion. Many of the arguments apply generically to any religion espousing belief in a personal God. Many divisions exist within the broad theistic framework of Judeo-Christianity, rendering some of my arguments more or less relevant based on one's religious affiliation.

Freedom and Dignity (Skinner, 1971) as "the theory and practice of hell" (Rubenstein, 1971).[2]

The problems with acceptance by the Judeo-Christian culture might be viewed by some behaviorists as establishing the need to assert their arguments in favor of science. Behaviorists might be more effective in communicating in the culture at large, however, if they emphasized similarities between behaviorism and Judeo-Christianity. Gould (1999) provided several examples of how a mutual respect forged by honest intellectual debate has been productive for both science and religion. Within the science of behavior, Sidman (1960) has argued that science matures more so by emphasizing similarities than dissimilarities among divergent areas of research.

Consistent with this view, this chapter seeks commonalities between the philosophy of behaviorism and Judeo-Christianity. The common theme is pragmatic: Both behaviorists and Judeo-Christians have a common goal of solving socially significant problems. As part of this, they both spend considerable resources working with disadvantaged populations. Behaviorists have developed effective methods for addressing some of these social problems. The religious community has developed particularly effective means of mobilizing people to work on social issues. By combining these strengths, both Judeo-Christians and behaviorists may be more effective in minimizing societal problems. To obtain such cooperation, however, requires examining the issues that have kept it from occurring to this point. Several key issues including free will, moral responsibility, ethics, and the status of an intervening God will be examined. Philosophical differences undoubtedly exist, and will be briefly described emphasizing their practical implications. Although behaviorists and theists ultimately disagree on several metaphysical issues, it may be profitable to "agree to disagree" and move on to more pragmatic questions. As such, in the final section of the chapter the focus will shift from the relation between the philosophy of behaviorism and Judeo-Christianity to the role that a science of behavior (behavior analysis) could play in a Judeo-Christian culture.

Free Will and Determinism

The term *free will* is defined traditionally as the partial freedom of the agent, in acts of conscious choice, from environmental and phylogenic determinants (Durant, 1926/1960). The concept of free will is at the heart of

---

[2] For examples of negative reactions to *Beyond Freedom and Dignity* (Skinner, 1971), see Chein (1972) and Wheeler (1973). For a review of these reactions and a behaviorist reply, see Dinsmoor (1992).

Western philosophy and religion.[3] St. Irenaeus (125–202 A.D.) wrote, "Man is rational and therefore like God; he is created with free will and master over his acts" (Catechism of the Catholic Church, 1994, p. 481). Free will seems to be required within the Judeo-Christian worldview for at least three reasons. First, God created people in God's own image, granting them mastery over nature and all the animals (Genesis 1: 26–29; New International Version).[4] Second, God bestowed on humankind free will so they would be free to choose to love and worship God (Catechism of the Catholic Church, 1994, p. 481). Finally, free will is required within the Judeo-Christian system of ethics. For example, a just God could not condemn the sinful to eternal damnation if those people were not free to choose evil over good (Drange, 1998).

The philosophy of behaviorism posits that behavior is the product of the environment and phylogeny of the organism. Thus, behaviorism denies the existence of free will and aligns itself with the physical sciences in assuming a deterministic worldview. As Skinner (1953) argued:

> Science is more than the mere description of events as they occur. It is an attempt to discover order, to show that certain events stand in lawful relation to other events.... If we are to use the methods of science in the field of human affairs, we must assume that behavior is lawful and determined. (p. 6)

According to metaphysical determinism, every event that occurs in the universe is the necessary outcome of antecedent conditions (Slife, Yanchar, & Williams, 1999). One consequence of metaphysical determinism is that if all the relevant antecedents were known, human behavior could be predicted with perfect accuracy and the notion of free will could be disproved. Perfect prediction, of course, has eluded science. Within a metaphysical deterministic framework, the inability to make perfect predictions arises from two sources. The first is ignorance of the controlling variables (Baum, 1994; Sidman, 1960). As knowledge of the controlling variables increases, predictions become more refined. Second, predictions may be constrained due to limitations in measurement. Within physics, Heisenberg (1958) discovered that it is physically impossible to measure both the exact position and exact momentum of an atomic particle at any given time. Because it is impossible to measure the exact state of a

---

[3] Although free will is a fundamental assumption of most Judeo-Christian religions, there are several exceptions. Luther, for example, stated that the will was not free when it came to spiritual matters, referred to as the "bondage of the will" (Plass, 1959). Calvin denied the existence of free will altogether, espousing a religion based on predetermination. For the purposes of the present analysis, however, the assumption is that most people of the Judeo-Christian faith embrace traditional notions of free will.

[4] All biblical citations refer to the New International Version Bible.

physical system, it may be impossible to predict the future of that system with perfect accuracy.

Some behaviorists have abandoned metaphysical determinism in favor of *metaphysical probabilism* or *probabilistic determinism* (Slife et al., 1999; see Marr, this volume; Neuringer, this volume). This philosophical position stems from viewing behavior as a stochastic system incorporating random events. In practice, both metaphysical determinism and probabilistic determinism can only couch predictions in terms of probability. Because of this, some theorists have attempted to insert free will as a source of behavioral variability (Howard, 1994; Rockwell, 1994; Rychlak, 1992; for a review, see Slife et al., 1999). This insertion is incompatible with behaviorism. Echoing the metaphysical determinist stance, Baum (1994) labeled free will as "an illusion based on ignorance of the factors determining behavior" (p. 15). Moreover, Slife et al. (1999) argued that lawful processes determine the random variation viewed as inherent in stochastic models of behavior, leaving no room for an autonomous agent. Because both metaphysical and probabilistic determinism reject traditional notions of free will, the term determinism will be used generically throughout the rest of this chapter.

Within philosophy, workers have been attempting to integrate free will and determinism for hundreds of years. *Compatibilist* arguments attempt to incorporate free will into a deterministic account of behavior. The early Judeo-Christian leaders initially desired such arguments to reconcile the discrepancy between human free will and God's apparent foreknowledge of their actions.[5] Later, the success of Newtonian mechanism compelled many theistic philosophers, such as Kant, to posit compatibilist accounts of determinism and free will. Whereas a recounting of compatibilist arguments is beyond the scope of this chapter, many define free will in such a way so as to be compatible with behaviorism. Dennet (1984), for example, defined free will as deliberation before action. As Baum (1994) noted, deliberation is a class of behaviors (thinking, feeling, etc.) that ultimately is determined by genetic and environmental factors. Because deliberating itself is a determined event, Dennet's definition of free will does not pose a conceptual problem for behaviorism. Thus, one way to diffuse the free will/determinism controversy would be to adopt a compatibilist viewpoint. Unfortunately, most compatibilist arguments that are consistent with behaviorism define free will in such a limited way as to be incompatible with Judeo-Christian views of free will (Baum, 1994).

---

[5] For several dozen examples of God's foreknowledge of human actions, see Drange (1998, p. 323) and McKinsey (1995, pp. 322–328).

These arguments illustrate some of the futility both behaviorists and theists have encountered when engaging in philosophical debate over the free-will/determinism issue. Rather than find a position compatible to each, it may be wise to "agree to disagree" on metaphysical issues and adopt a more methodological position on the subject of determinism. In doing so, determinism is used in its simplest form to examine whether one or more events influence another event. Invoking determinism, thus, is not necessarily a reflection of any fundamental truth regarding the ultimate status of universe (Gazda & Corsini, 1980; Mazur, 1994; Slife et al., 1999; Vorsteg, 1974), but rather a tactical decision. Behaviorists thus avoid many points of contention with the Judeo-Christian culture. As Mazur (1994) wrote:

> Is it necessary to be a determinist to pursue the sort of scientific analysis that is described in this book? Certainly not. Regardless of your religious beliefs or your philosophical convictions, you can profit from reading this book as long as you are willing to observe that there is some regularity and predictability in the behaviors of both humans and nonhumans.... We can proceed in this fashion without taking any particular position on the free-will/determinism controversy. (p. 17)

Meanings of Freedom

By adopting a methodological approach to determinism, behaviorists and theists can begin to address more practical issues, such as the types of freedoms valued by each worldview. A search for the words "free" and "freedom" in the New International Version of the Bible revealed 72 verses with respect to freedom from slavery, captivity, imprisonment, bondage, or servitude. In addition, another 28 verses referred to freedom from other aversive events, such as disease, pain, fear, and violence. Thus, the most common biblical interpretation of freedom involves freedom from aversive control (accounting for over 60% of all references to "free" and "freedom").

Freedom from aversive control is a value shared by behaviorists (Baum, 1994; Sidman 1989; Skinner, 1971) and theists alike, and is evident in many of Skinner's writings, particularly *Beyond Freedom and Dignity*. It is important to note that conceptualizations of freedom are largely independent of the free will/determinism controversy. The similarities between the Judeo-Christian and behaviorist conceptualization of freedom—and the importance each attaches to the concept—should be emphasized.

In most religions embracing the notion of free will, freedom from aversive control is only the first step in achieving a more complete freedom.

The biblical view of freedom also is associated with choosing one course of action over another. This is the type of freedom most commonly associated with free will and its implications with respect to moral responsibility and ethics will be discussed in subsequent sections.

Another use of the word "freedom" is in the context of *spiritual freedom*. On one level, spiritual freedom refers to the freedom to love and worship God. There are 25 verses in the Bible that refer to "freewill offerings" in which people offer prayers and sacrifices to God. Functionally, this interpretation of spiritual freedom is the same as that associated with choice. Baum (1994), however, defined spiritual freedom as freedom from worldly wants and desires. Thus conceived, spiritual freedom refers to escape from or avoidance of events that others find to be positive reinforcers. The Bible refers to freedom from various types of sin, for example the love of money (Hebrews 13: 5). St. Paul agonized over the conflicting repertoires of wanting to serve the Lord and the (potentially) sinful nature of satisfying worldly desires (Romans 7: 7–25). Interestingly, many of these worldly desires may have deleterious long-term effects (Baum, 1994). For example, behaving "greedily" may lead to many short-term consequences (e.g., new cars, vacations, lavish homes), but ultimately may hurt interpersonal relationships. In many respects, spiritual freedom resembles the self-control paradigm of behavioral research; that is, choosing a larger delayed reinforcer over a smaller immediate reinforcer. Behaviorists recognize the importance of such a freedom and are in a unique position to offer insight into how it can be obtained. Indeed, Platt (1973) argued that the pragmatic resolution of St. Paul's dilemma potentially afforded by a science of behavior "may be the most important contribution to ethical practice in 2000 years" (p. 48).

In specifying the instances in which the Judeo-Christian culture uses the word "free," it becomes obvious that behaviorists strive for many of the same freedoms valued by most religions. Far from wanting to strip people of their freedom and dignity, behaviorists value the types of freedom that improve the quality of life. In a discussion about marketing applied behavior analysis in educational settings, for example, Bailey (1991) concluded, "Instead of trying to sell determinism... we need to promote the view that behavioral technology gives children dignity and cultivates freedom" (p. 447).

Moral Responsibility

Free will often is viewed as a prerequisite for moral responsibility. People are not held morally responsible for their actions if it is impossible for them to behave otherwise, as in the examples of coercion or mental illness. Moral responsibility plays a prominent role in Judeo-Christian theology. People are held accountable for their actions. Ultimately, good deeds result in eternal happiness in heaven whereas evil deeds lead to eternal suffering in hell. Within the behaviorist framework, however, people never are truly responsible for their actions because their choices are determined by previous conditions such that they could not act otherwise. At first blush, it appears that in denying that people are morally responsible for their actions, behaviorism is fundamentally incompatible with a Judeo-Christian worldview, not to mention a threat to the validity of current legal and political systems.

This is not necessarily the case. Far from having no use for the concept, behaviorists take a practical viewpoint on moral responsibility. Holding someone responsible, Baum (1994) stated, "comes down to a decision on whether to impose consequences" (p. 169). This decision is determined by evaluating the behavior in context and predicting the likelihood that consequences would be effective in punishing undesirable behavior or reinforcing desirable behavior. To this end, Schnaitter (1977) argued that a person is morally responsible for an event if the likelihood of the person again causing the event can be modified by contingencies of reinforcement or punishment.

In some ways, the actual practice of assigning moral responsibility is similar to Judeo-Christian practices. A culture that places the cause of behavior outside the individual still has pragmatic grounds for punishing those who break the law; although in such a culture the stigma associated with committing a crime might decrease. This is consistent with the Judeo-Christian ideals of forgiveness and compassion. If anything, behaviorism emphasizes the use of positive reinforcement and rehabilitation, and promotes a more tolerant justice system using punishers selected for their function in reducing undesirable behavior (see Chiesa, this volume). This is consistent with the move from the "eye for an eye" philosophy of the Old Testament to Christ's teachings in the New Testament.

Although practical problems of assigning moral responsibility may be resolved, there remains a fundamental philosophical conflict between behaviorism and Judeo-Christianity over the nature of moral responsibility. As mentioned above, if people are not truly responsible for their actions, the idea that some people are eternally punished for their actions seems inconsistent with the notion of a just God. As in the case of the free will debate, it may be best for behaviorists and those of the Judeo-Christian faith to focus on the practical issue of assigning moral responsibility (where commonalities exist).

Ethics

I have argued that behaviorists and theists share common commitments to values such as freedom, dignity, forgiveness, and compassion. Despite the philosophical differences between the two positions, is it possible that behaviorists and Judeo-Christians share a common system of ethics? The existence of such an ethical system would facilitate the integration of behaviorism and Judeo-Christian culture.

On the surface, it appears as if the search for a common ethical system is misguided. The basis for the system of ethics in the Judeo-Christian culture ultimately is derived from the Word of God or the teachings of Christ, as codified in the Bible. Biblical literalists believe these revelations are absolute, unchanging across time and place. Although religious nonliteralists may modify their beliefs based on contextual variables or scientific findings, they too generally believe in moral absolutes: the endpoints represented in Judeo-Christian teachings by the workings of God and Satan. On the other hand, behaviorists take a more pragmatic approach to ethics (see Chiesa, this volume; Lattal & Laipple, this volume; Staddon, this volume). Skinner (1971) defined *values* in terms of contingencies of reinforcement. Things that function as positive reinforcers usually are labeled "good," whereas things that function as negative reinforcers are labeled "bad." At the level of the individual, Skinner's conceptualization of values, however, does not lead to a reasonable ethical system. For example, if stolen goods function as positive reinforcers, then stealing is good. As can be seen, this line of reasoning leads to a moral relativism devoid of universal values and is diametrically opposed to the morality of the Judeo-Christian faith.

That behaviorism implies an extreme moral relativism is, however, unfounded. Skinner's analysis of ethics also included the use of a selectionist framework at the level of the culture (Baum, 1994; Day, 1977; Zuriff, 1987). Behaviors that have been beneficial to the survival of the culture tend to be selected, and over time, becomes codified into laws and ethical systems. Ethical systems derived in this manner are known as natural laws or natural ethics because they were derived through natural or cultural selection (see Staddon, this volume, for additional discussion of natural ethics).

The religious community often is unlikely to accept this conceptualization of ethics because of the conspicuous absence of a divine influence. St. Thomas Aquinas (trans. 1963), however, provided roles for both natural ethics and divine law within one ethical system. In his *Summa Theologica* (trans. 1963), Aquinas distinguished between natural moral laws and divine laws. Divine laws concerned matters of supernatural significance, such as the afterlife, and could become known only through divine revelation and religious belief. All other ethical laws were classified as natural moral laws, established through a process akin to cultural selection. From this view, natural moral laws also had divine origins, but no religious belief was necessary to obtain knowledge of these laws or to behave morally (Arnhart, 1998).

Aquinas's position on the natural law contains several similarities to Skinner's treatment of natural ethics. Aquinas referenced Ulpian[6] as describing the natural law as "what nature has taught all animals" (Sigmund, 1988, p. 50). Moreover, Aquinas stressed the role of consequences and social desirability as measures of the relative "goodness" of an action. Consider the following quote from the *Summa Theologica* (trans. 1963): "An action is called good because it is conducive to a good effect; in this way an action's bearing on an effect is the measure of its goodness" (p. 13). This conceptualization of natural ethics and divine law is quite compatible with the behaviorists' views. First, it relegates divine law to the realm of the metaphysical, where behaviorists and theists need not quarrel over its ultimate status. Second, all other ethical systems are the result of cultural selection that may or may not have been divinely inspired (depending on one's beliefs).

Given the arguments above, it would seem that Skinner's ethical system could be integrated within a Judeo-Christian worldview. Skinner's ethical system, however, is not limited to an analysis of the conditions under which people report that behavior is good or bad. Skinner (1971) went further, and argued that a science of behavior could determine what people *ought* to do. People ought to behave in ways that support the long-term survival of the culture. As Skinner stated:

> Questions of this sort seem to point toward the future, to be concerned not with man's origins but with his destiny. They are said, of course, to involve "value judgments"—to raise questions not about facts, not about what a man *can* do but about what he *ought* to do. It is usually implied that the answers are out of the reach of science. . . . It would be a mistake for the behavioral scientist to agree. (p. 102)

Skinner's ethical system thus attempts to usurp the authority of what he called the traditional view of ethics based, in the Western culture, on Judeo-Christian teachings (Day, 1977). Skinner's system can be objected to on several grounds. First, Skinner committed the *naturalist*

---

[6] Ulpian was a Roman jurist, d. 228.

fallacy, that is, attempting to derive an *ought* statement from an *is* statement. This premise is universally regarded as a logical fallacy and even has been criticized from within the behaviorist camp (Staddon, 2001, this volume; Zuriff, 1987). Second, even if the naturalist premise is accepted, Skinner's ethical system provides little guidance as to how behaviorists should go about making ethical decisions, as the survivability criterion seems to require foreknowledge (Staddon, 2001). Moral dilemmas exist precisely because people disagree as to what is in the long-term best interests of society. Finally, Skinner's conceptualization of ethics is in violation of NOMA. Behaviorists must be careful not to use the factual authority of science to make moral claims (Gould, 1999). To be sure, behavior analysis can shed light on many ethical issues, but so can traditional religious teachings. In some respects the two are complementary and examine ethics in different ways. Begelman (1977) provided an appropriate analogy:

> ...the way in which a taxidermist views a zebra contrasts markedly with the way the animal is viewed by a zoologist, physiologist, or interior decorator. But none of these separate outlooks competes with others, nor is aimed at supplanting them. It appears that the same is true for moral philosophy and functional analysis. (p. 25)

The Status of an Intervening God

In discussing the above issues, debate often emerges over the very existence of God. It is important to note that there is nothing within the behaviorist philosophy that requires a nonbelief in God. Behaviorism, however, does seem to limit God's ability to intervene in people's daily lives. Behaviorism posits that all behavior is the product of genetic and environmental determinants, leaving no room for God to intervene as a causal entity in human affairs. A science of behavior cannot exist if behavior is subject to the influences of supernatural forces.

The concept of an intervening God lies at the heart of the Judeo-Christian faith. It is the stuff of miracles and the reason for prayer. Behaviorists will find it futile attempting to convince those of faith that God is powerless to intervene in their lives. Rather, it is essential to examine exactly what it means to speak of divine interventions. I will discuss two possible meanings: Miraculous interventions and interventions mediated via the natural world.

Gould (1999) defined *miracle* as "a unique and temporary suspension of natural law to reorder the facts of nature by divine fiat" (p. 85). By definition, miracles cannot be attributed to natural sources. The Roman Catholic Church, for example, employs skeptics to investigate claims of miracles. Only when no natural causes are discovered is a phenomenon classified as a miracle. Miraculous interventions are not only incompatible with behaviorism; they are incompatible with the philosophy of science (Gould).

A second conceptualization of divine intervention states that although God may be the ultimate cause of some event, God chooses to work through the natural world. This is probably how Judeo-Christians would characterize most workings of God. Even devout theists usually can identify physical causes associated with an apparent divine intervention. For example, the parents of a gravely ill child may pray to God that the doctors are blessed with the skills needed to save the child's life. If the child recovers, the parents may credit both the doctors (proximally) and God (ultimately) as determinants of the child's improved health.[7]

In an intervention mediated by the natural world, God need not suspend the laws of nature to accomplish God's will. Rather, the workings of God may be predetermined. With perfect foresight, God created the laws of nature such that prayers would be answered, and the sick child in the above example would recover. This interpretation of God is deistic, and advocates of an intervening (in the miraculous sense) God may reject such an interpretation. Gould (1999) countered, echoing the views of philosopher and theologian Thomas Burnett:

> Do we not have greater admiration for a machine that performs all its appointed tasks (both regular and catastrophic) by natural laws operating on a set of initial parts, than for a device that putters along well enough in a basic mode, but requires a special visit from its inventor for anything more complex. (p. 23)

I conclude this section by noting that some behaviorists may wish to reject even the second conceptualization of divine intervention (and for that matter, perhaps the existence of God altogether) on the basis of several philosophical grounds including parsimony, burden of proof, and Sagan's balance (the idea that extraordinary claims call for extraordinary evidence). They are free to do this. While cooperating with those of the Judeo-Christian faith to achieve societal change, however, it may be more profitable not to challenge this conceptualization of God's workings, as it does not necessarily conflict with behaviorism.

---

[7] Notable exceptions to this example include those of the Christian Science faith.

Behavior Analysis and Judeo-Christianity

The purpose of this chapter has been to seek commonalities between the philosophy of behaviorism and Judeo-Christianity. Commonalities were found in the kinds of freedoms valued by behaviorists and theists, the practical methods for establishing moral responsibility, and commitments to values such as freedom, dignity, forgiveness, and compassion. Moreover, the chapter argues that there is nothing within a behaviorist philosophy that requires nonbelief in God. A final commonality is that both are intervention-oriented, committed to eradicating many of the problems that face society today. Theologians often speak of a moral decay in the fabric of society, pointing to a loss in spirituality as the major controlling variable. Although behaviorists may disagree with the causes of such a moral decay, there is no doubt that the religious community is identifying something real. Issues such as poverty, violent crime, terrorism, AIDS, and the failures of the educational system continue to plague society. Ideally, a science of behavior should be in the position to engage the Judeo-Christian community in productive discourse, united by a common goal of minimizing these societal problems.

In interactions with those of the Judeo-Christian faith, it is important for behaviorists to remember that science and religion ask different questions about human behavior. Behavior analysis identifies functional relations between behavior and environment. Religion seeks to answer more ultimate questions about human behavior, such as questions associated with morality and the afterlife. Although the philosophy of behaviorism and Judeo-Christianity may differ on metaphysical grounds, these differences need not prevent a productive working relationship, as the domains of behavior analysis and religion are independent of one another.

Science and religion *can* work together to solve problems of social importance. For example, in my community a number of churches of different faiths cooperated with a local hospital to sponsor two babies from Ethiopia in need of life-saving surgery. The hospital provided the necessary medical care while the churches provided homes for the families to live in while the babies recovered. Together, the churches and the hospital saved two lives. It is doubtful that similar results would have been achieved if the churches and the hospital had decided instead to focus their energy on debating the ethics of modern medical science.

Behavior analysts provide products and services in a culture dominated by the ideals of religion and free will. Providing these products and services probably is hindered by a heavy-handed pitch for determinism. The terms used in technical communication such as "control," "manipulate," "intervene," and "subjects" can be abandoned when communicating with the public (Bailey, 1991). This is not to imply that behaviorists abandon their behavioral data language in the laboratory or the classroom (Hineline, 1980). Communication within a discipline is a different class of behavior than communication outside of the discipline. To this end, Geller (1995a, 1995b) has advocated an "actively caring" model of community based treatment and environmental protection. In this model, behavioral principles are used to modify humanistic goals, such as increasing self-esteem, decreasing depression, and achieving socially desirable outcomes such as environmental protection. Such an approach ultimately advances communication between behavior analysts and others because more individuals are able come into contact with behavioral-based interventions.

Changing the way behaviorists interact with potential consumers of their services is only the first step in increasing the role a science of behavior can play in solving societal problems. The influence of a science of behavior will increase as more behavior analysts become active in their communities, schools, and hospitals. Often this will involve working with people who do not share their philosophical convictions in order to accomplish a common goal. These relationships will be more likely to endure if they are grounded in the principles of NOMA. Theists need not accept the philosophical tenets of behaviorism to endorse the practices of behavior analysis. Behavior analysts need not challenge the domain of religion in addressing ultimate questions of human existence. In this way, behavior analysts can begin to engage the Judeo-Christian community in a mutually reinforcing relationship.

Acknowledgements

I thank Michael Perone, Susan Schneider, and Carol Pilgrim for reviews on an earlier version of this manuscript.

References

Aquinas, T. (1963). *Summa theologica* (Vol 18). Blackfriars: Cambridge.
Arnhart, L. (1998). The search for a Darwinian science of ethics. *Science and Spirit, 9*, 4–7.
Bailey, J. S. (1991). Marketing behavior analysis requires different talk. *Journal of Applied Behavior Analysis, 24*, 445–448.
Baum, W. M. (1994). *Understanding behaviorism: Science, behavior, and culture.* New York: Harper Collins.

Begelman, D. A. (1977). Commentary. In J. E. Krapfl & E. A. Vargas (Eds.), *Behaviorism and ethics* (pp. 24–28). Kalamazoo: Behaviordelia, Inc.

Catechism of the Catholic Church (1994). New York: Doubleday.

Chein, I. (1972). *The science of behavior and the image of man.* New York: Basic Books.

Chiesa, M. (1994). *Radical behaviorism: The philosophy and the science.* Boston: Authors Cooperative, Inc.

Day, W. (1977). Ethical philosophy and the thought of B. F. Skinner. In J. E. Krapfl & E. A. Vargas (Eds.), *Behaviorism and ethics* (pp. 7–23). Kalamazoo: Behaviordelia, Inc.

Dennett, D. C. (1984). *Elbow room: The varieties of free will worth wanting.* Cambridge: MIT Press.

Dinsmoor, J. A. (1992). Setting the record straight: The social views of B. F. Skinner. *American Psychologist, 47,* 1454–1463.

Drange, T. M. (1998). *Nonbelief & evil: Two arguments for the nonexistence of God.* Amherst: Prometheus Books.

Draper, J. W. (1897). *History of the conflict between religion and science.* New York: Appleton & Company. (Original work published in 1874)

Durant, W. (1960). *The story of philosophy* (8th ed.). New York: Pocket Books. (Original work published in 1926)

Gazda, G. M., & Corsini, R. J. (1980). *Theories of learning: A comparative approach.* Itasca, IL: F. E. Peacock Publishers.

Geller, E. S. (1995a). Actively caring for the environment: An integration of behaviorism and humanism. *Environment and Behavior, 27,* 184–195.

Geller, E. S. (1995b). Integrating behaviorism and humanism for environmental protection. *Journal of Social Issues, 51,* 179–195.

Gould, S. J. (1999). *Rocks of ages: Science and religion in the fullness of life.* New York: Ballentine.

Grunbaum, A. (1953). Causality and the science of human behavior. In H. Fiegl & M. Brodbeck (Eds.), *Readings in the philosophy of science* (pp. 766–778). New York: Appleton-Century-Crofts.

Heisenberg, W. (1958). *Physics and philosophy: The revolution in modern science.* New York: Harper and Brothers.

Hineline, P. N. (1980). The language of behavior analysis: Its community, its functions, and its limitations. *Behaviorism, 8,* 67–86.

Howard, G. S. (1994). Some varieties of free will worth practicing. *Journal of Theoretical and Philosophical Psychology, 14,* 50–61.

Mazur, J. E. (1994). *Learning and behavior.* (3rd ed.). Englewood Cliffs, NJ: Prentice Hall, Inc.

McKinsey, C. D. (1995). *The encyclopedia of biblical errancy.* Amherst: Prometheus Books.

New International Version Bible. Retrieved from http://www.niv.org/ on January 11, 2002.

Plass, E. M. (1959). *What Luther says: An anthology.* (Vol III). St. Louis: Concordia Publishing House.

Platt, J. R. (1973). The Skinnerian revolution. In H. Wheeler (Ed.), *Beyond the punitive society* (pp. 22–56). San Francisco: W. H. Freeman and Company.

Rockwell, W. T. (1994). Beyond determinism and indignity: A reinterpretation of operant conditioning. *Behavior and Philosophy, 22,* 53–66.

Rubenstein, R. L. (1971, September). Beyond freedom and dignity by B. F. Skinner. *Psychology Today,* pp. 28–31, 95–96.

Rychlak, J. F. (1992). Free will: "Doing otherwise all circumstances remaining the same." In B. Slife & J. Rubinstein (Eds.), *Taking sides: Clashing views on controversial psychological issues* (7th ed., pp. 65–71). Guilford, Connecticut: Dushkin Publishing Group.

Schnaitter, R. (1977). Behaviorism and ethical responsibility. In J. E. Krapfl & E. A. Vargas (Eds.), *Behaviorism and ethics* (pp. 29–47). Kalamazoo: Behaviordelia, Inc.

Sidman, M. (1960). *Tactics of scientific research.* New York: Basic Books. (Reprinted, 1988. Boston: Authors Cooperative.)

Sidman, M. (1989). *Coercion and its fallout.* Boston, MA: Author's Cooperative.

Sigmund, P. E. (Ed.). (1988). *St. Thomas Aquinas on politics and ethics.* New York: W. N. Norton & Company.

Skinner, B. F. (1948). *Walden two.* New York: MacMillan.

Skinner, B. F. (1953). *Science and human behavior.* New York: MacMillan.

Skinner, B. F. (1971). *Beyond freedom and dignity.* New York: Bantam.

Skinner, B. F. (1974). *About behaviorism.* New York: Alfred A. Knopf.

Slife, B. D., Yanchar, S. C., & Williams, B. (1999). Conceptions of determinism in radical behaviorism: A taxonomy. *Behavior and Philosophy, 27,* 75–96.

Staddon, J. E. R. (2001). *The new behaviorism: Mind, mechanism, and society.* Philadelphia: Psychology Press.

Vorsteg, R. H. (1974). Operant reinforcement theory and determinism. *Behaviorism, 2,* 108–119.

Wheeler, H. (Ed.). (1973). *Beyond the punitive society.* San Francisco: W. H. Freeman and Company.

White, A. D. (1960). *A history of the warfare of science with theology in Christendom.* New York: Dover Publications. (Original work published in 1897)

Zuriff, G. (1987). *Naturalist ethics.* In. S Modgil & C. Modgil (Eds.), B. F. Skinner: Consensus and controversy (pp. 309–318). New York: Fulmer Press.

15

Behavior Analysis and a Modern Psychology
PROGRAMS OF DIRECT ACTION

Edward K. Morris

Psychology has purportedly undergone two revolutions since becoming a science—one in the first decades of the 20th century, the other a half-century later. These were the behavioral and the cognitive revolutions, respectively. Although behaviorism is now presumably dead and cognitivism ascendant, cognitivism is not today modern in psychology. It is not modern because (a) it is not naturalistic, placing behavior and mind in different ontological categories—material and immaterial; (b) it adheres to a world view better fitted to the physical than the life sciences—mechanism; and (c) it is, ironically, little more than a standard form of behaviorism—methodological behaviorism. Not even behaviorism, though, naturalized psychology, for two reasons. First, where behaviorism was a stimulus-response (S->R) psychology, it was unable to account for purposive or intentional action, especially in language and cognition. Second, although objective, behaviorism has vacillated between being metaphysical and methodological. In *metaphysical* behaviorism, behavior is what psychology studies, as well as its subject matter, whereas in *methodological* behaviorism, behavior is what psychology studies, but it is not its subject matter—its subject matter is generically the mind. In the end, mainstream behaviorism became a methodological behaviorism,

Edward K. Morris • Department of Human Development, University of Kansas, Lawrence, KS 66045-2133.

whose dominant form was, by mid-century, *mediational* behaviorism (e.g., Hull, Spence, Tolman) where hypothetical constructs (e.g., expectancies, drives) mediated the relation of stimuli to responses in an S->O->R psychology.

The received view about the cognitive revolution notwithstanding (see Baars, 1986; Gardner, 1985), more recent, less presentist accounts of psychology's history tend to refute it. Such accounts argue that the purported revolution was little more than the evolution of mediational behaviorism (e.g., Leahey, 1992b; Moore, 1995). To be sure, psychology's evolution was punctuated by a distinct change in its surface structure, for instance, in its language and its models; however, its deep structure—its explanatory practices—were little affected. For instance, although *input* and *output* replaced stimulus and response, and information processing became the predominant mediational model, cognitivism is still an S->O->R psychology, a methodological behaviorism (Lee, 1988a).

Cognitivism, of course, sought to be scientific, and thus embraced the standard "isms" of science: materialism, determinism, and positivism. It did so, however, in ways that were more scientistic than naturalistic. For instance, cognitivism is rarely materialistic without being reductionistic, that is, without seeking explanations of mind and behavior in biology (e.g., physiology, neurology). It is rarely deterministic without being mechanistic, for instance, characterizing the mind as a machine (e.g., a computer) and mental processes as the action of formal, immutable entities (i.e., bytes). And, it is rarely positivistic without being dualistic, making behavioral relations *indexes* of operationally defined psychological constructs, not *instances* of descriptively defined psychological concepts, where *cognitive* refers to hypothetical structures and processes (e.g., cognitive structures, information processing), not to a quality of action (e.g., cognitive behavior, public or private). Cognitivism's attempt to remake mentalistic Western folk psychology into a scientific psychology on the pattern of the physical sciences has proved to be a daunting task.

Those behaviorisms that might have made psychology naturalistic were metaphysical, not methodological or mediational, in nature. They eschewed Western folk psychological traditions and adopted assumptions and methods more consistent with the life sciences. These behaviorisms, however, were incomplete and inconsistent in themselves, and thus remained a minority program. Watson's (1913a, 1913b) classical behaviorism, for instance, vacillated between being a metaphysical and methodological behaviorism, and in either case was largely mechanistic in worldview. Kantor's (1924, 1926, 1959) interbehavioral psychology offered naturalistic postulates and perceptive interpretations of psychology's content domains, but no accompanying and validating empirical program of research. And, although Skinner (1938, 1945, 1953, 1974) provided both a naturalized philosophy (i.e., radical behaviorism) and a natural science (i.e., basic behavioral processes discerned through the experimental analysis of behavior), his behaviorism never systematically engaged the natural history of behavior. That is, it never offered an empirical account of the content domains of behavior in individual, social, and cultural context, for instance, of perceptual and cognitive, emotional and motivated, and verbal and social behavior. These classes of behavior, though, along with individual differences within and between them, are generally regarded as the essence of what it is to be human. They are what mainstream psychology describes and what it offers to explain in its myriad content-specific domains. Thus, although Skinner's philosophy and his science had important things to say about psychology (e.g., selection by consequences, contingencies), it usually said them about unimportant behavior (i.e., generic responses; e.g., bar pressing). This is not necessarily a criticism of a young science, but rather an observation about what Skinner's science—or, more broadly, *behavior analysis* (see Michael, 1985; Reese, 1986)—has yet to offer mainstream psychology. It is also an observation about what the culture expects of its psychology.

In any event, throughout the history of Western civilization, a naturalistic psychology has been an unfulfilled promise, at least as proffered by these behaviorisms. These behaviorisms, though, have not been the only attempts to naturalize psychology; other programs have sought the same end. In this chapter, I describe five such programs, programs of "direct action." In the main, they share significant features with behavior analysis, but unfortunately, they and behavior analysis have proceeded independently of one another, unaware of their common critiques of mainstream psychology (Costall & Still, 1987) and of their like-minded alternatives (Still & Costall, 1991). After describing the five programs, I then note some points on which they are at variance, but mainly I emphasize the symmetries between them and behavior analysis, except on one point. After this, I describe how behavior analysis and the programs of direct action are complimentary on a broader, more disciplinary dimension—the former as natural science, the latter as natural history—and describe how both are necessary for a naturalized psychology. In closing, I consider the possibilities of their integration and the politics of their alliance, finding reason for optimism and pessimism alike. Before beginning, however, I provide a brief historical overview.

An Historical Overview

The history of mainstream psychology reaches back into ancient Greece, wherein psychology embraced, for instance, the reality of Plato's

universal forms, as against a materialist ontology, as well as the atom-
ists' copy theories of perception, as against a realist epistemology. Two
millennia later, these views were formalized into Cartesian mind-body
dualism, and two hundred years afterward were made scientific in psychology's first system—structuralism—the introspective study of the mind.
When structuralism gave way to classical behaviorism, mentalism was set
aside, but not everywhere dismissed. It was later reintroduced as the O in
mediational S->O->R behaviorism, which is today the cognition in
cognitivism—a psychology of "indirect" action.

A history of the programs of direct action has, in contrast, yet to be
written, perhaps because the programs failed to become unified as an alternative to mainstream psychology. Their long past, though, can be traced
to Aristotle's naturalistic psychology, wherein action was the essence of
mind, not independent of it (Moore, this volume; Rachlin, 1994). Aristotelian psychology, however, was eclipsed for over 2000 years (Kantor,
1963, 1969), until the short history of direct action formally commenced
with the Scottish school of common sense realism (e.g., Reid, Stewart)—a
direct, unmediated psychology. Aspects of this program were later manifested in several forms of act psychology, Gestalt psychology, and phenomenology (see Day, 1980), but these never became mainstream because,
ironically, they were eclipsed by classical behaviorism whose epistemology
was of course "direct," but whose ontology was generally mechanistic. Not
until the articulation of radical empiricism (e.g., James) and its subsequent
elaboration by the neorealists (e.g., Holt, Perry, Singer) did psychology
have an evolutionary, functional, and philosophically pragmatic program
of direct action, but even this program failed in its own time. Today, though,
several instantiations of it are found as alternatives to mainstream mediational behaviorism and cognitive psychology (Heft, 2001), to which I now
turn.

Programs of Direct Action

Although these programs do not reflect a unified body of work,
they share a strong family resemblance in their approaches to psychological science, which are variously referred to as non-representational,
non-mediational, ecological, selectionist, and systems-like. These are
S<->R psychologies of codefining functional relations. In this section,
I describe five of these programs, each instantiated in one of psychology's content domains: perception, memory, cognition, intelligence, and
development.

A Nonrepresentational Approach to Perception

The first program is the most well-established, Gibson's (1979) "theory of direct perception." As in most of these programs, Gibson took both a destructive and a constructive stance, the former critical of a mainstream view, the latter an alternative to it. Gibson's destructive stance was to dismantle "the myth of the ghost in the machine" (cf. Ryle, 1949). In particular, he sought to dismantle the representational theory of perception—the theory that individuals do not perceive the world directly, but only indirectly, through internal, mental representations of it. On this view, objects and events have no meaning until they are mentally represented.

Representational theories, Gibson (1979) argued, are supported by two longstanding assumptions, Cartesian dualism and the mechanistic worldview. Cartesian dualism is the view that nonmaterial minds inhabit material bodies and are in direct contact with those bodies, not with the world. Mechanism, in turn, as adopted from classical physics, assumes that effects must have immediate, physically contiguous causes. On this view, objects and events at a spatial distance from an organism cannot cause its actions because the objects are not physically contiguous with the organism's body. The spatial gap between them must be filled, which is what representations are said to do. They fill the gap between "there" and "here," bringing objects to mind, where they are contiguous with bodies and can cause action.

Gibson's constructive alternative was to treat perception as action, that is, as a functional relation between the perceiver and the perceived. As action, not merely a physical response, perception involves both the organism and the environment (see Johnston, 1985), wherein their relation is said to be "mutual." The value of one for the other lies in this relation, a direct, nonrepresentational relation, with no spatial gaps to be filled because functional relations have no gaps. At the heart of this alternative is Gibson's concept of "affordances." As Gibson (1979) described it: "The perceiving of an affordance is not a process of perceiving a value-free physical object to which meaning is somehow added . . . ; it is a process of perceiving a value-rich ecological object" (p. 140). In other words, organisms do not first sense the physical structure of the environment, then mentally represent and give it meaning, and later act on the representation. Instead, given biological, psychological, and socio-cultural histories, an object's value is perceived directly, that is, what it affords behavior. People perceive, for instance, the graspability of a hammer, the kindness of strangers, and orderliness of data. This does not mean that they perceive an object as others perceive it, only that when it is perceived, it is perceived directly.

A Nonmediational Approach to Memory

A newer program of direct action—a non-mediational perspective—is found in Watkins (1990) "direct memory perspective." In his destructive stance, Watkins criticizes logical positivism and the mechanistic world-view. The underlying problem, he argues, is mediationism, which is "the doctrine that remembering an event requires that a representation of that event be embodied in a 'memory trace' that is retained over time between the event's occurrence and its recollection" (Watkins, p. 329). The flaw in mediationism is that the three-stage theorizing among the occurrence of an event, its mediation, and its later recollection constitutes a level of complexity in which memory can be hypothetically accounted for in more ways than data can discriminate among (see Jenkins, 1974; Watkins, 1981; cf. Malcolm, 1977). Theories of memory thus proliferate, but remain so underdetermined by the data that knowledge does not emulate.

Mediationism, Watkins (1990) argues, retains a strong hold on memory research for three reasons. First, the mind is complex, and so psychologists must have complex theories. Second, formal theories are necessary to generate research, and so psychologists must have them. And third, mediation satisfies the mechanistic requirement that action-at-a-temporal distance must be accounted for by unbroken chains of contiguous causes and effects. In the case of memory, this involves bridging the temporal gap between an event's occurrence and its later recollection, which is what the hypothetical mediators—the mental traces—are said to do.

Watkins (1990) takes exception to these reasons and argues that psychologists can indeed meaningfully study "the effect that an experience at one point in time can have on experience or behavior at another point in time without invoking a physical substrate to bridge their temporal separation" (p. 331). The benefits are several. First, "by ceasing to look inward to the [memory] trace, theorists would be more likely to look outward to the context in which memory occurs" (p. 331). This would strengthen the search for controlling variables, as well as the relation between basic and applied research. Second, functional explanations involving "empirical laws" would replace mechanistic explanations of action that invoke mediators to bridge temporal gaps between "then" and "now." And third, the direct memory perspective would intensify the "study of stimulus control over the remembering process, and of how external stimuli interact with willful control in determining memory" (p. 332).

With respect to the study of stimulus control, this involves research on what Watkins (1990) calls "contingency relations" between classes of memory cues. These relations are formulated as " 'cuegrams,' or descriptions merely of the relations between classes of cues, rather than of the nature of hypothetical memory traces. [On this view,] changes of memory...are nothing more nor less than changes in cuegrams" (p. 332). As for the willful control of remembering, Watkins suggests that psychologists should consider more carefully the conditions that occasion remembering. Where remembering is weak, they should investigate strategies and heuristics for remembering what needs to be remembered (e.g., remembering related antecedents, consequences, and contexts).

An Ecological Approach to Cognition

Another descriptor of the nonrepresentational and nonmediational programs of direct action is "ecological" (see Gibson, 1979), especially as it applies to cognition (e.g., Neisser, 1984; Still & Costall, 1991; Wilcox & Katz, 1981b). Wilcox and Katz (1981b), for example, take an ecological approach to cognitive development. Their key observation is that, over time and occasion, one-and-the-same input into system, instance, into a cognitive state, yields different outputs. The mainstream account of this one-to-many discrepancy is that the cognitive state is changed by the first input, with the changed state thereby yielding different outputs for the next input, even when the next input is formally the same. Wilcox and Katz's destructive program is similar to Gibson's and Watkins': Cognitive explanations in terms of states lead to an infinite regress, are circular, and are superfluous.

Wilcox and Katz's (1981b) constructive alternative to the traditional explanation of the input-output discrepancy is not to presume any change in some hypothetical cognitive state, but instead to redefine the nature of the input, that is, of the environment. Their redefinition "involves expanding the temporal size of the input" (p. 251) such that the " 'present' situation is perceived in relation to an unfolding past" (p. 256). In the context of an unfolding, and thereby ever-changing past, formally identical, one-and-the-same inputs are different inputs, their physical form notwithstanding. These inputs function differently because they are embedded in a system of continuously ongoing changes in organism-environment interactions. In this view, cognitive development knows no internal states, but rather is a function of ongoing changes in the relation between organism and environment. What develops in cognitive development, then, is the environment—not the physical environment but the functional environment (see Still & Costall, 1991).

Wilcox and Katz's (1981b) alternative to the mechanistic information-processing theories of cognitive development is not just a program of direct action, but also an exemplar of the worldview of contextualism (cf. Hayes, Hayes, Reese, & Sarbin, 1992), wherein contextualism is Pepper's (1942/1960, pp. 232–279) term for philosophical pragmatism. The root metaphor of contextualism is the "historic event," wherein each action is unique in its historical context, that is, unique in the context of an ever-changing historical stream of events, as the present continuously becomes the past for more present (see Rosnow & Georgoudi, 1986). This is the lineage from James's radical empiricism (cf. Lattal & Laipple, this volume; Marr, this volume) to Holt's neorealism, then to Gibson's theory of direct perception, and finally to modern ecological (Noble, 1991) and cognitive psychology (see Hoffman & Nead, 1983).

A Selectionist Approach to Intelligence

Another approach of some programs of direct action is "selectionist" with respect to causation. Here, selectionism does not refer to the intentional design of purposeful agents in "selecting" what actions to take, but rather, to the selection by the consequences of action, which in turn explains intentionality, as in, for example, Darwin's (1871) analysis of how natural selection explained Lamark's teleological account of evolutionary biology and Hineline's (this volume) analysis of intentional language. Selectionism—wherein the consequences of present actions differentially strengthen their future probabilities—has long been influential in biology, but only recently has it emerged as a means for understanding the mental, in particular, intelligence. In understanding intelligence, selectionism is fundamental to the "adaptive network theory" of how the nervous system operates, for instance, the parallel distributed processing (PDP) approach to intelligent action as described by Rumelhart, McClelland, and their colleagues (McClelland, Rumelhart, & the PDP Research Group, 1986; Rumelhart, McClelland, & the PDP Research Group, 1986; see also Donahoe, this volume).

The selectionist accounts of intelligent action question the sufficiency, even the necessity, of preprogrammed (e.g., storage), rule-governed (e.g., mediational), computational models of the mind (e.g., information processing). Their alternative is to demonstrate that intelligent action emerges from more basic, lower-level processes (e.g., the strengthening of connections between processing units) whose cumulative outcome depends on their initial conditions and the historical consequences of action. In particular, the PDP accounts demonstrate that intelligent action (e.g., perceiving, knowing, problem solving) can be constructed through processes that reduce the discrepancy between (a) a PDP's output and (b) the output appropriate for a situation. These processes involve the passing of information about the discrepancies back through the PDP network to change the weights of the connections between the inputs and outputs until the output is appropriate (i.e., it works, it solves the problem). The networks do not represent or store the discrepancies in any traditional sense; instead, the strengths of their interconnections are changed. They are changed through the selective action of historical contingency on the computational system, that is, through experience.

A Systems Approach to Development

A fifth program of direct action goes further than the others in illustrating the pervasiveness of the representational and mediational accounts of action throughout the life sciences. This is the "developmental systems" approach to biological and psychological ontogeny (see Gottlieb, 1992; Oyama, 1982, 1985, 1989). Developmental systems seeks to dismantle the mainstream view that genes mediate the effects of (a) the natural selection on species for (b) individual development through processes that involve the representation (e.g., encoding, transmission, and retrieval) of the past for the present. That is, developmental systems denies that the temporal gap between natural selection and current individual development must be filled in this or any manner. In particular, it rejects genetic metaphors couched in terms of "symbols" "instructions," "programs," and "blueprints" because they imply a "gene-environment dualism" (Gottlieb; Oyama, 1982, 1985, pp. 46–72), a dualism in which genes are self-actional agents, "the ghosts-in-the-ghost-in-the-machine" (Oyama, 1985, p. 73) that represent and mediate nature for individual development.

In the developmental systems' constructive program, genes do not represent or mediate the interactions between natural selection and development, or between phylogeny and ontogeny. Instead, from biological conception onward, genetic activity is as much a function of genes as it is of the historical (timing) and current context (place) in which the genes are embedded. That is, genetic activity is importantly a function of (a) what has been developed or constructed to that point in time through ontogenesis and (b) what else has been inherited (e.g., nongenetic cellular materials). Genes, then, are but one among many "developmental interactants," and thus no more represent or mediate the effects of heredity for development than any other interactant, including the environment. Where every interactant mediates the effects of every other interactant, mediation becomes a meaningless concept. The interactants are also not a blueprint for development, but instead their interactions constitute the nurture out of which individual biological and psychological natures are constructed (cf. the ingredients for a recipe, D. B. Miller, 1988). On this view, the nature-nurture dichotomy is a false dichotomy. In Oyama's (1989) words: "Nature and nurture are... not alternative sources of... causal power. Rather, nature is the *product* of the *process* of developmental interactions we call nurture" (p. 5), that is, a function of individual biological and psychological ontogenetic history.

Conclusion

These foregoing programs of direct action do not exhaust the set of these and related perspectives (see, e.g., Delprato, 1987, in press; Hineline, 1990a, 1990b); still others could be included. Schafer (1976), for example, has argued that psychoanalysis should cease using psychological nouns—for instance, personality, knowledge, and depression—to explain action, and instead seek explanations in the language of verbs and adverbs. That is, psychoanalysis should use the language of action—action unmediated by nouns referring to hypothetical explanatory constructs. Another program of direct action may be found in those phenomenological and existential psychologies that are non-dualistic, that is, those that accept experience as directly given and reject the possibility of stepping outside the stream of consciousness to assess Reality or Truth (see, e.g., Merleau-Ponty, 1962, 1963; Sartre, 1956). Still other programs may be found in several forms of social constructionism, postmodernism, and hermeneutical inquiry (see, e.g., Gergen, 1985; Packer, 1985; Rorty, 1979).

Variation and Symmetry

I now have described five programs of direct action and noted some others that converge explicitly or implicitly on a common perspective and that bear a family resemblance on some other dimensions (e.g., functionalism, contextualism). These conceptual symmetries notwithstanding, the variations among the programs should not be overlooked. In so newly elaborated an approach to the behavioral, social, and cognitive sciences, variation is to be expected (cf. Hull, 1988). Although I mention some of the variations in this section, I shall concentrate more on the conceptual symmetries between these programs and behavior analysis because behavior analysis is arguably also a program of direct action. Behavior analysis, however, is still evolving (Hayes, Barnes-Holmes, & Roche, 2001; Morris, 1992), and thus is not unexpectedly at variance with some aspects of the programs of direct action, especially developmental systems on one point.

Variations Across the Programs of Direct Action

That today's programs of direct action vary among themselves should not be surprising given some of the variation among their antecedents. Pragmatism, for example, comes in several varieties, ranging from those in which "successful working" meant effective action in the world (e.g., Peirce) to those in which it meant intellectual coherence (e.g., James; see Hayes et al., 1992; see also Lattal & Laipple, this volume). Neorealism likewise varied across its proponents (e.g., Holt, Perry, Singer; see Heft, 2001). The legacy of these differences remains, and today includes variations in (a) worldviews (e.g., mechanistic vs. contextualistic), (b) emphases on statistical prediction as opposed to experimental control (e.g., hypothetical-deductive vs. empirical-inductive theory construction), and (c) treatments of the environment as internal or external to the units of analysis. For example, some programs of direct action take the unit of analysis to be the interaction of organism and environment—perceiving, remembering, and behaving in historical and current context—while in others, action is located in the actor, that is, in the perceiver, rememberer, and behaver. In the former programs, the environment is internal to the unit of analysis, a unit of functional relations, whereas in the latter, the environment is external—the organism is psychologically independent of the environment. This latter perspective is actually inconsistent with a thoroughgoing program of direct action and, again, illustrates the enduring influence of Cartesian dualism and Western folk psychology on the discipline of psychology as a cultural practice (Kantor, 1963, 1969).

Symmetries with Behavior Analysis

Although these programs of direct action vary on several dimensions, as a group they are viewed as standing in unwavering opposition to behaviorism however construed. On careful examination, however, behavior analysis reveals itself as a program of direct action (Lee, 1988a; Morris, 1992; see also interbehavioral psychology, Kantor, 1959), and thus it evinces some conceptual symmetries with the other programs. Let me here describe some of the symmetries in the context of the programs' content domains, except for developmental systems wherein behavior analysis is not seen as a program of direct action in every regard.

Perception

Of the programs of direct action, Gibson's (1979) nonrepresentational approach to perception is the one most commonly related to behavior analysis (see, e.g., Costall, 1984). In their destructive stances, both programs are critical of Cartesian dualism and the mechanistic worldview. For Skinner (1963, 1974, pp. 89–95), these yielded the "copy theory" of perception wherein mental copies are made of stimulus objects and then given meanings to be acted upon. Skinner's (1953, pp. 129–140) constructive alternative was to treat perceiving as a functional relation between responses and stimuli, said relations subject to lawful description in their own right (see Rachlin, this volume). On this account, the between- and within-individual differences in responding to stimulus objects are accounted for by biological and behavioral histories, and by current context and contingencies, not by mental representations. As for "affordances," they are akin to the concept of stimulus function (Morris, 1989, pp. 62–64), about which Costall (1984) wrote, "We can properly be said to immediately perceive the functions that objects serve for our activities" (pp. 112–113). Where one does not immediately perceive the function of an object (e.g., a set of data points), then further public and private perceptual action may occur in the stream of behavior (e.g., mentally rotating the coordinates) that then produces a function for the object (e.g., a correlation), but this is more action, not a mental representation.

Memory

Watkins' (1990) critique of mediationism has several affinities with behavior analysis, for instance, their common reservations about (a) logical positivism (see Smith, 1986, pp. 259–297), (b) the sufficiency of formal hypothetical-deductive theorizing (Skinner, 1956), and (c) mediational constructs bridging temporal gaps (Marr, 1983). Both also propose nonreductionistic accounts of action (Skinner, 1950, 1974), offer unmediated functional relations and empirical laws (Skinner, 1935, 1947), and point to environmental sources of those relations, especially in terms of contingencies (e.g., stimulus control; see Branch, 1977). Indeed, the two programs are so closely aligned that Watkins' (1990) article, "Mediationism and the Obfuscation of Memory," was reprinted in *The Behavior Analyst* (Watkins, 1996).

Cognition

Wilcox and Katz's (1981a, 1981b) ecological approach to cognitive development parallels behavior analysis in its critique of the circularity and infinite regress of cognitivist explanations, as well as in its constructive alternative to mechanistic state-change theories of cognitive development. Both conceptualize cognitive change as change not in hypothetical structures, but in ever-evolving functional relations between organisms and environments. Moreover, the behavior-analytic melding of Pepper's

(1942/1960) root metaphor of the "historic event" with a functionally-defined unit of analysis (Chiesa, 1992; Moxley, 1992) and a pragmatic criterion of truth (Zuriff, 1980) makes behavior analysis, like the ecological approach to cognition, a variety of contextualism (Hayes, Hayes, & Reese, 1988; Hayes et al., 1992; Morris, 1988, 1991, 1992, 1993; cf. Noble, 1981).

Intelligence

Both the PDP theory of intelligence and behavior analysis question preprogrammed, rule-governed explanations of action, as well as the existence of cognitive constructs (e.g., representations), albeit not cognitive concepts (e.g., intelligence) (Donahoe, this volume; Donahoe & Palmer, 1989, 1994). Likewise, their alternatives involve syntheses and analyses of how the processes and products of such action can emerge through selection by consequences (Skinner, 1981). Intelligent systems and behavioral repertoires change—they adapt. They adapt in accord with the selective action of current contingencies on the products of historical contingencies. Everything else being equal, causation is environmental, and mind and consciousness have no independent or unique ontological status (Donahoe & Palmer, 1989).

Developmental systems

As mentioned, behavior analysis can be expected sometimes to be at variance with these programs of direct action. In particular, it differs with the developmental systems perspective on nature and nurture. For instance, whereas developmental systems analysis points out that the nature-nurture dichotomy is a false one (see Oyama, 1982, 1991), Skinner's (1966, 1981) view on nature and nurture was conventional (Midgley & Morris, 1998). He maintained a dichotomy between phylogenic (or evolutionary) and ontogenic (or behavioral) contingencies, with the former transmitted to the latter via genes. On this view, genes account for action-at-a-phylogenic distance. That is, they represent or mediate the effects of phylogenic contingencies for individual development; they fill the temporal gap between a species' phylogeny and the behavioral ontogeny of its members. Generally lacking an account of biological ontogeny, behavior analysis has adopted this representational and mediational perspective on how evolution affects individual behavior (Midgley & Morris, 1992). As a consequence, it fails in some sense as a thoroughgoing program of direct action.

As for the additional programs of direct action mentioned before—among them, some forms of psychoanalysis, phenomenology and existentialism, and constructionism, postmodernism, and hermeneutics—their affinity to behavior analysis has been noted by others. See, for example, Day (1969a, 1988), Fallon (1992), Freeman and Locurto (1994), Giorgi (1975), Guerin (1992), Kvale and Grenness (1967), Lee (1988b), and H. L. Miller (1994).

Complementarity

Behavior analysis and these programs of direct action also differ in a more general way, but one in which they compliment each other, such that their integration and alliance would broaden the scope of a naturalized psychology and unify it. Their complementarity lies in their respective provinces of knowledge: Behavior analysis, or at least the experimental analysis of behavior, is a natural *science*, whereas the programs of direct action are natural *histories*. Not only are they complimentary, but psychology requires both provinces of knowledge—science and history. Let me elaborate on this natural science-natural history distinction and the point of complementarity, both in general and then with respect to behavior analysis and the programs of direct action. Afterward, I consider some points regarding their integration and alliance.

Natural Science and Natural History

By *natural science*, I refer to basic processes, principles, and laws that are presumably ahistorical and universal across time and place, albeit subject to initial and boundary conditions. The typical exemplars of such science are physics, chemistry, and molecular biology, but their subject matters (e.g., gravity, electricity) are not those of psychology, and thus their assumptions (e.g., atomism), models (e.g., machines), and methods (e.g., hypothetical-deductive theory construction; structural analyses; see Kantor, 1959) should not be uncritically adopted. By *natural history*, or historical science, I refer to historical processes that are "situated," contingent on time and place, and subject even further to initial and boundary conditions. Among the historical sciences are astronomy, climatology, cosmology, ecology, evolutionary biology, geology, and paleontology. Again, these represent different subject matters than that of psychology (e.g., the growth of river deltas, the extinction of species, global warming), and the same caveats apply to their assumptions, models, and methods.

Within most scientific disciplines, complementary specializations in natural science and natural history may be characterized as *provinces* of knowledge, some of which will overlap and merge. Biology, for example, includes distinctive natural sciences such a molecular biology, as well as historical sciences such as ecology. Because they share fundamental assumptions (e.g., naturalism; contra. vitalism), and define their subject matters in complimentary ways, they proceed in a mutually informative manner, sometimes overlapping and merging. The latter occur at the points where natural science undertakes synthesis and natural history engages analysis. For instance, given knowledge of sufficient scope and precision, natural science attempts to synthesize historical processes and their products (e.g., tornadoes, chemical agents, and new breeds of animals) in order to test and extend the understanding of basic processes. Likewise, in order to test and extend our understanding of historical processes (e.g., natural and human-made events such as avalanches, metal fatigue, sudden population shifts), natural history attempts to analyze them. Where synthesis requires analysis, and analysis requires synthesis—which they usually do—natural science and natural history become difficult to differentiate.

Behavior Analysis and the Programs of Direct Action

Distinctions

The foregoing distinctions and complimentarities between natural science and natural history find parallels in behavior analysis and the programs of direct action. As for the distinctions, the experimental analysis of behavior is mainly a natural science, whereas the programs of direct action are mainly natural histories. More specifically, the former is a natural science of basic behavioral processes (e.g., stimulus control, stimulus equivalence, reinforcement, and the matching law; see Catania, 1998; Mazur, 1998), while the latter are natural histories of psychology's content domains (e.g., perception, memory, intelligence). As such, the behavioral processes are, presumably, ahistorical and general across the behavior of species, individuals, and groups, as well as across psychology's content domains (e.g., cognitive, social, and motivational psychology), albeit subject to initial and boundary conditions (e.g., biological constraints), while the historical processes are situated in time and place, and thus specific to species, individuals, and cultural practices (cf. Gergen, 1973) and subject even further to initial and boundary conditions.

Complimentarities

With few exceptions, behavior analysis has not much analyzed the natural history of psychology's content domains (e.g., perception, memory, cognition, intelligence, development), that is, of behavior in individual, social, and cultural context. Likewise, the programs of direct action have not much engaged a natural science of behavioral processes that apply to all domains of behavior, that is, to behavior independent of individual, social, and cultural context. Although behavior analysis and the programs of direct action differ in these regards, they are complimentary provinces of knowledge. Behavior analysis describes ahistorical processes that help explain action in any domain, while the programs of direct action describe historical processes that help explain action in specific domains. Behavior analysis and the programs of direct action are mutually informative in these regards.

In addition, where behavior analysis undertakes synthesis and the programs of direct action engage analysis, they may overlap and merge. Behavior analysis, for example, has synthesized psychology's content domains, for example, social, verbal, and cognitive behavior—using basic behavioral processes in both laboratory and natural settings (e.g., Epstein, 1984; Hake, 1982; Gewirtz & Pelaez-Nogueras, 1991; Whitehurst & Valdez-Menchaca, 1988). In turn, the programs of direct action have analyzed their content domains, albeit only with concepts drawn from natural history (e.g., affordances, cuegrams), not in terms of basic behavioral processes. The latter, though, may be found, on occasion, in applied behavior analysis, for example, in the analysis of teacher-child interactions (e.g., stimulus control; see Atwater & Morris, 1988), chronic aberrant behavior (e.g., establishing operations; see Iwata, Dorsey, Slifer, Bauman, & Richman, 1982), and antisocial behavior (e.g., aversive control; see Patterson, DeBaryshe, & Ramey, 1989). Together, synthesis and analysis inform us maximally about the behavior of organisms as individuals. This is where science and history, behavioral and historical processes, and the interests of scientists and practitioners overlap and merge, and where psychology most thoroughly understands its subject matter.

In summary, taken alone, neither behavior analysis nor the programs of direct action, that is neither natural science nor natural history, offers an account of psychology of sufficient scope or precision, or an account that can unify the discipline. Together, though, they may contribute to a complete, thoroughgoing, unified, and naturalized psychology.

Integration and Alliance

Integrating and allying behavior analysis and the programs of direct action in this manner is a form of consilience—"the linking of facts and fact-based theory across disciplines, to create a common groundwork for explanation" (Wilson, 1999, p. 8). Mainstream psychology, however, is likely to resist it for several reasons. First, psychology's content domains would lose some measure of their independence from one another, becoming less the mini-sciences of the psychological sciences, and more the subdisciplines of one science. Second, what is now "basic research" in these domains would be properly seen as natural history or historical science, not natural science. And third, psychology would have to ally with a form of the behaviorism it nominally overthrew in the cognitive revolution.

The programs of direct action also may resist integration and alliance with behavior analysis for the same reasons, but presumable less so because they are aligned in two significant ways. First, they both challenge explanations of action that appeal to hypothetical constructs from nondimensional systems (e.g., information processing) or that appeal to real interactants operating in unreal ways (e.g., genes). In particular, they challenge explanations of action that invoke representational and mediational constructs to account for the effects of objects and events on behavior over space and time. Second, their explanations are generally cast in terms of functional relations between organism and environment, relations that emerge and remain stable or change as a function of their biological and behavioral histories and of their environments more broadly construed. How much behavior analysis and these programs of direct action vary in these regards affects the possibilities of their integration, while how much these variations are emphasized affects the politics of their alliance.

The Possibilities of Integration

As for the possibilities of integration, to date the programs of direct action have seen little or no correspondence between themselves and behavior analysis—or they disavow it. Watkins (1990), for example, disclaimed,

> In our case, accusations of "rank Skinnerism" have been common. It may be true that ours is a radically functional approach to the study of memory and that it contains more than a germ of behaviorism. But Skinner and his followers have no place for mental life, whereas we consider memory to be, of its very essence, a mental phenomenon. (pp. 332–333)

Wilcox and Katz (1981b) likewise commented: "As our remarks indicate, the ecological approach, unlike radical behaviorism, does not involve the rejection of ordinary mental concepts. They can typically be treated as output" (p. 259). And, Rumelhart and McClelland (1986) remarked: "Our models must be seen be seen as completely antithetical to the radical behaviorist program" (p. 121). Watkins (1990), however, misunderstands the behavior-analytic account of private events and of remembering as a form of problem solving (see Palmer, 1991). Wilcox and Katz overlook the affinity between radical behaviorism and ordinary-language, analytic philosophy (see Day, 1969b). And, Rumelhart and McClelland have too narrow a view on the breadth of a selectionist account in natural history (Skinner, 1981).

The possibility of integration is not, however, everywhere unappreciated. For instance, Leahey (1992a) observed that Skinner's (1977, 1985, 1990) complaints about cognitivism parallel or converge on those of ecological psychologists such as Neisser (1984). I quote from Leahey (1992a), who quotes with ellipses from Neisser on the ecological approach to cognition:

> Like the radical behaviorist, the "ecological psychologist [begins] ... with a careful description of the environment and people's ordinary activities within it." Like the radical behaviorist, the ecological cognitive scientist "tak[es] the environment seriously." Like the radical behaviorist, "ecological psychologists are generally reluctant to construct models or to postulate hypothetical events." Like the radical behaviorist, the ecological psychologist believes that "introspection does not reveal [the] structures" in the environment to which people respond. (p. 468)

Leahey (1992a) concluded: "Neisser does not discuss the parallels between his descriptions of ecological psychology and radical behaviorism, but they are there" (p. 468). Integration, then, remains a possibility, even if Leahey (2000) no longer addresses the point.

The Politics of Alliance

As for the politics of alliance, independent of integration, some arguments are in its favor. First, the programs of direct action might ally with one another in order to fend off common criticisms and misunderstandings from mainstream psychology, as they evolve toward a nonmediational, nonrepresentational natural science of psychology. Second, alliance might also strengthen the viability of the programs of direct action within the discipline overall (see Heft, 2001). To borrow from Donohoe and Palmer (1989), where alliance is welcome, the programs might ally themselves proactively—"A friend in need is a friend indeed." Where alliance is not welcome, but the programs face similar criticisms and misunderstandings, they might ally themselves reactively—"The enemy of your enemy is your friend."

Conclusion

Behavior analysts have reasons to be both optimistic and pessimistic about integration and alliance, about the future of a naturalized psychology, and about their role and status within it. As for the optimism, consider again the received view in psychology that cognitivism overtook behaviorism and was a purported revolution. On this account, classical and mediational behaviorism are dead, and behavior analysis is but a minority program (Coleman & Mehlman, 1992; Leahey, 2000). In the more recent accounts of this history, however, there was no revolution; cognitivism was but an extension of mediational behaviorism (Leahey, 1992b). If anything revolutionary has occurred in the last half century, it may be the emergence of the programs of direct action, behavior analysis among them (see Moore, 1995). In rejecting mental representations and mediationism, they are qualitatively distinct from mediational behaviorism and cognitivism. They offer both a natural science and a natural history of psychology, are complimentary in this regard, and overlap and merge in their syntheses and analyses. If this is the next stage in the evolution of psychology as a science, then psychology will become more behavior-analytic in its method, process, content, and metatheory.

As for the pessimism, behavior analysis has reason to be concerned about its role and status in the future of this psychology because this psychology is not likely to be called "behavior analysis" for at least two reasons. First, the behavior-analytic conceptual system is already being reinvented by the programs of direct action, all the while these programs misunderstand, misrepresent, and dismiss it. Second, many of these programs are cognitive in content, wherein it would be politically incorrect to see or acknowledge any likeness with behavior analysis or concede any credit at all. Behavior analysts will likely chaff at this, thinking their system vindicated by its symmetries with the programs of direct action and by its complementarity with them, and feeling discredited where credit is due but not proffered. As the inventor, Charles F. Kettering, observed, "First they tell you you're wrong, and they can prove it. Then they tell you you're right, but it's not important. Then they tell you it's important, but they've known it for years" (see Ayllon & Azrin, 1968, p. 1).

This pessimism, however, is in part misplaced; indeed, it suggests an unflattering vanity. What matters most in the evolution of psychology is that it achieve consilience across its provinces of knowledge—across psychology as a natural science and natural history. What matters least is what that psychology is eventually called. In the end, as I suggested, it is not likely to be called "behavior analysis." This point is consistent with two of Skinner's observations. Early in his career, he wrote: "It would be an anomalous event in the history of science if any current system should prove ultimately the most convenient (and hence, so far as science is concerned, correct)" (Skinner, 1938, p. 438). Later in his career, he observed: "Behaviorism, as we know it, will eventually die—not because it is a failure, but because it is a success. As a critical philosophy of science, it will necessarily change as a science of behavior changes" (Skinner, 1969, p. 267). If behavior analysis becomes a less convenient system or if it changes because its science changes, then so too, may be what it is called. Where the convenience and change are consistent with the programs of direct action, then behavior analysts might seek integration and alliance with them, and invite the same in return. In doing so, they may contribute to the evolution of naturalistic psychology, one that is complete, thoroughgoing, and unified—a modern psychology. In the process, they may retain something of the name and the legacy, but more importantly, the prescience and the promise of behavior analysis—and advance them.

References

Atwater, J. B., & Morris, E. K. (1988). An observational analysis of teachers' instructions in preschool classrooms. *Journal of Applied Behavior Analysis, 21*, 157–167.

Ayllon, T., & Azrin, N. H. (1968). *The token economy*. New York: Appleton-Century-Crofts.

Baars, B. J. (1986). *The cognitive revolution in psychology*. New York: Guilford.

Branch, M. (1977). On the role of "memory" in the analysis of behavior. *Journal of the Experimental Analysis of Behavior, 28*, 171–179.

Catania, A. C. (1998). *Learning* (4th ed.). Upper Saddle River, NJ: Prentice-Hall.

Chiesa, M. (1992). Radical behaviorism and scientific frameworks: From mechanistic to relational accounts. *American Psychologist, 47*, 1287–1299.

Coleman, S. R., & Mehlman, S. E. (1992). An empirical update (1969–1989) of D. L. Krantz's thesis that the experimental analysis of behavior is isolated. *The Behavior Analyst, 15*, 43–49.

Costall, A. P. (1984). Are theories of perception necessary? A review of Gibson's *The ecological approach to visual perception*. *Journal of the Experimental Analysis of Behavior, 41*, 109–115.

Costall, A. P., & Still, A. (Eds.). (1987). *Cognitive psychology in question*. New York: St. Martin's Press.

Darwin. C. (1871). *The descent of man*. London: Murray.

Day, W. F. (1969a). Radical behaviorism in reconciliation with phenomenology. *Journal of the Experimental Analysis of Behavior, 12*, 315–328.

Day, W. F. (1969b). On certain similarities between the philosophical investigations of Ludwig Wittgenstein and the operationism of B. F. Skinner. *Journal of the Experimental Analysis of Behavior, 12*, 489–506.

Day, W. F. (1980). The historical antecedents of contemporary behaviorism. In R. W. Rieber & K. Salzinger (Eds.), *Psychology: Theoretical-historical perspectives* (pp. 203–262). New York: Academic Press.

Day, W. F. (1988). Hermeneutics and behaviorism. *American Psychologist, 43*, 129–131.

Delprato, D. J. (1987). Developmental interactionism: An integrative framework for behavior therapy. *Advances in Behavioral Research and Therapy, 9*, 173–205.

Delprato, D. J. (in press). Converging movements in psychology. In B. D. Midgley & E. K. Morris (Eds.), *Modern perspectives on J. R. Kantor and interbehaviorism*. Reno, NV: Context Press.

Donahoe, J. W., & Palmer, D. C. (1989). The interpretation of complex human behavior: Some reactions to *Parallel distributed processing*, edited by J. L. McClelland, D. E. Rumelhart, and the PDP research group. *Journal of the Experimental Analysis of Behavior, 51*, 399–416.

Donahoe, J. W., & Palmer, D. C. (1994). *Learning and complex behavior*. Boston: Allyn & Bacon.

Epstein, R. (1984). Simulation research in the analysis of behavior. *Behaviorism, 12*, 41–59.

Fallon, D. (1992). An existential look at B. F. Skinner. *American Psychologist, 47*, 1433–1440.

Freeman, M., & Locurto, C. (1994). In Skinner's wake: Behaviorism, poststructualism, and the ironies of intellectual discourse. *New Ideas in Psychology, 12*, 39–56.

Gardner, H. (1985). *The mind's new science: A history of the cognitive revolution*. New York: Basic Books.

Gergen, K. J. (1973). Social psychology as history. *Journal of Personality and Social Psychology, 26*, 309–320.

Gergen, K. J. (1985). The social constructionist movement in modern psychology. *American Psychologist, 40*, 266–275.

Gewirtz, J. L., & Pelaez-Nogueras, M. (1991). The attachment metaphor and the conditioning of infant social protests. In J. L. Gewirtz & W. M. Kurtines (Eds.), *Intersections with attachment* (pp. 123–144). Hillsdale, NJ: Erlbaum,

Gibson, J. J. (1979). *The ecological approach to visual perception*. Boston: Houghton-Mifflin.

Giorgi, A. (1975). Convergences and divergences between phenomenological psychology and behaviorism. *Behaviorism, 3*, 200–212.

Gottlieb, G. (1992). *Individual development and evolution: The genesis of novel behavior*. New York: Oxford.

Guerin, B. (1992). Behavior analysis and the social construction of knowledge. *American Psychologist, 47*, 1423–1432.

Hake, D. F. (1982). The basic-applied continuum and the possible evolutions of human operantsocial and verbal behavior. *The Behavior Analyst, 5*, 21–28.

Hayes, S. C., Barnes-Holmes, D., & Roche, B. (Eds.). (2001). *Relational frame theory: A post Skinnerian account of human language and cognition*. New York: Kluwer Academic/Plenum Publishers.

Hayes, S. C., Hayes, L. J., & Reese, H. W. (1988). Finding the philosophic core: A review of Stephen C. Pepper's *World hypotheses*. *Journal of the Experimental Analysis of Behavior, 50*, 97–111.

Hayes, S. C., Hayes, L. J., Reese, H. W., & Sarbin, S. R. (Eds.). (1992). *Varieties of scientific contextualism*. Reno, NV: Context Press.

Heft, H. (2001). *Ecological psychology in context*. Mahwah, NJ: Erlbaum.

Hineline, P. N. (1990a). Message from the president. *The ABA Newsletter, 13*(2), 2–3.

Hineline, P. N. (1990b). Message from the president. *The ABA Newsletter, 13*(3), 7–8.

Hoffman, R. R., & Nead, J. M. (1983). General contextualism, ecological science, and cognitive research. *The Journal of Mind and Behavior, 4*, 507–560.

Hull, D. L. (1988). *Science as a process: The evolutionary account of the social and conceptual development of science*. Chicago: University of Chicago Press.

Iwata, B. A., Dorsey, M. F., Slifer, K. J., Bauman, K. E., & Richman, G. S. (1982). Toward a functional analysis of self-injury. *Analysis and Intervention in Developmental Disabilities, 2*, 3–20.

Jenkins, J. J. (1974). Remember that old theory of memory? Well, forget it! *American Psychologist, 29*, 785–795.

Johnston, T. D. (1985). Environmental constraints and the natural context of behavior: Grounds for an ecological approach to the study of infant perception. In G. Gottlieb & N. A. Krasnagor (Eds.), *Measurement of audition and vision in the first year of postnatal life: A methodological overview* (pp. 91–108). Norwood, NJ: Ablex.

Kantor, J. R. (1924). *Principles of psychology, Vol. 1*. Chicago: Principia Press.

Kantor, J. R. (1926). *Principles of behavior, Vol. II*. Chicago: Principia Press.

Kantor, J. R. (1959). *Interbehavioral psychology*. Chicago: Principia Press.

Kantor, J. R. (1963). *The scientific evolution of psychology, Vol. 1*. Chicago: Principia Press.

Kantor, J. R. (1969). *The scientific evolution of psychology, Vol. 2*. Chicago: Principia Press.

Kvale, S., & Grenness, C. E. (1967). Skinner and Sartre: Towards a radical phenomenology. *Review of Existential Psychology and Psychiatry, 7*, 129–150.

Leahey, T. H. (1992a). *A history of psychology: Main currents in psychological thought* (2nd ed.). Englewood Cliffs, NJ: Prentice-Hall.

Leahey, T. H. (1992b). Mythical revolutions in the history of American psychology. *American Psychologist, 47*, 308–318.

Leahey, T. H. (2000). *A history of psychology: Main currents in psychological thought* (4th ed.). Englewood Cliffs, NJ: Prentice-Hall.

Lee, V. L. (1988a). *Beyond behaviorism*. Hillsdale, NJ: Erlbaum.

Lee, V. L. (1988b). The language of action: A review of Schafer's *A new language for psychoanalysis*. *Journal of the Experimental Analysis of Behavior, 49*, 429–436.

Malcolm, N. (1977). *Memory and mind*. Ithaca, NY: Cornell University Press.

Marr, M. J. (1983). Memory: Models and metaphors. *The Psychological Record, 33*, 12–19.

Mazur, J. E. (1998). *Learning and behavior* (4th ed.). Upper Saddle River, NJ: Prentice-Hall.

McClelland, J. L., Rumelhart, D. E., & the PDP Research Group (Eds.). (1986). *Parallel distributed processing: Explorations in the microstructure of cognition: Vol. 2. Psychological and biological models*. Cambridge, MA: MIT Press.

Merleau-Ponty, M. (1962). *The phenomenology of perception*. New York: Humanities Press.

Merleau-Ponty, M. (1963). *The structure of behavior*. New York: Beacon Press.

Michael, J. (1985). Behavior analysis: A radical perspective. In B. L. Hammonds (Ed.), *The G. Stanley Hall Lecture Series, Vol. 4: Psychology and learning* (pp. 99–121). Washington, DC: American Psychological Association.

Midgley, B. D., & Morris, E. K. (1992). Nature = f (nurture): A review of Oyama's *The ontogeny of information: Developmental systems and evolution*. *Journal of the Experimental Analysis of Behavior, 58*, 229–240.

Midgley, B. D., & Morris, E. K. (1998). Nature and nurture in Skinner's behaviorism. *Mexican Journal of Behavior Analysis, 24*, 111–126.

Miller, D. B. (1988). The nature-nurture issue: Lessons from the Pillsbury doughboy. *Teaching of Psychology, 15*, 147–149.

Miller, H. L. (1994). Taking hermeneutics to science: Prospects and tactics suggested by the work of B. F. Skinner. *The Behavior Analyst, 17*, 35–43.

Moore, J. (1995). Some historical and conceptual relations among logical positivism, behaviorism, and cognitive psychology. In J. T. Todd & E. K. Morris (Eds.), *Modern perspectives on B. F. Skinner and contemporary behaviorism* (pp. 51–84). Westport, CT: Greenwood.

Morris, E. K. (1988). Contextualism: The world view of behavior analysis. *Journal of Experimental Child Psychology, 46*, 289–323.

Morris, E. K. (1989). Questioning psychology's mechanism: A review of Costall and Still's *Cognitive psychology in question*. *The Behavior Analyst, 12*, 59–67.

Morris, E. K. (1991). The contextualism that is behavior analysis: An alternative to cognitive psychology. In A. Still & A. Costall (Eds.), *Against cognitivism: Alternative foundations for cognitive psychology* (pp. 123–149). Hemmel Hempstead: Harvester-Wheatsheaf.

Morris, E. K. (1992). The aim, progress, and evolution of behavior analysis. *The Behavior Analyst, 15*, 3–29.

Morris, E. K. (1993). Behavior analysis and mechanism: One is not the other. *The Behavior Analyst, 16*, 25–34.

Moxley, R. A. (1992). From mechanistic to functional behaviorism. *American Psychologist, 47*, 1300–1311.

Neisser, U. (1984). Toward an ecologically oriented cognitive science. In T. M. Shlechter & M. P. Toglia (Eds.), *New directions in cognitive science* (pp. 17–32). Norwood, NJ: Ablex.

Noble, W. (1981). Gibsonian theory and the pragmatist perspective. *Journal for the Theory of Social Behavior, 11,* 65–85.

Noble, W. (1991). Ecological realism and the fallacy of "objectification." In A. Still & A. Costall (Eds.), *Against cognitivism: Alternative foundations for cognitive psychology* (pp. 199–223). Hemmel-Hempstead: Harvester-Wheatsheaf.

Oyama, S. (1982). A reformulation of the idea of maturation. In P. P. G. Bateson & P. H. Klopfer (Eds.), *Perspectives in ethology: Ontogeny* (Vol. 5, pp. 101–131). New York:Plenum.

Oyama, S. (1985). *The ontogeny of information: Developmental systems and evolution.* New York: Cambridge University Press.

Oyama, S. (1989). Ontogeny and the central dogma: Do we need a concept of genetic programming in order to have an evolutionary perspective? In M. R. Gunnar & E. Thelen (Eds.), *Systems and development: The Minnesota symposium on child development* (Vol. 22, pp. 1–34). Hillsdale, NJ: Erlbaum.

Oyama, S. (1991). Bodies and minds: Dualism in evolutionary theory. *Journal of Social Issues, 47,* 27–42.

Packer, M. (1985). Hermeneutic inquiry in the study of human conduct. *American Psychologist, 40,* 1081–1093.

Palmer, D. C. (1991). A behavioral interpretation of memory. In L. J. Hayes & P. N. Chase (Eds.), *Dialogues on verbal behavior* (pp. 261–279). Reno, NV: Context Press.

Patterson, G. R., DeBaryshe, B. D., & Ramey, E. (1989). A developmental perspective on antisocial behavior. *American Psychologist, 44,* 329–325.

Pepper, S. C. (1960). *World hypotheses: A study in evidence.* Berkeley, CA: University of California Press. (Original work published 1942)

Rachlin, H. (1994). *Behavior and mind: The roots of modern psychology.* New York: Oxford University Press.

Reese, E. P. (1986). Learning about teaching from teaching about learning: Presenting behavior analysis in an introductory survey course. In W. P. Makosky (Ed.), *The G. Stanley Hall Lecture Series* (Vol. 6, pp. 69–127). Washington, DC: American Psychological Association.

Rorty, R. (1979). *Philosophy and the mirror of nature.* Princeton, NJ: Princeton University Press.

Rosnow, R. L., & Georgoudi, M. (Eds.). (1986). *Contextualism.* New York: Praeger.

Rumelhart, D. E., & McClelland, J. L. (1986). PDP models and general issues in cognitive science. In D. E. Rumelhart, J. L. McClelland, & the PDP Research Group (Eds.). (1986). *Parallel distributed processing: Explorations in the microstructure of cognition: Vol. 1. Foundations* (pp. 110–146). Cambridge, MA: MIT Press.

Rumelhart, D. E., McClelland, J. L., & the PDP Research Group (Eds.). (1986). *Parallel distributed processing: Explorations in the microstructure of cognition: Vol. 1. Foundations.* Cambridge, MA: MIT Press.

Ryle, G. (1949). *The concept of mind.* New York: Barnes and Noble.

Sartre, J. P. (1956). *Being and nothingness.* New York: Philosophical Library.

Schafer, R. (1976). *A new language for psychoanalysis.* New Haven, CT: Yale University Press.

Skinner, B. F. (1935). The generic nature of the concepts of stimulus and response. *Journal of General Psychology, 12,* 40–65.

Skinner, B. F. (1938). *The behavior of organisms: An experimental analysis.* Englewood Cliffs, NJ: Prentice-Hall.

Skinner, B. F. (1945). An operational analysis of some psychological terms. *Psychological Review, 52,* 270–277, 291–294.

Skinner, B. F. (1947). Experimental psychology. In W. Dennis (Ed.), *Current trends in psychology* (pp. 16–49). Pittsburgh: University of Pittsburgh Press.

Skinner, B. F. (1950). Are theories of learning necessary? *Psychological Review, 57,* 193–216.

Skinner, B. F. (1953). *Science and human behavior.* New York: Macmillan.

Skinner, B. F. (1956). A case study in scientific method. *American Psychologist, 11,* 221–233.

Skinner, B. F. 1963). Behaviorism at fifty. *Science, 140,* 951–958.

Skinner, B. F. (1966). The phylogeny and ontogeny of behavior. *Science, 153,* 1204–1213.

Skinner, B. F. (1969). *Contingencies of reinforcement: A theoretical analysis.* New York: Appleton-Century-Crofts.

Skinner, B. F. (1974). *About behaviorism.* New York: Knopf.

Skinner, B. F. (1977). Why I am not a cognitive psychologist. *Behaviorism, 5,* 1–10.

Skinner, B. F. (1981). Selection by consequences. *Science, 213,* 501–504.

Skinner, B. F. (1985). Cognitive science and behaviorism. *British Journal of Psychology, 76,*502–510.

Skinner, B. F. (1990). Can psychology be a science of mind? *American Psychologist, 45,* 1206–1210.

Smith, L. D. (1986). *Behaviorism and logical positivism: A reassessment of the alliance.* Berkeley, CA: University of California Press.

Still, A., & Costall, A. P. (Eds.). (1991). *Against cognitivism: Alternative foundations for cognitive psychology.* Hemmel-Hempstead: Harvester-Wheatsheaf.

Watkins, M. J. (1981). Human memory and the information processing metaphor. *Cognition, 10,* 331–336.

Watkins, M. J. (1990). Mediationism and the obfuscation of memory. *American Psychologist, 45,* 328–335.

Watkins, M. J. (1996). Mediationism and the obfuscation of memory. *The Behavior Analyst, 19,* 91–103.

Watson, J. B. (1913a). Image and affection in behavior. *Journal of Philosophy, Psychology, and Scientific Methods, 10,* 421–428.

Watson, J. B. (1913b). Psychology as the behaviorist views it. *Psychological Review, 20,* 158–177.

Whitehurst, G. L., & Valdez-Menchaca, M. C. (1988). What is the role of reinforcement in early language acquisition? *Child Development, 59,* 430–440.

Wilcox, S., & Katz, S. (1981a). A direct realistic alternative to the traditional conception of memory. *Behaviorism, 9,* 227–239.

Wilcox, S., & Katz, S. (1981b). The ecological approach to development: An alternative to cognitivism. *Journal of Experimental Child Psychology, 32,* 247–263.

Wilson, E. O. (1999). *Consilience.* New York: Vintage.

Zuriff, G. E. (1980). Radical behaviorist epistemology. *Psychological Review, 87,* 337–350.

III

**Extensions to Research
and Application**

16

Verbal Governance, Verbal Shaping, and Attention to Verbal Stimuli

A. Charles Catania

Whence comes the power of words? Citizens of purportedly civilized nations have come under the sway of the rhetoric of demagogues. Soldiers have killed and been killed following the orders of military superiors. Leaders of some religious sects have put people to death for utterances labeled blasphemous or heretical. Leaders of others have taken their own and their followers' lives with words of salvation on their lips. Yet were my next words to promise you immortality in good health and prosperity in a world of intellectual challenge, amusement, and good fellowship, asking nothing more in return than a portion of your current worldly goods, I doubt you would take up my offer. Some in our culture, however, do give things over to or do things for those who say they guarantee eternal bliss in exchange. Why are so many so susceptible to such verbal behavior?

In 1919, Hitler became an education officer for squads about to be discharged from the German army after the end of the First World War: "For the first time in his life, he had found something at which he was an unqualified success. Almost by chance, he had stumbled on his greatest talent. As he himself put it, he could 'speak'" (Kershaw, 1998, p. 124). Appealing to charisma will not do. Many political and cultural contingencies contributed to Hitler's rise to power (Kershaw, 1998, 2000), but

---

A. Charles Catania • Department of Psychology, University of Maryland/Baltimore County, Baltimore, MD 21250 USA.

he could not have brought Germany to Nazism, the Holocaust, and the Second World War without words, though sometimes what was not said also made a difference (Cornwell, 1999).

The power of words, of course, is not all bad. Students have been inspired by the words of wise teachers, and the speeches of visionary leaders have sometimes drawn their followers to nonviolent protest rather than violent revolution, to creation rather than desecration. In the service of social and political organizations, much of human moral and ethical behavior is codified in a web of maxims and laws and other verbal traditions. But what makes words work as they do?

Scientists are only beginning to learn about their functions. It is difficult even to think consistently about words as behavior. This chapter first reviews the nature of verbal behavior and what can be said about its origins. Plausible accounts of those origins are severely constrained by what is known about how behavior is selected in phylogeny, ontogeny, and cultural transmission. Having considered those issues as prerequisites for further analysis, the chapter then considers the contemporary functions of verbal behavior, examining how the variables that determine it can combine to produce potent effects on subsequent behavior, both verbal and nonverbal. The focus is on three major topics: (a) verbal governance, in the contingencies, mainly social, that lead not only to instruction-following, but also to correspondences between what one does and what one says about what one does; (b) verbal shaping, in the natural and artificial contingencies that arrange consequences for verbal behavior and thereby raise or lower the probabilities of different verbal classes; and (c) attention to verbal stimuli, in which reinforcing and aversive properties of these stimuli affect not only whether they will be noted, but also whether they will become incorporated into one's own verbal behavior. An essential feature of the analysis is the combination of these processes in the multiple causation of verbal and nonverbal behavior.

The Nature and Origins of Verbal Behavior

Verbal behavior is any behavior involving words, without regard to whether the words are spoken, written or gestural. It involves both speaker behavior shaped by its effects on the behavior of listeners and listener behavior shaped by its effects on the behavior of speakers. The functional units of verbal behavior (such as words) are maintained by the practices of verbal communities. Spellings and pronunciations in dictionaries and rules in grammar books summarize those practices by describing standard structures of verbal units. The distinction between functional and structural concerns is to a large extent captured by the distinction between the terms *verbal behavior* and *language* (sentences with similar structures may have different functions and sentences with different structures may have similar functions).

The most basic consequence of verbal behavior is that through it speakers change the behavior of listeners. Verbal behavior is a way to get people to do things; it is "effective only through the mediation of other persons" (Skinner, 1957, p. 2; see also pp. 224–226). Sometimes its effects are nonverbal, as when someone is asked to do something; sometimes its effects are verbal, as when people change what they have to say about something. The effect of verbal behavior on others is primary because other functions gain their significance only through it. What more important reason to describe one's feelings than that others may treat them differently? What more important reason to give information than that others may act upon it? Could some social function more general than changing what someone else does have provided the selective contingencies under which human language evolved? Transmitting information and describing feelings are functions of language, but these secondary functions matter only if they sometimes make a difference by changing the behavior of others. Verbal behavior does not transmit information or ideas or feelings; the verbal behavior itself is what is transmitted.

Speculations about the origin and evolution of verbal behavior have a long and controversial history (e.g., Catania, 1985), but discriminating the behavior of others was presumably a crucial prerequisite. Verbal behavior is quintessentially social and can emerge only in organisms whose behavior is or can become sensitive to social contingencies. Discriminating the behavior of other organisms, whether of one's own or of other species, has selective advantages. Predators that can distinguish whether they have been seen by their prey, like prey that can distinguish whether they have been seen by their predators, have substantial advantages over ones that cannot.

Any account of the origins and evolution of language must be consistent with selection as it operates at three different levels: phylogenic selection, as populations of individuals (and their genes) are selected by evolutionary contingencies; ontogenic selection, as populations of responses are selected by their consequences over the lifetime of an organism; and cultural or memetic selection, as behavior passed on from one organism to another is selected by social contingencies (Catania, 1994; Darwin, 1859, 1871; Dawkins, 1976, 1982; Skinner, 1981; cf. Donahoe, this volume, and Glenn, this volume).

The behavior of one organism may allow another to act on the basis of stimuli available only to the first, as when one monkey's vocal call allows another to escape from a predator it had not seen. In monkeys, predator calls vary with kinds of predator and the response to the call depends on who the caller is and who the listener is (e.g., Gouzoules, Gouzoules, & Marler, 1984; Seyfarth, Cheney, & Marler, 1980). Elicited cries produced by predator attack provide one of several plausible starting points for the selection of precursors of verbal behavior by phylogenic and ontogenic contingencies. Imagine a band of preverbal hominids with a minimal repertory of fixed action patterns elicited by vocal releasers, so that speakers' calls reliably determine some behavior of other members of the band. If just a single utterance with effects corresponding to the contemporary word *stop* prevents out-of-reach offspring from wandering into danger, those participating in such vocal control will have, over the long run, a reproductive advantage over those who do not (the benefit would accrue to the shared genes of both the individual and the individual's kin).

From such a start, a vocabulary of releasers limited at first to just a few calls, not yet qualifying as verbal behavior, but with relatively simple effects (keeping together during movement; coordinating aggression or flight; etc.), could evolve over millennia into a richly differentiated repertory involving mothers and offspring, mates, and other subgroups of the hominid social unit (contemporary human vocalizations with strong phylogenic components include laughter and yawning: Provine, 2000). If human impact on the habitats of other primates is anything to go by, the species differentiating such repertories soonest and most rapidly is likely to cut off the opportunities for others to do so.

This scenario presupposes speaker and listener behavior evolving in parallel. Primatological evidence implies that the discriminative capacities of listeners increased as speaker vocalizations became more finely differentiated. Contemporary primates, for example, discriminate vocal calls along many dimensions: caller identity, gender, kinship, emotional variables (e.g., Rendall, Owren, & Rodman, 1998; Rendall, Rodman, & Emond, 1996). Small changes in capacities for differential vocalizations would allow selection of finer capacities for discriminations among vocalizations, and vice versa. The contingencies for their parallel evolution would be maintained as long as the distributions of each included overlapping spectra of vocalizations (cf. Skinner, 1986: "The human species took a crucial step forward when its vocal musculature came under operant control in the production of speech sounds," p. 117; see also Provine, 2000, on how bipedalism, freeing respiration from locomotion, allowed more finely differentiated vocalizations).

If the properties of these protoverbal calls were weakly determined phylogenically or varied along dimensions orthogonal to those that made them effective releasers, ontogenic contingencies could begin to supplement this rudimentary vocal control. For example, dominant speakers might learn to attack listeners who failed to respond to calls, thereby punishing disobedience (presumably the contemporary effectiveness of verbal governance, maintained by reinforcing the following of instructions and/or by punishing deviations from it, depends mainly on ontogenic rather than phylogenic contingencies).

Once vocal behavior had expanded to ontogenically as well as phylogenically determined calls, idiosyncratic repertories developed by individuals would ordinarily be lost to later generations unless reproduced in the speakers' successors. Thus, a critical feature of this evolutionary scenario is the listener's repetition of the speaker's verbal behavior (cf. Jaynes, 1976). Such repetition is key to the cultural selection of verbal behavior. Once some individuals begin to repeat what others say, verbal behavior becomes behavior maintained by cultural as well as ontogenic contingencies and thereby can survive across generations (one kind of repetition is called echoic, distinguished from simple vocal imitation by its replication of phonetic units rather than mere acoustic properties: Catania, 1998, pp. 241–243; Risley, 1977; Skinner, 1957, pp. 55–65).

Vocal behavior replicates itself in such repetition, but what selective advantages can repetition provide? As vocal behavior became more finely differentiated, only repetition accompanied by other more immediate and significant consequences could maintain functional ontogenic features of vocal repertories over generations. One was that a listener's repetitions created conditions under which a speaker's instructions might be followed in the speaker's absence, at later times and in other places. In effect, governance was gradually transferred from the speaker's verbal behavior to the listener's replication of it. Repetition had to come first, but once in place powerful contingencies could maintain it. The scope of verbal governance could expand to those remote in time or space from the original speaker, and coordinated human groups could spread beyond the range of a single human voice, thereby setting the stage for wide dissemination of human cultural practices (repetition is also a prerequisite for verbal memory: Catania, 1998).

As human groups expanded, contact with different and conflicting speakers no doubt made it important for listeners to discriminate among different sources of verbal behavior (e.g., group members versus outsiders, rankings within dominance hierarchies). In particular, once the speaker's direct verbal control was supplanted by indirect control via the listener's repetition of the speaker's utterance, listeners must eventually have learned to discriminate themselves from others as sources of verbal stimuli. Responding directly to what someone has said differs from responding to one's own repetition of the other's utterance, which in turn differs from producing one's own novel utterance. Presumably such complex discriminations emerged only as a consequence of contingencies that made such discriminations important.

Once in place, verbal governance would necessarily evolve in complexity in parallel with the increasing complexity of other human activities, such as the production and distribution of food and goods (cf. Skinner, 1953, 1969). Individuals could learn from each other through verbal behavior. For example, they could be told about contingencies instead of observing them. Verbal governance is eventually attenuated, however, if instructions have little relation to current contingencies. Cultural contingencies no doubt concurrently shaped verbal behavior with respect to environmental events, in classes eventually called naming and describing, and characterized in terms of truth, falsity, accuracy, and reliability.

Once verbal governance is well-established in a culture, a speaker can instruct what another says as well as what the other does. Giving a definition or stating a fact instructs with respect to verbal behavior just as giving an order instructs with respect to nonverbal behavior. Speaking affects the behavior of others whether or not it is grammatically an imperative; to the extent that a declarative makes another behave with respect to some event, it includes an implicit "look" or "see" or "listen" (cf. Horne & Lowe, 1996). Whether an instance of verbal behavior is an instruction does not depend on its grammatical form: All utterances are, usually in multiple senses, ways of telling someone else what to do.

Obviously, much still needs filling in (for more detailed treatments, see Catania, 1990, 1995c, 2001). For example, transitions from single- to multiple-word utterances not only demand syntactic coordinations, but also allow a dramatic expansion in the functions of verbal behavior, perhaps analogous to the dramatic expansion of varieties of living systems in the Cambrian transition from single-to multiple-celled organisms. Once speakers could instruct the verbal behavior of listeners who could in turn instruct nonverbal behavior, the prerequisites for human political and religious institutions were firmly in place. The invention of writing, perhaps initially a matter of record-keeping, moved verbal governance further from the behavior of individual speakers. Human behavior throughout the world has been and still is heavily influenced by records of long-past verbal behavior: *The Analects of Confucius, Bhagavad Gita, The Old and New Testaments, The Koran, The Book of Mormon*, to mention just a few (fortunately, *Mein Kampf* failed to achieve a comparably enduring status). Religious behavior provides particularly compelling examples of the verbal phenomena about to be reviewed: verbal governance in the following of religious precepts, the generation and shaping of verbal behavior in recitations of scripture and other verbal rituals, and differential attention to verbal stimuli in prescribed and proscribed religious texts.

Verbal Governance

Verbally governed behavior is behavior, either verbal or nonverbal, controlled by verbal antecedents (such behavior has been called *rule-governed behavior*, but the definition of rules, based sometimes on structural and sometimes on functional criteria, is ambiguous; therefore the term *verbally governed behavior* will be used here). Control is maintained not so much by consequences arranged for particular responses given particular verbal stimuli, but rather by social contingencies that generate higher-order classes of behavior characterized by correspondences between verbal antecedents and subsequent behavior (as in the following of orders in the military, where obedience extends across many different possible orders, some perhaps never even given before).

Operant behavior is behavior that is sensitive to its consequences. A higher-order class of behavior is an operant class that includes within it other classes that can themselves function as operant classes (as when generalized imitation includes all component imitations that could be separately reinforced as subclasses). Higher-order classes of behavior are held together by the common contingencies shared by their members, just as the various topographies of a rat's food-reinforced lever pressing (e.g., left paw, right paw, both paws) are held together by the common contingencies according to which they produce food.

Within higher-order classes, relations between responses and their consequences at the higher-order level need not be compatible with those at the more local level of the subclasses. In the case of verbal governance, social contingencies maintain the higher-order class, but other contingencies act on specific instances. In the military, for example, social contingencies maintaining obedience may conflict with nonsocial contingencies prevailing on the battlefield, as when the aversive nonsocial consequences of advancing under fire oppose the aversive social consequences of retreat. When social consequences prevail, the component responses remain consistent with the higher-order class (orders are obeyed) and the behavior is called verbally governed; it is relatively insensitive to the nonsocial contingencies. When nonsocial consequences dominate (retreat occurs against orders), the behavior is called *contingency-governed* or *contingency-shaped* (the former usage emphasizes maintaining contingencies and the latter origins: cf. Skinner, 1969).

This vocabulary of verbal governance and contingency governance is convenient, but it is important to recognize that contingencies operate at both levels, the *higher-order* and the *local* levels, and that the distinction between higher-order and local levels is orthogonal to that between verbal and nonverbal behavior. In other words, verbal behavior is defined by certain social contingencies, but such contingencies can operate either on higher-order classes or locally.

Nevertheless, social contingencies, especially in verbal behavior, can have arbitrary properties that free higher-order classes from the constraints imposed by nonsocial contingencies (cf. Skinner, 1957: "Abstraction is a peculiarly verbal process because a nonverbal environment cannot provide the necessary restricted contingency," p. 109). The point is that verbally governed behavior is often determined more strongly by higher-order social contingencies than by more local (often nonsocial) contingencies, and therefore is often less likely than contingency-governed behavior to change when the local contingencies change. It is also worth noting that verbal behavior includes other higher-order classes along with verbal governance (e.g., naming, as in Horne & Lowe, 1996; relational responding, as in Hayes, Barnes-Holmes, & Roche, 2001), and that along with or instead of their own discriminative and/or instructional functions (Schlinger & Blakely, 1987), verbal antecedents may alter the functions of other stimuli (e.g., as when something neutral becomes a reinforcer after one is told it is worth having: cf. Hayes, Zettle, & Rosenfarb, 1989, on augmenting stimuli).

Verbally governed behavior may be established by verbal communities precisely because of the relative insensitivity of such behavior to local contingencies. People often give instructions when natural consequences are weak (e.g., telling children to study), remote (e.g., telling drivers to wear seat belts), or likely to lead to undesirable behavior (e.g., warning against drug abuse). People do not ordinarily tell other people to do what they would do even without being told (which suggests that children are advised that hurts produced by words matter less than those of sticks and stones precisely because words can have powerful effects).

Performances maintained by reinforcement schedules provide a convenient index of verbal governance, because verbal governance tends to make human operant behavior relatively insensitive to local contingencies that produce large and reliable effects on nonhuman behavior. For example, with nonverbal species ratio schedules, which deliver a reinforcer for the last of some fixed or variable number of responses, reliably produce higher response rates than interval schedules, which deliver a reinforcer for the first response occurring after some fixed or variable interval, but they fail to do so reliably with humans. Verbal governance is implicated in this human insensitivity to local schedule contingencies because human schedule performances often vary more with changes in verbal behavior than with changes in schedule contingencies.

Verbal governance begins early. With consequences arranged according to various schedules, children under 2 behave much like nonverbal organisms such as pigeons, between about 2 and 4 or 5 their behavior becomes variable, and by the age of 5 most children behave in the relatively stereotyped ways that characterize adult verbally governed performance (Bentall & Lowe, 1987; Bentall, Lowe & Beasty, 1985; see also Catania, Lowe, & Horne, 1990). Insensitivity to local contingencies produced by verbal behavior is pervasive (e.g., Hayes, Brownstein, Zettle, Rosenfarb, & Korn, 1986; Matthews, Shimoff, Catania, & Sagvolden, 1977; Svartdal, 1989) and extends far beyond schedule performances. Contingencies operating on higher-order verbal classes override those operating on local subclasses in many different tasks (e.g., Maki, 1979; Reber, 1976; Schooler & Engstler-Schooler, 1990; Shimoff & Catania, 1998; Skinner, 1969).

Verbal antecedents in verbal governance are most obvious in the form called instructions, as when one is told to do or say something. "I'm thirsty," a declarative, however, may have the same function as "Please give me a drink of water," an imperative. Furthermore, verbal antecedents may specify contingencies, as when one is told what will happen if one does or says something. People often tell others about contingencies operating in some environment, assuming that descriptions of contingencies will somehow produce behavior appropriate to them. Descriptions of contingencies having implications for performance, however, are not equivalent to explicit descriptions of performance. Effects depend on the listener's verbal repertory, so descriptions of contingencies and descriptions of performances need not have comparable instructional effects.

Verbal governance, like any other operant class, may be conditional on other events. Humans learn to follow instructions from some individuals, but not others. Humans often talk to themselves, usually silently, but occasionally, as when following complex instructions, out loud. Thus, verbal antecedents may lead to other verbal behavior, as when implications and courses of action are derived from something said. And because humans often can distinguish between what they have been told and what they have arrived at without being told, the most effective verbal antecedents may be those that they generate themselves. In such cases, they may fail to recognize the remote origins of what they generated, in the verbal behavior of others that initiated their own self-talk.

Local contingencies may also generate verbal behavior that in turn produces nonverbal behavior consistent with natural consequences (as when making calculations based on measurements). Behavior then may become sensitive to its consequences because an effective verbal account of contingencies and related performances has been formulated; in such cases, the indirect sensitivity, mediated by verbal behavior, is functionally different from contingency-governed behavior (Skinner, 1969; cf. Catania, Matthews, & Shimoff, 1982; Danforth, Chase, Dolan, & Joyce, 1990).

In many contexts, human performance is determined by higher-order verbal contingencies rather than by local contingencies, but of course some of the time human behavior must be directly determined by local contingencies. Many skilled motor performances (e.g., tying shoelaces) are not conducive to verbal mediation, and verbal behavior seems eventually to drop out of some skills that begin with large instructional components (e.g., driving a stick-shift car).

Ironically, one class of human behavior more likely to be locally than verbally governed is verbal behavior itself. Our everyday language does not include an effective vocabulary dealing with the functional properties of our own verbal behavior, so one rarely talks about the variables that determine it. In other words, many properties of verbal behavior are typically not verbally governed. That may be why the shaping of human verbal behavior often appears to be easier than the shaping of human nonverbal behavior. Furthermore, if verbal contingencies have established correspondences between saying and doing (cf. Baer, Detrich & Weninger, 1988; Risley & Hart, 1968), the shaping of verbal behavior, saying, may sometimes be accompanied by changes in related nonverbal behavior, doing.

Verbal Shaping

Verbal behavior is a function of antecedents and consequences, and the fact of verbal shaping (Greenspoon, 1955; Rosenfeld & Baer, 1970; Skinner, 1957) is itself evidence that verbal behavior is often governed by local contingencies. Shaping creates new behavior through the selective reinforcement of other behavior that more and more closely approximates it. The shaper adjusts the reinforcement criteria to the current population of responses, in successive approximations to the behavior to be shaped (Eckerman, Hienz, Stern, & Kowlowitz, 1980; Galbicka, Kautz, & Jagers, 1993; Platt, 1973). Behavior analysts are most familiar with examples of shaping from the laboratory, but natural contingencies may produce shaping, as when differential parental attention inadvertently shapes an infant's annoying cries (the distinction is analogous to Darwin's distinction between artificial and natural selection in phylogeny: Catania, 1994, 1995b).

Shaping is effective because behavior is variable. Reinforcement of a response produces a spectrum of responses that differ from the reinforced response along such dimensions as topography, magnitude, and force. Verbal shaping is of special interest because verbal behavior can vary along semantic and syntactic dimensions as well.

Shaping typically involves quantitative changes along one or more dimensions of an organism's behavior, but sometimes it produces qualitative changes. Consider a rat producing food by pressing on a counterweighted lever so high that the rat must stand on its hind legs to reach it (Catania & Harnad, 1988, p. 476). With a modest weight, the rat presses easily with one or both forepaws on the lever. When the increasing weight requirement exceeds the rat's weight, pressing the lever with the forepaws no longer works because the hind paws come up off the floor. Further pressing will be effective only if a new topography emerges. Hanging on the lever, the rat must lift its hind paws to the chamber wall where a wire mesh allows a firm grip. If the rat does so, it can operate the lever by pulling between forepaws and hind legs. This example illustrates two kinds of transitions in ontogenic selection, one gradual (with a requirement below the rat's own weight) and the other relatively abrupt (with the rat's weight exceeded). Analogously, in phylogenic selection the gradual changes produced by selection relative to a population mean are sometimes contrasted with more abrupt changes (sometimes called saltations) produced by catastrophic environmental events. Analogies in the shaping of verbal behavior by natural contingencies might be those dramatic changes called religious conversions or epiphanies.

Correspondences between verbal behavior and nonverbal operant behavior in humans have been studied during performances maintained by reinforcement schedules. The direction of effect in the relation between verbal and nonverbal behavior is ambiguous when verbal reports are sampled during operant performances (did changes in response rate occasion an accurate report, or did the report occasion changes in response rate?). With shaping, however, the experimenter knows which came first.

If left-button presses during one stimulus produce points worth money according to ratio contingencies and right-button presses during an alternating stimulus produce points according to interval contingencies, verbal shaping can be carried out during periodic interruptions that provide opportunities for verbal behavior (e.g., filling in questionnaires, with points depending on the answers). The rate difference reliably produced by ratio and interval contingencies with nonverbal organisms is often absent in human behavior, but successful shaping of relevant verbal behavior (e.g., "Press the left button fast" or "The red light means press slowly") typically produces rates of pressing conforming to the new verbal behavior. Verbal governance by shaped verbal behavior usually works even when the outcome is incompatible with the schedules (e.g., "press slow" leading to low rates during ratio contingencies), though the effects are eventually attenuated with increasing discrepancies between verbal and nonverbal contingencies. Pitting verbal against nonverbal contingencies lets an experimenter determine their relative potencies.

Just as verbal governance by instructions can be conditional on other variables, so also for verbal governance by shaped verbal behavior. For example, it makes a difference whether what is shaped describes behavior or describes contingencies operating for that behavior (Catania, Shimoff, & Matthews, 1989). Descriptions of what one does differ from descriptions of how an environment works. Someone correctly identifying two schedules as depending on response number and time intervals might go on to say that point deliveries should increase with faster pressing in the former, but not in the latter; another, also correctly identifying the schedules, might instead go on to say that rate of pressing does not matter because points in both are unpredictable. Only the first is likely to show rate differences appropriate to the schedules.

Verbal shaping involves treating successive verbal responses as varying along semantic or other verbal dimensions, but judgments of which are closer or farther from the behavior to be shaped can be tricky. For example, an experimenter trying to shape descriptions of rates of button pressing can easily select words related to *fast, slow, time* or *number* for reinforcement, but someone coming up with a phrase like "four fast presses and then three slow ones" and following it thereafter mainly with variations of just the two numbers may be caught in a sort of verbal trap, because the possibilities for varying the numbers are unlimited. In this case, further attempts to shape simpler verbalizations might be difficult and perhaps even unsuccessful. Instructions in what to say could of course be introduced, but instructing is not functionally equivalent to shaping.

The shaping of verbal behavior is a potent technique for changing human behavior. A practical implication is that shaping what people say about their own behavior may be a more effective way to change their behavior than either shaping their behavior directly or telling them what to do (cf. Lovaas, 1964; Luria, 1961; Zivin, 1979). Therapists may sometimes be effective simply by shaping clients' talk (Truax, 1966). Therapies that invoke cognitive behavior modification or cognitive efficacy are said to modify client behavior by changing the client's cognitions, but this is ordinarily done by changing the client's verbal behavior through instructions or verbal shaping (though verbal shaping is more likely to be incidental than deliberate). Such therapies are sometimes effective, but probably for reasons other than those claimed (cf. Catania, 1995a; Chadwick, Lowe, Horne, & Higson, 1994; Truax, 1966).

The implications bear repetition: The fact of verbal shaping implies that verbal behavior itself is sensitive to local contingencies even when it governs other behavior; furthermore, if much nonverbal behavior is verbally governed it may in general be easier to change human behavior by shaping what someone says than by shaping what someone does. The greater effectiveness of verbal shaping relative to instructions may depend in part on the speaker's failure to discriminate the sources of the verbal behavior. Someone whose descriptions of schedule performances have been shaped is more likely to say "I figured out how the buttons worked and was told I was right," than to say "By giving me points you got me to say how the buttons worked." In other words, even speakers who accurately discriminate among various sources of verbal behavior when following instructions usually call their own shaped verbal behavior self-generated. To change beliefs is to change verbal behavior, but it matters whether one has been told what to say or has come to say it in other ways.

Audiences provide discriminative stimuli that set the occasions on which verbal behavior may have consequences and provide reinforcers that shape verbal behavior. Different audiences set the occasion for different verbal classes. The examples here of verbal shaping have been mainly experimental, but anyone who has observed drifts in the content of conversation as attention to particular topics or speakers picks up or flags has seen it in a natural setting. Verbal shaping is difficult to track in natural environments: a wide range of social reinforcers enters into it (e.g., eye contact, changes in facial expression or posture, continued verbal behavior) and their effectiveness changes over time (e.g., a comment that works early in a conversation may be totally irrelevant later on).

Some of the most interesting reinforcers of verbal behavior are themselves verbal: an answer to a question, an acknowledgment, a continuation of a line of thought, and so on. If some verbal consequences are more effective reinforcers than others, however, it follows that some command more attention than others. Verbal stimuli are discriminative stimuli, and people attend to them, as they attend to nonverbal ones, not on the basis of the information they carry, but rather as a function of their correlation with reinforcers. What follows provides some evidence in support of this role of reinforcement in the maintenance of attention.

Attention to Verbal Stimuli

Some discriminative stimuli are correlated with the delivery of reinforcers and others with periods of extinction. Only the former are likely to acquire reinforcing functions of their own and when they do they are called conditional or conditioned reinforcers. The effectiveness of discriminative stimuli as occasions for behavior depends on whether the organism attends to them, which in turn depends on their status as conditional reinforcers (Dinsmoor, 1995). Looking at or attending to a stimulus is reinforced when the stimulus is correlated with reinforcers, but not otherwise. An informative stimulus is also a discriminative stimulus, in the sense that different contingencies operate when the stimulus is present than when it is absent, but it is not necessarily a conditional reinforcer (e.g., it may be correlated solely with extinction or with aversive events). Thus, informativeness alone is not sufficient to maintain attention to discriminative stimuli.

An observing response produces or clarifies a discriminative stimulus and is maintained by the effectiveness of that stimulus as a conditional reinforcer (Dinsmoor, 1983, 1995; Kelleher, Riddle, & Cook, 1962). For example, assume the irregular alternation of extinction and ratio reinforcement of a pigeon's key pecks, with a single white stimulus present throughout so that the pigeon usually pecks in both conditions. Now add a second key on which pecks produce stimuli correlated with the two conditions (the observing key). During extinction, pecks on the observing key turn the first key red for a while; during ratio reinforcement, they turn it green. Soon the pigeon comes to peck infrequently during red (extinction) and frequently during green (reinforcement). Whenever either red or green turns back to white the pigeon quickly shifts to pecking the observing key and brings the appropriate color back.

The red and green stimuli are equally informative, even though one is correlated with extinction and the other with reinforcement. If observing responses produce green on the main key during reinforcement, but do nothing during extinction, the pigeon still pecks the observing key. If, however, observing responses produce red during extinction, but do nothing during reinforcement, the pigeon stops pecking the observing key, even though turning on red in this new procedure should be just as useful as turning on green only or both red and green. Red is bad news. The pigeon does not work to look at it. Similarly, stimuli correlated with differential punishment (reinforcement in one condition and reinforcement plus punishment in the other) do not maintain observing responses very well; informative effects, if any, are overridden by the aversiveness of the stimulus correlated with reinforcement plus punishment, even though that stimulus would allow the pigeon to respond more efficiently by concentrating its responding in the reinforcement-only condition (Dinsmoor, 1983).

In other words, organisms do not attend to stimuli because they are informative. Instead, they attend to informative stimuli only if those stimuli are conditional reinforcers. This finding, which undercuts the appeal to information processing as a primary cognitive process, has implications for what happens when stimuli are verbal, because it follows that the effectiveness of a message depends more on whether its content is reinforcing or aversive than on whether it is correct or complete or consistent. The phenomenon has long been recognized in folklore, as in accounts of Cassandra's fate and the unhappy treatment of a messenger who brings bad news. It is no surprise that people often hesitate to ask about medical diagnoses. That humans attend at all to bad news or that sometimes they reach conclusions even when the answer is not what they wanted to hear are what need explanation. Presumably bad news does sometimes allow effective avoidance behavior and many stimuli are correlated with sufficient reinforcers that they can maintain attention even when they are also correlated with occasional aversive events.

Verbal behavior has a variety of functions, some of which may amplify the effects of differential attention to verbal stimuli relative to cases where the stimuli are totally nonverbal. For example, humans repeat to themselves what they hear and what they read. Once they have done so their own verbal behavior is likely to summate with other verbal antecedents that participate in the verbal governance of their subsequent behavior. If these verbal stimuli were reinforcing in the first place, then behavior producing contact with more or similar instances will be strengthened, in turn providing even more related initiating instances (cf. Parsons, Taylor, & Joyce, 1981; Rosenfarb, Newland, Brannon, & Howey, 1992). It is no surprise, for example, that people turn to news media that are biased toward political views they already hold; conservative magazines do not count on generating income from liberal subscribers. Once again the repetition of verbal behavior plays a critical role.

The individual who generates varied verbal stimuli some of which are more potent reinforcers than others may be producing conditions for automatic verbal shaping (e.g., Joyce & Chase, 1990; cf. Skinner, 1957, on poetry and other literary verbal behavior, and any issue of *Skeptical Inquirer* for examples that are more bizarre). Thus, differential attention to verbal stimuli may lead to self-generated verbal behavior that is somewhat independent of current environments, so that verbal governance becomes a pervasive feature of an individual's behavior across a range of different situations. As contact with particular antecedents and contingencies becomes more tenuous (it is after all difficult to disprove claims of heaven and hell, parallel universes, and alien abduction), higher-order verbal contingencies may generate idiosyncratic verbal behavior that appears to be virtually autonomous. When such concentrated effects show up in the behavior of individuals, they are sometimes called interests or obsessions; when they extend across groups, they are sometimes called fads or cults.

The Multiple Causation of Verbal and Nonverbal Behavior

Multiple causation has been implicit throughout this treatment of the converging effects of verbal governance, verbal shaping, and attention to verbal stimuli. It has been crucial to distinguish among verbal and nonverbal antecedents, responses and consequences, because verbal units can serve as any term in the three-term contingency (on the symmetrical status of words as stimuli and as responses, see Horne & Lowe, 1996, on naming; Sidman, 1994; Sidman, Wynne, Maguire, & Barnes, 1989, on equivalence classes; Hayes, Barnes-Holmes, & Roche, 2001, on relational framing).

Various combinations of social and nonsocial antecedents, responses, and consequences might be examined, but a classification solely in such terms probably would be of limited value. For example, it takes social contingencies to create higher-order classes of verbal behavior occasioned by nonverbal antecedents, but such classes, once established, may be maintained by nonsocial contingencies, as when a situation occasions a description of contingencies that alters someone's subsequent nonverbal behavior. Similarly, governance by verbal antecedents is established by social contingencies, but once established it can be maintained either by nonsocial consequences, as when someone makes a repair by following a service manual, or by social ones, as when someone complies with a request (respectively tracking, or instruction-following based on correspondences between verbal behavior and environmental events, and pliance, or instruction-following based on social contingencies: Zettle & Hayes, 1982). Although social consequences are the glue that holds together everyday conversation, the contingencies that involve nonsocial consequences of verbal governance are essential features of the ways in which people act upon their environments (e.g., in science and technology). And what about dimensions of behavior such as the distinction between natural and artificial contingencies, the different functional properties of local and higher-order classes, and the relative phylogenic and ontogenic contributions to antecedents and responses and reinforcers?

Behavior analysis must do more than provide pigeonholes for purposes of classification. It must put the pieces together. Here are some of them: Verbal antecedents affect both what is said and what is done; People tend to reproduce verbal behavior that they come in contact with and therefore produce their own verbal antecedents; People seek out or maintain contact with verbal antecedents correlated with relatively more potent reinforcers, including those that they themselves have produced; The saying and doing that follows are further differentiated by new consequences; People continue to reproduce it, again providing their own verbal antecedents, which are now among those that they seek out or maintain contact with; Saying and doing follow from them and are further differentiated, producing still more verbal antecedents; These in turn affect both what people say and what they do. . . .

That is already more than once around: been there, done that. The point is not only that the pieces fit well together, but also that they become components of cycles within which they strengthen and build upon each other. Omit any one and the cyclicity is significantly attenuated. Even if the social reinforcers that participate in these functions are ordinarily small, they operate on behavior day in and day out over weeks and months and years. Behavior analysts know how much behavior can be shaped in just a few minutes with a nonverbal organism, so should anyone be surprised at the effects of interlocking verbal contingencies operating over human lifetimes? These are powerful variables, and it is easy to imagine how they could sometimes produce verbal behavior that is dull and highly stereo-typed and sometimes verbal behavior that is flexible and highly creative. Verbal governance and verbal shaping and attention to verbal stimuli make separate contributions, but their synergistic effects produce complex behavior that is much more than just the sum of its parts.

Conclusion

So what about Hitler? From a wealth of evidence only a little can be sampled here. Verbal governance is easy enough to identify through-out Hitler's Germany, but it is especially prominent in German military traditions. Coercion obviously played a major role, but of special relevance to our account is the phenomenon of "working toward the Führer" (Kershaw, 1998, 2000). Except in his increasing control of the military as the war progressed, Hitler did not so much give orders as allow those who answered to him to "work toward the Führer," to formulate policies and directives consistent with what they saw as his objectives. They made their offerings and he selected among them, necessarily attending to some more than others. The result was that those who acted on Hitler's behalf were acting in conformity with verbal behavior that they had generated themselves.

The effects of verbal shaping are particularly evident in the early days of Hitler's oratorical career. Over time, in front of mirrors and cameras as well as before actual audiences, he adapted his speeches in content, uniform, posture, and manner of delivery to the reactions of his audiences (Kershaw, 1998, 2000). The audience reactions shaped his oratory in large part because his pronouncements incorporated much that his audience was ready to hear. He spoke, they cheered, he spoke more, they cheered more, and so on. As he rose to power, he gave frequent speeches, so there were ample opportunities for variation and selection along the way. Hitler and his audiences were tragically involved in a reciprocal reinforcement relation that led them and their innumerable victims to disaster.

Hitler's speeches provided content that, unlike the economic and political bad news of the time, maintained attention in his receptive audience. Those who may wonder about the reinforcers involved in antisemitism and other varieties of persecution need only note that Germany was recovering from a lost war and hyperinflation, among other social and economic problems, and that under aversive circumstances opportunities for aggression can serve as reinforcers (Azrin, Hutchinson, & Hake, 1966; Azrin, Hutchinson, & McLaughlin, 1965). Effects of verbal stimuli more or less correlated with reinforcers are prominent throughout the history of the Third Reich. News of easy victories—the occupation of the Sudetenland, the march into Vienna, the fall of France—were quickly and widely disseminated, but not so news of failures or embarrassments—the German defeat at Stalingrad, Rommel's support of an unsuccessful attempt at Hitler's assassination. This other side of the phenomenon increasingly revealed itself as the tides of war turned against Germany. For example, Hitler was not awakened for the news of the D-Day invasion of the Normandy beaches, and even as the Soviets tightened their vise around Berlin in the last weeks of the war he continued to speak of opportunities for counterattack, secret weapons yet to be deployed, and miraculous victories.

Something like Hitler could happen again. In fact, those who look at subsequent years of the twentieth century in Iraq or Cambodia or Jonestown or Rwanda or the former Yugoslavia or Waco or Afghanistan, among many other places, may well conclude that it already has. More routine instances of human behavior might have been considered, but scientists usually learn the most about the functional relations in which they have an interest by including the most extreme values in their analyses. If these interpretations are relevant even to such extreme cases, then they may also be useful when applied to more ordinary ones, like the behavior of children and teachers, doctors and patients, religious leaders and their congregations, salespeople and their customers, executives and employees, lawyers and clients, citizens and elected officials, and maybe even the behavior of the scientists who try to figure out how it all works.

References

Azrin, N. H., Hutchinson, R. R., & Hake, D. F. (1966). Extinction-induced aggression. *Journal of the Experimental Analysis of Behavior, 9,* 191–204.
Azrin, N. H., Hutchinson, R. R., & McLaughlin, R. (1965). The opportunity for aggression as an operant reinforcer during aversive stimulation. *Journal of the Experimental Analysis of Behavior, 8,* 171–180.

Baer, R. A., Detrich, R., & Weninger, J. M. (1988). On the functional role of the verbalization in correspondence training procedures. *Journal of Applied Behavior Analysis, 21,* 345–356.

Bentall, R. P., & Lowe, C. F. (1987). The role of verbal behavior in human learning: III. Instructional effects in children. *Journal of the Experimental Analysis of Behavior, 47,* 177–190.

Bentall, R. P., Lowe, C. F., & Beasty, A. (1985). The role of verbal behavior in human learning: II. Developmental differences. *Journal of the Experimental Analysis of Behavior, 43,* 165–181.

Catania, A. C. (1985). Rule-governed behavior and the origins of language. In C. F. Lowe, M. Richelle, D. E. Blackman, & C. Bradshaw (Eds.), *Behavior analysis and contemporary psychology* (pp. 135–156). Hillsdale, NJ: Erlbaum.

Catania, A. C. (1990). What good is five percent of a language competence? *Behavioral and Brain Sciences, 13,* 729–731.

Catania, A. C. (1994). The natural and artificial selection of verbal behavior. In S. C. Hayes, L. Hayes, M. Sato, & K. Ono (Eds.), *Behavior analysis of language and cognition* (pp. 31–49). Reno, NV: Context Press.

Catania, A. C. (1995a). Higher-order behavior classes: Contingencies, beliefs, and verbal behavior. *Journal of Behavior Therapy and Experimental Psychiatry, 26,* 191–200.

Catania, A. C. (1995b). Selection in biology and behavior. In J. T. Todd, & E. K. Morris (Eds.), *Modern perspectives on B. F. Skinner and contemporary behaviorism* (pp. 185–194). Westport, CT: Greenwood Press.

Catania, A. C. (1995c). Single words, multiple words, and the functions of language. *Behavioral and Brain Sciences, 18,* 184–185.

Catania, A. C. (1998). *Learning* (4th Ed.). Englewood Cliffs, NJ: Prentice-Hall.

Catania, A. C. (2001). Three varieties of selection and their implications for the origins of language. In G. Györi (Ed.), *Language evolution: Biological, linguistic and philosophical perspectives* (pp. 55–71). Frankfurt am Main: Peter Lang.

Catania, A. C., & Harnad, S. (Eds.). (1988). *The selection of behavior: The operant behaviorism of B. F. Skinner.* New York: Cambridge University Press.

Catania, A. C., Lowe, C. F., & Horne, P. J. (1990). Nonverbal behavior correlated with the shaped verbal behavior of children. *Analysis of Verbal Behavior, 8,* 43–55.

Catania, A. C., Matthews, B. A., & Shimoff, E. (1982). Instructed versus shaped human verbal behavior: Interactions with nonverbal responding. *Journal of the Experimental Analysis of Behavior, 38,* 233–248.

Catania, A. C., Shimoff, E. H., & Matthews, B. A. (1989). An experimental analysis of rule-governed behavior. In S. C. Hayes (Ed.), *Rule-governed behavior: Cognition, contingencies and instructional control* (pp. 119–150). New York: Plenum.

Chadwick, P. D. J., Lowe, C. F., Horne, P. J., & Higson, P. J. (1994). Modifying delusions: The role of empirical testing. *Behavior Therapy, 25,* 35–49.

Cornwell, J. (1999). *Hitler's pope.* New York: Viking.

Danforth, J. S., Chase, P. N., Dolan, M., & Joyce, J. H. (1990). The establishment of stimulus control by instructions and by differential reinforcement. *Journal of the Experimental Analysis of Behavior, 54,* 97–112.

Darwin, C. (1859). *On the origin of species.* London: John Murray.

Darwin, C. (1871). *The descent of man.* London: John Murray.

Dawkins, R. (1976). *The selfish gene.* New York: Oxford University Press.

Dawkins, R. (1982). *The extended phenotype.* San Francisco: Freeman.

Dinsmoor, J. A. (1983). Observing and conditioned reinforcement. *Behavioral and Brain Sciences, 6,* 693–728.

Dinsmoor, J. A. (1995). Stimulus control. *Behavior Analyst, 18,* 51–68, 253–269.

Eckerman, D. A., Hienz, R. D., Stern, S., & Kowlowitz, V. (1980). Shaping the location of a pigeon's peck: Effect of rate and size of shaping steps. *Journal of the Experimental Analysis of Behavior, 33,* 299–310.

Galbicka, G., Kautz, M. A., & Jagers, T. (1993). Response acquisition under targeted percentile schedules: A continuing quandary for molar models of operant behavior. *Journal of the Experimental Analysis of Behavior, 60,* 171–184.

Gouzoules, S., Gouzoules, H., & Marler, P. (1984). Rhesus monkey (*Macaca mulatta*) screams: Representational signalling in the recruitment of agonistic aid. *Animal Behaviour, 32,* 182–193.

Greenspoon, J. (1955). The reinforcing effect of two spoken sounds on the frequency of two responses. *American Journal of Psychology, 68,* 409–416.

Hayes, S. C., Barnes-Holmes, D., & Roche, B. (2001). *Relational frame theory: A post-Skinnerian account of human language and cognition.* New York: Kluwer Academic/Plenum.

Hayes, S. C., Brownstein, A. J., Zettle, R. D., Rosenfarb, I., & Korn, Z. (1986). Rule-governed behavior and sensitivity to changing consequences of responding. *Journal of the Experimental Analysis of Behavior, 45,* 237–256.

Hayes, S. C., Zettle, R. D., & Rosenfarb, I. (1989). Rule-following. In S. C. Hayes (Ed.), *Rule-governed behavior: Cognition, contingencies, and instructional control* (pp. 191–220). New York: Plenum.

Horne, P. J., & Lowe, C. F. (1996). On the origins of naming and other symbolic behavior. *Journal of the Experimental Analysis of Behavior, 65,* 185–241.

Jaynes, J. (1976). *The origin of consciousness in the breakdown of the bicameral mind.* Boston, MA: Houghton Mifflin.

Joyce, J. H., & Chase, P. N. (1990). Effects of response variability on the sensitivity of rule-governed behavior. *Journal of the Experimental Analysis of Behavior, 54,* 251–262.

Kelleher, R. T., Riddle, W. C., & Cook, L. (1962). Observing responses in pigeons. *Journal of the Experimental Analysis of Behavior, 5,* 3–13.

Kershaw, I. (1998). *Hitler 1889–1936: Hubris.* New York: Norton.

Kershaw, I. (2000). *Hitler 1936–1945: Nemesis.* New York: Norton.

Lovaas, O. I. (1964). Cue properties of words: The control of operant responding by rate and content of verbal operants. *Child Development, 35,* 245–256.

Luria, A. R. (1961). *The role of speech in the production of normal and abnormal behavior.* New York: Liveright.

Maki, R. H. (1979). Right-left and up-down are equally discriminable in the absence of directional words. *Bulletin of the Psychonomic Society, 14,* 181–184.

Matthews, B. A., Shimoff, E., Catania, A. C., & Sagvolden, T. (1977). Uninstructed human responding: Sensitivity to ratio and interval contingencies. *Journal of the Experimental Analysis of Behavior, 27,* 453–467.

Parsons, J. A., Taylor, D. C., & Joyce, T. M. (1981). Precurrent self-prompting operants in children: "Remembering." *Journal of the Experimental Analysis of Behavior, 36,* 253–266.

Platt, J. R. (1973). Percentile reinforcement: Paradigms for experimental analysis of response shaping. In G. H. Bower (Ed.), *The psychology of learning and motivation. Vol. 7* (pp. 271–296). New York: Academic Press.

Provine, R. R. (2000). *Laughter: A scientific investigation.* New York: Viking.

Reber, A. S. (1976). Implicit learning of synthetic languages: the role of instructional set. *Journal of Experimental Psychology: Human Learning and Memory, 2,* 88–94.

Rendall, D., Owren, M. J., & Rodman, P. S. (1998). The role of vocal tract filtering in rhesus monkey (*Macaca mulatta*) vocalizations. *Journal of the Acoustic Society of America, 103,* 602–614.

Rendall, D., Rodman, P. S., & Emond, R. E. (1996). Vocal recognition of individuals and kin in free-ranging rhesus monkeys. *Animal Behaviour, 51,* 1007–1015.

Risley, T. R. (1977). The development and maintenance of language: An operant model. In B. C. Etzel, J. M. LeBlanc, & D. M. Baer (Eds.), *New developments in behavioral research* (pp. 81–101). Hillsdale, NJ: Erlbaum.

Risley, T. R., & Hart, B. (1968). Developing correspondence between the non-verbal and verbal behavior of preschool children. *Journal of Applied Behavior Analysis, 1,* 267–281.

Rosenfarb, I. S., Newland, M. C., Brannon, S. E., & Howey, D. S. (1992). Effects of self-generated rules on the development of schedule-controlled behavior. *Journal of the Experimental Analysis of Behavior, 58,* 107–121.

Rosenfeld, H. M., & Baer, D. M. (1970). Unbiased and unnoticed verbal conditioning: The double agent robot procedure. *Journal of the Experimental Analysis of Behavior, 14,* 99–107.

Schlinger, H., & Blakely, E. (1987). Function-altering effects of contingency-specifying stimuli. *Behavior Analyst, 10,* 41–45.

Schooler, J. W., & Engstler-Schooler, T. Y. (1990). Verbal overshadowing of visual memories: Some things are better left unsaid. *Cognitive Psychology, 22,* 36–71.

Seyfarth, R. M., Cheney, D. L., & Marler, P. (1980). Vervet monkey alarm calls: Semantic communication in a free-ranging primate. *Animal Behaviour, 28,* 1070–1094.

Shimoff, E., & Catania, A. C. (1998). The verbal governance of behavior. In K. A. Lattal, & M. Perone (Eds.), *Handbook of research methods in human operant behavior* (pp. 371–404). New York: Plenum.

Sidman, M. (1994). *Equivalence relations and behavior: A research story.* Boston, MA: Authors Cooperative.

Sidman, M., Wynne, C. K., Maguire, R. W., & Barnes, T. (1989). Functional classes and equivalence relations. *Journal of the Experimental Analysis of Behavior, 52,* 261–274.

Skinner, B. F. (1953). *Science and human behavior.* New York: Macmillan.

Skinner, B. F. (1957). *Verbal behavior.* New York: Appleton-Century-Crofts.

Skinner, B. F. (1969). An operant analysis of problem solving. In B. F. Skinner *Contingencies of reinforcement* (pp. 133–171). New York: Appleton-Century-Crofts.

Skinner, B. F. (1981). Selection by consequences. *Science, 213,* 501–504.

Skinner, B. F. (1986). The evolution of verbal behavior. *Journal of the Experimental Analysis of Behavior, 45,* 115–122.

Svartdal, F. (1989). Shaping of rule-governed behavior. *Scandinavian Journal of Psychology, 30,* 304–314.

Truax, C. B. (1966). Reinforcement and nonreinforcement in Rogerian therapy. *Journal of Abnormal Psychology, 71,* 1–9.

Zettle, R. D., & Hayes, S. C. (1982). Rule-governed behavior: A potential theoretical framework for cognitive-behavioral therapy. In *Advances in cognitive behavioral research and therapy. Vol. 1* (pp. 73–118). New York: Academic Press.

Zivin, G. (1979). *The development of self-regulation through private speech.* New York: Wiley.

17

Creativity and Reinforced Variability

Allen Neuringer

Campbell (1960) argued that random variations are essential for creativity because, if an act is truly novel or original, it cannot be anticipated or preformulated. A random process implies, according to Campbell, that generation of variations cannot be accounted for by knowledge of prior environmental events. (Ultimately the environment selects from among the variations [see Donahoe, this volume], but Campbell's focus, and that of the present paper, is on the variation process itself.) Campbell was convincing that variability is necessary for creativity—replication is not creative—but contemporary research shows that the process by which variations are generated is in fact influenced by the environment. Variable versus repetitive actions, levels of variability, the set of possible variants, and the probability of unlikely combinations; all of these are directly affected by consequences. Stated simply, behavioral variability can be reinforced. To the extent that variability is necessary, creativity may wither in the absence of environmental support. This claim is both controversial, because many believe that reinforcement is detrimental to creativity, a claim to which I shall return, and important, because it indicates a direction for educational and social policy.

There were many anticipators of Campbell's (1960) theory, and I will cite three of the most important: Epicurus, Fechner, and Skinner. Democritus in the 4th century BC was one of the first to claim that atoms were the bases for all physical matter, and that it was interactions of these indivisible, basic atoms that could explain all else. Epicurus, although agreeing with

Allen Neuringer • Psychology Department, Reed College, Portland, OR 97202.

Democritus' atomic theory, objected to the strict determinism implied. If all things were determined, there would be no room for creativity, argued Epicurus, and he proposed that atoms, although normally determined in their movements, occasionally swerved randomly. Random swerves solved, he thought, not only the problem of creativity, but also that of originality and the initiation of action.

More than two thousand years later, Gustav Fechner (an influential progenitor of contemporary psychophysics and cognitive psychology) fleshed out the Epicurean theory (Heidelberger, 1987). Psychological/behavioral phenomena were collectives of instances, with general laws describing the collectives—for example, as an average of many instances—but chance governing the instances. That is, psychological laws were manifestations of classes, or sets, of events. Within the set, chance, or probability reigned. For Fechner, such probabilistic instances were a real part of the real world, and not due simply to faulty knowledge. Fechner, like Epicurus, posited chance to explain the richness that underlies novel and creative behavior, and thus he also invoked both deterministic and probabilistic processes.

It may surprise some that B. F. Skinner held views that paralleled Fechner's. Both Fechner and Skinner were determinists regarding general laws, but both argued that individual instances could not be predicted from knowledge of the current state of the environment. Skinner's work, more than any other, is responsible for current research and theory on reinforced variability, but at least his early work argued that the origination of behavioral variability was not in the environment (Skinner, 1938; see also Moxley, 1997). Skinner distinguished between Pavlovian reflexes, or respondents, and operant responses. Pavlovian reflexes were determined by prior environmental events, conditioned and unconditioned stimuli. Operants could be predicted and controlled by reinforcement contingencies, but only at the level of the "class" of responses. Indeed, Skinner argued that each instance of an operant response was a member of a generic class (Skinner, 1935/1961), and that whereas the class could be functionally related to environmental events, the instance could not. For example, the class of lever-press responses, defined by microswitch closures, could be predicted and controlled, given knowledge of conditioning history and current reinforcement contingencies. Predictions could *not* readily be made, however, concerning the member of the class that would emerge at any given point of time, e.g., presses with right paw, left paw, or mouth. These seemed to occur randomly. Thus, at one and the same time, Skinner held to a determinist's belief in prediction and control of operant classes, but maintained that exemplars of the class could not be predicted.

This point is sufficiently important that I will rephrase it. Operant classes are defined by the fact that different responses have the same effect on the environment. A given class may contain many different types of instances. For example, reaching one's hand to get the salt, and uttering the words "please pass the salt," may both be members of a single operant class, each member occurring probabilistically. (As in the example just given, probabilities of instances may differ, one from the other, depending upon the momentary context, but their emission is probabilistic nonetheless.) Language is another example of deterministic relations at the level of class, but probabilistic at the level of instance. Chomsky's (1959) objections notwithstanding (he argued that operant analyses cannot account for the richness of language-see Catania, this volume, and Chase, this volume), the operant nature of language helps to explain its creativity because all operants are (at the level of instance) probabilistic and therefore potentially generative (see Neuringer, 2002, for further discussion). This conceptualization of Skinner's position captures his distinction between instance and operant class. A single intellectual line connects Epicurus, Fechner, Skinner, and Campbell: sets of probabilistic instances are necessary to explain the creativity of thought and action, and the instance cannot be explained by the environment.

Influences on Variability

These four great thinkers agreed that variability is characteristic of psychological phenomena, but research over the past 40 years has gone beyond their claim of an omni-present variability in order to search for specific sources. Three important influences on variability will be identified, with the focus on the third. First, variability is influenced by states of illness and well-being: by clinical states (e.g., depressed individuals and those with autism vary less than do normals), by injury to the CNS (e.g., Alzheimer dementia and damage to the frontal cortex lower variability) and by drugs (e.g., alcohol, opioid antagonists, and benzodiazepine) (see Brugger, 1997, for a review). In most of these examples, which are representative, effects are to lower variability, working in a direction opposite to that needed for creativity, with normal behavior manifesting relatively high levels of the requisite variability.

The second source is variability elicited by adversity, e.g., resulting from a sudden decrease in reinforcement (Balsam, Deich, Ohyama, & Stokes, 1998). In particular, many studies have indicated that extinction elicits variability (but see Neuringer, Kornell, & Olufs, 2001, for a discussion of both the variability-inducing and stability-maintaining aspects of extinction). Adversity-elicited variability is found across species, from bacteria to people, but the resulting variability is generally short-lived, because responding decreases to low, and sometimes zero levels. Variability is also reported to be elicited by constraints placed on the acceptable response class (see, e.g., Stokes, 2001). But temporarily increased variability, due to adversity or constraints, may not suffice to maintain creative activity.

The third source is direct reinforcement. When contingent upon a particular level of behavioral variability, reinforcement generates and maintains it. Because this source has been largely ignored, research will be described to show that high variability can be reinforced, including levels approaching randomness, and maintained indefinitely. This research is important for an understanding of creative behavior.

The Control of Variability

Maltzman (1960) began this work by asking, "How can the reinforcement of one bit of uncommon behavior increase the frequency of other uncommon behaviors which by definition are different" (p. 231). Part of his answer was an empirical demonstration that when human subjects were trained to generate free associations, novelty of the associations increased and transfer occurred, e.g., to tests that required that subjects identify unusual uses for common objects. Goetz and Baer (1973) reinforced novel block constructions by children and observed that originality increased. During the same period, supportive results were obtained in animal laboratories. Blough (1966) rewarded pigeons for generating Poisson distributions of interpeck durations, or that expected from a random process. The pigeons' pecks came to approximate the output of a Geiger counter's response to the random emissions of atomic particles, among the most random of phenomena. Pryor, Haag, and O'Reilly (1969) reinforced novel jumps, turns, and swims by porpoises, resulting in behaviors never before observed by any of the trainers. In light of Campbell's claim, these early studies, and there were many others, showed that a component of creativity, namely variability, could in fact be increased and maintained by reinforcement.

Important objections, however, were raised. A series of experiments appeared to show that reinforcement decreased creativity (see below) and, more to the point, Schwartz (1982) argued that the experiments described above may have been misinterpreted. According to Schwartz, variability may have increased for reasons other than its reinforcement. Perhaps short-term extinction was responsible, because the reinforcement operation involves both presenting reinforcers, when there is an approximation to a goal response, and withholding reinforcers, when approximations are not forthcoming. According to Schwartz and others, reinforcers increase the behaviors that are being reinforced, and therefore lead to stereotypy, not variability. One critical test was needed: to compare reinforced variability with a control condition in which exactly the same reinforcers were provided and withheld, but independently of the variability. This would control for extinction and any other correlated effects.

Page and Neuringer (1985) performed the critical experiment with pigeons pecking two response keys for food rewards. In one condition, sequences of 8 responses across left (L) and right (R) keys had to differ from each of the last 50 sequences in order for the birds to be reinforced. For example, if the pigeons happened to peck LLRRLLLL in the current trial, food reinforcement was provided only if that sequence had not been emitted during any of the previous 50 trials (including, at the beginning of the current session, those from yesterday's session). The pigeons readily varied and maintained high levels of variability across more than 30 sessions. When reinforcers were then presented independently of variability in the yoked control condition, but at exactly the same frequency and pattern as during the previous phase, levels of variability dropped and stayed low: the pigeons tended to repeat one or two sequences again and again. Return to the variability-reinforcing phase resulted in regaining high levels of sequence variability. These results strongly support the operant nature of variability, and were soon followed by confirming evidence from other laboratories (e.g., Machado, 1989).

How did the pigeons accomplish their task? The hypothesis was offered that ability to vary was basic, and not derived from other competencies, such as discriminative control by prior responses, or what is referred to as memory. It was unlikely that the pigeons were remembering each of their last 50 sequences (they do not have that good a memory), but to further rule out a memory hypothesis, Page and Neuringer (1985) showed that levels of variability increased when number of responses per trial increased, a prediction consistent with the pigeons acting as a stochastic, or random, generator, but inconsistent with a memory hypothesis. Here is the reasoning. Assume that reinforcement accrues whenever the sequence of L and R responses in the current trial differs from the sequence in the previous trial, a Lag 1 variability contingency. Let us now ask about the effects of number of responses per trial. Because memory varies with amount of information to be recalled, trials consisting of 2 responses should exert better control, according to a memory hypothesis, than trials consisting of 8 responses. Speaking informally, it would be easier to remember and not repeat an LR sequence, than an RLLLRLRL sequence. Thus, if the pigeons were using the previous sequence as the controlling discriminative stimulus, then with increasing numbers of responses per trial, performances should be degraded. On the other hand, if the pigeon were responding in random fashion, the probability that the current trial would repeat the previous trial equals 0.25 for the 2-response case (there are 4 different possible sequences, LL, LR, RL and RR), whereas the probability in the 8-response case for repetition is 0.004 (there are 256 different sequences of length 8). Thus, the stochastic-generator hypothesis predicts that as number of responses per trials increases, a random generator would be reinforced increasingly. Memory predicts poorer performance, stochastic generator, better. The results supported the stochastic-generator hypothesis, i.e., performance improved as responses per trial increased.

Also against memory were findings that as the time between responses in a sequence was systematically increased (through imposition of time-out periods), pigeons and rats were better able to meet a variability contingency (Neuringer, 1991). When other subjects were reinforced for repeating a particular sequence, e.g., LLRR, it was found that as interresponse times increased, performances were degraded. Thus, as expected, repetitions depended upon memory, but the variable operant appeared not to be based on memorial processes; rather memory for past responses may have interfered with operant variability (Weiss, 1964).

That variable responding is, in fact, an operant, controlled in ways that are similar to other voluntary operants, is indicated by four additional findings:

1. Variability is precisely controlled by contingencies of reinforcement (Machado, 1989; Page & Neuringer, 1985).
2. Discriminative stimuli influence it; e.g., rats and pigeons learn to respond variably in the presence of one stimulus (light or tone) and repetitively in another (Denney & Neuringer, 1998).
3. Rats and pigeons vary vs. repeat as a function of relative reinforcement frequencies; i.e., they "match" their vary vs. repeat "choices" to reinforcement frequencies, as is the case for other operants (Neuringer, 1992).
4. What is varied also depends upon the reinforcement contingencies, i.e., the subjects do not do just anything. This was shown by all of the above findings and also, more explicitly, by defining a subset of response sequences (e.g., only those beginning with LL...) and reinforcing variations only among that subset. Animals successfully delimit the domain of variations (Mook, Jeffrey, & Neuringer, 1993).

Variability is multidimensioned (Knuth, 1969), requiring many different tests to establish highest levels. In most of the above studies, one or two measures sufficed to establish that variability is sensitive to consequences. In one study, however, the results of many more statistical tests were simultaneously provided to humans as reinforcing feedback. The question was whether humans can approach the level of a random generator (Neuringer, 1986). High-school and college students were asked to respond as randomly as possible on two keys of a computer keyboard. When reinforcing feedback was withheld in the initial baseline phase of the experiment, performances were readily distinguished from random, a results consistent with hundreds of previous studies of this sort (e.g., Brugger, 1997; Wagenaar, 1972). The subjects were then given feedback—this being the first experiment in which an attempt was made to reinforce random responding—first from one statistical test, then another, until they saw feedback from 10 separate tests following each series of 100 responses. The feedback was in the form of a table, indicating how performances compared to distributions generated by the random generator. The result (after many sessions of training and tens of thousands of responses) was sequences that did not differ statistically from random according to all 10 tests, i.e., the subjects learned to approximate a random generator. This result differs from all of the previous findings, but as indicated, this was the first experiment in which such behavior was explicitly reinforced. When people are simply asked to respond randomly, they fail, but when reinforced, they successfully approximate a random generator.

Is Reinforcement Detrimental to Creativity?

The argument to this point is that variability is a necessary part of creativity; that behavioral variability is an operant, it can be reinforced; and therefore that explicit reinforcement of variability may contribute importantly to creativity (see also, Stokes, in press). In support are studies in which creativity is directly reinforced (e.g., Eisenberger & Armeli, 1997). In opposition, however, are other studies indicating that reinforcement is detrimental to creative work (e.g., Amabile, 1983). This is a deeply controversial literature that has been reviewed in a number of places (e.g., Cameron & Pierce, 1994; Cameron, Banko, & Pierce, 2001; Deci, Koestner, & Ryan, 1999), and I will not try to describe many of the issues involved. My students and I, however, have conducted two studies that may contribute to a resolution of some of the issues, and I shall describe these. Both confront the hypothesized detrimental effects of reinforcement. To anticipate the results of both studies, detrimental effects are real—reinforcement has complex effects, some of which are to decrease response strength—but the effects can be explained by reinforcement theory.

A common finding in operant laboratories is that as reinforcement is approached, e.g., under fixed-interval and fixed-ratio schedules, animals and people respond faster and faster. When reinforcement depends upon accuracy, as in discrimination learning or matching to sample, that too is found to increase within the fixed interval or ratio (Nelson, 1978; Nevin, 1967). Cherot, Jones, and Neuringer (1996) asked whether the same pattern would hold for variability: would variability increase as reinforcement for varying was approached? The question is related to real-world cases where a composer is rushing to complete a composition before the scheduled performance, or an artist to finish a painting before an exhibition. With rats and pigeons serving as subjects, and a fixed-ratio 4 contingency (the subjects had to meet a variability contingency 4 times to be reinforced) the opposite result was observed: as the reinforcer was approached, the subjects varied *less and less*, that is, the probability of meeting the variability contingency *decreased*. For comparison, with other animals repeating a particular sequence was reinforced, once again under the fixed-ratio 4. For these animals, probability of correct repetitions *increased* with proximity to reinforcement, a finding opposite to that for the variability group, but consistent with the previous literature. Thus, to the extent that creativity is based on variability, these results imply that approach to, or anticipation of, reinforcement interferes with creativity, a result consistent with those who argue that reinforcement exerts detrimental effects. Can these results be reconciled with reinforcement theory?

One additional piece of information from Cherot et al. (1996) helps to resolve the inconsistency. The animals whose varying responding was reinforced engaged in much more variably overall than those reinforced for repeating. (Other studies, some mentioned above, show that animals rewarded for varying responded much more variably overall than those rewarded for repeating.) Reinforcement of variability appears to exert simultaneously two effects: overall variability is elevated, sometimes to the highest levels; but approach to (and possibly focus on) the reinforcers constrains, or lowers, variability. The overall enhancement of variability was of much greater magnitude than the decrease with approach, but both effects were statistically significant. Disagreement concerning whether reinforcement helps or harms creativity may partly be due to exclusive emphasis on one or the other of these effects. Reinforcers have a multiplicity of effects, and all must be taken into account.

The second experiment similarly involves detrimental effects, and the question can best be introduced by describing a representative experiment.

Williams (1980) measured the time that 4th and 5th grade children spent playing with toys during Phase 1 of an experiment. In Phase 2, the children received comic books as reinforcers contingent upon playing with the same toys. The third phase was a return to the conditions in Phase1, i.e., the same toys were available, but the comic book reinforcers were no longer provided. Performances in this experimental group were compared to a group that received the Phase 1 conditions throughout the experiment, i.e., they were never reinforced with comic books for playing. The main question was whether the two groups differed during Phase 3, and the answer was yes: the experimental subjects played less with the toys in Phase 3 than did the control subjects. Some have interpreted this finding as indicating that the addition of an *extrinsic reinforcer*, comic books, detracts from the *intrinsic reinforcement* derived from playing with toys. (Note that interpretation of such results has been hotly debated, including by Williams, the author of the just-described study.) This experiment represents a large number of similar cases, including those involving creative and artistic behaviors. For example, Lepper, Greene, and Nisbett (1973) rewarded preschool children with gold stars for drawing with felt-tipped colored pens. When the rewards were no longer provided, percentage of time that the children chose to draw was significantly lower than in a control condition in which gold stars had not been provided. In many other cases, adding an extrinsic reinforcer is found to have detrimental effects on intrinsically maintained performances, including, as mentioned above, creative behaviors. The question is whether the decreases in performance can be explained by reinforcement principles.

Examples of extrinsic reinforcers are gold stars, toys, money, and praise. Examples of intrinsic reinforcers are the consequences of pressing piano keys, or the results seen on a sheet of paper of drawing with colored pens. Some have emphasized the qualitative differences between these, and have posited that extrinsic reinforcers uniquely degrade intrinsic motivations (Deci & Ryan, 1985). Just as hammers and nails have different qualities, enabling the hammer to pound the nails into wood, but not vice-versa, extrinsic and intrinsic reinforcers are hypothesized to have unique qualities, resulting in extrinsic reinforcers weakening behaviors maintained by intrinsic reinforcers, but presumably not vice-versa. The next experiment shows that reinforcement may have detrimental effects, indeed, but that these effects can be explained by reinforcement theory generally, without hypothesizing a difference between the intrinsic vs. extrinsic nature of the events. The research was done by Aleksandra Donnelly in collaboration with me, parts of which served as her senior thesis at Reed College, and because the data have not previously been published, the experiment will be described in some detail.

Children moved an unusual pen across a page of paper: the pen contained no ink. This "colorless drawing" response was maintained by extrinsic reinforcers, colored stickers, which the children enjoyed collecting. Because the sheet of paper remained blank, we assumed that no intrinsic reinforcement was present. In a second phase, we assessed the effects of adding the intrinsic reinforcer: we placed visible ink in the pens so that the children could now see their drawings as they were being created. In the previous research described above, responding was maintained by intrinsic reinforcers throughout all three phases (e.g., the drawings themselves), and Phase 2 presented both intrinsic plus extrinsic (e.g., drawings plus gold stars). In the Donnelly experiment, the same design was employed, but extrinsic reinforcers (stickers) were provided throughout the three phases and Phase 2 contained both extrinsic and intrinsic reinforcers (stickers and the colored drawings). Thus, Donnelly's design was identical to previous work, but intrinsic and extrinsic reinforcers were reversed. The question was whether the same results would be observed under these reversed conditions.

The details of the experiment were as follows. Sixty-five preschool children, ages 3 to 6, were divided into three groups. In Phases 1 and 3, all subjects in all groups were rewarded with colored stickers for "drawing" with colorless markers on 8.5 × 11 in white paper. If the child drew with the markers, that is, the tip of the marker touched the paper at any time during a trial, the trial ended with a sticker reward. The intervening phase, or Phase 2, differed among the groups. For subjects in the Experimental group, the colorless markers were replaced by colored markers that left bright colors on the page. In all other respects, Phase 2 was identical to Phases 1 and 3 and subjects continued to be rewarded with stickers for drawing at any time during a trial. For subjects in the Control-Same group, Phase 2 was identical to Phases 1 and 3, i.e., drawing with a colorless marker continued to be rewarded with stickers. Because Control-Same and Experimental groups differed in two ways—the experimental subjects experienced colored markers during Phase 2 and also experienced a change in procedure between Phases 1 and 2—a second control group was added. In Phase 2, the Control-Erase subjects were provided with an eraser and told to erase pencil marks on sheets of paper. Sticker rewards were now contingent upon having touched the eraser to the sheet at any time during a trial. We hypothesized that erasing has minimal intrinsic attraction but provided a control for change. The main question was whether providing the Experimental subjects with intrinsic rewards for drawing in phase 2 would decrease drawing when the intrinsic rewards were removed in phase 3. For some of the subjects, each of the 3 phases consisted of 10 trials, i.e., 10 drawings, with each trial lasting 60 s. For others, trials were 45-s in duration, and 6 trials were provided in phases 1 and 3, with 10 trials in phase 2. There were other minor differences in procedure, but as will be seen, the two procedural variants yielded the same results.

Each subject's time spent working, touching colorless or colored pens or eraser to paper, was summed across the trials within each phase and the time spent working was divided by the maximum total time that a subject could have been working, i.e., proportion of maximum time was the main measure. This proportion is referred to as *work time*. A $2 \times 3 \times 3$, mixed-design ANOVA compared work times across (a) the two procedural variants of the experiment, (b) the Experimental, Control-Same, and Control-Erase conditions, and (c) the three phases, this last being a repeated measures variable. The main results were: (a) performances did not differ across the two procedural variants (no main effect or interaction involving the procedures were significant)(p > .10); (b) performances differed significantly across the three phases, $F(2, 110) = 15.17, p < .0001$; and, (c) most importantly, a significant phase $\times$ condition interaction was observed, $F(4,110) = 10.70, p < .0001$.

Figure 1 shows the interaction between phase and condition. Most striking is the similarity of these functions to those previously obtained when extrinsic rewards were manipulated. The Experimental subjects' work times were influenced by phase, $F(2,110) = 36.07, p < .001$, with work time increasing when the colorless markers were replaced by colored markers in Phase 2 ($p < .01$) and then decreasing during Phase 3 when the colorless markers were reintroduced ($p < .01$). Most importantly, the Experimental subjects' work time during Phase 3 was significantly lower ($p < .01$) than during the identical conditions of Phase 1. Adding and then removing intrinsic rewards had a detrimental effect on drawing. On the other hand, neither control group was affected significantly by phase, $F(2,110) = 1.83$, p > .10 for Control-Same and $F(2,110) = .519$, p > .10 for Control-Erase.

As noted above, Phases 1 and 3 were identical to one another and identical across all groups. Of main interest were differences in work time between these two phases, and thus planned comparisons were done on difference scores (Phase 1 minus Phase 3 work times). The three groups differed significantly, $F(2, 58) = 4.44, p < .05$, with the Experimental subjects showing larger change scores than either of the control groups (Newman-Keuls, $p < .05$). Thus, adding and taking away an intrinsic reinforcer produced detrimental effects in the Experimental subjects.

The present findings indicate that the extrinsic/intrinsic distinction may be unimportant in explaining detrimental (and facilitating) effects. Given that intrinsic rewards affect extrinsically motivated behavior in the same way that extrinsic rewards affect intrinsically motivated behavior,

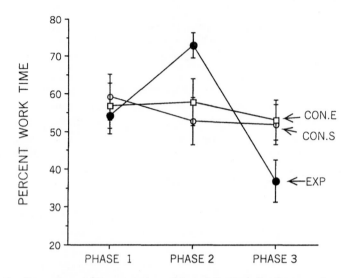

Figure 1. Percentage of time spent working at the task for the experimental subjects (Exp) and two groups of control subjects, Con.S and Con.E, across the three phases of the experiment. During phases 1 and 3, drawing with *colorless* markers was extrinsically reinforced with presentations of children's "stickers." During phase 2, drawing with normal coloring markers was rewarded for the Exp group, this presumed to provide intrinsic reinforcement. In phase 2, colorless markers continued to be present for the Con.S group, and erasing of pencil marks was rewarded for the Con.E group. Error bars show standard errors.

it is unnecessary to hypothesize unique effects of either. But the question still remains: how are detrimental effects—produced by either intrinsic or extrinsic reinforcers—to be explained?

When the value of a reward is increased relative to a baseline phase, return to the original reward results in decreased responding relative to baseline, at least temporarily (Porac & Salancik, 1981). Such effects are discussed in terms of the relativity of reward: the value of a currently experienced reward being relative to the value of the reward previously experienced for the same response (see Flaherty, 1996). The results of all studies in which reinforcers are temporarily increased and then decreased—whether manipulations are of intrinsic or extrinsic reinforcers—are consistent with these same relative-value explanations, an observation made previously by others (Bandura, 1986; Flora, 1990).

Furthermore both detrimental and incremental effects of reinforcers are functional, selected by evolutionary pressures. For example, decreases in reward magnitude, as in the transition for the experimental subjects from Phase 2 to Phase 3 in the current work, may result in exploration or behavioral variation, thereby possibly increasing the likelihood of discovering alternative sources of reward. Behavioral variations caused by decreased rewards are found in organisms as simple as bacteria (Staddon, 1983) through rats (Notterman & Mintz, 1965) to humans (Balsam, Paterniti, Zechowy & Stokes, 2002). Equally general are findings that reinforcement of one activity results in decrements in other, concurrently available activities (Herrnstein, 1997), and that intermittent schedules of reinforcement, such as fixed-interval and fixed-ratio, result in marked postreinforcement decrements in responding, often referred to as postreinforcement pauses. All of these effects indicate that response decrements are basic consequences of the interchange of an organism with rewards in its environment. Both the increases and decreases in behaviors upon which rewards are contingent serve important functions for the success and survival of organisms. The take-home message is that reinforcement theory can help to explain both increases and decreases in the behaviors required for creative output. Reinforcement sometimes directly engenders the variability necessary for creative work, and other times elicits such variability, but it is not necessary to invoke intrinsic and extrinsic concepts to explain these effects.

Conclusions

As indicated above, the work of B. F. Skinner provides the foundation for many of the studies reported in this chapter. Variability played an important role in Skinner's life, as well as the work he motivated, and I will conclude with a brief review of his writings on this matter. Skinner wrote explicitly about accidents, serendipity, and the importance of variability, in his life and work. "The main course of my life was set by a series of accidents" (Skinner, 1983, p. 400), he wrote; and "Custom is ... the villain. It stales our lives.... We tend to do what we are accustomed to do because we have done it successfully, but we suffer from the sameness" (Skinner & Vaughan, 1983, pp. 91–93). With respect to his research, three of the five basic principles described in "A Case History in Scientific Method" involve variability produced by accidents: "... it is no exaggeration to say that some of the most interesting and surprising results have turned up first because of ... accidents" (Skinner, 1935/1961, p. 86); and he concludes that "science is a continuous and often a disorderly and accidental process" (Skinner 1935/1961, p. 98). More than most, however, Skinner tried to identify and generate conditions that maximized such accidents: "... there are calculated ways of generating accidents ... " (Skinner, 1980, p. 216); "Creative people know ... how to encourage variations in their work..." (Skinner, 1983, pp. 74–75); "One way to be original is to make deliberate changes in the ways in which you do things" (Skinner, 1983, p. 75); and "[The student] can learn not only to take advantage of accidents, following Pasteur's well-known dictum, but to produce them" (Skinner, 1968, p. 180). These musings provide only informal evidence, as is the case with much about creativity, but Skinner clearly believed—and his life exemplified—that variability-producing environments can be established, a view consistent with current research showing that variability can be reinforced in order to provide the necessary substrate for creativity.

References

Amabile, T. M. (1983). *The Social psychology of Creativity*. New York: Springer-Verlag.

Balsam, P. D., Deich, J. D., Ohyama, T., & Stokes, P. D. (1998). Origins of new behavior. In W. O'Donohue (Ed.) *Learning and Behavior Therapy* (pp. 403–420). Boston: Allyn and Bacon.

Balsam, P. D., Paterniti, A. Zechowy, K., & Stokes, P. D. (2002). *Outcomes and behavioral variability: Disappointment induced variation*. Manuscript submitted for publication.

Bandura, A. (1986). *Social foundations of thought & action*. Englewood Cliffs, NJ: Prentice-Hall.

Blough, D. S. (1966). The reinforcement of least frequent interresponse times. *Journal of the Experimental Analysis of Behavior, 9*, 581–591.

Brugger, P. (1997). Variables that influence the generation of random sequences: An update. *Perceptual and Motor Skills, 84*, 627–661.

Cameron, J., Banko, K. M., & Pierce, D. W. (2001). Pervasive negative effects of rewards on intrinsic motivation: The myth continues. *The Behavior Analyst, 24*, 1–44.

Cameron, J., & Pierce, W. D. (1994). Reinforcement, reward, and intrinsic motivation: A meta-analysis. *Review of Educational Research, 64*, 363–423.

Campbell, D. T. (1960). Blind variation and selective retention in creative thought as in other knowledge processes. *Psychological Review, 67*, 380–400.

Cherot, C., Jones, A., & Neuringer, A. (1996). Reinforced variability decreases with approach to reinforcers. *Journal of Experimental Psychology: Animal Behavior Processes, 22*, 497–508.

Chomsky, N. (1959). Verbal Behavior. By B. F. Skinner. *Language, 35*, 26–58.

Deci, E. L., Koestner, R., & Ryan, R. M. (1999). A meta-analytic review of experiments examining the effects of extrinsic rewards on intrinsic motivation. *Psychological Bulletin, 125*, 627–668.

Deci, E. L., & Ryan, R. M. (1985). *Intrinsic motivation and self-determination in human behavior*. New York: Plenum Press.

Denney, J., & Neuringer, A. (1998). Behavioral variability is controlled by discriminative stimuli. *Animal Learning & Behavior, 26*, 154–162.

Eisenberger, R., & Armeli, S. (1997). Can salient reward increase creative performance without reducing intrinsic creative interest? *Journal of Personality and Social Psychology, 72*, 652–663.

Flaherty, C. F. (1996). *Incentive relativity*. Cambridge: Cambridge University Press.

Flora, S. R. (1990). Undermining intrinsic interest from the standpoint of a behaviorist. *The Psychological Record, 40*, 323–346.

Goetz, E. M., & Baer, D. M. (1973). Social control of form diversity and emergence of new forms in children's block building. *Journal of Applied Behavior Analysis, 6,* 209–217.

Heidelberger, M. (1987). Fechner's indeterminism: from freedom to laws of chance. In Kruger, L. et. al (Eds.). *The Probabilistic Revolution, Vol. 1: Ideas in History* (pp. 117–156). Cambridge, MA: MIT Press.

Herrnstein, R. J. (1997). (H. Rachlin & D. I. Laibson, Eds.). *The Matching Law.* Cambridge, MA: Harvard University Press.

Knuth, D. E. (1969). *The art of computer programming.* Reading, MA: Addison-Wesley.

Lepper, M. R., Greene, D., & Nisbett, R. E. (1973). Undermining children's intrinsic interest with extrinsic rewards: A test of the 'overjustification' hypothesis. *Journal of Personality and Social Psychology, 28,* 129–137.

Machado, A. (1989). Operant conditioning of behavioral variability using a percentile reinforcement schedule. *Journal of the Experimental Analysis of Behavior, 52,* 155–166.

Maltzman, I. (1960). On the training of originality. *Psychological Review, 67,* 229–242.

Mook, D. M., Jeffrey, J., & Neuringer, A. (1993). Spontaneously Hypertensive Rats (SHR) readily learn to vary but not repeat instrumental responses. *Behavioral and Neural Biology, 59,* 126–135.

Moxley, R. A. (1997). Skinner: from determinism to random variation. Behavior and Philosophy, 25, 3–27.

Nelson, T. D. (1978). Fixed-interval matching-to-sample: Intermatching time and intermatching error runs. *Journal of the Experimental Analysis of Behavior, 29,* 105–113.

Nevin, J. A. (1967). Effects of reinforcement scheduling on simultaneous discrimination performance. *Journal of the Experimental Analysis of Behavior, 10,* 251–260.

Neuringer, A. (1986). Can people behave "randomly"?: The role of feedback. *Journal of Experimental Psychology: General, 115,* 62–75.

Neuringer, A. (1991). Operant variability and repetition as functions of interresponse time. *Journal of Experimental Psychology: Animal Behavior Processes, 17,* 3–12.

Neuringer, A. (1992). Choosing to vary and repeat. *Psychological Science, 3,* 246–250.

Neuringer, A. (2002). Operant Variability: Evidence, functions, and theory. *Psychonomic Bulletin & Review, 9,* 672–675.

Neuringer, A., Kornell, N., & Olufs, M. (2001). Stability and variability in extinction. *Journal of Experimental Psychology: Animal Behavior processes, 27,* 79–94.

Notterman, J. M., & Mintz, D. E. (1965). *Dynamics of response.* New York: John Wiley.

Page, S., & Neuringer, A. (1985). Variability is an operant. *Journal of Experimental Psychology: Animal Behavior Processes, 11,* 429–452.

Porac, J. F., & Salancik, G. R. (1981). Generic overjustification: The interaction of extrinsic rewards. *Organization Behavior and Human Performance, 27,* 197–212.

Pryor, K. W., Haag, R., & O'Reilly, J. (1969). The creative porpoise: Training for novel behavior. *Journal of the Experimental Analysis of Behavior, 12,* 653–661.

Schwartz, B. (1982). Reinforcement-induced stereotypy: How not to teach people to discover rules. *Journal of Experimental Psychology: General, 111,* 23–59.

Skinner, B. F. (1938). *The Behavior of Organisms.* New York: Appleton-Century-Crofts.

Skinner, B. F. (1961). The generic nature of the concepts of stimulus and response. In B. F. Skinner, *Cumulative Record (pp. 347–366).* New York: Appleton-Century-Crofts (Reprinted from *Journal of General Psychology, 12,* 40–65, 1935).

Skinner, B. F. (1968). *The Technology of Teaching.* New York: Appleton-Century-Crofts.

Skinner, B. F. (1976). *About behaviorism.* NY: Random House.

Skinner, B. F. (1980). *Notebooks.* Englewood Cliffs, NJ: Prentice-Hall.

Skinner, B. F. (1983). *A Matter of Consequences.* New York: Alfred A. Knopf.

Skinner, B. F., & Vaughan, M. E. (1983). *Enjoy Old Age: A Program of Self-Management.* New York: Norton.

Staddon, J. E. R. (1983). *Adaptive Behavior and Learning.* Cambridge: Cambridge University Press.

Stokes, P. D. (in press). Creativity and operant research: Selection and reorganization of responses. In M. A. Runco (Ed.) *Handbook of creativity research.* Cresskill, NJ: Hampton Press.

Stokes, P. D. (2001). Variability, constraints, and creativity. *American Psychologist, 56,* 355–359.

Wagenaar, W. A. (1972). Generation of random sequences by human subjects: A critical survey of literature. *Psychological Bulletin, 77,* 65–72.

Weiss, R. L. (1964). On producing random responses. *Psychological Reports, 14,* 931–941.

Williams, B. W. (1980). Reinforcement, behavior constraint, and the overjustification effects. *Journal of Personality and Social Psychology, 39,* 599–614.

18

In the Analysis of Behavior, What Does "Develop" Mean?

Donald M. Baer and Jesús Rosales-Ruiz

The concept of development is an old one in behavioral science. Indeed, Developmental Psychology was the seventh division of the American Psychological Association, which "developed" into 45 more divisions. To be seventh in a sequence of 52 implies the concept is basic (or that children are important), and the current size and complexity of the division imply the concept is durable (or that children are important).

The development concept is also extraordinarily complex (Reese, 1991). The basic phenomena that evoke it, however, are simple enough: Over the life span of most of the organisms that have been studied, behavior, structure, physiology, and biochemistry seem to change in orderly, predictable, and, therefore, systematic ways (Bijou & Baer, 1961). Describing that breadth of change in detail creates a very large taxonomy. Relating the details of that change to age creates a large developmental science; and indeed, those details do relate very well to age. Stating what happens as a function of age is also stating it as a matter of sequences; and indeed, many of the details of development can be stated as sequences (and because sequences take time, they have some correlation with age). So, if variance-accounted-for were the end-goal of science, stating all forms of organismic development as a function of age or as a matter of sequences would be a scientific triumph.

Donald M. Baer • (deceased) formerly of the Department of Human Development, University of Kansas, Lawrence, KS 66045-2133.   Jesús Rosales-Ruiz • Department of Behavior Analysis, University of North Texas, P.O. Box 310919, Denton, Texas 76203.

Developmental psychologists, however, tend to go beyond description, and try to explain why that development relates so thoroughly to age; or why it so often comes in those apparently invariant sequences; or why those sequences sometimes are matters of not just one behavior changing, but large classes of behavior changing together. Then something quite different from a triumph emerges. Put pessimistically, no explanation has succeeded very well; put optimistically, many different explanations have succeeded equally well. Among the many alternative explanations of development, stage theories are seen as the "lesser evil" (Siegler, 1992). To explain why behavior changes at particular ages, stage theories postulate developing organizations of the mind that enable behavior change at those ages. Each state of development represents an internal change in the child. How this internal change produces the change in behavior, and what caused the internal change itself, are often unclear. When they are unclear, the problem of explaining development has produced not an explanation, but the invention of a different level at which explanation is needed, and at which its absence may not be noticed.

Explanations sometimes tend to postulate an end point to development as if that explained it—as if teleology were a respectable form of explanation (cf. Overton & Reese, 1973; Spiker, 1966). Teleologically, development is whatever it takes to reach that end point. The end point, however, has prerequisites, and the prerequisites have prerequisites, which in turn have prerequisites, and so forth. That is why dependable sequences are observed—sequences that are so lengthy that age becomes a reasonable unit of time. The problem then is to specify an end point such that all the sequential, age-related details of development can be seen as how to get to just that end point. This is obviously difficult. The end points offered, in trying to explain so much, tend to be global and vague (Rosales-Ruiz & Baer, 1996). Candidates such as "complexity" are nominated, but such concepts are likely to be embarrassed by one or another part of the dependable observable details of development that happen not to fit that concept. Too much of that embarrassment engenders a more contextual solution: to specify numerous end points, each designed to explain only some respectably interesting domain within the totality of development (e.g., Siegler, 1981; cf. also reviews by Flavell, 1982, 1992; Siegel, 1991; Siegler, 1989). That strategy tends to weaken the concept of development a little more with each subdivision found to require its own special explanation. "Development" devolves into "developments." The ultimate case, in which every detail is explained by a different mechanism, approaches the ultimate destruction of the development concept as such—depending on how different is "different."

Whatever their focus or breadth, these theories still explain behavior change in terms of other, hypothetical changes within the organism. For them, what develops is not behavior, but an innate capacity of the organism. Behavior is seen as the product of that changed capacity. Thus, these theories claim that what children know, regardless of their environment, is sufficient to predict when behavior change should occur. Yet the only available evidence is that behavior (including knowledge), structure, physiology, and biochemistry seem to change in an orderly, predictable, and systematic way across the life span of most organisms. When explanations of those changes must be made empirical, and the empirically demonstrable explanations tend to look different in different cases, rather than systematically alike across them all, there is a superb irony: An apparently cohesive process needs explanation; abundant cohesive theories arise, but the provable explanations of various parts of that process do not seem cohesive. That leaves developmental psychology with a great deal of empirical knowledge that behavior changes, a set of purported explanatory mechanisms that cannot be empirically tested (e.g., equilibrium, Piaget, 1975), and an explanatory logic that assumes one given change leads to another until a final point is reached.

Unlike those approaches, behavior analysis examines the relation between the environment and the behavior of the organism to account for behavior change in any sequence. Suppose behavior really does change systematically across the life span. Behavior analysis knows a good deal about how to change behavior. The mechanisms it knows are the environmental contingencies: the relations among behavior, its consequences, and its antecedents; and the past history of those relations and relations physically like them (stimulus and response generalization) or made like them (functional classes and equivalence classes) (cf. Baum, 1994). This knowledge does not establish the only ways to change behavior, it only proves that these ways are dramatically powerful and general. They also appear to be equally powerful and general at almost all points in the life span. Thus, if these ways are relied on to explain orderly, predictable, and systematic behavior change across the life span, it must be assumed that not these ways, but the application of these ways, changes in a correspondingly orderly, predictable, and systematic way across the life span.

How could the application of the environmental contingencies differ in an orderly, predictable, and systematic way across the life span? Perhaps the power of some consequences to reinforce or punish varies in an orderly, predictable, and systematic way across the life span. Perhaps the discriminability of some antecedents does. And, perhaps most powerful of all, culture changes those contingencies in an orderly, predictable, and systematic way across the life span (see Glenn, this volume). For example, perhaps culture teaches parents, teachers, and peers that certain responses of children (and adults) should be taught only at certain ages and in certain sequences; perhaps culture teaches them to use different reinforcers, punishers, and antecedents to do that, depending on the child's age or the place of the behavior in some sequence; perhaps culture tells them when to rely on old antecedents and consequences and when to condition new ones; perhaps culture tells them when to rely most on consequences and when to rely most on antecedents—when and what to reward, punish, or extinguish, and when and what to explain.

To whatever extent this explains what is orderly, predictable, and systematic in behavioral development, then the proper study of behavioral development is not so much the behavior of the person being taught, but the behavior of the people doing the teaching. That is, if development is behavior change, and if it is to be explained by the principles of behavior management—which are so dramatically effective at behavior change— and if the behavior called developmental is orderly, predictable, and systematic, behavior analysts might well look for a corresponding order, predictability, and system in how the behavior-management techniques are managed by whoever and whatever manages them.

If one's only tool is a hammer, then all problems are nails. If development is orderly behavior change, and if the only way behavior change is explained is by behavior management, then the responsible behavior management must be as orderly as the behavior change. Therefore, the study should be primarily of the development not of behavior, but of behavior management across the life span. It also should be acknowledged that in doing so the consequent is being affirmed, a serious error in logic. (Behavior management changes behavior; therefore, if behavior changes, it must be behavior management doing it. Logical? No. True? Sometimes, sometimes not.) Still, the logical error of affirming the consequent is often made deliberately in science, because, although it certainly is an error in logic, it need not always be one in fact.

The question is, do the facts support affirming the consequent, even if it is illogical? If the development of behavior management in the natural environment is observed, and any powerful relations between age and sequence and the behavior-management techniques usually applied is found, there would be a correlational endorsement of the thesis that behavior develops in an orderly way across the life span because it is taught in an orderly way across the life span.

Unfortunately, being correlational, it would also be just as good an endorsement of the opposite thesis that: behavior-management techniques change in that orderly way because behavior and behavior-changeability change in just that orderly way. Perhaps it is, after all, still the development of behavior that must be studied, because perhaps it is the development of behavior that drives what management techniques will be applied to it.

Then why not make the study experimental, to see if one of those two distressingly opposite interpretations can be avoided (both of which are true sometimes)? Ethics, especially for the human case, prohibit much of that kind of experimental analysis. When one takes experimental control of the behavior-management techniques to be applied to someone's case (especially a child's case), it is to remediate a serious problem, not to clarify some theories of development. Experimental control of how real-world people will manage trivial or inconsequential behaviors is always acceptable, of course. Control of trivial behaviors, however, is correspondingly trivial proof that one view of development is better than another. Ethics and practicality limit testing experimentally with real-world people the possibility that important, serious, and valuable behavior develops in an orderly, predictable, and systematic way across the life span only because culture moves us to teach them in a correspondingly orderly, predictable, and systematic way across that life span. Experimental control of what amounts to a lifetime of a lifestyle of how to teach what to whom cannot be obtained (Lest this be interpreted as a statement of regret, we affirm here that we would not want to live in or allow a society in which that possibility could be tested experimentally.)

Indeed, this problem of proof pervades the developmental issue. The essential fact necessitating the concept is that whole, coherent classes of behavior change in an orderly, predictable, and therefore presumably systematic way across the life span. Apart, however, from theories that say it must be, what is the proof that behavior change is indeed orderly and predictable across the life span? The simplest assertion is the pervasive correlation of behavior change with age. Behavior analysis, however, has too often changed behaviors at ages much too early, according to the simplistic timetables that once made up the introductory texts of the field. That allows a presumption: The fact that so much behavior change is correlated with age may testify to little more than an absence of systematic attempts to undo that correlation with the most powerful behavior-analytic tools available for that job.

A more sophisticated set of facts is the frequent appearance of uniform sequences of behavior change, indeed, sequences of change of unified classes of behavior, called stages, only loosely tied to age. The argument is that the uniformity of these stage sequences, and their size, may testify to their necessity; that necessity is the key fact of development, even if not yet the explanation of it. In effect, necessary sequence means that each behavior, or each stage, in that sequence is somehow a prerequisite for the next. How can one prove that a sequence is a necessary one? Again, the uniformity of the sequence, obvious to naturalistic observation, may testify to little more than a lack of systematic attempts to change the sequence with the most powerful behavior-analytic tools. To *prove* the sequence is necessary, it must be shown that the second behavior or class never emerges until the first has appeared. That is, *every* conceivable way to make the second behavior or class appear in the absence of the first must have been tried, and have failed. In the days when little was known about shaping and diverse task analyses, that might have seemed a feasible criterion. Today, there are simply too many conceivable ways of making the second behavior or class appear in the absence of the first, to ever say that all ways have been tried, and that they all have failed.

Thus, the assertion that any sequence is a necessary sequence is not provable. To prove that a sequence is not necessary, however, one need only show once that the second behavior or class can be made to appear in the absence of the first. That transforms the question from, "Is this a necessary sequence?" to, "Under what conditions does the emergence or shaping of the first behavior or class make the emergence or shaping of the second more probable, and under what conditions does it not?" If the conditions under which the presence of the first behavior or class maximizes the probability of the second are more common than the conditions under which the presence of the first behavior does not maximize the probability of the second, then that will explain why the sequence was thought to be a necessary sequence. It also will continue, however, to affirm that the sequence is not necessary.

Similarly, one may well ask how unified are the behaviors that together make up a stage? The classing of behavior so that it covaries as a class when change operations are applied to only some of the elements is a well known problem in behavior analysis; and the removal of members from such a class is also a well known problem (cf. Baer, 1982). As a result, classes, and therefore the unity of the covarying behavior that defines stages, should be thought of as provisional: some classes can be made and unmade at will; that leaves the possibility that any of them can be made or unmade, if it were ethical and if there was available the time and environmental control it would require. Thus stage, like sequence, is a fragile, vulnerable concept, because it is based on a fragile, vulnerable set of behavioral covariations.

In our opinion, the essence of behavior analysis is its derivation from and steady if not perfect dependence on proof through experimental analysis. To a remarkable extent, as behavioral sciences go, behavior analysis has been a proof-driven enterprise. To a considerable extent, as just argued, the questions of behavioral development are not suitable for experimental analysis. Too much of development will remain a problem for only conceptual analysis, not experimental analysis. (See Skinner's 1957 book, *Verbal Behavior*, to consider language acquisition as a case in point; also see Palmer, this volume, on interpretation). Thus it can be concluded that the analysis of behavioral development is not a perfect behavior-analytic problem. Two recent texts (Novak, 1996; Schlinger, 1995) show admirably that behavior-analytic principles can be applied as well as cognitive, dynamic, or genetic ones. They cannot show proof, however, that the behavior-analytic principles are the best of them, should any student-reader value proof.

From the point of view of proof, it is viable and apparently fruitful to question the extent to which behavior does in fact change in an orderly, predictable, and thus presumably systematic manner across the life span. Exceptions have been found, and surely more will, one after another. The question is how far that will go—how much order and prediction will be left after well informed, energetic, programmatic attempts at undoing that orderly predictability have been pursued at length. It is possible to prove that there is less order and predictability than seems true at present. This may not be proved, of course, but it is possible. By contrast, it is not possible to prove that behavior changes in an orderly, predictable way across the life span; that is only a disprovable, not a provable, proposition. To defend the concept of development, one can only, at any moment, point to the behavior changes that have not yet been taken under enough experimental control to change their apparent order and predictability across the life span. That is a terribly vulnerable definition of development.

An astonishingly arrogant question can be imagined: If scientists knew enough about managing behavior, would they still think that in addition to being managed, it also did something called "develop?" Behavior analysts will know more and more about behavior management, so a less arrogant question arises as well: Will scientists ever think the first question was not so arrogant after all? The fruitful course is to proceed as if to find out.

Acknowledgments

Donald M. Baer died on April 29, 2002, before this volume was completed. Don participated vigorously in the conference, honoring his colleague Hayne W. Reese, that was the basis for this book. At that conference, perhaps more than any of the other presenters, he spoke directly to the issues and concerns Hayne had studied throughout his career. Ironically, Don died shortly after the University of Kansas celebrated his career with a similar conference in honor of his retirement. The material in this chapter is reprinted with permission of the authors and the *Mexican Journal of Behavior Analysis* (where it appeared in volume 24, 1998, pp. 127–136).

The article was the primary basis for Don's presentation at the conference. Slight modifications in the original text were made by the editors to make it stylistically consistent with the other chapters.

References

Baer, D. M. (1982). The imposition of structure on behavior, and the demolition of behavioral structures. In D. W. Bernstein (Ed.), *Response structure and organization: Nebraska symposium on motivation* (pp. 217–254). Lincoln, NE: University of Nebraska Press.

Baum, W. (1994). *Understanding behaviorism: Science, behavior, and culture*. New York: Harper Collins.

Bijou, S. W., & Baer, D. M. (1961). *Child Development I: A systematic and empirical theory*. New York: Appleton-Century-Crofts.

Flavell, J. H. (1982). Structures, stages, and sequences in cognitive development. In W. A. Collins (Ed.), *The concept of development: The Minnesota symposium on child psychology* (pp. 1–28). Hillsdale, NJ: Erlbaum.

Flavell, J. H. (1992). Cognitive development: Past, present, and future. *Developmental Psychology, 28,* 998–1005.

Novak, G. (1996). *Developmental psychology: Dynamical systems and behavior analysis*. Reno, NV: Context Press.

Overton, W., & Reese, H. W. (1973). Models of development: Methodological implications. In J. R. Nesselroade & H. W. Reese (Eds.), *Life-span developmental psychology: Methodological issues* (pp. 65–86). New York: Academic Press.

Piaget, J. (1975). *The development of thought: Equilibration of cognitive structures*. Oxford: Blackwell.

Reese, H. W. (1991). Contextualism and developmental psychology. In H. W. Reese (Ed.), *Advances in child development and behavior* (Vol. 23, pp. 187–230). New York: Academic Press.

Rosales-Ruiz, J., & Baer, D. M. (1996). A behavior analytic view of development. In E. Ribes & S. W. Bijou (Eds.), *Recent approaches to behavioral development*. Reno, NV: Context Press.

Schlinger, H. (1995). *A behavior analytic view of child development*. New York: Plenum Press.

Siegel, L. (1991). On the maturation of developmental psychology. In F. S. Kessel, M. H. Bornstein, & A. J. Sameroff (Eds.), *Contemporary constructions of the child: Essays in honor of William Kessen* (pp. 251–264). Hillsdale, NJ: Erlbaum.

Siegler, R. (1981). Developmental sequences within and between concepts. *Monographs of the Society for Research in Child Development, 46,* 1–13.

Siegler, R. (1989). Mechanisms of cognitive development. *Annual Review of Psychology, 40,* 353–379.

Siegler, R. (1992). What do developmental psychologists really want? In M. R. Gunnar & M. Maratsos (Eds.), *Modularity and constraints in language and cognition: The Minnesota symposia on child psychology* (Vol. 25, pp. 221–232). Hillsdale, NJ: Erlbaum.

Skinner, B. F. (1957). *Verbal behavior*. Englewood Cliffs, NJ: Prentice-Hall.

Spiker, C. C. (1966). The concept of development: Relevant and irrelevant issues. In H. W. Stevenson (Ed.), *Concept of development: A report of a conference commemorating the fortieth anniversary of the Institute of Child Development, University of Minnesota* (pp. 40–54). *Monographs of the Society for Research in Child Development, 31* (5, Serial No. 107).

19

Behavioral Education

PRAGMATIC ANSWERS TO QUESTIONS ABOUT NOVELTY AND EFFICIENCY

Philip N. Chase

Behavioral education is one example of work on socially significant problems that illustrates the consistency among philosophical, experimental, interpretive, and applied behavior analyses. Behavioral education is concerned with studying how the environment, particularly the social environment, affects long-lasting changes in behavior (Skinner, 1968; Sulzer-Azaroff & Mayer, 1991). Successful instructional programs and curricula have been developed by behavior analysts for a wide range of populations including people with developmental disabilities (e.g., Cuvo,1978), children who have trouble with language arts skills and quantitative skills (e.g., Carnine & Silbert, 1979; Silbert, Carnine, & Stein, 1981), college students and other normally developing learners (e.g., Johnson & Ruskin, 1977), and employees, staff, and managers in organizational settings (e.g., Ford, 1984).

Despite these successes, behavior analysts continue to struggle to convince the public that excellent teaching and training could be obtained through the use of behavioral interventions. Although behavioral education has been in conflict with other approaches to education since its inception, current conflicts are often based on outdated views of behavior analysis. These older views have failed to recognize that some of the

Philip N. Chase • Department of Psychology, West Virginia University, Morgantown, WV 26506-6040.

problems that seemed intractable when first encountered forty years ago are being solved.

The purpose of this chapter, therefore, is to make three points related to how behavior analysis has evolved to answer critical educational questions. First, I will comment briefly on how behavioral education is internally consistent with the philosophical, experimental, and interpretive analyses that have advanced behavior analysis in the past forty years. Second, I will address some of the questions that have been raised about behavioral education. Of the many such issues, two are identified that were valid and important when first identified years ago: Behavioral solutions to educational problems are often inefficient and they do not prepare students to engage in novel or adaptive behavior. Having identified these problems, I will turn to an interpretation of the experimental and applied literatures as they apply to addressing these two problems. Based on this interpretation I will conclude that behavior analysts have made substantial progress in answering these questions. By providing these arguments the chapter demonstrates how behavior-analytic concepts meet the pragmatic criterion of successful working at an applied level of analysis. As a result, this chapter serves as another illustration of behavior analysis as a logically consistent, parsimonious, and aesthetically integrated field of inquiry.

Philosophical, Experimental, and Interpretive Consistency

The emphasis on identifying the environmental influences of observable behavior ties behavioral education *philosophically* to a pragmatic (Lattal & Laipple, this volume), modern mechanistic (Marr, 1993, and this volume), and selectionist (Donahoe, 1991, and this volume) world view that characterizes behavior analysis. These philosophical influences have led to an emphasis on measuring observable behavior, detailed analysis of the component responses needed to engage in complex behavior, sequencing of environments that instruct both component and complex behavior, and careful arrangement of consequences that select and maintain the behavior. In particular, the pragmatic aspects of a behavior-analytic world view are evident in the strong emphasis on demonstrating success. Success has been achieved for individuals and society (Lattal & Laipple, this volume), and in answering critical questions that have been posed for the field (e.g., the questions posed for behavioral education that are addressed in this chapter). As repeated throughout this chapter, the concepts of behavior analysis applied to education are shown to work through continued testing and evolution of these concepts using the experimental criteria of prediction and control, the applied criteria of efficiency and client efficacy, and the interpretive criteria of uniformity and parsimony.

Consistent with these philosophical perspectives, many of the successful instructional programs developed by behavior analysts share characteristics derived from the *experimental analysis of behavior*. For example, behavioral educators select consequences that are functional for the individual, provide an initial arrangement of rich schedules of consequences to promote acquisition, and gradually change the consequences so that they promote maintenance of behavior (Sulzer-Azaroff & Mayer, 1991). Behavioral educators also apply findings from the research on stimulus control. Examples of stimulus control include the use of differential reinforcement to establish discriminative control, stimulus fading to transfer discriminative control from one stimulus to another, and matching-to-sample procedures to establish conditional discriminations (Sulzer-Azaroff & Mayer).

The experimental *methods* developed by behavior analysts also have been applied to educational problems to better assure that the solutions work. Markle (1967), for example, defined a program of instruction in pragmatic terms by insisting that programs have to be demonstrated empirically to work. She described a research strategy that begins with intensive intrasubject research to establish the internal validity of the instruction and group research to investigate the generality of the instruction for the targeted population of students. Focusing on internal validity before addressing questions of external validity has become a defining feature of behavior-analytic research methods (Sidman, 1960). Markle's methodological recommendations are similar to recent calls for developing technology transfer (Johnston, 2000). These calls harken the integration of scientific and technological methods for solving socially significant problems concerning behavior, which in turn is directly related to the pragmatic criteria of successful working used by behavior analysts (Lattal & Laipple, this volume).

Behavioral education also *interprets* complex environment-behavior relations as analogous to experimentally analyzed relations. For example, the Personalized System of Instruction (PSI) was derived from such interpretation (Johnson & Ruskin, 1977). PSI is characterized by features that can be mapped onto environmental manipulations that basic and applied research has found to affect behavior (Keller, 1968). For example, the stress on the written word as the main means of conveying information is interpreted as a form of discriminative control. Lectures and demonstrations are used as establishing operations to motivate the students. Peer proctors provide immediate consequences for the students' performance in the class. The level of complexity of PSI prohibited determining how its individual features functioned with respect to behavior (although, see Johnson & Ruskin), but the interpretation of these features as illustrations of behavioral principles is compelling enough to foster both support for the use of PSI from the behavior-analytic community and criticism from nonbehaviorists.

This interaction among philosophy, basic research, applied experimentation, and interpretation has led to many successful educational programs. Examples of behavioral education have shown repeatedly that when one can identify the target behavior needed by a population and arrange for the population to contact direct training on the behavior, behavioral strategies and tactics will succeed in reliably producing the target behavior.

Problems with Behavioral Education

Regardless of the successes of behavioral education and its conceptually aesthetic integration of philosophy, research, application, and interpretation, one question has plagued behavior educators for years: Why more educators do not adopt behavior-analytic practices and procedures? One reason is that the philosophical influences of behavioral education have placed it at odds with a number of other movements in education.

Behavioral education's mechanistic and selectionist influences have emphasized part-to-whole instruction that defines complex performance in terms of the product of simpler component performances. In contrast, much of the focus on complexity in modern education has been influenced by holistic, gestalt, or constructivist perspectives. One such contrast has occurred in the development of curriculum for language arts and mathematics. One of the best documented behavioral curricula in these areas is *direct instruction* (Engelmann & Carnine, 1982). The curriculum of direct instruction is analyzed into component environmental-behavior relations, for example, phonemic responses, that are taught to mastery before moving onto the synthesis of these relations in complex behavior, for example, blending. Direct instruction is often contrasted with *whole language curriculum* with its emphasis on holistic, relevant, and complex behavior. Whole language approaches de-emphasize the analysis of component skills and start instruction with examples of behavior at a level of complexity represented by relevant tasks. For example, reading instruction starts at the level of whole words, sentences, and stories that are selected for their relevance to the population. The criticism of the part-to-whole approach of behavioral education from holistic approaches has focused primarily on the complexity of behavior that students learn from behavioral instruction. According to these holistic approaches, instruction that is too analytic, precisely programming the component skills and their composites, is not likely to lead to adaptive behavior. I will return to this problem below.

Another aspect of behavioral education that puts it at odds with other approaches is its emphasis on active responding. Behavioral curricula are developed and implemented with the pragmatic assumption that one cannot be sure learning has occurred unless one observes it occurring. Focusing on active responding, however, demands increased attention to evaluation and accountability. Critics of accountability have pointed out the difficulty of measuring complex behavior and the resulting emphasis on evaluation of overly simplistic behavior (cf. Atkins, 1969; Popham, 1969).

Behavioral instruction has also supported a number of unpopular practices. For example, in college-level education behaviorists have suggested that lectures are a poor way to communicate what a student is to learn (Johnson & Ruskin, 1977; Keller, 1968; Skinner, 1963). Lectures have been de-emphasized because they: (a) do not leave a permanent product to function as stimuli for the students' behavior, (b) are not individualized, and (c) foster infrequent student activity. Most educators, however, have had instructors throughout their education who lectured as their primary method of teaching. These lectures have become the models of exemplary teaching (Johnson & Ruskin, 1977). With so many educators imitating these models, and so many classrooms designed to utilize lectures, it has been too costly in the short term for colleges to stop using lectures as the primary method of communicating with students.

The differences between behavioral education and more popular approaches to education have contributed to teachers not adopting the strategies developed by behavioral educators. These differences have also led to a reaction from teachers that the amount of work necessary to use behavioral practices is too great for the gains in learning that typically occur. This reaction can be summarized by two of the most important questions asked about behavioral analytic approaches: "How does one efficiently teach all of the target skills?" and "How does one program a maximally adaptive repertoire for changing environments?" Each of these questions has been asked of behavioral work for a long time (Atkins, 1969; Ebel, 1969; Chomsky, 1959) and formed two specific pragmatic challenges for behavior analysis. The answers to these challenges lie in adopting teaching strategies derived from research on novel and adaptive behavior. This work demonstrates that it is not necessary to directly train all target skills and that some behavioral training strategies produce adaptive behavior.

The Efficiency Question

The first question is reasonable given the length of time it takes a teacher to develop a sound program of instruction according to the pragmatic criterion of demonstrating successful working. For example, Markle (1967) recommended the following set of procedures: During early stages in the development of instructional materials a few representative students go through the materials one-on-one with an instructor. The student and instructor discuss places where students have problems as the problems arise. The teacher adds instruction as needed to solve these problems and collects frequent pre and postinstruction data to find what the students have learned or not. These intensive interactions often involve intrasubject experimental designs, frequent assessment of student preference, measuring rate or latency to respond, as well as measuring accuracy of behavior, all of which are used to find precisely where students learn and have difficulty learning.

After the materials for a course have been shaped by such intensive interaction with a few subjects, the course is tried out with a few more students and various parts of the instruction are manipulated to determine what features are necessary for successful learning (Markle, 1967). Holland & Kemp's (1965) blackout technique is one of many such manipulations. With this technique, parts of the instruction are eliminated or "blacked-out" to determine the effects on student performance. If students learn without the blacked-out material, then it is not necessary to include in the curriculum.

The final stage of development is a check on the external validity or generality of an instructional program as it is systematically replicated with different students, instructors, and organizations (Markle, 1967). Instructional programs developed through such methods lead to changes in the consequences arranged to select and maintain performance, changes in the amount of practice required to learn the material, changes in the stimuli used to instruct and occasion the behavior, and changes in the general environment or context so that it closely approximates the environment in which the behavior is targeted to occur.

Estimates vary widely for how long following such a set of procedures takes to produce a program of instruction, but even the most conservative will make a busy teacher pause. Attempts in my laboratory have indicated that if the total time is tracked from conception to measured success with the target population, it takes approximately 200 development hours for every hour of instruction. Such figures are daunting. Unless the learning achieved is significant, such development times are prohibitive for most educators.

Answers to the efficiency question, however, are complicated by the problem of false economies. Some may think that because students sometimes learn without evidence of direct training that direct training is not necessary. For example, an elementary school teacher gives the students a reading task from a popular book, quizzes the students on their comprehension, and finds that two thirds of the class pass the quiz. The teacher concludes that instruction was successful and that direct training on the component skills required of reading the popular book was not necessary. Such evidence is not sufficient because teachers rarely know enough about the history of students outside of their classrooms to say whether the students have had direct training or not. Maybe the successful students were instructed at home or maybe these students have had the kinds of learning histories, which will be discussed later, that make it more likely that new skills are learned easily.

Confirmation from students who do learn also creates problems for the students who do not. The students who have not learned continue through the curriculum and continue to make mistakes. Small mistakes or misunderstandings often become compounded into larger problems. The larger and more complex the problems, the harder they are to alleviate. Work on teaching mathematics skills to college students who are ill prepared for college level mathematics is a good example. Approximately 15% of students who enter a typical state university have not learned to solve problems with fractions, ratios, signed numbers, and simple abstract algebraic statements (Mayfield & Chase, 2002). Often even many hours of intensive work on a carefully developed and tested curriculum is not sufficient to learn these skills. Colleges have to provide alternative instruction, counseling, and appropriate evaluation procedures for determining how to assign students to different courses to assist the students. For some students, the skill deficiencies have become so enmeshed with emotional reactions to quantitative stimuli that therapy will have to be combined with skill training to make headway. The costs of this time and effort have to be added to the costs of middle and high school curricula that only teaches some of the students some of the time. Thus, instruction is not more efficient when only some of the students learn, it has hidden the problem.

The views of behavior analysts on student failure are linked to their pragmatic orientation. Behavior analysts state their research and applied goals in terms of the individual subject, student, or client. Behavior analysts often say, "the student is always right" based on a quote from Skinner (1948): "Eventually I realized that the subjects were always right. They always behaved as they should have behaved" (p. 240). This does not mean, of course, that the student always knows the right answer or has engaged in the right behavior for a given teacher arranged situation. These rights and wrongs are determined by the teacher and the teacher's culture. Skinners observation means that students only engage in behavior for which they are prepared to perform. In basic research this observation suggests that the experimenter does not understand the principles that govern behavior until the behavior can be produced in any animal with the appropriate physiological capabilities. In applied educational work, saying that the student is always right suggests that if the student does not engage in behavior expected by the teacher, then the teacher examines what could be changed to increase the likelihood of the behavior. If some students learn with one arrangement of instruction, but others do not, then behavioral educators seek changes in their instruction in order to get these latter students to learn. This perspective is at the heart of the behavior-analytic approach to individual differences in education.

False economies also appear when one does not have an adequate evaluation of student learning. Many teachers state that they are interested in teaching behavior that maintains over time, that endures under situations that are less then ideal, that occurs under a range of appropriate situations, and that can be combined with other behavior when the need arises. Achieving these outcomes is a behavioral definition of fluency (Johnson & Layng, 1992). For example, fluent sailors *maintain* their knowledge of rigging from one summer to the next. Their rigging skills *endure* even when the wind is high. They are able to *apply* their rigging skills to a variety of boats. And they can *combine* their rigging skills with their knot-tying skills when a piece of equipment breaks. These outcomes are based on behavior-analytic ties to selectionism (i.e. selecting repertoires that are adaptive for the individual, see Johnson & Layng). The outcomes also specify pragmatic criteria for testing whether instruction is successful.

When teachers measure whether the student has learned, however, they rarely measure all or even a subset of these four outcomes. In many classrooms only the most rudimentary responses are evaluated. For example, Johnson and Chase (1981) examined eight studies on the kinds of objectives met in college classrooms and other courses for adults and found typically more than 50% of the objectives and in some cases over 90% of the objectives could be completed simply by copying from the text or other study materials provided to the student. Given such weak evaluation, it is likely that even fewer students are learning what teachers claim they are learning.

The false economies of teaching some of the students some of the time have to be separated from the real question of efficiency if progress is to be made in resolving the question of whether an effective instructional program can be designed in a reasonable amount of time. The answer to the real efficiency problem lies in whether there are strategies and tactics of designing instruction that do not require direct training on every skill. Many of these instructional practices may be derived from the experimental, applied, and interpretive work that behavior analysts have done over the last 40 years. Before I turn to these strategies and tactics, however, I will introduce the second question.

The Novelty Question

The second question "How does one program a maximally adaptive repertoire for changing environments?" also has been asked of behavior analysts for a long time. Chomsky (1959) may not have been the first to ask such a question, but his critique of Skinner (1957) resonated in the psychological and educational communities when he argued that behavioral psychology could not account for *novelty*. Chomsky asked a simple question: how is it that people can read and understand a newspaper when they undoubtedly come upon countless sentences that are dissimilar in a physical sense from any that they have seen before? (Shahan & Chase, 2002). His question illustrates the general problem many have had with understanding environmental influences on behavior: how can a model based on concepts like discrimination, reinforcement, deprivation, and so forth help society understand the complex adaptive behavior of individuals in dynamic environments (i.e., novelty).

Although I do not agree with Chomsky's (1959) solution, to go inside the organism to find innate structures responsible for novelty (see Palmer, 1986), nor his criticism of Skinner (see MacCorquodale, 1970), his skepticism that the existing behavior-analytic concepts could be applied to understanding complexity was probably justified for the time. By 1959 behavioral researchers did not have much to say about conditional discrimination, about alternatives to generalization gradients for predicting stimulus control by novel stimuli, and methods other than extinction for producing behavioral variability. Research that has occurred since that time, however, has addressed these issues and begins to complete the environmental account of complex adaptive behavior. The answers behavior analysts have given to these questions of novel behavior come from work that has addressed stimulus control, emergent behavior, problem solving, and operant variability. By maintaining a consistent pragmatic and selectionist position for answering these questions about novelty, behavior analysts have integrated experimental, applied, and interpretive work to generate procedures that produce significant, complex adaptive behavior. At the same time, this work has shown that one does not have to directly reinforce every relation between the environment and behavior.

These literatures might be useful to review in order to apply the full range of behavior-analytic concepts to answer both the efficiency and the novelty questions. These questions have challenged whether behavior analysis is successful in solving educational problems and it is questions like these that form the substance of meeting pragmatic criteria. This review will illustrate how questions like these form the goals of a pragmatically driven field and the continued refinement of goals when questions begin to be answered. If these questions can be answered, they extend the contexts in which behavior-analytic concepts can be used successfully.

A Behavior-Analytic Reply to Questions of Efficiency and Novelty

Classes of Stimuli

Behavioral educators have found that they can apply what is known about *classes of stimuli* to eliminate the need to teach every environment-behavior relation they plan for students to learn. Though Chomsky's (1959) challenge referred to classes of events that are not physically similar, many classes of stimuli can be formed from physical similarities. The behavioral concepts of stimulus generalization and conceptual behavior or, in Skinner's (1957) terms, tact extension, rely on the finding that behavior that has previously been brought under discriminative control may occur in the presence of other stimuli that share physical features with the discriminative stimuli (Alessi, 1987). This experimental finding is critical to behavioral educators because it allows them to predict the likelihood that a response will occur in the presence of some stimuli even when the response has not been reinforced in the presence of these stimuli.

The procedures that produce stimulus generalization and extension are sufficiently precise to enable behavioral educators to describe educational practices that produce novel responding where the physical features and the range of contexts that vary can be predicted (Becker, Englemann, and Thomas, 1975; Englemann & Carnine,1982; Herrnstein, 1990). In addition, these concepts can be combined to predict and control behavior occurring in situations where the defining stimulus features may vary across some measurable physical dimension as well as occurring in a novel context. For a simple example, a teacher might ask a child to calculate the area of the red rug in a doll house. The shade of red is one the child has never encountered before and the size, texture etc. of the rug are contexts for which the child has never calculated the area. As long as the child has been provided with discrimination training for the color names and differential reinforcement on a range of problems calculating the areas of rectangles, one can predict that the child will respond correctly to the problem. That some subset of the stimuli in the classes can be trained and others will still occasion the relevant behavior also makes it possible for thorough instruction to be efficient.

Crucial to understanding the kind of novelty discussed by Chomsky (1959), however, is the finding that classes of stimuli can be formed through conditional discrimination procedures that produce different consequences when stimuli are presented together than when they are presented apart (Layng & Chase, 2001; Sidman, 2000; Wetherby & Striefel, 1978). For these classes of stimuli, whether or not the stimuli share physical features is irrelevant to the formation of the class. Often this irrelevance has been described as arbitrary, in the sense that the stimuli in the class are not related by color, size, or other physically measurable dimensions, but rather they are related by the conditioning history of the individual's behavior arranged by the culture. Such arbitrary or culturally defined classes composed many of the stimulus classes that teachers are trying to teach. The novel sentences that Chomsky challenged behaviorists with explaining are composed of such classes including semantic classes such as synonyms and syntactic classes such the word order.

The most recent and powerful set of procedures that produce *arbitrary classes* are those that produce stimulus equivalence. *Stimulus equivalence* is usually obtained through a matching-to-sample procedure with three or more stimuli in a class (A, B, and C) and two or more classes (1. and 2.). In the simplest case, selecting B1 in the presence of A1 is reinforced and selecting C1 in the presence of B1 is reinforced. Selecting B2 in the presence of A1 is not reinforced and similarly selecting C2 in the presence of B1 is not reinforced. After this training three types of emergent relations are tested: *reflexivity* (e.g., A1 = A1), *symmetry* (e.g., B1 = A1), and *transitivity* (e.g., A1 = C1) (Sidman & Tailby, 1982). When reflexivity, symmetry, and transitivity are obtained, the stimuli involved are said to be members of an equivalence class and are interchangeable. As interchangeable members of a class, behavior that is directly reinforced in the presence of one member will occur in the presence of other members without a history of reinforcement.

This finding expands the methods that behavioral educators use to design efficient instruction that produces novelty. One example is the use of stimulus equivalence procedures to produce coin equivalences with individuals with developmental disabilities (McDonagh, McIlvane, & Stoddard, 1984). In one experiment, McDonagh et al. taught a student to match nickels to the written price "five cents" and match five pennies to the price "five cents" through differential reinforcement. After this training, the student learned to match dimes to the price "ten cents" and ten pennies to the price "ten cents." Finally, the student learned to match ten pennies to the price "five cents and five cents" as well as two nickels to the price "five cents and five cents." Matching-to-sample tests were used to test the emergence of novel matches that had not been directly trained, but were consistent with the prediction that the training had produced coins, prices, and sets of change as equivalent stimuli. For example, the student was able to match a nickel to five pennies, two nickels to 10 pennies, and a dime to two nickels without direct training. In subsequent experiments, further training and testing resulted in the development of a full range of equivalences among pennies, nickels, dimes, prices, and combinations of change.

Shahan and Chase (2002) suggested that research on stimulus equivalence can be applied to problems of novel linguistic stimuli like those used in the question asked by Chomsky (1959). Shahan and Chase stated:

> Thus, individuals may learn to use a few instances of adjectives before nouns (e.g., "red truck," green ball"). They may also learn that words in one class are interchangeable as adjectives (e.g., colors, shapes, heights, weights), and words in another class are interchangeable as nouns (e.g., objects, people, animals). Finally, they *may* even learn to describe words as adjectives and nouns, although this step is not required. At this point, they only have to be told whether a word is an adjective or noun to use it properly in a sentence or to hear the word used in a sentence to classify it properly as an adjective or a noun. (p. 182)

The accounts of how to efficiently teach novelty discussed so far describe situations in which the antecedent stimuli that control behavior are novel whereas the class of behavior remains stable. The consequences in these situations are important as well. Without differential reinforcement or differential reinforcement/punishment, the behavior would not be selected during training with the stimuli. In addition, without reinforcement the behavior occurring under novel conditions would not be maintained. What has not been described, however, is that to teach novelty it is necessary to describe how the responses may also vary. For this account I turn to the literature on variability in responding.

Variability in Responding

As stated above, behavioral education is consistent with a selectionist perspective. This perspective relies on the concept of *response variability* (cf. Donahoe, this volume; Donahoe & Palmer, 1994). Reinforcement as a selection process, for example, could not occur without variability in responding from which behavior can be selected. In fact, variation is a defining feature of the operant. The *operant* is a class of responses that result in a characteristic consequence and as a class each operant involves variation across members of the class (Skinner 1935). Catania (1973) clarified the role of variability in defining operants by describing responding in terms of distributions. Contingencies of reinforcement do not select single topographies of behavior, but distributions of responses. In addition, these distributions shift with changes in the contingencies that select which responses will produce reinforcement (Catania).

Skinner's (1969) account of problem solving uses the observation of response variability and shifting response distributions as the defining features of how novel solutions to problems occur. According to Skinner a problem exists when stimuli occasion responses that previously have been reinforced in similar situations, but that are currently not reinforced, i.e., they currently do not produce the solution. If the solution has been established as a reinforcer it is likely that responses that were part of the distributions previously produced by similar situations will now occur.

For example, the students are given the following novel equation on a test: $[(3g^5 \cdot 8g^9)/4g^8]^2 =$. This equation may be novel in at least two ways. First, the students may never have seen this particular arrangement of numbers and symbols. Second, the *synthesis* of multiplying and dividing variables and coefficients with exponents, raising variables and coefficients with exponents to a power, and ordering operations may not have been reinforced. Teachers have reinforced answering problems illustrating each of the component responses, but the components had never been combined in their presence. Therefore, one may assume that the both the stimuli and the behavior are novel (but see page 353 of the current chapter for warnings about this assumption).

Under the conditions described in the paragraph above, the equation is a problem for the students: any simple, previously reinforced response will not produce the solution. The stimuli in the problem (i.e. the exponents, variables, numbers, division and multiplication signs), however, share characteristics with other problems the students have solved. Using the stimulus control concepts of generalization, extension, and the conditioning of arbitrary relations among stimuli, one can predict whether these stimuli will occasion the appropriate component responses. Given the recognition of variability as a defining feature of an operant and the description of problem solving provided by Skinner, a behavior analyst might also predict that the problem will set the occasion for the student to vary the component responses until the solution is found.

The combination of response variability with the concepts of stimulus control has been described as *resurgence* (Epstein,1985). Resurgence attempts to describe the set of contingencies that give rise to novel behavior in problem-solving situations. Resurgence relies heavily on the observation that extinction increases response variability (Antonitis, 1951) to help explain how novel responses to problem situations occur. The increased variability produced by extinction in the problem situation is likely to contain responses that are under stimulus control, that is they were reinforced previously in environments related either by similarity or arbitrary class formation (Epstein, 1983). Extinction produces variation, the variation that occurs includes the resurgence of previous responses, this results in an increase in the likelihood that the previous responses will combine to form novel responses, and some subset of this novelty may produce the solution.

The contribution of resurgence to problem solving has been demonstrated by training various responses individually, extinguishing these responses, and then setting up a problem, the solution of which requires recurrence of responses that were previously reinforced. As a replication of Birch's (1945) work that resulted in an experiential explanation of insightful problem solving in chimpanzees, Epstein (1987) arranged conditions that produced novel behavior with pigeons. Epstein trained a pigeon to engage in several separate responses including pushing a box toward targets, climbing onto a box, and pecking a plastic banana. After all the responses were established separately, the plastic banana was presented out of reach and only pecks to the banana were reinforced. Under the extinction conditions arranged by this problem situation, the previously trained response reappeared to produce a sequence of pushing the box under the banana, standing on the box, and pecking the banana.

Although this demonstration was based on the prediction that responses that are under partial stimulus control will reoccur under extinction, the concepts of stimulus control and resurgence are probably not sufficient to account for the novel behavior that occurs in other problem situations. For example, students who have mastered each of the multiplication operations described above differ in terms of their success in solving new problems (Mayfield & Chase, 2002). Some students engage in each behavior that they have mastered, and still do not solve the problem. Others combine and recombine responses until the solution appears. Still others engage in emotional responses or quit the situation (an alternative problem-solving repertoire). Resurgence may help account for the recurrence of each of these sets of behavior, but what variables account for the set that solves the problem: combining and recombining the previously reinforced behaviors. Understanding how novel behavior required for solving some real-world problems requires describing the conditions that give rise to combining and recombining previous behavior.

The combination of previous responses in the presence of a new contingency has been labeled *contingency adduction* or more simply as *adduction*

(Andronis, 1983; Catania, 1998). As it is currently described in the literature, adduction occurs as a result of combinations of stimuli. The evidence that supports this conclusion, however, is not complete and further research is needed to examine the variables that produce adduction. Regardless of what variables are necessary and sufficient to produce adduction, it would seem to be made more likely if it were treated as a general class of responding, like imitation, or following rules, that has to be established in a range of contexts in order for it to occur reliably under extinction conditions. Behavior analysts have a set of concepts that address the procedures that are likely to produce this kind variability. The literature on reinforced variability suggests some additional procedures for the educator to use to teach novel combinations of previously reinforced behavior.

Reinforced Variability

Part of the problem suggested above may be solved by the finding that variability is a dimension of behavior like many others (e.g., force, duration, location) that is sensitive to reinforcement (e.g., Machado, 1997; Neuringer, this volume; Page & Neuringer, 1985; Pryor, Haag, & O'Reilly, 1969; Schoenfeld, Harris, & Farmer, 1966). Neuringer (this volume) reviews and extends this work, particularly its relevance to issues of creativity, and I will not repeat it here. Suffice to say that when reinforcement is made contingent on variability, variability increases, and increased variability can be brought under stimulus control.

Although variability may be induced by the extinction arranged by problem situations as well as other methods (Balsam, Deich, Ohyama, & Stokes, 1998; Layng, 1991), the finding that variability in operant behavior is also sensitive to its consequences and can be brought under stimulus control suggests that educators can design instruction that increases the likelihood that behavior will vary in problem-solving situations. If variable behavior is under discriminative control of problem situations, then not only will the individual component responses resurge under these conditions, but variability in responding will also resurge. Skinner (1953) suggested the possibility of *discriminated variable responding* in a discussion of problem solving:

> An example of problem solving in the sense of finding a solution appears in connection with trial-and-error learning when the organism "learns how to try." It emits responses in great numbers because of previous success and perhaps according to certain features of the problem. (p. 248)

Skinner's "learning to try" is synonymous with discriminated variable responding.

Adding this observation to the concepts that have been suggested earlier to predict novel responding furthers the usefulness of the present account to solve relevant educational problems. For example, in the algebra example above, the responses that are likely to occur would be determined not only by the person's history with respect to multiplication, division, and related stimuli, but also by whether the individual has a history of reinforcement for varying these and other related responses. Research that has demonstrated discriminated variability suggests that in addition to assuring that students master the individual operations, teachers need to make sure that reinforcement contingencies are in place for discriminated variable responding. At least some initial findings suggest that one way to achieve this variability in responding is by cumulative practice.

Cumulative Practice

One method for producing resurgence and combinations of behavior relevant for solving particular classes of problems is *cumulative practice or review* (Mayfield & Chase, 2002). Cumulative review begins by independently training two skills to a criterion and then practicing them together, usually by mixing practice on both skills in the same practice set. After a criterion is met on the cumulative set, a third skill is introduced, trained to a criterion, and then added to reviews involving all three skills. This procedure of adding new skills to old skills is continued until all skills in a set of related skills have been trained to a criterion independently as well as in conjunction with the other skills (Becker, Engelmann, & Thomas, 1975; Carnine, 1997; Carnine, Jones, & Dixon, 1994).

Mayfield and Chase (2002) suggested that cumulative review produces problem solving because it combines behavioral procedures that produce responding to variations in stimuli as well as variability in behavior. Practice and mastery of each of the individual skills assured that each involves stimuli that are discriminated from other stimuli. For example, multiplication operations were contrasted with addition, subtraction, and division operations. Practice that varies the stimuli for which the skills were used also assured generalization and extension. Rules were also taught that made it likely that the skills would occur whenever a particular operation was called for by its relevant signs. The effect of rules like this can probably best be understood in terms of arbitrary stimulus classes (Chase & Danforth, 1991).

Once the basic component skills were mastered, then variability in behavior was repeatedly induced across cumulative reviews by the juxtaposition of two or more sets of stimuli that set the occasion for different component skills within the same review sessions. Mayfield and Chase

(2002) indicated that this juxtaposition of different kinds of problems may facilitate discriminating when to apply each rule and also when to switch between rules. This multiple discrimination then may facilitate the novel combinations of these rules in the presence of the problem-solving items. Switching between the use of different rules on successive problems in the review sessions approximates the combining of these rules during problem-solving tests. Thus, similarities between the stimulus conditions of cumulative practice and the problem-solving items during testing may facilitate the transfer of stimulus control from the former to the latter.

The findings of Mayfield and Chase (2002) are consistent with procedures that have produced novel responding in research on direct instruction (Engelmann & Carnine, 1982), miniature linguistic systems (Wetherby & Striefel, 1978), and stimulus equivalence (Sidman, 2000). As a critical part of the evolving behavioral account of educational practices, it appears that cumulative practice is a component of training complex novel behavior.

Conclusions

The premise of this chapter was that in order for behavioral education to meet its own pragmatic goal of successful working that behavioral educators had to answer two fundamental and oft repeated questions: "How does one arrange instruction without directly teaching every skill in every environment?" and "How does one teach a maximally adaptive repertoire for environments that change?" I have suggested that to address these questions behavior analysts have examined how to teach novel behavior, for example problem solving. Both basic and applied research can now be interpreted to say that the extinction introduced by novel situations is likely to increase the variability of behavior and make the resurgence of previously reinforced behavior more likely. In addition, this body of research has suggested that not just any behavior occurs under these circumstances, rather, it is behavior that is under stimulus control of the novel situation.

Stimulus control research has developed a number of concepts that are relevant for an accounting of the conditions under which behavior will occur in novel environments (e.g., generalization, conditional discrimination, extension, and arbitrary stimulus class formation). The findings from the resurgence literature, then, can be combined with the research on stimulus control, and subsequent interpretation demonstrates the scope of a behavior-analytic account of the ways stimuli in a current situation influence the responses that occur. The variability in behavior that results will be constrained by the stimuli present in any given problem situation and the responses occasioned by these stimuli or stimuli related by generalization, extension, and/or equivalence (i.e., the current stimuli will determine what behavior resurges).

Further, although variability may be induced by the extinction arranged by the problem, the finding that variability is also sensitive to its consequences and can be brought under stimulus control is important for understanding novel behavior. Skinner (1953) described the phenomenon of "learning to try" that is characterized by the occurrence of variation in responding. This may be the outcome of discriminated variable responding. Finally, it may that one kind of variability, combining and recombining different responses to produce new responses may be engendered through cumulative review. A history of producing solutions that result from the increased variability in behavior and novel combinations makes it likely that novel situations in general will occasion variable behavior.

Thus, behavioral theory, basic research, applied research, and interpretation have produced concepts that help educators understand how they can answer the question of how to make teaching and training more efficient. Teachers do not have to reinforce every response in the presence of every stimulus. They can apply the concepts of generalization, extension, and stimulus equivalence to produce responding to classes of stimuli.

Behavioral theory, research, and interpretation have also suggested how adaptive behavior can be taught. The concepts of response class, extinction induced variability, resurgence, and reinforced variability can be applied to produce behavior that varies and changes in the presence of a dynamic environment. The last concept, that variability can be conditioned, may also answer questions related to teaching behavior that will adapt to situations that cannot be predicted. If teachers do not know exactly what behavior will be required by a changing environment, then they might do well to put reinforcement contingencies in place for combining and recombining responses when problems arise. Particularly in those disciplines where problems or changing environments are frequent or important, like mathematics, such educational practices are likely to be useful.

The conclusion that adaptive behavior can be taught efficiently through the application of a full range of behavioral concepts and principles illustrates a specific instance of pragmatic success that has been achieved by behavior analysis. This example of the useful application of behavioral concepts fits the theme of the current book to evaluate behavior analysis in terms of its integration of philosophical, experimental, interpretive, and applied levels of analysis. If behavioral concepts make a difference for the individual and society; if behavioral concepts provide precise definitions of terms; if behavioral concepts continue to evolve to meet the goals of adaptation, prediction, control, and verification, then the field has been successful (Lattal & Laipple, this volume). Examples like those provided in this chapter, which demonstrate the consistency, power, and parsimony of behavioral concepts to meet specific goals, establish the utility of behavior theory and philosophy.

References

Alessi, G. (1987). Generative strategies and teaching for generalization. *Analysis of Verbal Behavior, 5,* 15–27.

Andronis, P. (1983). *Symbolic aggression by pigeons: Contingency adduction.* Unpublished doctoral dissertation, University of Chicago.

Antonitis, J. J. (1951). Response variability in the white rat during conditioning, extinction, and reconditioning. *Journal of Experimental Psychology, 42,* 273–281.

Atkins, J. M. (1969). Behavioral objectives in curriculum design: A cautionary note. In R. C. Anderson, G. W. Faust, M. C. Roderick, D. J. Cunningham, & T. Andre (Eds.), *Current research on instruction* (pp. 60–65). Englewood Cliffs, NJ: Prentice-Hall.

Balsam, P. D., Deich, J. D., Ohyama, T., & Stokes, P. D. (1998). Origins of new behavior. In W. T. O'Donohue (Ed.), *Learning and behavior therapy* (pp. 403–420). Boston: Allyn & Bacon.

Becker, W. C., Engelmann, S. E., & Thomas, D. R. (1975). *Teaching 2: Cognitive learning and instruction.* Palo Alto: Science Research Associates.

Birch, H. G. (1945). The role of motivational factors in insightful problem-solving. *Journal of Comparative Psychology, 38,* 295–317.

Carnine, D. (1997). Instructional design in mathematics for students with learning disabilities. *Journal of Learning Disabilities, 30,* 130–141.

Carnine, D., Jones, E., & Dixon, R. (1994). Mathematics: Educational tools for diverse learners. *School Psychology Review, 23,* 406–427.

Carnine, D., & Silbert, J. (1979). *Direct instruction reading.* Columbus, OH: Charles E. Merrill.

Catania, A. C. (1973). The concept of the operant in the analysis of behavior. *Behaviorism, 1,* 103–116.

Catania, A. C. (1998). The taxonomy of verbal behavior. In K. A. Lattal & M. Perone (Eds.), *Handbook of Research Methods in Human Operant Behavior* (pp. 405–433). New York: Plenum.

Chase, P. N., & Danforth, J. S. (1991). The role of rules in concept learning. In L. J. Hayes & P. N. Chase (Eds.), *Dialogues on verbal behavior* (pp. 205–225). Reno, NV: Context Press.

Chomsky, N. (1959). Verbal Behavior. By B. F. Skinner. *Language, 35,* 26–58.

Cuvo, A. J. (1978). Validating task analyses of community living skills. *Vocational Evaluation and Work Adjustment Bulletin, 11,* 13–21.

Donahoe, J. W. (1991). The Selectionist approach to verbal behavior: Potential contributions of neuropsychology and connectionism. In L. J. Hayes & P. N. Chase (Eds.), *Dialogues on verbal behavior* (pp. 119–145). Reno, NV: Context Press.

Donahoe, J. W., & Palmer, D. C. (1994). *Learning and complex behavior.* Needham Heights, MA: Allyn and Bacon.

Ebel, R. L. (1969). Some limitations of basic research in education. In R. C. Anderson, G. W. Faust, M. C. Roderick, D. J. Cunningham, & T. Andre (Eds.), *Current research on instruction* (pp. 15–21). Englewood Cliffs, NJ: Prentice-Hall.

Engelmann, S. E., & Carnine, D. (1982). *Theory of instruction: Principles and applications.* New York: Irvington.

Epstein, R. (1983). Resurgence of previously reinforced behavior during extinction. *Behavior Analysis Letters, 3*, 391–397.

Epstein, R. (1985). Extinction-induced resurgence: Preliminary investigations and possible applications. *The Psychological Record, 35*, 143–153.

Epstein, R. (1987). The spontaneous interconnection of four repertoires of behavior in a pigeon (*Columbia livia*). *Journal of Comparative Psychology, 101*, 197–201.

Ford, J. E. (1984). Applications of a personalized system of instruction to a large personnel training program. *Journal of Organizational Behavior Management, 5* (3/4), 57–65.

Herrnstein, R. J. (1990). Levels of stimulus control: A functional approach. *Cognition, 37*, 133–166.

Holland, J. G., & Kemp, F. D. (1965). A measure of programming in teaching machine material. *Journal of Educational Psychology, 56*, 264–269.

Johnson, K. R., & Chase, P. N. (1981). Behavior analysis in instructional design: A functional typology of verbal tasks. *The Behavior Analyst, 4*, 103–121.

Johnson, K. R., & Layng, T. V. J. (1992). Breaking the structuralist barrier: Literacy and numeracy with fluency. *American Psychologist, 47*, 1475–1490.

Johnson, K. R., & Ruskin, R. S. (1977). *Behavioral instruction: An evaluative review.* Washington, D.C.: American Psychological Association.

Johnston, J. M. (2000). Behavior analysis and the R & D paradigm. *The Behavior Analyst, 23*, 141–148.

Keller, F. S. (1968). "Goodbye teacher...." *Journal of Applied Behavior Analysis, 1*, 79–89.

Layng, T. V. J. (1991). A selectionist approach to verbal behavior: Sources of Variation. In L. J. Hayes & P. N. Chase (Eds.), *Dialogues on verbal behavior* (pp. 146–150). Reno, NV: Context Press.

Layng, M., & Chase, P. N. (2001). Stimulus-stimulus pairing, matching-to-sample testing, and emergent relations. *The Psychological Record, 51*, 605–628.

MacCorquodale, K. (1970). On Chomsky's review of Skinner's verbal behavior. *Journal of the Experimental Analysis of Behavior, 13*, 83–99.

Machado, A. (1997). Increasing the variability of response sequences in pigeons by adjusting the frequency of switching between two keys. *Journal of the Experimental Analysis of Behavior, 68*, 1–25.

Mayfield, K. H., & Chase, P. N. (2002). The effects of cumulative practice on mathematics problem solving. *Journal of Applied Behavior Analysis, 35*, 105–123.

Markle, S. M.. (1967). Empirical testing of programs. In P. C. Lange (Ed.),*Programmed instruction* (pp. 104–138). Chicago: University of Chicago Press.

Marr, M. J. (1993). Contextualistic mechanism or mechanistic contextualism? The straw machine as tar baby. *The Behavior Analyst, 16*, 59–65.

McDonagh, E. C., McIlvane, W. J., & Stoddard, L. T. (1984). Teaching coin equivalences via matching to sample. *Applied research in mental retardation, 5*, 177–197.

Page, S., & Neuringer, A. (1985).Variability is an operant. *Journal of Experimental Psychology: Animal Behavior Processes, 11*, 429–452.

Palmer, D. C. (1986). Chomsky's nativism: A critical review. In P. N. Chase & L. J. Parrott (Eds.), *Psychological aspects of language: The West Virginia Lectures* (pp.44–60). Springfield, IL: Charles C. Thomas.

Popham, W. J. (1969). Probing the validity of arguments against behavioral goals. In R. C. Anderson, G. W. Faust, M. C. Roderick, D. J. Cunningham, & T. Andre (Eds.), *Current research on instruction* (pp. 66–76). Englewood Cliffs, NJ: Prentice-Hall.

Pryor, K. W., Haag, R., & O'Reilly, J. (1969). The creative porpoise: Training for novel behavior. *Journal of the Experimental Analysis of Behavior, 12*, 653–661.

Schoenfeld, W. N., Harris, A. H., & Farmer, J. (1966). Conditioning response variability. *Psychological Reports, 19,* 551–557.

Shahan, T. A., & Chase, P. N. (2002). Novelty, stimulus control, and operant variability. *The Behavior Analyst, 25,* 175–190.

Sidman, M. (1960). *Tactics of scientific research.* New York: Basic Books.

Sidman, M. (2000). Equivalence relations and the reinforcement contingency. *Journal of the Experimental Analysis of Behavior, 74,* 127–146.

Sidman, M., & Tailby, W. (1982). Conditional discrimination vs. matching to sample: An expansion of the testing paradigm. *Journal of the Experimental Analysis of Behavior, 37,* 5–22.

Silbert, J., Carnine, D., & Stein, M. (1981). *Direct instruction mathematics.* Columbus, OH: Charles E. Merrill.

Skinner, B. F. (1935). The generic nature of the concepts of stimulus and response. *Journal of General Psychology, 12,* 40–65.

Skinner, B. F. (1948). *Walden two.* New York: Macmillan.

Skinner, B. F. (1953). *Science and human behavior.* New York: Macmillan.

Skinner, B. F. (1957). *Verbal Behavior.* Englewood Cliffs, NJ: Prentice-Hall.

Skinner, B. F. (1963). Reflections on a decade of teaching machines. *Teachers College Record, 65,* 168–177.

Skinner, B. F. (1968). *Technology of Teaching.* Englewood Cliffs, NJ: Prentice-Hall.

Skinner, B. F. (1969). *Contingencies of reinforcement: A theoretical analysis.* Englewood Cliffs: Prentice-Hall.

Sulzer-Azaroff, B., & Mayer, G. R. (1991). *Behavior analysis for lasting change.* Fort Worth, TX: Holt, Rinehart and Winston.

Wetherby, B., & Striefel, S. (1978). Application of miniature linguistic systems or matrix training procedures. In R. L. Schiefelbusch (Ed.) *Language intervention strategies* (pp. 318–356). Baltimore: University Park.

20

Developmental Disabilities
SCIENTIFIC INQUIRY AND INTERACTIONS IN BEHAVIOR ANALYSIS

Nancy A. Neef and Stephanie M. Peterson

Behavior analysis has had a pervasive influence on the field of developmental disabilities. This is evident from the proliferation of behaviorally based interventions for individuals with developmental disabilities; from course content and textbooks on behavior approaches included in the curricula of training programs in special education; from the number of advertisements for positions in developmental disabilities in which skill in behavior analysis is a qualification; from the results of litigation mandating provision of services based on behaviorally based practices; and from policy, regulatory standards, and legislation regarding use of behaviorally based assessment and treatment in various situations (e.g., Reid, 1991). That is surely good news. On the other hand, there have been, and continue to be, notable failures and sources of dissatisfaction. We conclude that this is also good news because these failures force the field to continue to improve. This chapter will argue that continued interaction among basic science/theory, applied research, technology, and applied practice will provide the best source of improvement. In order to make this point, this chapter will (a) illustrate different types of interactions between basic science/theory, applied research, technology, and applied practice; (b) examine them in the context of developments in behavioral analysis and developmental disabilities; and (c) consider what they suggest for further advances.

Nancy A. Neef and Stephanie M. Peterson • College of Education, The Ohio State University, Columbus, OH 43210.

Types of Interactions

In the most advanced fields of science, there is a relation between its conceptual and technological arms. A hierarchical perspective holds that the organization of data into theories, principles, or qualified statements of uniformity in basic areas of science provide the foundation for practical solutions to human problems through better prediction and control. For example, medicine applies the data, principles, and theories from physiology in treating illness; engineering applies those from physics in construction; pharmacy applies those from chemistry in developing effective drugs; agriculture applies those from botany in enhancing crops; and weather forecasting applies those from meteorology and astronomy.

Applied research, in turn, can establish the social utility of the basic principles of science, provide further validation or qualification of the observed relations in context, as well as suggest new areas for experimental scrutiny through either basic or applied research. This can occur through research that (a) examines the relevance or robustness of a basic research finding in an applied setting, (b) refines an applied procedure, and/or (c) solves a socially significant problem for the participants. The information derived from this process can ultimately contribute to more effective practices because it leads to technology development. Indeed, Skinner (1968) noted that, "As science itself has so abundantly demonstrated, the power of any technology depends upon an understanding of its basic processes" (p. 704).

Technologies are "dependable ways of ameliorating societal problems" (Johnston, 2000, p. 142) through the application of technical knowledge. Johnston (1993) defined behavioral technologies as "behavior change procedures whose mechanisms have been established by experimental analysis in the terms of natural science of behavior and for which applied empirical evaluation has established reliable and general effects" (p. 333). Technologies are a true test of a science's subject matter. That is, a scientist's solution to a societal problem is often judged according to the extent to which it is practical and uncompromising (Johnston, 2000; see also Lattal & Laipple, this volume). Whereas the priority of applied research is in building technological capacity, the priority of technology is to evaluate the conditions under which a procedure works in realistic situations so that the technology becomes an applied practice (i.e., the customary or usual way of doing things). Everyday use of technology through applied practice then contributes to solution of the socially significant problem.

The relation between basic science, applied research, technology, and applied practice, however, is not always hierarchical (i.e., in which the stimulus controls proceed linearly from theory and basic science to applied research to technology and practice). In fact, the relations are dynamic in nature. These relations also illustrate the inductive nature of behavior analysis, whereby theory is driven by the observable outcomes of scientific research and, therefore, is continually modified as the results of research are analyzed and interpreted. Skinner maintained that "theories are based upon facts; they are statements about organization of facts" (Skinner, 1972, p. 302).

Given this position that theory more profitably derives from empirical events than vice versa, Moxley (1989) pointed out that "It seems an odd behavioral inconsistency that the technologist should be more under the control of theory than the scientist and less under the control of practical events than the scientist" (p. 49). Basic science is not always the parent (although it is often the grandparent) of technology development. In fact, applied research is not always the parent of technology development. Occasionally, social problems lead directly to technology development. Behavior analysis and developmental disabilities reflect these diverse influences as well as opportunities for influence between basic science, applied research, technology, and applied practice.

Figure 1 shows different relations (A-J) between basic science/theory, applied research, technology, and applied practice. These relations occur on a continuum and can be conceptualized in terms of their source(s) of control. Again, these sources of control are not mutually exclusive (nor exhaustive), but instead are dynamic and suggest relative emphasis.

Applied Research Informed by Basic Science

Applied research can derive from basic research and theory. This is represented by (A) in Figure 1. This relation typified much of the initial applied behavior-analytic research in developmental disabilities. Behavioral research progressed from extensions of behavioral principles to persons with developmental disabilities for the sake of demonstrating generality in the 1950s to applying those principles to the analysis and treatment of problems and teaching adaptive skills in the 1960s. Indeed, a defining characteristic of applied behavior analysis is striving for relevance to principle (Baer, Wolf, & Risley, 1968); showing how procedures derive from basic principles can serve to make "a body of technology into a discipline rather than a collection of tricks" (p. 96).

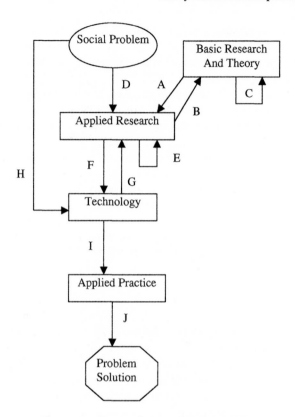

Figure 1. Types of research interactions.

In developmental disabilities, applied research on functional analysis illustrates this relation. Functional analysis (Iwata, Dorsey, Slifer, Bauman, & Richman, 1994/1982) is an assessment methodology derived from basic operant principles of behavior that allows researchers to determine the environmental variables maintaining problem behavior. Its conceptual and empirical foundations derived from basic behavioral science as outlined by Skinner (1953). In addition to introducing fundamental principles that specify the behavioral function of certain kinds of environmental events, Skinner described how "The external variables of which behavior is a function provide for what may be called a causal or functional analysis" (p. 35), and he described methods for experimentally isolating those relations.

Carr (1977) hypothesized that self-injurious behavior (SIB) might be learned as a function of a history of positive or negative reinforcement. For example, head banging might have produced attention from adults attempting to soothe and comfort the individual, or resulted in the termination of aversive stimuli as in withdrawal of difficult tasks or demands. Subsequently, Iwata et al. (1994/1982) formulated a comprehensive, conceptually systematic, and standardized assessment of the variables that controlled the SIB of individuals with developmental disabilities. The functional analysis included conditions in which the following variables were present versus absent: play materials, experimenter demands, and social attention. In addition, the consequences for SIB varied across condition (e.g., when high demands were in place, self-injurious behavior was followed by brief breaks from task demands). Results showing that higher levels of SIB were associated with a specific environmental condition indicated that SIB was maintained in different individuals by different sources of reinforcement. Identifying the function of the problem behavior led to the development of more effective and acceptable treatments; the identified source of reinforcement could be rearranged to favor selection of adaptive behavior alternatives relative to the problem behavior.

The relation between basic (or conceptual) science and applied research occurs on a continuum and may not always represent distinct activities. For example, basic and applied research sometimes are bridged by experimental analyses of human behavior (Baron & Perone, 1982), which become closer to applied depending on whether the subjects, target behaviors, and/or settings are analogues or represent those in which the problems typically occur. In addition, applied research can involve not only replication of basic research procedures and findings in an applied setting, but also interpretation of basic research at a conceptual level.

This is illustrated by research on matching theory and choice making. There is a large body of basic research on the matching law (Herrnstein 1961, 1970), a quantitative description of the functional relation between relative rates of reinforcement and relative rates of responding across multiple response alternatives (see Davison & McCarthy, 1988, and Pierce & Epling, 1983, for reviews). The matching law provided an experimental paradigm and conceptual framework for studying choice behavior in humans. Because most human behavior can be conceptualized as choices between competing contingencies or schedules, this was heralded as an important development for applied investigations (McDowell, 1988; Myerson & Hale, 1984). Although subsequent applied research indicated that the matching law may not always yield adequate quantitative predictions or descriptions of how individuals distribute their responding across alternatives in changeable natural environments (e.g., Mace, Neef, Shade, & Mauro, 1994), matching theory has been imported into applied work at a conceptual level in many important ways. By viewing all behavior as choices, applied investigators have begun to examine behavior in relation to the reinforcement (and the dimensions of reinforcement, such as rate, quality, and delay) for competing response alternatives within a concurrent schedules paradigm (Cooper et al., 1999; Mace, McCurdy, & Quigley, 1990; Martens, Halperin, Pummel, & Kilpatrick, 1990; Martens & Houk, 1989; Martens, Lochner, & Kelly, 1992; Neef, Mace, & Shade, 1993; Neef, Mace, Shea, & Shade, 1992; Neef, Shade, & Miller, 1994; Peck et al., 1996). This, in turn has led to increased knowledge about how contingencies can be altered to promote allocation to desirable versus less desirable alternatives, and to improved interventions (e.g., Binder, Dixon, & Ghezzi, 2000; Neef & Lutz, 2001).

For example, recognition that the rate of a behavior is a function of reinforcement for that behavior relative to the reinforcement obtained for concurrently available alternatives has led to applied research on attenuating problem behavior in at least two ways: First *noncontingent reinforcement* which increases the total amount of reinforcement available, has been shown to decrease levels of severe behavior problems in individuals with developmental disabilities (e.g., Fisher, Iwata, & Mazaleski, 1997; Vollmer, Ringdahl, Roane, & Marcus, 1997). Second, increasing reinforcement for alternative behaviors relative to the reinforcement for problem behavior, such as SIB, have been successful, as illustrated by Peck et al. (1996).

In the Peck et al. (1996) study, functional analyses were conducted to identify the operant function of the problem behavior of 6 children with developmental disabilities. Next, functional communication training packages (Carr & Durand, 1985) were implemented to increase adaptive responding (i.e., communication) and decrease problem behavior. Typically, functional communication training involves providing the same consequence that was identified as the reinforcer in the functional analysis contingent upon communication and withholding the reinforcer contingent on problem behavior. For example, if a child's problem behavior served to obtain adult attention in the functional analysis, functional communication training typically involves providing adult attention contingent on communication and withholding adult attention contingent on problem behavior.

In the Peck et al. (1996) study, however, the participants' problem behavior was so severe that the reinforcer could not be withheld when the problem behavior occurred. For example, one participant's problem behavior consisted of pulling on his central-venous line (a plastic tube that delivered nutrition and medication directly to his venous system), which was maintained by attention. Line pulling, however, could not be ignored because it was a life-threatening behavior. Instead of ignoring him when he pulled on his line, adults provided brief (10-s), neutral attention to remove his hand from the line. In addition, the researchers implemented functional communication training and taught the student to press a microswitch that activated the pretaped message "Someone come and play with me." Contingent upon this display of communication, adults provided enthusiastic attention for 2 min. Thus, the student could choose between two responses, each of which resulted in attention: Communication resulted in higher quality attention of longer duration relative to line pulling. All of the participants allocated their choice responding to the alternative (functional communication) that resulted in higher quality and/or amount (duration) of reinforcement.

Basic Science Informed by Applied Research

Applied research, in turn, has the potential to inform theory and basic research. This is diagrammed as (B) in Figure 1. In fact, basic research would logically be more relevant to, and perhaps more likely to spur, applied research if the relation were bidirectional. An example of this type of relation is applied investigations involving individuals with developmental disabilities which suggested that bouts of sleep deprivation served as an establishing operation that affected escape from or avoidance of demands as a negative reinforcer for SIB and aggression (Kennedy & Itkonen, 1993; Kennedy & Meyer, 1996; O'Reilly, 1995). This possibility was suggested by the results of functional analyses implemented both when the individual had adequate sleep and when the individual had a bout of sleep deprivation as a result of natural sleep patterns. In these studies, however, the relation between disrupted sleep and increased problem behavior was correlational and therefore tentative. Kennedy, Meyer, Werts, and Cushing (2000) therefore conducted basic research to experimentally analyze this relation. The results showed that rates of avoidance responding in rats increased after 48 hr of sleep deprivation, and that shock avoidance increased with sleep deprivation as an inverse function of the response-shock interval. These findings "suggest a role for sleep deprivation in increasing rates of negatively reinforced behavior and offer a starting point from which to clarify the findings of previous applied studies" (Kennedy et al., 2000, p. 344).

There are numerous potential benefits of basic research informed by problems identified by applied investigators. Application can yield confirmation and support of laboratory findings or limits to their generality suggesting additional complexities in need of investigation (Michael, 1980). By disentangling and addressing issues suggested by application under controlled laboratory conditions, basic research can better illustrate its value to the culture that supports it. Despite strong advocacy for such interaction (e.g., Mace, 1991, 1994), however, this type of research is rare. In fact, applied research is, for the most part, disregarded by basic scientists; less than 2% of the citations in *the Journal of the Experimental Analysis of Behavior (JEAB)* have cross-citations to its applied counterpart, *Journal of Applied Behavior Analysis (JABA)* (Poling, Alling, & Fuqua, 1994). Similarly, basic human operant research has had little impact on nonhuman animal research. Perone (1985) sampled research in *JEAB* from 1972 through 1982 and found that the former accounted for only 3% of the references in the latter.

Basic Science Informed by Basic Science

Although basic research (e.g., with nonhuman animals) can play an important role in furthering understanding of human behavior, it need not always be conducted for, or justified by, that purpose (Lattal, 2001). Basic research has been largely controlled by its own subject matter and research, as represented by (C) in Figure 1; from 30% to 47% of citations in *JEAB* have been self-citations (Poling et al., 1994). For example, basic research on the matching law, such as whether estimates based on it would vary systematically with the order in which different reinforcement schedules are presented within a session (Belke, 2000) is derived from previous basic research on matching and schedules.

Although both basic and applied research are open to serendipity, Cardwell (1994) distinguishes basic science and applied research based on the latter's emphasis on purpose. Basic scientists are interested in data for their own sake independent of immediate utility. For example, electricity was known and studied for many centuries preceding its practical application. The basic scientists concerned with understanding electrical phenomena, and whose names today are associated with it (e.g., Galvani, Volta, Ohm), were dead or near the end of their lives before a system of electrical telegraphy was developed in 1836 that permitted its use for any practical purpose; thus, purposes such as illumination, communication, or energy sources could hardly have been envisioned when electricity was first studied. In basic research it is often the case that the ultimate achievements could not have been foreseen, and were quite different from the original objectives, whereas "it would be difficult to imagine how an engineer setting out to design a new type of bridge or to build a revolutionary new heat engine could end up producing a new type of ship, or freezer" (Cardwell, 1994, p. 487). It is perhaps this difference that accounts, in part, for the relative lack of basic research deliberately addressing issues of concern to applied researchers.

Applied Research Informed by Social Problems

Very often, applied research focuses on delivering a service to solve a problem that arises in specific circumstances (shown as D in Figure 1). The emphasis on solving the problem may even supercede understanding the underlying basic behavioral processes that caused the problem (Johnston, 1996). Applied behavior analysis is distinguished by the fact that "The behavior, stimuli, and/or organism under study are chosen because of their importance to man and society, rather than their importance to theory" (Baer et al., 1968, p. 92).

Much of the applied behavioral research in the 1970s was characterized by this focus. Although it appealed to the demand for practical solutions to human problems, concerns developed. Despite the recognition that behavior was learned through a history of environmental contingencies (A in Figure 1), these reinforcement histories were generally disregarded in developing interventions prior to the use of functional analyses. Instead, research and intervention in developmental disabilities involved teaching new repertoires or altering existing ones by superimposing reinforcement or punishment contingencies onto the unknown contingencies that maintained the behavior. This often involved reliance on default technologies of punishment or contrived reinforcement that posed several problems for technology (F in Figure 1). First, by superimposing contingencies onto unknown operative ones, there was no consistent basis for being able to predict their effectiveness. Second, once the superimposed contingencies were removed, the behavior remained under the control of the operative unchanged contingencies, creating dependence on default technologies for maintenance. These difficulties led to a sequence of increasingly intrusive interventions that were unsatisfactory to consumers (Lattal & Neef, 1996; Mace, 1994; Neef, 2002).

Applied Research Informed by Applied Research

Applied investigations seeking solutions to social problems often lead to additional research for improved outcomes, as represented by (E) in Figure 1. Just as with patent searches in which an inventor searches for artifacts designed to address the same problem, but which need further refinement to do so adequately, the applied researcher often finds studies that relate to the same problem of interest, but which suggest a need for further exploration of the independent variables. Often experience with the subject matter will also enable the researcher to tact further needs for improvement, leading to additional research by the same investigator.

For example, with respect to functional analysis, the Iwata et al. (1994/1982) article stimulated a wide variety investigations on the assessment and treatment of problem behavior in individuals with developmental disabilities. Additional studies evaluated whether functional analysis procedures could be applied to problem behaviors other than SIB, such as aggression (Northup et al., 1991), pica (e.g., Mace & Knight, 1986; Piazza, Hanley, & Fisher, 1996), stereotypic behavior (e.g., Repp, Felce, & Barton, 1988), bizarre speech and inappropriate verbal behavior (e.g., Dixon, Benedict, & Larson, 2001; Mace & Lalli, 1991), tantrums (e.g., Repp & Karsh, 1994), elopement (e.g., Piazza et al., 1997), and multiple topographies of problem behavior (e.g., Day, Horner, & O'Neill, 1994; Derby et al., 1994, 2000). Applied researchers have sought to better understand variability in functional analyses by studying the specific antecedent stimuli used in the analysis (e.g., Carr, Yarbrough, & Langdon, 1997; Lalli & Kates, 1998; Mueller, Wilczynski, Moore, Fusilier, & Trahant, 2001; Van Camp et al., 2000) and the establishing operations that precede analyses (e.g., Berg et al., 2000; Kennedy & Meyer, 1996; O'Reilly & Carey, 1996). Researchers have sought to further refine functional analysis procedures by clarifying the effects of equal versus unequal reinforcer duration (e.g., Fisher, Piazza, & Chiang, 1996) and the content of verbal attention provided (e.g., Fisher, Ninness, Piazza, & Owen-DeSchryver, 1996). Applied research continually informs applied research because each study raises questions in the process of answering others.

Technology Informed by Applied Research

In basic research, as we have shown, social significance of the outcomes of research is not a concern. In fact, concerns about social significance may even hinder discovery in basic science by constraining what is investigated (Deitz, 1978). In applied behavioral research, however, the social importance of the goals, procedures, and effects of applied research are critical to adoption of technology (Schwartz & Baer, 1991; Wolf, 1978), and "practical importance, specifically ... power in altering behavior enough to be socially important, is the essential criterion" of the extent of its contribution or effectiveness (Baer et al., 1968, p. 96). This influence is represented by (F) in Figure 1. It is not always necessary that demand precede technology, however. Many advances in the field of developmental disabilities occurred because applied behavior analysis had shown it was possible, and until the possibility existed, there was no precedent for seeking it as a solution.

Mace (1991) suggested an investigative sequence for technology development that involves (a) initial experimental demonstration of the effects of a procedure on a single subject, (b) systematic replications that vary subject, setting, and response variables, (c) demonstrations of short- and long-term maintenance of intervention effects with a small number of participants, (d) detailed analysis of favorable and unfavorable responses to intervention, (e) large-scale studies documenting the effectiveness in the population, and (f) large-scale studies comparing the effectiveness of alternative interventions. This sequence of investigation implies that numerous applied studies must be conducted in order to develop a technology. The abundance of applied research in the area of functional analysis as described above is somewhat illustrative of the line of research suggested by Mace in order to advance a technology.

Applied Research Informed by Technology

Technological application does not focus on asking experimental questions (Johnston, 1991). Instead, efforts in technological application consist primarily of delivering a service and most typically involve assessment, selection and adjustment of procedures, and continuing field evaluation. Experimental questions, however, sometimes will arise when procedures fail to produce the desired effects (Johnston). New research questions may develop as a result of the application of technology. This relation is shown by (G) in Figure 1. Thus, applied research has not derived exclusively from basic research; it is also derived from the demands that technology places on it.

For example, although a technology for functional analysis now exists, some argue that this technology is limited because of the resources and expertise necessary for practitioners (e.g., school personnel) to correctly implement, analyze the outcomes of, and interpret the findings of such assessments. Applied researchers therefore have begun to address the issue of practitioner training. Iwata et al. (2000) and Pindiprolu, Peterson, Rule, and Lignuaris/Kraft (2003), for example, examined the effects of different training procedures on the design and implementation of functional analyses.

Technology Informed By Social Problems

Joseph Henry (1886), one of the American founders of science as a profession, stated that 'in order that an important invention may be successful... the scientific principle on which it is to be founded must be known" (p. 315). This position is contradicted, however, by the fact that medieval cathedrals in regular use today were constructed without benefit of established theories of engineering and physics, just as Aristotle's description of why beds were corded with ropes side-to-side rather than diagonally occurred before principles of forces at right angles had been formally articulated. Advances in technology did and do proceed even when they precede scientific explanation of it. As pointed out by Cardwell (1994) "it would be ridiculous to suppose that invention has to wait humbly, cap in hand, for science to open the door before it can proceed. Technology is purposive and it tends…to be positivist. The criterion is simply, does it work?" (pp. 492–493). Technology also can be used without knowledge of its existing theories and principles.

As demonstrated by Petroski's (1992) examination of the histories of forks, zippers, screws, and scoops to nuts, contemporary artifacts typically evolved as a result of someone's dissatisfaction with a current state of affairs. Similarly, solutions to problems in developmental disabilities are to a large extent influenced by concerns identified by those responsible for these individuals' care, education, and habilitation (e.g., parents, teachers, service providers), as represented by both (H) and (A) in Figure 1.

The development of the Self-Injurious Behavior Inhibiting System (SIBIS) technology provides an example of social problems informing technology (H). In his article on controversial default technologies, Iwata (1988) relates the story of the development of SIBIS. This technology was developed as a direct result of the problem faced by Leslie and Moosa Grant, the parents of a girl with autism who engaged in face and head hitting so severe that it had produced lacerations to the bone and almost severed an ear. After repeated unsuccessful attempts for many years to treat their daughter's SIB based on professional recommendations, they built their own device for delivering contingent mild electric shock, which was cumbersome, but effective in eliminating their daughter's SIB. They approached Johns Hopkins Applied Physics Laboratory (APL) to help them build a better device. Although the impetus for the development of SIBIS was the Grant's need to effectively and rapidly attenuate their daughter's SIB (relation H), the technology was served when it in turn led to systematic examination through applied research. APL enlisted the help of several professionals in the fields of behavioral science and the treatment of SIB, who designed clinical studies that evaluated each new component of the system as it was developed (relation G). This led to additional components being suggested and developed (relation F).

Applied Practice Informed By Technology

In the end, no matter how well grounded in basic science and effective a procedure might be, it will not be widely used if it does not benefit society in a meaningful way. The adoption of behavior analysis in developmental disabilities occurred to a large extent because it provided effective, practical technologies that solved the problems and concerns identified by society in the education and treatment of those citizens. The adoption and use of behavioral techniques by society is often referred to as *technology transfer* (indicated by I in Figure 1).

As a result of the abundance of applied research and technology development activities, functional analysis has been shown to be a fairly reliable solution to an applied problem, permitting the development of more consistently effective reinforcement-based treatments (Iwata, Pace, et al., 1994; Pelios, Morren, Tesch, & Axelrod, 1999). This has led to functional analysis being adopted by members of the public as a useful tool. For example, after examining the current research on destructive behaviors in individuals with developmental disabilities, the conclusion of the NIH Consensus Development Conference (National Institutes of Health, 1991) was that treatments for SIB should be based on an analysis of environmental situations and consequences (in addition to medical and psychiatric conditions and skills deficits). Furthermore, when Congress passed the 1997 Amendments to the Individuals with Disabilities Education Act, they included a mandate that functional behavior assessments be conducted for all students with disabilities for whom an educational placement change was being considered as a result of problem behavior. Additional evidence of widespread adoption of the functional analysis technology is the recent publication of books and materials, such as *Functional assessment: Strategies to prevent and remediate challenging behavior in school settings* by Chandler and Dahlquist (2002), a textbook designed to provide the general public (i.e., general educators, special educators, parents) with information on how to conduct a functional assessment.

Some argue that behavior analysis has few, if any, technologies that have sufficiently matured to be transferred to the larger market (Pennypacker & Hench, 1997). Pennypacker (1986) noted that there is often a gap between a technique that has practical potential and delivery of the technique to the marketplace. Johnston (2000) suggested that this gap is often not closed because of the academic research style used by most investigators. That is, research often evolves from the experimenters' own histories and opportunities with respect to the subject matter (as shown by E in Figure 1), similar to the manner in which basic research evolves from previous basic research (as shown by C in Figure 1). Although this may result in a large and varied literature documenting the effective application of procedures and ultimately lead to their adoption (as shown by F and I, respectively, in Figure 1), it may not be the most efficient, focused, or coordinated way to pursue technology development. Pennypacker (1986) proposed that the pathway indicated on Figure 1 as (I) could be strengthened if research for the purpose of technology development was driven by the specific outcomes or deliverables (i.e., technology) needed.

Facilitating Future Failure and Success

As noted by Azrin (1977) "...the public that pays for our research believes that understanding will result in personal benefit. A 'promissory note' is implicit that basic research will lead to application" (p. 141). "Personal benefit" through "application" is indicated by (J) in the figure; a solution to the social problem. Both development (through discovery) and growth (through demonstrations) are necessary to that purpose (Morris, 1991), and each of the research relations outlined above contributes to it. The dynamic relations illustrated above have played an important role in the development of behavior analysis in developmental disabilities, and may be worthy of promotion.

To the extent that course corrections have been or are needed, the issues are of degree and balance for, as Petroski (1992) noted, 'what constitutes a useful improvement to one person may represent a deterioration to another" (p. 248). With respect to degree, there remain gaps in both the connection between basic and applied research (A and B in Figure 1) and between applied research, technology, and practice (F and I in Figure 1; Neef, 1995). In order to help address those gaps, it is useful to examine areas in which there have been relative successes. The matching law and functional analysis are good examples of these respective connections. In fact, in research citations in *Journal of Applied Behavior Analysis* (*JABA*) over the last 15 years, the Herrnstein (1961) and Herrnstein (1970) articles on matching law are two of the most frequently cited articles from basic research, and Iwata et al. (1994/1982) on functional analysis is the most frequently cited study in applied research.

Both functional analysis and matching were supported by an extensive research base. Matching had been the subject of decades of basic research, followed by "bridge" studies that examined whether the variables identified in laboratory research operated similarly under more naturalistic conditions (Fisher & Mazur, 1997). Functional analyses of self-injury were reported for 152 cases in an experimental epidemiological analysis (Iwata, Pace, et al., 1994), and have been the topic of numerous additional investigations.

Second, that research base was made accessible to its potential users. Potential applications of basic research on matching to human performance were described and published in journals read by applied researchers (e.g.,

Epling & Pierce, 1983; McDowell, 1988; Myerson & Hale, 1984; Pierce & Epling, 1995, Strand, 2001). Likewise, research on functional assessment methodologies was summarized in practitioner-oriented journals (e.g., *School Psychology Review*) and books (e.g., Chandler & Dahlquist, 2002) and was translated in terms that required little response effort for the consumer.

That is no small task, either in importance or difficulty. The developer's research is initially controlled by a problem or discovering a relation independent of how that information can be best packaged for the consumer. For example, cans were developed as a solution for preserving food long before attention was given to how the consumer might gain access to the contents (the first patent for a can opener was obtained almost 50 years later). Prior to that time, Petroski (1992) reports that a tin carried by an explorer on one of Parry's Arctic expeditions bore the instructions, "Cut round on the top with a chisel and hammer" (p. 186). Similarly, the content of research articles is typically not presented or "packaged" in a way that makes the information accessible to consumers not equipped with specialized "tools" (e.g., the finding that inverse response rates with the subtraction ratio, indicating negative sensitivity to the negative slope conditions, and analyses showing a two state pattern, do not support molar maximization [Jacobs & Hackenberg, 2000]). In addition, through the process of experimentation, developers have an extensive history of behavior under the control of the subject matter that the consumer does not. The developer's behavior has been shaped by contingencies of extensive interaction with the subject matter, whereas the potential consumer is provided only with the developer's verbal stimuli culminating from that history. Even if understood, implementation or application would not be as facile for the consumer as for the developer who has that history.

A third potential factor that may have facilitated connections is that both matching and functional analysis had potential to address a significant problem or issue of relevance to consumers. Matching provided applied researchers with both a methodological and conceptual framework to better analyze target behaviors in their areas and populations of interest. Functional analysis provided a means of developing more effective interventions for behavior problems that were of significant concern to parents, teachers, and administrators, particularly given that inclusion policies in special education discouraged simply referring students with behavior problems for alternative placements.

Fourth, the methods could be tailored to local conditions to match the needs of its consumers. As discussed above, matching was imported at more of a qualitative than quantitative level when mathematical predictions proved limited in applied situations. Similarly, brief functional analyses and alternative functional assessment methods were developed when available resources rendered extended experimental analyses in analogue situations impractical for use by school personnel. Those decisions involve compromises (e.g., precision versus practicality) because it is a logical impossibility for all requirements to be met when those requirements are in conflict. Because all developments imply a degree of failure along some dimension that cannot be satisfied without sacrificing another dimension (e.g., in terms of cost, resources, scope, precision, utility, accessibility, control, relevance, etc.), usage necessitates choices concerning to what extent and along which dimensions that failure will be manifest.

Conclusions

The above factors pertaining to transfer are similar to some of those that have been cited by others (e.g., Stolz, 1981); they are illustrative rather than exhaustive, and may prove not to be the most important ones. Much has been written about the process of technology transfer, but such accounts themselves remain largely theoretical. It would seem, however, that whatever applies to dissemination and adoption of applied technology to practice would have parallels in the transfer from basic science to applied research.

In terms of balance, models have been proposed, including those adopted from medicine (Mace, 1991) and research and development (Johnston, 2000), for coordinated progression and systematic, purposeful interaction. Although there would appear to be a great deal to be gained from such efforts, it is not clear that contingencies operate or could easily be arranged to support them, as the above examination suggests. Many applied researchers' activities, for example, are controlled by the practical needs and nature of the problems in the human service settings in which their research is conducted (Michael, 1980; Reid, 1991), whereas many basic researchers' activities are controlled by lawful relations among features of behavior seemingly irrelevant to human problems; it is not clear that either basic or applied researchers are prepared to forsake their current interests to address a different agenda or a common goal.

Fortunately, each of the types of research interactions described above has its proponents and, just as fortunately, most of those proponents are modeling or otherwise facilitating the type they advocate. Our discipline (behavior analysis) and the fields in which it operates (e.g., developmental disabilities) have been well served by such variation and diversity.

References

Azrin, N. H. (1977). A strategy for applied research.: Learning based but outcome oriented. *American Psychologist, 32,* 140–149.

Baer, D. M., Wolf, M. M., & Risley, T. R. (1968). Some current dimensions of applied behavior analysis. *Journal of Applied Behavior Analysis, 1,* 91–97.

Baron, A., & Perone, M. (1982). The place of human subject in the operant laboratory. *The Behavior Analyst, 5,* 143–158.

Belke, T. W. (2000). Studies of wheel-running reinforcement: Parameters of Herrnstein's (1970) response-strength equation vary with schedule order. *Journal of the Experimental Analysis of Behavior, 73,* 319–331.

Berg, W. K., Peck, S., Wacker, D. P., Harding, J., McComas, J., Richman, D., & Brown, K. (2000). The effects of presession exposure to attention on the results of assessments of attention as a reinforcer. *Journal of Applied Behavior Analysis, 33,* 463–477.

Binder, L. M., Dixon, M. R., & Ghezzi, P. M. (2000). A procedure to teach self-control to children with attention deficit hyperactivity disorder. *Journal of Applied Behavior Analysis, 33,* 233–237.

Cardwell, D. S. L. (1994). *The Norton history of technology.* London: Fontana Press.

Carr, E. G. (1977). The motivation of self-injurious behavior. *Psychological Bulletin, 84,* 800–816.

Carr, E. G., & Durand, V. M. (1985). Reducing behavior problems through functional communication training. *Journal of Applied Behavior Analysis, 18,* 111–126.

Carr, E. G., Yarbrough, S. C., & Langdon, N. A. (1997). Effects of idiosyncratic stimulus variables on functional analysis outcomes. *Journal of Applied Behavior Analysis, 30,* 673–686.

Chandler, L. K., & Dahlquist, C. M. (2002). *Functional assessment: Strategies to prevent and remediate challenging behavior in school settings.* Columbus: Merrill Prentice Hall.

Cooper, L. J., Wacker, D. Brown, K., McComas, J. J., Peck, S. M., Drew, J., Asmus, J., & Kayser, K. (1999). Use of a concurrent operants paradigm to evaluate reinforcers during treatment of food refusal. *Behavior Modification, 23,* 3–40.

Davison, M., & McCarthy, D. (1988). *The matching law: A research review.* Hillsdale, NJ: Erlbaum..

Day, H. M., Horner, R. H., & O'Neill, R. E. (1994). Multiple functions of problem behaviors: Assessment and intervention. *Journal of Applied Behavior Analysis, 27,* 279–289.

Derby, K. M., Hagopian, L., Fisher, W. W., Richman, D., Augustine, M., Fahs, A., & Thompson, R. (2000). Functional analysis of aberrant behavior through measurement of separate response topographies. *Journal of Applied Behavior Analysis, 33,* 113–117.

Derby, K. M., Wacker, D. P., Peck, S., Sasso, G., DeRaad, A., Berg, W., Asmus, J., & Ulrich, S. (1994). Functional analysis of separate topographies of aberrant behavior. *Journal of Applied Behavior Analysis, 27,* 267–278.

Deitz, S. M. (1978). Current status of applied behavior analysis: Science versus technology. *American Psychologist, 33,* 805–814.

Dixon, M. R., Benedict, H., & Larson, T. (2001). Functional analysis and treatment of inappropriate verbal behavior. *Journal of Applied Behavior Analysis, 34,* 361–363.

Epling, W., F., & Pierce, W. D. (1983). Applied behavior analysis: New directions from the laboratory. *The Behavior Analyst, 6,* 27–37.

Fisher, S. M., Iwata, B. A., & Mazaleski, J. L. (1997). Noncontingent delivery of arbitrary reinforcers as treatment for self-injurious behavior. *Journal of Applied Behavior Analysis, 30,* 239–249.

Fisher, W. W., & Mazur, J. E. (1997). Basic and applied research on choice responding. *Journal of Applied Behavior Analysis, 30,* 387–410.

Fisher, W. W., Ninness, H. A. C., Piazza, C. C., & Owen-DeSchryver, J. S. (1996). On the reinforcing effects of the content of verbal attention. *Journal of Applied Behavior Analysis, 29,* 235–238.

Fisher, W. W., Piazza, C. C., & Chiang, C. L. (1996). Effects of equal and unequal reinforcer duration during functional analysis. *Journal of Applied Behavior Analysis, 29,* 117–120.

Henry, J. (1886). *Scientific writings of Joseph Henry.* Washington: Smithsonian Institution.

Herrnstein, R. J. (1961). Relative and absolute strength of response as a function of frequency of reinforcement. *Journal of the Experimental Analysis of Behavior, 4,* 267–272.

Herrnstein, R. J. (1970). On the law of effect. *Journal of the Experimental Analysis of Behavior, 13,* 243–266.

Iwata, B. A. (1988). The development and adoption of controversial default technologies. *The Behavior Analyst, 11,* 149–157.

Iwata, B. A., Dorsey, M. F., Slifer, K. J., Bauman, K. E., & Richman, G. S. (1994). Toward a functional analysis of self-injury. *Journal of Applied Behavior Analysis, 27,* 197–209. (Reprinted from *Analysis and Intervention in Developmental Disabilities, 2,* 3–20, 1982).

Iwata, B. A., Pace, G. M., Dorsey, M. F., Zarcone, J. R., Vollmer, T. R., Smith, R. G., Rodgers, T. A., Lerman, D. C., Shore, B. A., Mazaleski, J. L., Goh, H. L., Cowdery, G. E., Kalsher, M. J., McCosh, K. C., & Willis, K. D. (1994). The functions of self-injurious behavior: An experimental-epidemiological analysis. *Journal of Applied Behavior Analysis, 27,* 215–240.

Iwata, B. A., Wallace, M. D., Kahng, S., Lindberg, J. S., Roscoe, E. M., Conners, J., Hanley, G. P., Thompson, R. H., & Worsdell, A. S. (2000). Skill acquisition in the implementation of functional analysis methodology. *Journal of Applied Behavior Analysis, 33,* 181–194.

Jacobs, E. A., & Hackenberg, T. D. (2000). Human performance on negative slope schedules of points exchangeable for money: A failure of molar maximization. *Journal of the Experimental Analysis of Behavior, 73,* 241–260.

Johnston, J. M. (1991). We need a new model of technology. *Journal of Applied Behavior Analysis, 24,* 425–427.

Johnston, J. M. (1993). A model for developing and evaluating behavioral technology. In R. Van Houten & S. Axelrod (Eds.), *Effective behavioral treatment: Issues and implementation* (pp. 323–343). New York: Plenum.

Johnston, J. M. (1996). Distinguishing between applied research and practice. *The Behavior Analyst, 19,* 35–47.

Johnston, J. M. (2000). Behavior analysis and the R & D paradigm. *The Behavior Analyst, 23,* 141–148.

Kennedy, C. H., & Itkonen, T. (1993). Effects of setting events on the problem behavior of students with severe disabilities. *Journal of Applied Behavior Analysis, 26,* 321–327.

Kennedy, C. H., & Meyer, K. A. (1996). Sleep deprivation, allergy symptoms, and negatively reinforced problem behavior. *Journal of Applied Behavior Analysis, 29,* 133–135.

Kennedy, C. H., Meyer, K. A., Werts, M. G., & Cushing, L. S. (2000). Effects of sleep deprivation on free-operant avoidance. *Journal of the Experimental Analysis of Behavior, 73,* 333–345.

Lalli, J. S., & Kates, K. (1998). The effect of reinforcer preference on functional analysis outcomes. *Journal of Applied Behavior Analysis, 31,* 79–90.

Lattal, K. A. (2001). The human side of animal behavior. *The Behavior Analyst, 24,* 147–161.

Lattal, K. A., & Neef, N. A. (1996). Recent reinforcement-schedule research and applied behavior analysis. *Journal of Applied Behavior Analysis, 29,* 213–230.

Mace, F. C. (1991). Technological to a fault or faulty approach to technology development? *Journal of Applied Behavior Analysis, 24,* 433–435.

Mace, F. C. (1994). Basic research needed for stimulating the development of behavioral technologies. *Journal of the Experimental Analysis of Behavior, 61,* 529–550.

Mace, F. C., & Knight, D. (1986). Functional analysis and treatment of severe pica. *Journal of Applied Behavior Analysis, 19,* 411–416.

Mace, F. C., & Lalli, J. S. (1991). Linking descriptive and experimental analysis in the treatment of bizarre speech. *Journal of Applied Behavior Analysis, 24,* 553–562.

Mace, F. C., McCurdy, B., & Quigley, E. A. (1990). A collateral effect of reward predicted by matching theory. *Journal of Applied Behavior Analysis, 23,* 197–205.

Mace, F. C., Neef, N. A., Shade, D., & Mauro, B. C. (1994). Limited matching on concurrent-schedule reinforcement of academic behavior. *Journal of Applied Behavior Analysis, 27,* 585–596.

Martens, B. K., Halperin, S., Pummel, J. E., & Kilpatrick, D. (1990). Matching theory applied to contingent teacher attention. *Behavioral Assessment, 12,* 139–156.

Martens, B. K., & Houk, J. L. (1989). The application of Herrnstein's law of effect to disruptive and on-task behavior of a retarded adolescent girl. *Journal of the Experimental Analysis of Behavior, 51,* 17–27.

Martens, B. K., Lochner, D. G., & Kelly, S. Q. (1992). The effects of variable-interval reinforcement on academic engagement: A demonstration of matching theory. *Journal of Applied Behavior Analysis, 25,* 143–151.

McDowell, J. J. (1988). Matching theory in natural human environments. *The Behavior Analyst, 11,* 95–109.

Michael, J. (1980). Flight from behavior analysis. *The Behavior Analyst, 3,* 1–24.

Morris, E. K. (1991). Deconstructing "technological to a fault." *Journal of Applied Behavior Analysis, 24,* 411–416.

Moxley, R. A. (1989). Some historical relationships between science and technology with implications for behavior analysis. *The Behavior Analyst, 12,* 45–57.

Mueller, M. M., Wilczynski, S. M., Moore, J. W., Fusilier, I., & Trahant, D. (2001). Antecedent manipulations in a tangible condition: The effects of stimulus preference on aggression. *Journal of Applied Behavior Analysis, 34,* 237–240.

Myerson, J., & Hale, S. (1984). Practical implications of the matching law. *Journal of Applied Behavior Analysis, 17,* 367–380.

National Institutes of Health. (1991). *Treatment of destructive behaviors in persons with developmental disabilities.*

Neef, N. A. (1995). Research on training trainers in program implementation: An introduction and future directions. *Journal of Applied Behavior Analysis, 28,* 297–299.

Neef, N. A. (2002). The past and future of behavior analysis in developmental disabilities: When good news is bad and bad news is good. *Behavior Analyst Today.*

Neef, N. A., Mace, F. C., & Shade, D. (1993). Impulsivity in students with serious emotional disturbance: the interactive effects of reinforcer rate, delay, and quality. *Journal of Applied Behavior Analysis, 26,* 37–52.

Neef, N. A., Mace, F. C., Shea, M. C., & Shade, D. (1992). Effects of reinforcer rate and reinforcer quality on time allocation: Extensions of matching theory to educational settings. *Journal of Applied Behavior Analysis, 25,* 691–69.

Neef, N. A., & Lutz, M. N. (2001). Assessment of variables affecting choice and application to classroom interventions. *School Psychology Quarterly, 16,* 239–252.

Neef, N. A., Shade, D., & Miller, M. S. (1994). Assessing influential dimensions of reinforcers on choice in students with serious emotional disturbance. *Journal of Applied Behavior Analysis, 27,* 575–583.

Northup, J., Wacker, D., Sasso, G., Steege, M., Cigrand, K., Cook, J., & DeRaad, A. (1991). A brief functional analysis of aggressive and alternative behavior in an outclinic setting. *Journal of Applied Behavior Analysis, 24,* 509–522.

O'Reilly, M. F. (1995). Functional analysis and treatment of escape-maintained aggression correlated with sleep deprivation. *Journal of Applied Behavior Analysis, 28,* 225–226.

O'Reilly, M. F., & Carey, Y. (1996). A preliminary analysis of the effects of prior classroom conditions on performance under analogue analysis conditions. *Journal of Applied Behavior Analysis, 29,* 581–584.

Peck, S. M., Wacker, D. P., Berg, W. K., Cooper, L. J., Brown, K. A., Richman, D., McComas, J. J., Frischmeyer, P., & Millard, T. (1996). Choice-making treatment of young children's severe behavior problems. *Journal of Applied Behavior Analysis, 29,* 263–290.

Pelios, L., Morren, J., Tesch, D., & Axelrod, S. (1999). The impact of functional analysis methodology on treatment choice for self-injurious and aggressive behavior. *Journal of Applied Behavior Analysis, 32,* 185–195.

Pennypacker, H. S. (1986). The challenge of technology transfer: Buying in without selling out. *The Behavior Analyst, 9,* 147–156.

Pennypacker, H. S., & Hench, L. L. (1997). Making behavioral technology transferable. *The Behavior Analyst, 20,* 97–108.

Perone, M. (1985). On the impact of human operant research: Asymmetrical patterns of cross-citation between human and nonhuman research. *The Behavior Analyst, 8,* 185–189.

Petroski , H. (1992). *The evolution of useful things.* New York: Alfred A. Knopf.

Piazza, C. C., Hanley, G. P., Bowman, L. G., Ruyter, J. M., Lindauer, S. E., & Saiontz, D. M. (1997). Functional analysis and treatment of elopement. *Journal of Applied Behavior Analysis, 30,* 653–672.

Piazza, C. C., Hanley, G. P., & Fisher, W. W. (1996). Functional analysis and treatment of cigarette pica. *Journal of Applied Behavior Analysis, 29,* 437–449.

Pierce, W. D., & Epling, W. F. (1995). The applied importance of research on the matching law. *Journal of Applied Behavior Analysis, 28,* 237–241.

Pindiprolu, S. S., Peterson, S. M. P., Rule, S., & Lignuaris/Kraft, B. (2003). Using Web-Mediated Experiential Case-Based Instruction to Teach Functional Behavioral Assessment Skills. *Teacher Education in Special Education, 26,* 1–16.

Poling, A., Alling, K., & Fuqua, R. W. (1994). Self- and cross-citations in the Journal of Applied Behavior Analysis and the Journal of the Experimental Analysis of Behavior: 1983–1992. *Journal of Applied Behavior Analysis, 27,* 729–731.

Reid, D. H. (1991). Technological behavior analysis and societal impact: A human services perspective. *Journal of Applied Behavior Analysis, 24,* 437–439.

Repp, A. C., Felce, D., & Barton, L. E. (1988). Basing the treatment of stereotypic and self-injurious behaviors on hypotheses of their causes. *Journal of Applied Behavior Analysis, 21,* 281–289.

Repp, A. C., & Karsh, K. G. (1994). Hypothesis-based interventions for tantrum behaviors of persons with developmental disabilities in school settings. *Journal of Applied Behavior Analysis, 27,* 21–31.

Schwartz, I. S., & Baer, D. M. (1991). Social validity assessments: Is current practice state of the art? *Journal of Applied Behavior Analysis, 24,* 189–204.

Skinner, B. F. (1953). *Science and human behavior.* New York: Macmillan.

Skinner, B. F. (1968). *The technology of teaching.* New York: Appleton-Century-Crofts.

Skinner, B. F. (1972). *Cumulative record: A selection of papers.* New York: Appleton-Century-Crofts.

Stolz, S. B. (1981). Adoption of innovations from applied behavioral research: "Does anybody care?" *Journal of Applied Behavior Analysis, 14,* 491–505.

Strand, P. S. (2001). Momentum, matching, and meaning: Toward a fuller exploitation of operant principles. *Behavior Analyst Today, 2,* 170–175.

Van Camp, C. M., Lerman, D. C., Kelley, M. E., Roane, H. S., Contrucci, S. A., & Vorndran, C. M. (2000). Further analysis of idiosyncratic antecedent influences during the assessment and treatment of problem behavior. *Journal of Applied Behavior Analysis, 33,* 207–221.

Vollmer, T. R., Ringdahl, J. E., Roane, H. S., & Marcus, B. A. (1997). Negative side effects of noncontingent reinforcement. *Journal of Applied Behavior Analysis, 30,* 161–164.

Wolf, M. M. (1978). Social validity: The case for subjective measurement or how applied behavior analysis is finding its heart. *Journal of Applied Behavior Analysis, 11,* 203–214.

21

Corporate Cultures

Jon E. Krapfl

This chapter focuses on applications of behavior theory in organizational environments such as businesses, government agencies, hospitals, schools, and other nonprofit institutions. The use of behavior theory in the analysis, management, and direction of organizations represents a radical departure from more traditional approaches to the study of business in both management science and traditional psychology. The approach differs in two fundamental ways. First, the behavior-analytic approach uses the three-term contingency to analyze observable performance in the organization and its relation to the observable organizational environment. In contrast, more traditional approaches seek to explain the dynamic of the organization in terms of more hypothetical variables, (needs, motives, etc.). Second, even though behavior-analytic studies are organizational in nature, the focus remains on the behavior of the individual member of the organization across time, a unique feature of behavior analysis. In each of these aspects, the behavioral approach may be said to be orthogonal to the more traditional approaches.

Early behavior-analytic studies of organizations focused almost exclusively on the use of the three-term contingency model to study organizations. More recently contingency analysis has been combined with systems analysis, an approach that analyzes organizations in terms of input, process, and output variables. The combination of these two approaches has allowed behaviorists to deal with more complex organizations, to do so on a much larger scale, which is essential in most business interventions, and,

---

Jon E. Krapfl • Williamsburg, VA 23185.

yet, maintain the focus on the behavior of the individual across time and its relation to the controlling environment.

With such a different approach to the subject matter, then, it is little wonder that the impact of behavioral psychology on corporate and organizational America, although positive, has been limited. This limited impact may be partly a matter of scale. There are millions of organizations whereas behavioral psychology is a relatively small discipline that has been focused primarily on nonorganizational issues. It is the author's contention, however, that the process research model, including the combined systems/three-term contingency analysis model, severely limits the impact that behavior analysis can have in organizations. It does so because it focuses more on identifying what behavior to change within a process or how to change the behavior required for process outcomes than it does on determining what behavior is required to insure organizational survival and well being. This is not to denigrate the work that behavior analysts have done in organizations. That work has proven to be both appropriate and valuable. If, however, organizational behavior analysts would take as much advantage of behavior theory and conceptual interpretation as they do of emerging interventions and technology, they would expand their range and level of impact considerably. There is precedent for this approach. Both chemistry and clinical psychology developed with application preceding rather than following rigorous experimental analysis.

Limited background in behavior theory and limited knowledge of the business environment prevents the use of a more conceptual approach. In order to develop behavioral science in this area, the behavior analyst should have a thorough grounding in behavior theory and in the business environment so that a more complex behavioral understanding of the business environment can emerge.

Historical Behaviorism in Business

It is, in some ways, curious that applied behavior analysis, a discipline dedicated to improving the well being of people, has focused so little on the business world. The business environment is one of the principal environments in which human behavior occurs. It is, as well, an environment strongly in need of attention by behaviorists. In our lifetime there has never been a time when people worked harder or enjoyed it less. Business environments are less stable and organizational survival is far less assured than ever before. The business environment is a high stress environment for nearly everyone employed in it. Furthermore, in recent years, the implicit contract between the worker and the organization has been shattered. Few employees expect to stay with the same employer for a lifetime, or even for a protracted period of time. Employers have come to view employees as an expense rather than an asset. These factors, combined with the accelerated pace of change have made the workplace an increasingly difficult place in which to function.

In spite of this increasing turmoil in the workplace, however, the business community does not see a need for behavioral services. With a few notable exceptions, behaviorists generally are viewed as fringe players in this world. Most decision makers in the business community are unaware of the existence of, much less the need for, behavioral interventions.

To a significant extent, this lack of impact is a function of the larger discipline out of which behavior analysis has grown. In both psychology and education the primary foci of applications has been in such areas as education, mental health, medicine, and developmental disabilities. The applied emphases of behavioral research would appear to mimic the larger fields of which they are a part. The author knows of no studies to support this point, but would ask readers to consider whether they ever walked into a medical facility, a mental health facility, a school, or a prison where staff did not know something about the behavior analyst's role and contribution. On the other hand, in 30 years of business consultation, the author never competed with a behaviorist competitor for a piece of business, and never proposed business to a prospective client who had previous knowledge of what behaviorists do.

It is likely, then, that disciplinary cultural norms have played a significant role in the limited impact that behavior analysis has had on business. The work that has been done, although often good, has not been sufficiently widespread to attract serious attention in the business world.

Behaviorism in Business—the Future

In addition to the relative size and cultural norms that control foci of interest, however, it would be to the advantage of behavior analysts to consider several other factors, if they are to proceed from the periphery to the center of the business world. Four of these will be reviewed below: business knowledge, intervention scale, approach to problem solving, and a focus on *how* rather than *what*.

Business Knowledge

Behaviorists typically have only a limited knowledge of either business principles or of specific important features of a particular business. This limited understanding of the business environment often puts behaviorists at a loss when it comes to identifying the controlling variables related to the effective performance of a business. This lack of understanding of what is critical to the success of a business, coupled with a failure to appreciate the stimulus control features of corporate direction and corporate infrastructure, limit the contribution that behaviorists make in the business community.

Everyone understands that businesses exist to make a profit. It is also important, however, to know that businesses are organized around such resources as a value proposition, money, people, specification of direction, and infrastructure, specified roughly in order of importance. As an example, the value proposition is the product or service offered and its associated costs. If an organization's value proposition is flawed, engaging in a behavioral intervention to improve individual performance may be contrary to both the organization's and the individual employee's interest. Value propositions are of considerable importance in understanding the reciprocal controlling relationships between customers and employees, employees and managers, and the organizational culture. The A. B. Dick Company provides a case in point. In the early 1960s this company was the major provider of "ditto" machines. With the invention of the Xerox machine, there was nothing that a behaviorist or anyone else could do to improve the sale, manufacture, service, or distribution of ditto machines that would save that business. Were a behaviorist to have entered the A. B. Dick environment at that time, and not appreciated a failing value proposition, that behaviorist would have faced a tidal wave of change with a small bucket.

Today, value propositions are changing constantly. Behaviorists must understand them both in principle and in terms of the specific features of the value proposition of a prospective client, a complex task that involves understanding the relation of a business to both customers and competitors. Behaviorists also need to understand that it is the value proposition that results in consulting companies often specializing in only one or two areas of business. In doing so, consultants are better prepared to enter a foreign culture and propose interventions that are compatible in and appreciated by that culture, an enormous advantage.

The behavioral consulting firm, Corporate Oranizational Behavior Analysts (COBA), built a business around the identification and implementation of changing value propositions in the financial services industry.

Relying more on a conceptual background in behaviorism than on any particular behavioral methodology, COBA helped financial services companies to recognize how changes in their industry (channel collapse,) would change the behavior of nearly every employee in the organization and devise strategies for implementing that change.

Space will not permit, but similar analyses can be made of resources of the organization other than the value proposition. Behaviorists must be able to read a balance sheet and a profit and loss (P&L) statement as well as understand how individual managers in individual companies are influenced by them. People and organization resources will receive further attention later in this chapter. In short, if the fundamentals of the business are not understood, behavioral interventions may be inappropriate. A behaviorist might, for example, set up a reinforcement system to generate increased output from workers when, in fact, deficiencies in the specification of organizational direction and/or poor infrastructure arrangements are the real culprits. If the latter holds, the burden on the worker is increased while the environment that suppresses performance remains intact. Results obtained in such an environment generally are not sustainable over the longer term. Further, these sorts of interventions tend to exacerbate cultural problems and, thus are harmful to the organization and its performance over the longer term.

Intervention Scale

To intervene effectively in an environment, one must have permission to enter it. The work of the behaviorist in business is, presumably, to help the organization and the individuals within it to achieve their goals as well as to do some good applied science. Businesses look at the matter differently. To the decision maker in the business, a person empowered to employ or allow the behaviorist to intervene, the case must be made for the intervention. The decision will be based on the relation between four variables, investment, risk, time, and projected return. It is important for the behaviorist to understand what is implied by these business concepts and how they control the behavior of the business decision maker.

There are many issues for the behaviorist here, but two broad themes are particularly important. The first is that behaviorists, to establish genuine credibility in the discipline for the business, must plan their interventions on a relatively large scale. This is not to say small studies or interventions are inappropriate. For interventions to bring the kind of investment/risk/return ratios that businesses seek, however, it is likely that the interventions will need to be sizable. Larger interventions, on the other hand, bring their own problems related to the general environmental context in which the worker must function. Organizational management and organizational cultures control much of the behavior of the organization through the metacontingencies (see Glenn, this volume) that the organization generates and maintains. When culture and management are ignored, the conditions that prevailed prior to intervention are as likely to undo interventions as weeds are to take over an untended landscape. Though little data are available, it is likely that behavioral interventions, like many others, are not durable and often are unable to survive in a prevailing nonsupportive culture unless cultural variables are considered in planning the intervention. Temporary changes in business are not highly valued.

Approach

It is in their approach to work and problem solving that behaviorists and business managers are most divergent. The behaviorist has a scientific background, appreciates careful measurement and data, focuses on process and control, and would rather be sure than quick. The business manager is focused on the relation of results to costs and speed, seeking to make correct decisions most of the time, but not willing to take the care to be correct all of the time.

The behaviorist seeks careful analysis to make a decision. The typical manager wants to make lots of decisions, quickly, and is willing to go with only a high probability of being correct. The businessperson wants to know the benefit; the behaviorist wants to explain how the benefit will be derived. The behaviorist strives to prove something with data, the businessperson strives for a clear result. What people do, and how the environment supports it is everything to a behaviorist. To most managers people are no more important than the other resources such as money and the value proposition. These differences present a problem because the behaviorist cannot compromise the scientific approach or no value is added. On the other hand, the manager is unlikely to change when to do so would not be supported by the environment that maintains the manager's behavior.

The implications for the behaviorist are many and cannot be discussed in detail. They can, however, be summarized succinctly. To enter into an organization and to secure a project, and to be successful in it, the behaviorist must approach the organization and analyze it the way that Frazier did in *Walden Two* (Skinner, 1948). That is, the behaviorist must view the organization as a culture with its own way of operating and its own value system. For example, the behaviorist need not compromise on rigor in the planned intervention, but the manager is more likely to be interested in what the benefit will be, what it will cost, how long it will take. Conversations with the manager should be in the manager's frame of reference, not the behaviorists. Benefit, by the way, may come in the form of measurement on a behavior chart, but the manager is more likely to be interested in measures of increased production, decreased costs, improved profits, fewer problems. One way to think about this is to not talk about what one is going to do, but talk about the benefit that the business will derive. In business marketing, there is a strong distinction drawn between benefit and attributes. Marketers say that to sell something, it is best not to focus on telling others what will be done for them, rather focus on what benefit they will derive from the intervention.

How vs. What

It may be that, from time to time, behaviorists are bent on solving the wrong problem, or solving the right problem, but in the wrong way. Their background and experience, as that of all others, predisposes a particular view the world. The point was driven home by a consulting experience with a rubber company that sought to improve productivity in its production line. After several years, and hundreds of thousands of dollars of expenditure, a behavioral intervention on a grand scale had resulted in an average 20% improvement in performance, a worthwhile endeavor, but not one without lifestyle costs for both management and labor. Meanwhile engineers were brought in to work on the same problem and, within six months they had produced a 200% improvement in performance while reducing stress on both labor and management. That lesson was never forgotten by the author, but may have a more general relevance.

Behaviorists know how to increase behavior, decrease it, pace it, initiate it, or change it in almost any way. There is not a great deal, in our research literature, however, that tells us about what behavior to select for change. Interestingly, when businesses think of consultants, they often think about hiring someone to tell them what should be done. Behaviorists, on the other hand, operating out of their frame of reference, are more likely prepared to tell others how to go about getting done whatever it is that the organization wants done. When the question of what to do arises, behaviorists cannot reference a particular body of research and are more likely to fall back on theory, something with which many of them have only a limited familiarity.

It can be argued, however, that behaviorists have something to offer to businesses by extending Skinner's concepts of community and organization into the business world (Skinner, 1953). This approach could provide an overall context in which to work not only in the business at large, but also across the organization's levels and functions. An example illustrates how this can be done. A client, the largest property and casualty insurer in the world at the time, asked the author's company to devise a nationwide program for reducing expenses while holding constant or improving quality of service. The author, and the senior management with whom he worked, were hesitant to focus on devising processes to make the existing work process more efficient because the company already had forced cost out of the company. Furthermore, a bonus system for expense reduction was in place, price competition was increasing, and revenues were down.

There is not space to describe the process in any detail. Suffice it to say that the author and management began a protracted period of discussion, including reading and discussing Skinner (1948). As a result, management began to conceptualize the company as a culture that existed in and was dependent upon the larger culture of which it was a part. Furthermore, management began to see that much of the internal turmoil and poor performance within the company might be a consequence of what was happening outside the company. In short, the value proposition might no longer be valid and any further attempts at expense reduction in the current work reduction might make the work environment and management tasks untenable. Extensive studies were developed in two areas. The first examined what the larger culture (in the form of customers) wanted. The second studied all participants involved in the insurance transaction process to determine where, in this larger culture, the organization did and should fit.

To carry out the first set of studies, a behaviorally derived interview process was developed. The studies, carried out by trained managers and employees, revealed a dichotomy in which larger customers no longer wanted insurance at all and smaller companies were demanding lower cost alternatives to their current insurance programs without diminution of coverage.

The second study examined what behavior was required by whom and at what cost to put an insurance program in place. This was the first time that anyone in the company had looked at all of the behavior required by all employees in the completion of an insurance transaction. (The reader should note that when an organization of any size buys insurance, they may buy many different kinds of insurance, e.g., property, casualty, directors and officers liability, marine, etc. Furthermore, insurance proceeds roughly in a channel from a retail broker to a retail insurer, and then on to a reinsurer and a wholesale insurer, each of which has its own brokers. All of these companies were involved in every sizable transaction.) This study showed that, although each of the individual companies might operate efficiently, the entire transaction was grossly inefficient. Much of the work was repeated again and again across the vertical chain of companies required to complete a single transaction. As a result, the company decided to reorganize as two separate companies. The first would focus on financial risk management consulting for the larger clients and the second would focus on a process of "mass customization" of insurance for the intermediate size companies who wanted insurance, but at a better price.

Building the first company required a new definition of the work behavior required and a reconfiguration of staffing. Establishing the second company involved setting up insurance programs that were industry specific and collapsed the insurance channel. In the new work model, all the participants in the transaction, except for the retail broker and insurer, were required to participate in the process only when setting up an industry wide program, i.e. for the road contractor's industry, rather than being involved in each individual road contractor's insurance placement. As a consequence, more than 50% of the work required to complete a transaction was eliminated. Huge efficiencies were obtained for all participants and enormous cost was taken out of the insurance transaction and out of the client company. Behaviorists played a strong part, analyzing behaviorally what clients wanted, what would or could change, who would be helped or hurt, how the company might need to treat or retrain employees, how to get individuals to accept different work tasks, training managers, setting up accountability systems, and so forth.

Although there were a number of managers and consultants involved in the above described process, the fundamental approach was based on a behaviorally derived concept of the organization and the environment in which it must function and behaviorists were involved in every stage of planning and implementation. In fact, the process was somewhat fragmented and many features of the intervention required adjustment and follow-up intervention, but the overall effort was a success.

This general model, designed to involve behavior analysis at the heart of the organization, has been deployed successfully in other industries. The work that was done relied significantly on conceptualizing the organization as a culture, operating in and depending upon a larger culture, much as illustrated in Skinner (1948). Further, the work frequently examined reciprocal controlling relations that existed between competitors, clients, managers and employees.

The advantages of the above described approach are many, but they may be summarized by saying that intervening at the heart of the organization secures the long-term future of the behaviorist in the organization and also opens up the possibility for a wide variety of more scientifically based observations in the organization. A mutually supportive arrangement is thus developed in which a theory based practice leads, eventually to scientifically valid investigations, not unlike the emergence of chemistry out of alchemy or the behavioral influence in clinical psychology. Some preliminary analyses on this approach are described below in the form of salient features. Much of it is extrapolation, interpretation, or extension of the social design concepts of Skinner (1948).

Organizations as Cultures

In considering the corporate world as Frazier looked at Walden Two, the following basic points about organization can be made: Organizations can be analyzed as cultures, cultures are systems of behavioral practices, cultures evolve by selection, organizational cultures function within a larger cultural context, subcultures are nested within the organizational culture, and organizational survival depends upon selection by the larger culture(s). Each of these points is elaborated below.

To say that organizations can be analyzed as cultures is to say that they can be analyzed as agencies of social control (cf. Glenn, this volume). These cultures consist, in part, of contingencies that exert significant control over the behavior of the organization employees. These contingencies can be described in terms of a number of characteristics and dimensions that are relevant to intervention. For example, the culture can be measured in terms of the pervasiveness and strength of control, predominant kinds of control, and so forth.

The best way to define cultures is in terms of behavioral practices: "the way things are done around here." Work routines, working relationships, organizational predilections and caveats, workplace focus and pace, views of external environments, approaches and reactions to customers, shareholders, managers, all of these are components of the organizational culture. The behavioral practices that define a culture are composed of contingencies of reinforcement that evolve by selection in terms of their effectiveness in accomplishing organizational goals. Only two of the many dimensions that could be examined here in terms of possible interventions will be reviewed.

First, cultures may be more or less explicit in terms of the controlling contingencies. Because cultures often control through the imposition of contingencies rather than through the articulation of rules, it is rare that descriptions of the actual controlling arrangements are available. And, typically, they are not even recognized by people in the organization as relevant to organizational functioning. Yet, failure to conform to controlling arrangements or efforts to change them can cause significant turmoil and generate fierce opposition when they are deeply rooted in the culture.

Second, as corporate cultures evolve, they may develop contingencies that are not supportive of the organization or of select components of the organization. There may be cultures that support survival over the short term at the expense of the long term such as, for example, cutting expenses by reducing those costs associated with generating future revenue. There also may be fractures in the culture that support suboptimization and prevent the cooperation required for the overall achievement of organizational goals, such as local office revenue/profit centers that impede the teamwork and cooperation required to service a national or international client.

Organizational cultures do not exist independently of, but rather are significantly a product of, the larger culture(s) of which they are a part. Significant aspects of any culture include the current viability of the value proposition, the markets in which the organization functions, its differentiated position in those markets, the customers whom the organization serves, and the external board members by whom the organization is governed. In any company, but especially one functioning in a global economy, the integrity of the organizational culture may be severely challenged by conflicting contingencies posed by any of these outside interests.

Factors such as geographic separation, management differences, and department or unit contingencies often produce significant variations or subcultures within an organizational culture. These subcultures, themselves, can be analyzed as cultures and must be understood in terms of both the larger organizational culture and the external cultures of which they are a part. They are especially likely to differ from the larger organizational culture as a function of leadership or local external cultural conditions.

To survive and be effective the organization and its subcultures, that is, the various organizational units and functions, must be selected by the larger culture(s) of which they are a part. They will survive or fail in the markets where they compete, or with the customers and corporate masters they serve. They are a typical example of survival of the fittest.

Essential Functions of Corporate Cultures

Survival

The primary function of a culture is to ensure its own survival. This is the primary message of Skinner (1948). The function of the leaders and the members of an organization is to ensure their future. The need for short-term survival is often recognized, but organizational subcultures often sacrifice for the longer term. Survival, in the modern business world, does not necessarily imply corporate independence, but it does imply a continuity of the organization in its relation with its employees and customers.

Control

Cultures are a source of control. As noted previously, cultures prescribe "the way things are done around here." The more pervasive and powerful the cultural contingencies, the greater the internal consistency in the organization. Powerful cultures are likely to be strong organizations and to insure the survival of the organization over the longer term unless the environment external to the organization changes. When this happens, the strong culture creates a potential for catastrophe.

Generally, though, strong cultures are good for the organization. Cultures themselves may be bureaucratic and overcontrolling, but cultural controls can also obviate the need for a bureaucracy and a controlling management style. For example, if taking the time to do things right the first time is a strong cultural ethic, new employees will be selected on their predilection to so behave. In addition, employees will support and correct the behavior needed to fit into the culture, thereby obviating the need for close supervision or excessive rules. Strong cultures are an alternative to excessive policies and memos. Strong cultures allow for individuals to make judgements on behalf of the organization at the point of the customer interface without "running it up the line." Individuals' jobs are enriched and more reinforcing. Customers are better served with decisions made at the point of the customer interface. Strong cultures generally allow for increased customer focus and responsiveness, improved efficiency, and greater profits.

Deeply rooted cultures, however, also fend off change. Individuals deeply enmeshed in a culture have a tendency to reject changes that conflict with the culture, e.g., IBM in the 1970's. Such changes are usually brought about by changes from outside the culture. When the larger culture, of which they are a part, usually in the form of paying customers, no longer supports the internal contingencies of reinforcement that define the organizational culture, the organization moves into crisis. The internal and external cultures become misaligned and the cultural practices, which had developed to ensure organizational survival begin to turn on the culture, and begin to destroy it. This is a common occurrence in today's business environment.

Goal Alignment

Cultures include a set of contingencies that serve to align goals across the organization across organizational levels, functions, and individuals. In this goal alignment function, cultures serve to focus the work of the organization and to insure that the resources and energy expended are going toward the same end(s). Everyone understands where the organization is headed, what it is trying to do, how it will do it, and how each unit and person in the organization fits into the larger picture. It would seem to follow, therefore, that the stronger the culture, the more aligned the goals would be. Although this may be true, it is not necessarily for the good of the organization. It depends upon what the specific contingencies are. A deeply enmeshed culture of cynicism and doubt about others in the organization, for example, may be strong, but not necessarily for the good. The culture is strong, but that organization may die, even, in part, as a result of a strong culture.

Source of Differential Reinforcement

Recognition by or even membership in the culture may itself function as a differential reinforcer. Being a part of a company, a corporate unit, or a team that is considered in some way distinguished can exert a great deal of control over the work behavior of the individual member. Such a relation might be described as: pride in the company, pride in being part of a collective performance, a member of a successful team, companionship of others trying to achieve the same things, or a pathway to future success. Cultures can be sources of all of these and probably many other forms of reinforcement.

Features of Successful Corporate Cultures

Behavior theory not only suggests that corporations can be described as cultures, but it also identifies a number of features that will enhance the likelihood of culture contributing to the success rather than the detriment of the organization. Some of the more valuable cultural features follow.

To ensure its survival the organizational culture should be arranged to *balance constituency interests*. The culture should support and serve each of the organization's principal constituencies, customers, employees, and shareholders. These constituencies are often in conflict with one another because each of them is more likely to take a short-term rather than a long-term view of the organization. Often one of the organizational constituencies gains excessive power, almost always to the detriment of one of the others. When this happens, organizational distress and upheaval tend to occur. Recall for example, the excessive control of the unions of the 1970's that resulted in American auto manufacturers losing their cost-competitive edge against imports, or more recently and prominently, the excessive control of the stockholders who have forced companies to provide a level of return that made it impossible for the company to secure its long-term future.

The rapidly changing external environment has caused a rapid acceleration of organizational pace. As a result of the forces of technology and globalization, the culture can achieve stability only with a culture that is flexible, that works to achieve *stability through vectoring, not stasis*. Cultures in the contemporary organization must not only be open to modification; they must actually foster continuous development and change. Organizational survival today requires adapting to rapid and dramatic changes in markets, consumer interests, technological applications, and global competition. Employees also must be open to continuous development and change. Holding tight and hunkering down almost certainly puts an organization in the same position as buggy whip manufacturers at the turn of the last century. Recall that there is absolutely nothing the ditto machine people could have done to survive in the face of the development of the Xerox machine short of fundamentally reinventing themselves. A rarity in the 1960's, this event portended a future to be faced by nearly every kind of company in more recent times.

The culture also needs to rely on *natural reinforcers*. At least some of the work of each individual must be reinforcing, either in the work process, itself, or in the results the work produces, and ideally in both. My experience suggests that artificial consequence manipulations, including bonuses, tend to have short-term and nonenduring effects. Where work tasks themselves are not reinforcing, the social reinforcers of the group and the community are critical.

The internal focus of the organization must be *externally driven* at all levels of the organization, thus propelling the culture ever toward a more satisfactory position and fit in the larger culture of which it is a part. Organizations that are internally focused tend to lose contact with the environments that must maintain them over the longer term.

The long-term viability of the organization is difficult to establish among employees as a goal. Both organizational rules and employee training must not only establish a corporate ethic and clarify corporate standards, but also must *bridge gap for deferred consequences* by indicating the relation between current performance and likely future outcomes beneficial to the organization.

Management must provide a focus and direction for the organization; it must *emphasize cultural conformity.* An organization with 25 priorities is an organization with no priorities, at least in so far as the control and direction of employee behavior is concerned. Management also must recognize that decisions have an impact on the culture and cultures have an impact on the implementation of decisions. When cultural norms are violated or when management behavior is inconsistent with the prevailing culture, the culture, itself, is weakened and the consequence is a deterioration of organizational performance. Yet, few managers attend to cultural variables and management behavior is often in conflict, especially when it occurs as a reaction to external factors. The most common form of management inconsistency, however, is between what management does and what those same managers say about what they do. This leads not only to organizational confusion, but also to a loss of confidence in management.

Finally, within the organizational context that consists of the organizational direction and culture designed and nourished by management, there needs to be *support for diversity within the structure.* In general, management needs to specify a range of desirable outcomes and place less emphasis on how these outcomes are achieved. The reinforcing of organizational diversity in terms of how the job is to be done supports organizational survival. This does not and must not extend to the point that the organization tolerates unethical behavior or behavior that sacrifices the long-term good of the organization for the sake of the short term.

Elements of Intervention

In the preceding description, organizations and corporations were described as cultures and a number of essential and desirable features of a culture were described. Having done so, the question arises as to how one might proceed to initiate and carry out interventions based on a cultural analysis. Undertaking such ventures may appear daunting, but the practical issues involved in such a venture are manageable. Securing corporate support for such intervention usually is a process of successive approximations. One useful way to proceed is through an organizational analysis. Rather than targeting a specific set of behaviors for change, this approach seeks to provide for management an understanding of the relations that maintain in an organization, or across individuals and/or units of the organization and how these support or do not support organizational goals.

Although such an analysis has been done on entire organizations, it is unlikely that an investigation of this magnitude and cost would be commissioned from an unfamiliar source. To begin, one might choose a smaller unit of the organization such as a local or regional office or a support unit such as information services or accounting.

The purpose of such an analysis would be to identify points of disconnect, that is, individuals and or units in the organization where the expected mutually reinforcing relations do not appear to hold. Space will not allow for a full explication of the intervention process here, but the reader is referred to Chase and Smith (1994) for examples of how this might be done. Their suggested processes are particularly helpful in identifying disconnect points in the strategic direction and execution sections below. A few features of such an appraisal that is more closely focused on critical features related to value propositions follow.

Analysis of External Environment

Any organization or organizational component interested in securing its long-term future must understand the external environment in which the unit must function. Every organization will claim to have this understanding. The question behaviorists must answer is whether the current behavior of the organization reflects that understanding. Relevant factors that compose this external environment include such things as markets, customers, competitors, industry changes and trends, and corporate board and regulations.

Developmental Stage

In the infancy of an organization it is typical for the leadership to determine the culture. The organization is small and the entrepreneur who starts the organization is involved in every aspect of the business. As the business matures and the culture becomes fixed, the culture determines the leaders. That is, the leaders come up the ranks immersed in the culture and very much a part of it. Finally, culture destroys organizations as it becomes complacent and disconnected from its external environment. Whereas corporate developmental stages are like human developmental stages in that they describe only statistical trends and probabilities, they are a good indicator of where the intervention needs to be focused.

Strategic Direction

Based on this external analysis the behavior analyst must determine the extent to which the organization has established a strategic direction. Further, this analysis must include a measure of the extent to which the verbally specified direction is reflected in the behavior of the organization across its various levels and functions, the most critical being the behavior of the senior management. The strategic direction should be analyzed in terms of the extent to which it specifies the markets in which it will compete, the basis upon which it will compete, (vision, strategy), and the benefits customers will obtain (value of products or services ÷ cost).

Executing

Following this specification of future direction the organization must execute. It does this by arranging its internal environment to support the behavior required to achieve its strategic initiatives. The essential steps in arranging this internal environment involve communicating the direction, identifying core features of the culture, arranging the infrastructure to support the direction, leading and managing the people, reacting to changes in the external environment, and reacting to organizational performance. When an initial analysis of this sort is carried out, more often than not, one or more of three phenomena are observed. One significant possibility is finding a lack of correspondence between verbal claims of corporate action, i.e. vision, mission, direction, and the behavior to support them. Misalignment of executive verbal behavior, (values, claims, directives) and operating management and organizational contingencies are a prime source of difficulty that can be clarified by an organizational analysis. A second significant possibility is finding a failure of specification of direction, in the form of unclear specifications, conflicting specifications, or failure to communicate direction. In this situation, the behavior required of employees is not clear and corporate behavior may or may not support the achievement of corporate goals. Finally, infrastructure arrangements may be poor, a situation that makes moot the point of directional specification because structures are not in place to execute the corporate mission.

Only after all of these issues are addressed is the organization in a position to begin manipulating the behavior of individual employees or organizational units to accelerate productive performance.

Conclusions

There is an important contribution being made by behavioral psychologists in the corporate environment and an even more important one to be made. To improve the position of the discipline in industry so that it can make a greater contribution will require a different approach. This approach cannot be a piecemeal or even a systems intervention with the managers and employees of the organization if that intervention is based simply on improving performance in the organization as it currently functions. Securing our own future in the business environment will require a more thoughtful approach to what is required to align features of the organizational culture, with each other and with the external contingencies that maintain them.

References

Chase, P. N., & Smith, J. M. (1994). *Performance analysis: Understanding behavior in organizations*. Morgantown, WV: Envision Development Group.

Skinner, B. F. (1948). *Walden Two*. New York: Macmillan.

Skinner, B. F. (1953). *Science and Human Behavior*. New York: Macmillan.

Author Index

Subject Index

Note: References to topics covered by entire chapters appear in bold.